"Eric Bogosian's *Operation Nemesis* takes us into the complex aftermath of the Armenian genocide and reminds us that genocide committed without ethical or legal accountability results in protracted trauma and open wounds that can lead to more violence in efforts to seek justice. A dramatic and important book."

—Peter Balakian, author of *Black Dog of Fate*

"Absorbing reading.... To his great credit, Bogosian recognizes [the moral contradiction] and refuses to portray Tehlirian or any of the other members of his group as heroes. He's aware of the gravitas of his story and the need to set it in context.... Where it matters most he delivers: in his gripping action accounts of Nemesis at work, and in the sober assessment of its terrible aftermath."

—Joseph Kanon, *New York Times Book Review*

"Hitler asked, 'Who remembers the Armenians?' Eric Bogosian, that's who. Read his potent, action-packed account of how a little-known assassination plot harkens back to a world-historical genocide and so will you. So take that, Hitler."

—Sarah Vowell, author of *Lafayette in the Somewhat United States*

"A dark and compelling tale of blood vengeance. In *Operation Nemesis,* Eric Bogosian tells the remarkable story of how a small group of powerless postwar assassins sought revenge against the all-powerful masterminds of the Armenian genocide."

—Annie Jacobsen, author of *The Pentagon's Brain*

"Bogosian dives passionately into an underreported piece of history, a surprisingly effective conspiracy to assassinate the planners of Turkey's Armenian genocide." —Boris Kachka, *Vulture*

"Absorbing and accessible. Bogosian presents this complex and multilayered history with a master dramatist's flair. *Operation Nemesis* is an engaging and provocative account of an unforgettable tragedy and a cathartic attempt at finding justice."

—Atom Egoyan, Academy Award–nominated writer
and director of *The Sweet Hereafter* and *Ararat*

"Eric Bogosian, actor, playwright, and novelist, can now add historian to his résumé with this carefully researched tale of organized revenge on the perpetrators of one of the most heinous state-engineered genocides in modern history—the murderous expulsion of the Armenian people from Ataturk's newly reconstituted Turkey."

—Richard Price, author of *The Whites*

"*Operation Nemesis* is a spellbinding book. It is written with both urgency and patience. Bogosian's chapter summarizing the 'variety of peoples who crossed and recrossed' Anatolia is as good as any of the half-dozen established accounts I've read. His play-by-play story of the Armenian assassins avenging the Armenian genocide (1915–20) is as gripping as a Graham Greene novel. The whole book is a significant contribution to the history of Asia Minor and its effect on our present world."

—John Casey, author of National Book Award winner *Spartina*

"In this resurrection of a lost story, Eric Bogosian vividly tells the story of the assassins who avenged the Ottoman mass killings of Armenians in 1915. Unfolding like a thriller, Bogosian's history brings to life long-forgotten events and the courageous people who set out in their own way to bring a kind of justice and peace to their shared past."

—Ronald Grigor Suny, professor of history and political
science, University of Michigan, and author of
They Can Live in the Desert but Nowhere Else

"A clear, concise view of Turkey's history in the twentieth century, and it's not pretty. Difficult reading, but an extremely well-written political statement about Turkey—not just then, but as it is now."

—*Kirkus Reviews*

OPERATION NEMESIS

THE ASSASSINATION PLOT
THAT AVENGED
THE ARMENIAN GENOCIDE

ERIC BOGOSIAN

BACK BAY BOOKS

Little, Brown and Company

New York   Boston   London

In memory of my grandparents,
Rose, Lucy, Karekin, and Megerdich

—⟋⟍—

Back Bay Books / Little, Brown and Company
Hachette Book Group
1290 Avenue of the Americas, New York, NY 10104
littlebrown.com

Originally published in hardcover by Little, Brown and Company, April 2015
First Back Bay paperback edition, February 2017

Back Bay Books is an imprint of Little, Brown and Company, a division of Hachette Book Group, Inc. The Back Bay Books name and logo are trademarks of Hachette Book Group, Inc.

The publisher is not responsible for websites (or their content) that are not owned by the publisher.

The Hachette Speakers Bureau provides a wide range of authors for speaking events. To find out more, go to hachettespeakersbureau.com or call (866) 376-6591.

Selections from *The Legacy* by Arshavir Shiragian reprinted with permission from Sonia Shiragian and Hairenik Association; and from *The Armenian Genocide: Testimonies from the Eyewitness Survivors* reprinted with permission from Verjiné Svazlian.

The photograph of Aaron Sachaklian, courtesy of Marian Mesrobian MacCurdy, is published in her book *Sacred Justice: The Voices and Legacy of the Armenian Operation Nemesis*, Transaction Publishers, 2015.

Maps by Jeffrey L. Ward

ISBN 978-0-316-29208-5 (hardcover) / 978-0-316-29210-8 (paperback)
LCCN 2015933033

10 9 8 7 6 5 4 3 2 1

Printed in the United States of America

CONTENTS

PART III

FOREWORD

Over a year has passed since the first publication of *Operation Nemesis*. During that time minority religious groups have been massacred, cities have been reduced to rubble, and a vast river of refugees has poured out of their homelands. The events of the past few years have been nothing less than a horrific replay of the genocidal policies of the Ottoman Empire in decline.

This book is about a group of Armenian nationals living outside Turkey who sought to avenge the massive bloodshed of their fellow Armenians during World War I. These men rose up from the most anonymous of lives to mete out lethal punishment upon the Ottoman leaders most responsible for this genocide.

This book is not a "thriller" so much as an attempt to fully reveal this incredible story and its historical context. It is not the last word on the subject, but for many reasons it is a story that had not been fully told. The Ottoman Empire ruled the Middle East for six centuries. It would become the Republic of Turkey after World War I. The Turks and the Russians have been at war for centuries. The Christian Armenian people, who have lived for millennia in the eastern areas of today's Turkey as well as in the Caucasus and northern Iran, have been inextricably bound to this ongoing conflict between Russia and Turkey as well as other conflicts of empire going back to the Roman Empire and even earlier.

Any attempt to understand what is happening in the Middle East today while remaining ignorant of Arab, Turkish, Armenian, Persian, Russian, and British history (not to mention the huge impact of American Protestant and other missionaries) is doomed to misunderstand how this region lives and breathes. To try to understand contemporary developments without revisiting a historical commitment to deportation and genocide is to miss the foundation of modern Middle Eastern politics.

All of these narrative lines find their nexus in the remarkable story of Operation Nemesis.

OPERATION
NEMESIS

INTRODUCTION

When I was a little kid, there was nothing I loved better than hanging out at my grandparents' house. In her sunny kitchen, my Grandma Lucy would fashion honey-drenched Armenian pastries, while out in the backyard Grampa Megerdich roasted lamb shish kebab under the apple trees. After dessert, Grampa might knock back a tiny glass of arak and tell me stories. I was held rapt by the horrific narratives he dredged up from his faraway past. In his sweetly accented English, Megerdich would describe burning churches and sadistic horsemen. The stories would always end the same way. My grandfather would instruct me, "If you ever meet a Turk, kill him."

I was no more than four years old when I first heard those words.

My grandfather had spent his boyhood in the troubled eastern frontier of the Ottoman Empire more than a century ago. He had plenty of reason to hate the Turks, who had killed his father and almost killed him. In 1915, when he was barely twenty-one years old, Megerdich escaped the genocide that would exterminate hundreds of thousands of his fellow Armenians. More than once he told me the story of how his village burned while he and his mother crouched down in the middle of a wheat field, hiding from the *zapiteh.* Under darkness of night they fled, managed to find passage to France, and in 1916 Megerdich and my great-grandmother immigrated to the United States from Le Havre. My grandfather claimed that he had survived because he was smarter than the rest. That's why I was such a smart little boy. But perhaps it was just luck.

Megerdich's own father was not so lucky. Ovygin Jamgochian, after successfully immigrating to the United States in the 1890s, had gained American citizenship. But he made the mistake of returning to "the old country" to find his wife and teenage son. The Young Turk government didn't recognize his American citizenship, and he was swept up with hundreds of thousands of other able-bodied men and drafted into the army. His conscription would become a death sentence. Within months of being drafted, Ovygin, like most of the Armenians in the Ottoman army, was disarmed, then forced into a labor battalion where Christian soldiers were worked to death. All we know is that his family never saw him again. My Grandma Lucy also lost her father, Koumjian the jeweler, who once worked in the Constantinople bazaar. As far as we know, Lucy's father, like Ovygin, also died violently.

I understood from a young age that I was an "Armenian," and this meant that my family, like countless other Armenian families, had lost loved ones at the hands of the Turks. But knowing this and embracing it were two different things. Most of my freckle-faced friends in Woburn, Massachusetts, were of Irish American ancestry, blissfully unaware of their own harsh history. Though I was olive-skinned and kinky-haired and attended the Armenian (not Roman Catholic) church, I saw myself, like them, as nothing more than a carefree American kid. The horrors that had touched the lives of my grandfather's generation had not touched me. I was not an immigrant, I spoke perfect English, and I had zero interest in emphasizing anything that would exaggerate the differences between me and my classmates.

Horrible things had happened back in "the old country," but there was a disconnect between that carnage and my sweet exis-

tence as a suburban teenager. My life growing up in a Massachusetts subdivision was filled with pot-smoking teenagers in torn
jeans who barely paid attention to school and in their spare time
protested the Vietnam War. In another universe, a long time ago,
Kurdish tribesmen armed with pistols and knives had terrorized
villagers and abducted young Christian women. My grandfather's
world was genuinely dangerous. The stories I had heard at his knee
were so intense they seemed mythic, unreal, more like adventure
stories than real life. These events had taken place in a land a million miles away, a place my grandfather called "Armenia." I loved
Armenian food, I loved Armenian weddings and the strange choral
music sung in our churches, but I was an American kid, not an
Armenian.

As I began my career as an author and actor, I refrained from
emphasizing my roots. I didn't want to be pigeonholed as an exotic
"ethnic" actor, and if I was going to write about the human condition, I would represent the world I *knew,* the leafy suburbs of New
England and, later, the streets of New York City, not the harsh
plains of Anatolia, of which I had no direct experience. The Armenian history that I had come to know through my grandfather's
stories was not *my* history. *I* had not suffered in the desert, I had not
lost loved ones there, I had not witnessed atrocities firsthand. Why
should I be the one to write about those sad events from so
long ago?

When I first heard about the assassination of Talat Pasha about
twenty years ago, the story seemed more like wishful thinking
than the truth. Mehmet Talat Pasha, a leader of the Ottoman
Empire (which became the modern Republic of Turkey) during
World War I, had been assassinated in 1921 in Berlin by a young
Armenian. The twist was that this young engineering student,
Soghomon Tehlirian, was acquitted and set free. A supreme act of
vengeance had seemingly been pardoned. To most Armenians this
made perfect sense. Talat was a monster, he was responsible for a

massive tragedy, and Tehlirian slew him, like David slew Goliath. Like my grandfather's stories, Talat's death brought to mind an episode from a nineteenth-century novel.

When I came upon a reference to Tehlirian again in Peter Balakian's *Black Dog of Fate* and a few years later in Samantha Power's Pulitzer Prize–winning book on genocide, *A Problem from Hell,* I realized that this was not some kind of Armenian urban legend. Peter Balakian (whose great-uncle had been a witness at Tehlirian's trial) and Samantha Power told the same tale: Tehlirian had been a survivor of the genocide who had seen his entire family brutally massacred by Turks. He had then chanced upon Talat, who was in hiding in Berlin after the war. After his arrest, Tehlirian explained to the police that he'd been driven to shoot Talat by the effect of all that he had witnessed. Incredibly, the judge and jury sided with the young assassin, sympathizing with his suffering and loss. The June 4, 1921, *New York Times* headline summed it up: "THEY SIMPLY HAD TO LET HIM GO!"

I found the transcript of Tehlirian's trial online. It was packed with gruesome details of Soghomon's ordeal as well as a blow-by-blow description of the assassination. Why wasn't there a book or a film based on Tehlirian, I wondered. Clearly, the killing of Talat and Tehlirian's exoneration were tailor-made source material for a motion picture. I could easily imagine the structure of a big film: Act 1: the deportations and massacres in the desert; Act 2: Berlin, the assassination; Act 3: the trial and the triumphant acquittal. A true story filled with pathos and complexity. And history. I had finally found an Armenian subject that would challenge me as a writer and memorialize my beloved grandfather. I decided to set aside a few months to write the screenplay.

As soon as I began to sketch out a draft, obvious questions came to mind. How does an engineering student manage to kill a man who has spent his life surrounded by bodyguards? And with one shot? In the middle of a busy street, in the middle of the day? How did Tehlirian, a man who could barely speak German, get his hands on a gun in postwar Berlin? Was Tehlirian really a student? There was no evidence of his attending classes or having any friends who were students. If he wasn't a student, what was he doing in Berlin in the first place? How did he support himself? He didn't seem to have had a job. I read the court transcript over and over again. Something was wrong with this picture.

Then I discovered *Resistance and Revenge,* a dense monograph published in France in the 1980s by the journalist Jacques Derogy, which explained that in fact, the young Armenian was not an engineering student at all. Nor, as it turns out, had he been a witness to the massacre of his family in the desert. At the time of their deportation he hadn't even been living in Turkey.

Derogy laid out an even more remarkable, almost unbelievable story: A small group of Armenian conspirators with headquarters in the United States, calling themselves "Operation Nemesis," had successfully organized the assassination not only of Talat but also of most of the Turkish leaders responsible for the genocide. Neither Peter Balakian nor Samantha Power had made much of the Nemesis conspiracy; neither had mentioned its long list of victims. They focused on Tehlirian and repeated the story he told in court. I needed to know more. Over the next seven years I immersed myself in an exploration of history and of horror, of what the judge at Tehlirian's trial called "a tradition of bloody vengeance." I found links to British intelligence, and I reviewed recent research on interference in the trial by German officials. I asked scholar Aram Arkun to translate Tehlirian's 1953 memoirs, originally published in Armenian, and his work allowed me to deepen my understanding of this complex conspiracy.

These men were contemporaries of my grandfather; some had grown up only a hundred or so miles from where my grandfather was born. But they were nothing like my grandfather. My grandfather could hate Turks, but could he ever have killed one? It is one thing to hate, to wish harm on one's enemy, but it is a very different thing to step up to someone on the street and put a bullet in his brain. And watch him die.

My grandfather wanted me to know what had happened to

him long before I was born. He wanted me to be ready for the worst. He wanted to save me. And so he told me terrible stories and he warned me about the Turks. I'm sure he could never have imagined his young grandson actually killing a Turk, but he had said what he'd said and it never left me. He shared his memory with me, the most valuable thing he owned.

Tehlirian and his cohorts were not simply avengers. They were a small group of men, including a Boston newspaper editor, a Syracuse CPA, and a Washington diplomat, who, through their actions, tried to offset in some way the anonymous deaths of hundreds of thousands of innocent civilians who died in the deserts and in their homes and in mountain wastelands. No headstones mark where those victims of Talat and his gang fell. Nothing is left of them but our memory of them. To the million and a half Armenians who perished at the hands of Ottoman Turks during the First World War, and to their countless descendants, the actions of Operation Nemesis shouted, "You existed. You are memorable. We remember you."

For almost one hundred years, the story of this controversial band of men has been clouded by myth. I wrote this book because I had no choice. The Nemesis story required more attention than a simple screenplay. I've done my best to tell it as honestly and completely as possible. In this way, I honor memory.

PROLOGUE

A round ten o'clock on the morning of March 15, 1921, a heavyset man wearing an overcoat emerged from his apartment house in the fashionable Charlottenburg district of Berlin. He carried a cane and was bareheaded despite the cool early spring weather. The man wasn't comfortable wearing a European-style hat. It didn't look right to him. But he wouldn't dare wear a fez in this anarchic city of spies. The last thing he wanted to do was call attention to his Turkishness. As he stepped onto the sidewalk, the fresh air lifted his spirits. The winter had been long and hard, but a thaw was coming. Soon this exiled Turk could return to his home in Constantinople. His fellow Young Turk, General Musta-pha Kemal, was finding success in the east; in months the war would finally be over.

The man in the overcoat, Talat Pasha, had been hiding in Germany under an assumed name, pretending to be a businessman. In the years prior to moving to the apartment on Hardenbergstrasse, Talat had achieved fame as the leader of the Ottoman Empire during the Great War. The name Talat was known to people all over the world, but for the present it was a liability. The British forces occupying Constantinople had arrested numerous Ottoman leaders, the sultan's government had held war crimes trials, and though he had evaded arrest, Talat had been found guilty and sentenced to death in absentia. For the time being, it would be wiser to go by the more humble "Salih Bey."

Exile had diminished but not extinguished Talat's power. He was still a very important man, looked up to by many for leadership. But he had no choice; he had to remain hidden. Only days before, in a secret meeting with the British agent Aubrey Herbert, Talat had been asked if he feared assassination. He had coolly responded, "I never think of it."[1] But he did think of it. He thought of it all the time. There were rumors that the Armenians were hunting for him, that there was a bounty on his head. Talat was accustomed to the fact that his very presence intimidated people, but he also knew that he had to be extremely careful.

What Talat did not know as he strolled down Berlin's fashionable Hardenbergstrasse on this cool spring morning was that his alias had already been discovered. Danger was much closer than he imagined. Even as he stepped lightly among the local Berliners on his way to the Tiergarten park, he was being followed. Across the street and parallel to his course, a young Armenian émigré from Turkish Anatolia tracked his route. Unlike Talat, Soghomon Tehlirian was almost invisible, figuratively and literally. No one knew his name, no one in Berlin would ever recognize him, and in the midst of this posh neighborhood of White Russian émigrés, he did not stand out at all. Tehlirian was the personification of anonymity. In a few moments, that anonymity would end.

Anticipating Talat's path, the assassin jogged across Hardenbergstrasse, then abruptly turned and strode back toward his quarry. The young Armenian found himself coming face-to-face with the heavyset Turk. His temples throbbing with excitement, Tehlirian focused on his breathing, slowing it, controlling it. This was no time to fall to pieces. Tehlirian searched Talat's eyes as the two men passed each other. Was there a reaction, a recognition? If there was, it lasted only a fraction of a second. "Fear came into his eyes," Tehlirian would later write, as an "amazing calmness engulfed my being."[2]

As Tehlirian stepped past Talat, the larger man adjusted his stride, slowing just slightly. The young soldier drew his pistol from his waistband, raised it to the nape of Talat's broad neck, and squeezed the trigger. The victim probably never heard the gun fire. The bullet cleaved Talat's spinal cord, entered the base of his skull, traversed his brain, and exited his temple just above his left eye. The shock set off a massive coronary, and the large man shuddered. Then, according to Tehlirian, "he fell on his face with a sound like a branch sawed off a tree." A woman a few feet ahead of them on the sidewalk screamed and fainted as a single thought popped into Tehlirian's mind: "So effortless!"

Tehlirian, whose sole raison d'être was to end the life of the man now lying on the ground before him, immediately understood that another bullet wouldn't be needed. Transfixed, the twenty-five-year-old Armenian refugee stood over the corpse, the pistol still clutched in his hand, as "the black thick blood flowed like kerosene out of a broken container." The killer then dipped the toe of his shoe into the pool of blood as shouting rose up all around him: "Someone has been murdered! Grab him!" Tehlirian broke out of his trance, reflex took over, and he ran, completely forgetting his handler's explicit instructions to stay put after the killing. "I passed by them, no one tried to stop me." Tehlirian sprinted twenty or thirty steps, then veered into the Fasanenstrasse.

The crowd, at first reluctant to chase a violent, perhaps deranged killer, caught up with the young man and surrounded him. Someone grabbed his shoulder. Another smacked him on the back of the head. More punches and slaps. People in the crowd were attacking Tehlirian because they mistakenly believed he had gunned down a famous German general. As he was being beaten, Tehlirian felt something hard and sharp tearing at his face. Later he would realize that someone had been hitting him with a key ring full of jagged keys. The blood dripped down onto his shirt. A man interceded and hauled him off to the local police outpost by the Tiergarten gate. Tehlirian shouted to the crowd, "What you want? I am Armenian, he, Turkish. What is it to you?"[3]

The police hauled the bleeding young man back to the scene of the crime. "Blood was flowing from my head. Other policemen arrived. They turned me toward Hardenberg. The monster had fallen in the same position on the sidewalk. The police, the crowd, at a certain distance, surrounded all sides. We passed on."[4] The crowd surged, still struggling to lay hands on the killer. A paddy wagon rolled up and Tehlirian was shoved into the back. Fifteen minutes later he was in his cell at the Charlottenburg police station.

A trial followed a little over two months later. Stunningly, Tehlirian was acquitted. In occupied Constantinople a few weeks after that, the Muslim Azeri leader Khan Javanshir was gunned down outside the Pera Palace Hotel by another Armenian. That assassin, Misak Torlakian, would also be set free after a two-month trial. In December, Said Halim Pasha, former Young Turk Grand Vizier of the Ottoman Empire, was shot dead as he was returning to his home only blocks away from the Borghese Gardens in Rome. This assassin would also evade arrest despite a massive manhunt.

The following spring in Berlin, Said Halim's killer, Arshavir Shiragian, teamed up with Aram Yerganian to assassinate both Dr. Behaeddin Shakir, former head of the organization that oversaw the genocide of Armenians in Turkey, and Djemal Azmi, the notorious former governor-general of Trebizond. Neither Shiragian nor Yerganian was caught. Finally, in July 1922, Djemal Pasha, one of the key members of the Young Turk government, was slain by Stepan Dzaghigian in Tiflis, Georgia. Dzaghigian was arrested by the Cheka, the Soviet secret police, and sent to Siberia, where he would remain until his death.

These assassinations and at least four others were a response to the genocide of the Armenians in the Ottoman Empire during World War I. As the war wound down, it appeared that those Turks responsible for the massive destruction of the Christian civilian population would face judgment.[5] Trials were held in Constantinople, but by that time the central leaders had already slipped out of Turkey and had found safe harbor in Berlin, Rome, Tiflis, and Moscow. President Woodrow Wilson proposed a protective "mandate" for the Armenian provinces of Turkey, providing a homeland to which survivors might return. The mandate never materialized. Instead, Turkish nationalists under General Mustapha Kemal successfully pushed back forces seeking to occupy Turkish territory. By 1922, any thoughts of reparations for the Armenians, an Armenian homeland, or even a right of return had been extinguished as the Soviets moved in to claim possession of the short-lived Republic of Armenia, the tiny sliver of territory in the Caucasus to which hundreds of thousands of refugees had fled.

Operation Nemesis was an unprecedented conspiracy designed to avenge an unprecedented modern genocide. With little training, resources, or experience in intelligence operations, this humble collection of businessmen, intellectuals, diplomats, and former soldiers virtually eradicated an entire former government. As a group, they complemented one another: the quiet, steadfast members collaborated with the romantic visionaries; the impetuous spurred on the cautious. Together they formed an international team, understaffed and underfinanced, at a time when communication was by cable and all travel by rail or steamship. This thin network spread out across Europe and the Near East before systematically and effectively dispatching its targets. In the end, "Operation Nemesis" would satisfy its ambitions while having repercussions far beyond its need for revenge. Then, as suddenly as they appeared, this small cadre of businessmen, editors, and veterans faded into the background of history, almost forgotten. This is their story.

PART I

CHAPTER ONE

The Rise of Empire

Ne mutlu Türküm diyene! [Happy is the man who can say, "I am a Turk!"]

—Kemal Ataturk

I am Armenian, he, Turkish. What is it to you?

—Soghomon Tehlirian

The Christian Armenians and the Muslim Ottomans claim rich and complex histories. The Armenians flourished in Asia Minor as early as the dawn of recorded history. In fact, an Armenian king established the first Christian state in AD 301, while the ancestors of the Ottoman Turks invaded the same region about seven hundred years later. By the seventeenth century, the Muslim Ottoman Empire had conquered and absorbed territory extending from Europe to Persia, including the ancient Armenian homeland. At their peak, the Ottomans displayed a cultural and scientific sophistication equal to the greatest premodern civilizations.

It is not an exaggeration to say that both peoples, the Muslim and Christian subjects of the sultans, shared a civilization for centuries. There is no greater demonstration of this fact than the awe-inspiring mosques of Istanbul, requisitioned by royalty and designed by an Armenian, Mimar Sinan. In these mosques are made manifest the grandeur of the Ottomans and the aesthetic perfection that Sinan envisioned. Neither could exist without the other.

The terms "Turk" and "Armenian," used continuously since the end of the nineteenth century, seem easy to understand: Turks are the people from Turkey and Armenians are the people from Armenia, right? In fact, Turks didn't always call themselves "Turks," and "Armenians" hail not only from the eastern marches of Asia Minor but also from the Russian Caucasus and would also settle the fertile region of Cilicia, just north of Syria. Aside from their respective religious faiths, the two peoples are in many ways congruent in their culture and style. Both peoples call roughly the same vast territory home.[1] In fact, over the last one thousand years, they have intermixed populations continuously via religious conversion, intermarriage, and the complex Ottoman practice of *devshirme,* the systematic forced conversion to Islam of a prescribed number of Christian young men. In the end, religion became identity.[2]

An interesting example of intermixture is the Hemshin, a Muslim people who make their home in the mountains near the Black Sea. It is believed that the Hemshin are the descendants of Armenians who fled Muslim raids centuries ago, settled in the region, and over time forgot their roots. As a result, they believe that they are Turks, though they speak an Armenian dialect and continue to practice certain rituals associated with Christianity (for example, rudimentary baptism). In the twentieth century, as railroads and automobiles made Asia Minor a much smaller place, these remote Hemshin villages began to integrate with the rest of Turkey. The Hemshin people started to migrate into larger population centers and as "Turks" were amazed to discover people who spoke their Hemshin mountain dialect.

Over the millennia, the armies of numerous empires invaded and re-invaded the peninsula that extends from the Mediterranean to the Caucasus, from the Syrian deserts to the Black Sea. The Hittites, the Greeks, the Persians, the Romans, the Byzantines, the Arabs, the Seljuks, the Mongols, the Russians, and finally the Ottomans all at one time or another invaded and settled here. Each empire brought its civilization as well as its subject people. Over thousands of years, not only did dozens of ethnic and religious groups such as Kurds, Turks, Arabs, Persians, and Greeks settle in the region but also Jews, Roma, Albanians, Uzbeks, Christian Arabs, Hemshin, Laz, Turkmen and Yoruks, Georgians, Chaldean people, Tajiks, Zaza, later "Tartars" and Circassians, Pomeks, Cossacks, and Uygurs. Unbelievably, even the Normans of France invaded eastern Anatolia at one point. Invaders melded with those who came before them as well as migrants who entered the region as they were chased from their far-off homelands. Before the modern era, a greater variety of peoples crossed and recrossed this region than anywhere else on earth. And as far as we know, going back to the earliest written history, through all these invasions and migrations, the Armenians lived here, as kings and as peasants.

Asia Minor is where the East meets the West, where Asia meets Europe, making the great city of Constantinople a point where most traffic moving eastward or westward, northward or southward, had to pass. The first humans must have traveled through this land northward from Africa. According to the Bible, Noah's ark finally came to rest on the holy mountain of Ararat, which rises up from the easternmost reaches of the Armenian plateau. The Silk Road traverses this territory. The Ottoman Empire knit together Europe and the Middle East, North Africa and the Balkans. Before it began to break apart, roughly one third of those ruled by the sultan were European, one third Anatolian, and one third Arabian/African. Just prior to World War I, Constantinople was both a

European and a Near Eastern capital. For centuries it had been populated by Muslims and Christians as well as Jews, and at the end of the nineteenth century, the mix, reflecting the makeup of the empire itself, was almost fifty-fifty Muslim-Christian. Asia Minor has always been a place of convergence.

After the earliest years of Ottoman conquest, when the Armenians became a subject people, it was the Muslim Turks who held power as military men, administrators, or clerics, as inheritors of a vast militaristic empire. Often the Christians and Jews performed those tasks the Muslims avoided. They became the artisans, the merchants, the traders, the bankers. In the earliest days of the Ottoman Empire, society was divided not so much by religion as by "those who fought in its wars and those who paid for them."[3] The people who belonged to the sultan's military-administrative machine were known as *askeri*. The taxpaying class, by contrast, was known as *raya* (from the Arabic meaning "flock"). In time, *raya* would refer to the Christian peasantry.

In the first century after the death of Jesus, long before the Ottomans arrived in Asia Minor, apostles of the new Jewish sect based on his teachings traveled to outlying lands spreading the "good news." It was natural that some would end up in the kingdom of Armenia, which around the time of Christ existed as an autonomous if subordinate region of the Roman Empire. According to legend, Saint Jude (also known as Thaddeus), one of the original twelve apostles, was the first to make his way to Armenia, whereupon he converted the king's daughters. A few years later, Saint Bartholomew also visited Armenia and made yet more conversions, including the king's sister. (In the early Christian era, women seemed to be attracted to conversion more often than men.) These missions did not end well for the apostles, both of whom ended up as martyrs, Jude in Beirut and Bartholomew at Albanopolis in Armenia. Bartholomew is traditionally depicted in religious imagery as crucified upside down or skinned alive, as in Michelangelo's *Last Judgment,* where he is seen clutching his own flayed skin. Because the first Christians in Armenia were converted by original apostles, Armenians named their form of Christianity "Apostolic."

By AD 200, according to Tertullian (widely considered to be the first Christian author of note), numerous Christian enclaves had been established in Armenia. The Armenian rulers at the time hewed to the policy of the Roman Empire and tried to root out these secret societies. They persecuted the followers of Jesus with increasing violence, just as the Romans attempted to extinguish the cult wherever it arose in the empire.

Around AD 300, two and a half centuries after the apostles arrived to make converts, the reigning Roman emperor, Diocletian, became one of the most energetic antagonists of the new faith. This was the era when Christians would be smeared with pine tar and set afire or forced to fight hungry lions in the Roman Colosseum for the entertainment of the masses. The reigning Armenian king, Trdat, being an ally of Diocletian, followed suit, and became notorious in his own right for torturing and killing Christians.

An itinerant Christian monk named Gregory arrived at Trdat's court. Here the story gets complicated, because not only was Gregory Christian but also, according to legend, he was the son of Anak, the assassin of King Trdat's father. (Some sources claim that Gregory specifically sought out Trdat as a way of atoning for his father's sin.) When Trdat learned that the young monk was Anak's son, he had him tortured and tossed into an underground stone cell littered with dead bodies and crawling with serpents. The cell is located at the Khor Virap monastery in Armenia, and to this day, pilgrims to the Armenian homeland delicately descend, one by one, into the gloomy chamber by means of a steep iron ladder.

The legend has Gregory remaining in solitary confinement for a full thirteen years while King Trdat continued to wreak havoc among the believers. According to the fifth-century historian Agathangelos, thirty-seven Christian virgins, fleeing Roman persecution, arrived in Trdat's kingdom during Gregory's imprisonment. The king lusted after one of the virgin nuns, Hripsime, a renowned beauty. Hripsime had, of course, taken a vow of chastity, so she resisted Trdat's advances. In a rage, the king tortured and killed Hripsime, then martyred the entire flock of young virgin nuns. (One did manage to escape: Saint Nino, patron saint of the Georgian Orthodox Church, who went on to found Christianity there.)

According to church history, as a result of his evil deeds, God struck Trdat with a sickness that left him crawling around on all fours, on the brink of madness. In some stories the king lost his mind; in others God literally turned Trdat into a wild boar. Willing to try anything to cure her brother, Trdat's Christian sister, Khosrovidukht, proposed freeing the Christian monk Gregory, who at this point had been imprisoned for over a decade. Gregory was dragged out of his filthy dungeon, cleaned up, and brought before Trdat. Gregory, full of Christian forgiveness, blessed Trdat, and the old king snapped back to perfect health. Overcome with joy, Trdat immediately declared Armenia a Christian nation and invited Gregory to be the first head of this new state church. Saint Gregory "the Illuminator" would assume the role of chief bishop[4] and leader of the new Armenian Christian faith. Trdat and Gregory demanded compliance with the new way of doing things; any resistance was met with violence. Throughout the kingdom, heathen sanctuaries and temples were leveled. (The only surviving pagan temple in Armenia is in Garni, a popular tourist spot.) Hundreds of churches and monasteries were established, and hundreds of priests and bishops were ordained.

While converting members of the existing priestly class to Christianity, Gregory negotiated terms in order to secure the allegiance of the formerly pagan priests. For example, Armenian priests are allowed to marry and the pagan ritual of animal sacrifice was also preserved, since this sacrament provided an important part of a priest's income. After the animals were dispatched, the pagan (and, later, Christian) priest would take a commission, bringing a chunk of the slaughtered animal home to his own family. In the early church writings, Gregory laid down the law to his priests: "Your portions of the offerings shall be the hide and right-hand parts of the spine, the limb and fat, and the tail and heart and lobe of the lungs, and the tripe with the lard; of the ribs and shank-bones a part, the tongue and the right ear, and the right eye and all the secret parts."[5] This ritual has survived to the present as the *madagh*. Anyone who has attended an Armenian funeral has partaken of this animal sacrifice in the form of a small sliver of cooked lamb on bread. In Armenia today, ritual slaughter of sheep is still common. *Madagh* has also become part of the annual ceremony memorializing the genocide on April 24.

While meditating in Trdat's capital city of Vagharshapat, Gregory had a vision of Jesus descending to earth and striking the ground with a hammer. In his vision, a great Christian church topped with a massive cross rose from that spot. Following what he understood to be a divine commandment, Gregory built a church, renaming the city Etchmiadzin (translated as "the place of the descent of the only begotten"). This complex of holy shrines and churches still stands, some seventeen hundred years later.

Around the same time that the Armenian Church was founded, circa AD 300, long before the Muslim Arabs, Turks, or Mongols invaded, the anti-Christian Diocletian stepped down, and Emperor Constantine took over the Eastern Roman Empire. Constantine's mother, Helena, had been a practicing Christian, encouraging his more tolerant attitude toward the new religion. In 313 he issued an edict "tolerating" the fledgling faith throughout the Roman Empire. Constantine also moved the center of the Eastern Roman Empire to the city of Byzantion and renamed it after himself. Thus Constantinopolis, or Constantinople, would carry Constantine's name until 1923, when Ataturk officially renamed the great city Istanbul.

There are at least three reasons why Constantinople grew to be the capital of an empire. First of all, it straddles the Bosphorus, the major strait connecting the Black Sea to the Mediterranean. It is the gatekeeper to all of Russia's warm-water ports as well as the Crimea. For this reason it has always been a key chokepoint for Russian trade. (At the onset of World War I, half of Russia's world trade moved via the Bosphorus.)[6] Second, this place where two seas join culminates in one of the world's greatest harbors. In places it is a hundred feet deep and is protected from weather by the vast, calm Sea of Marmara, lying just to the south. Farther south are the headlands of the Dardanelles, and beyond them the eastern Aegean littoral, an awesome collection of islands and inlets. "Not only did the site control trade between the Black and Mediterranean Seas, and between Asia Minor and the Balkans, but it also could potentially rely upon a vast and sea borne provisioning zone stretching from the Crimean peninsula to Egypt and beyond."[7]

Third, this magnificent harbor is naturally defensible thanks to the imposing rocky heights projecting over it. This massif was, until the time of aircraft, almost impregnable. Constantinople/Istanbul is perched atop seven hills of stone, ringed by walls and fortifications built by the Romans and the Byzantines and, later, the sultans. Any approaching warships must either pass the Dardanelles or come down the Bosphorus. Gallipoli peninsula, where tens of thousands of soldiers died during World War I, is the landmass flanking the Dardanelles straits.

In its early years, Armenians made up a significant segment of the burgeoning Christian society. But Armenian churches celebrated the liturgy in Greek or Syriac, not Armenian. The priesthood and various educational institutions widely used Greek and Syrian. A century after the Armenian Church was established, the Armenian king Vramshapouh and his reigning Catholicos, Sahak Partev, concluded that an Armenian alphabet was crucial to strengthening the national Christian Armenian identity.

The task of creating a new alphabet was assigned to a scholar-monk named Mesrob Mashtots, who invented the Armenian alphabet of thirty-six letters (two more were added later) in 405. After naming the characters and ordering them, Mesrob had the renowned calligrapher Rufinus add artistic refinements. The first sentence written down in Armenian by Mesrob is said to have been the opening line of Solomon's Book of Proverbs: "For learning about wisdom and instruction, for understanding words of insight." In 430 the Bible was translated into the Armenian language from copies imported from Constantinople and Edessa. Previously the Bible was available only in the Syriac, Latin, Coptic, and Abyssinian languages. The introduction of a written language unique to the Armenians triggered a cultural renaissance. More than that, it unified a people and permanently forged a bond between literacy and religion that has survived to this day.

In 451, a century and a half after the Armenians embraced Christianity, their faith was tested. During this era the Byzantines (who were the heirs to the Eastern Roman Empire) began to lose their grip on the farthest reaches of their empire and the Persians became the dominant power in the region. The Persians practiced Zoroastrianism, a religion and philosophy based on the teachings of the prophet Zoroaster (Zarathustra), and they were not pleased that the Armenians followed another faith. These religious differences resulted in a number of insurrections by the Armenians against the Persians.

On May 26, 451, a major battle took place on the Avarayr Plain in Vaspurakan. Thousands of Armenians fought the vastly superior Sassanid Persian troops. Though most of the Armenian princes, including their leader, Vartan Mamigonian, fell in battle, the encounter had enduring value. The Armenians lost the battle but won the war, so to speak, because after the "Battle of Vartanantz," the Persians, finding the Armenians too difficult to control, left them alone to practice their faith as they wished. Saint Vartan is revered to this day by Armenians all over the world.[8]

Armenians were participants in many of the early church councils in which Christian leaders from different regions and sects came together to hash out matters of doctrine. Of particular importance to the history of the Armenian Church was the Council of

Chalcedon, convened in 451, at which a key point of theology was debated. The gist of the argument came down to whether God/Jesus possessed two "natures" (godly and human) or only one. This was an important theological question, because if Jesus was *not* a man, then obviously his suffering on the cross was mitigated by his supernatural powers. You can't torture a god the way you can torture a human. The Armenians, distracted by their war with the Persians, were not represented at Chalcedon. Perhaps because they did not participate in deciding the issue, the Armenians did not agree with the outcome.

The Byzantine Christian establishment (and Rome) embraced the notion of Christ's *dual* nature—humanness and godliness—through which his suffering absolved humanity of its original sin. The Armenians (and other "schismatic" churches), by contrast, opted for *one* nature. God was holy and that was that. That is why the Armenians are labeled "monophysite."[9] Theological resistance morphed into political resistance to the Byzantine hegemony. This position would now set the Armenians in contrast to their fellow Christians as well as the Islamic empire in which they lived.

For the next thousand years, the rising power of Islam would threaten the Christian world. When the Arabs invaded parts of Asia Minor in the second half of the first millennium, they decimated the Greek and Armenian communities settled there. If you visit Cappadocia today, you can tour a vast collection of manmade caves, in some places descending twenty stories underground, where temporary tunnel cities once housed thousands of Christians hiding from the Arab raiders. The Arab followers of Muhammad (570–632) had always thought of their military ventures as holy wars. During the first centuries of Islam, religion and warfare defined the new Islamic empire. The world was divided into two camps: the House of Islam *(dar al-Islam)* and the House of War *(dar al-Harb)*. The House of Islam was congruent with the territorial empire of the Arabs (and the later caliphates, including the Ottomans). Everything beyond that border was considered a war zone.[10]

The Arab raiders would be followed by the Seljuk Turks in the eleventh century. Turkic tribes from the Central Asian region now called Kazakhstan (and farther east) swept into Persia and then Anatolia. Like the Mongols, the original Turks were highly mobile cavalrymen, agile masters of the composite bow and arrow (wood, horn, sinew, and glue). Turkic forces employed an early version of "shock and awe," combining surprise with overwhelming force, often completely annihilating opposing armies. Like the Mongols, Turkic forces insisted on complete surrender. Often resistance was met with total destruction. And like the Arabs and the Mongols, the Turkic tribes were Muslim. The Seljuk Turks, a tribal dynasty, established a foothold in Anatolia by defeating the Christian Byzantines at Manzikert in 1071. They then proceeded to disrupt the Byzantine Empire by raiding and controlling the territory lying between the major population centers. As each city was cut off, it became helpless and could then be taken by siege.[11]

The Islamic Turkish invasion of Byzantium and the Holy Lands prompted the Byzantines to ask for assistance from the Christians of Europe proper. Crusader knights from France and other parts of Europe, blessed by the pope, invaded the eastern Mediterranean littoral in an attempt to wrest the birthplace of Jesus from "the Saracens." The pope promised his holy legions that if they "took up the cross," he would vacate sins and guarantee an afterlife. For the commoners of Europe, the Crusades were one way to escape the grinding misery of medieval existence. In this way the concept of the "holy warrior" or Crusader also became a fixture in Christian thinking. At first the knights were successful and managed to occupy Jerusalem. Fiefdoms were established up and down the coast, and the Knights Hospitaller, the Knights Templar, the Teutonic Knights, and others became a presence in the Middle East. Themselves at odds with the Byzantines, Armenians sided with the

Crusaders (commonly known as "Franks"),[12] who arrived on the scene at the dawn of the second millennium.

The fury with which the Crusader knights attacked the East was not always aimed at Muslims. By the Fourth Crusade in 1202, the knights, motivated by treasure and glory, had become a powerful political body in their own right. In this Crusade, they never got as far as the Holy Land but instead attacked Constantinople, where the Christian Byzantines, no longer on friendly terms with the Catholics, ruled. The Catholic French and Venetian knights ransacked the holy Byzantine city. "The Latin soldiery subjected the greatest city in Europe to an indescribable sack. For three days they murdered, raped, looted and destroyed on a scale which even the ancient Vandals and Goths would have found unbelievable....The Greeks were convinced that even the Turks, had they taken the city, would not have been as cruel as the Latin Christians."[13]

Ravaging Constantinople, the Christian capital of the Byzantine Empire, the Franks and their confederates murdered the priests and raped the nuns. The Library of Constantinople was destroyed. Antiquities were looted. Much of the city was torched. Inside the magnificent Hagia Sophia, at the time the greatest church in Orthodox Christendom, the invaders smashed icons, tore holy books to shreds, and desecrated the altar while guzzling sacred wine from holy chalices. The rampage was followed by a massacre of the population. Islamic historians would later cite the actions of the Crusaders (as well as the Catholic conquistadors in the Americas) as evidence that Christians were as bloody as any Muslim army.

—⁂—

By 1200, the Seljuk Turks had solidly installed themselves in Asia Minor. In the thirteenth century, the even fiercer Mongols burst onto the scene and destroyed what the Seljuks had established. Some hundred years later, the Mongols relinquished their hold on Anatolia and various resilient Turkish *ghazi* emirates reestablished themselves, again moving westward and crowding the weakened Byzantines. One tribe in particular flourished. It was founded by a man named Osman (1258–1326). In time his descendants, the Osmanlis, controlled all of Anatolia to the east and as far as the Balkans to the west. Europeans called the Osmanlis "Ottomans."

Then, around 1400, in a final Turco-Mongol thrust into the region, Tamurlane (or Timur) invaded Armenia and Georgia. Over the next two years he retook all of Anatolia and defeated the Ottoman sultan Bayezid in the Battle of Ankara. Tamurlane continued onward to Smyrna and ousted the Knights Hospitallers, remnants of the surviving Crusader forces. Tamurlane's stay in the Ottoman lands was brief, but the damage done to the region, especially to the Armenians, was deep and permanent.

The Ottomans reconstituted themselves and expanded their Islamic empire in all directions. As the Ottoman Empire grew and flourished, it spread into territories all around Constantinople but could not take the imperial city itself. In 1453, after two years of preparation, Sultan Mehmed "the Conqueror" attacked the Christian city. The massive walls were hammered with artillery for weeks on end, only to be repaired as fast as they crumbled. In one of the most famous battles in history, Mehmed ordered Turkish warships physically lifted out of the water, carried overland, and dropped into the harbor on the other side of the Golden Horn. He then attacked from two sides at once and succeeded in taking the city, ending a thousand years of Christian rule. Sultan Mehmed repopulated the city by inviting, and sometimes forcing, people to move there. This included Christians and Jews.

The apogee of imperial Ottoman glory was achieved by Suleiman "the Magnificent" almost one hundred years after Mehmed the Conqueror took Constantinople. Suleiman was a sultan of immense authority who successfully led armies against Europe until his advance was checked at the Siege of Vienna in 1529. In this way, the Ottomans took control of most of eastern Europe as

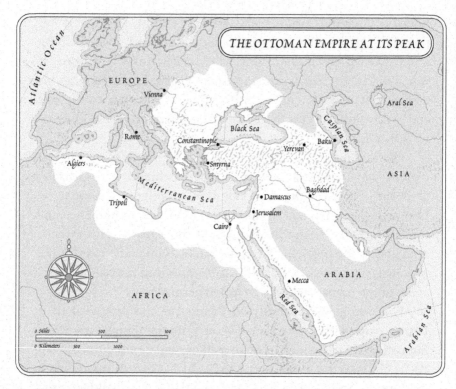

THE OTTOMAN EMPIRE AT ITS PEAK

In the sixteenth century, the Ottoman Empire under Sultan Suleiman the Magnificent reached its apogee. At its peak, the empire controlled most of the Middle East, Greece, the Balkans, Asia Minor, and North Africa.

well as all of Arabia and North Africa up to, but not including, Morocco. This Muslim imperium was populated by Turks as well as Slavic speakers of the Balkans.[14] The peoples of the empire also included Christian Greeks, Armenians, and Assyrians as well as Jewish refugees from the Inquisition in Spain. Perhaps the most remarkable thing about the Ottoman system was how successfully it incorporated the conquered peoples into its highest levels, enriching its cultural infrastructure. A slave girl from the most remote corner of the empire could become mother to a sultan. A Christian Bosnian could rise up through the ranks to the position of Grand Vizier.[15]

★   ★   ★

In the first centuries of the Ottoman Empire, Europeans had little contact with its people except during warfare or on the high seas. Europeans referred to them as "Musselmen" and erroneously regarded them as descendants of the ultra-violent Mongol Tamurlane. The Ottomans appeared, in the European imagination, as caricatures—hookah-smoking outlaws who abducted women into their harems, castrated young boys, or enslaved the crews of captured ships. Westerners pictured the Ottomans perched on pillows, ogling their odalisques while devouring roasted meat off skewers. (In fact, European traders introduced tobacco to the Ottomans. Muslim mullahs forbade its use, to no avail. The clerics labeled tobacco, wine, coffee, and opium as "the four legs of the couch of satan.")[16] The West indulged itself with fantasies of decadent sultans who wasted their days in lavish, cloistered extravagance. (Some did.) But this was a cartoonish view of an impressive civilization. Suleiman, the longest-reigning sultan, was intelligent and brave, instituting vast reforms in law, taxation, and education. A great patron of the arts, Suleiman oversaw the golden age of Ottoman architecture. His court was as complex and as sophisticated as any in Europe.

By the time Mozart was composing his opera *The Abduction from the Seraglio* (1782), set in an Ottoman harem, the "otherness" of the Ottomans had totally captivated the European imagination. The artists and storytellers of Europe expanded vague hearsay about the sultan's court into lush fantasies filled with naked slave girls and fierce eunuchs. Could there be a greater nightmare than getting caught by a Turk and being enslaved in his seraglio? The "Lustful Turk" represented the ultimate unfettered degenerate, a sadistic satyr with an enormous sexual appetite (and genitals), who would as soon drink blood as eat.

Ironically, in the middle of the sixteenth century, as the Ottomans were reaching their imperial apex under Suleiman, European kingdoms continued to fight tooth and nail amongst themselves. The advantage shifted from the Spanish to the English to the French to Hapsburg monarchs, with Russia waiting in the wings. The wars between the kingdoms were long and bloody. (Among the dozens of wars fought before, during, and after the European Renaissance were the Thirty Years' War, the Napoleonic Wars, and Britain's war with its North American colonies.) For over a hundred years, as Europeans wasted energy on hostilities, the Ottoman Empire loomed like a massive wall at one end of the continent, an enigmatic foe constantly threatening invasion. The Ottomans had been stopped at Vienna, but for how long?

With the discovery of "the New World," Europe fortified itself with plundered gold and silver, and the Ottoman Empire, laboring under its immense size, peaked. The Ottomans had no access to the treasure from across the Atlantic that was transforming Europe from a cluster of warring principalities into an interlocking quilt of very wealthy kingdoms. Moreover, Europeans were inventing new ways of utilizing their newfound wealth, as modern banking and transnational corporations superseded the outmoded feudal economic system. The Industrial Revolution dawned and manufacturing exploded, making Europe dominant in the art of war. The Ottomans, by contrast, remained mired in the old ways, leaving themselves at a distinct disadvantage. The Europeans used their money to construct fast ships and powerful new means of warfare, making the seemingly insuperable Ottoman armies vulnerable, and ultimately obsolete. As the empire loosened its grip on its vast territories, the balance of power shifted. Europe could now shove back at the formidable Turks.

What distinguished the Ottomans culturally from their contemporaries in Europe was not just their religious identity but their complex traditions and institutions, evolved over hundreds of years. Though the empire was ruled by a sultan who in almost every way seemingly paralleled the position of emperor, the similarities were in appearance only. Dynasties were forged in the harem in a manner completely unlike the system of primogeniture common in the West. The Ottoman military, heir to the Seljuk system, was from its earliest years organized in a unique fashion that made it fearsome. Finally and significantly as far as the history of the Armenians is concerned, religious minorities were tolerated under what was called the *millet* system, in contrast to the violent suppression of "heretics" common in Europe.

The sultan was not only the supreme political ruler; he was also caliph, leader of the Islamic world, the "shadow of God on earth" (in Arabic, *zill Allah fi'l-alem*),[17] and thus the entire empire belonged to him. Every ounce of gold, every acre, every slave was his property. Some of the highest dignitaries were legally his slaves. The first sultans were *ghazis,* warrior sultans who led their armies into battle. The sultan as caliph symbolically reigned beyond the borders of his empire: he was the leader of all Muslims, whether living as Ottomans or not.

In the Ottoman Empire, power flowed to the unknowable center. This was where the sultan held court and lived. There are almost no first-person accounts of the earliest sultans because few individuals were actually allowed to be in the royal presence— certainly not Westerners or anyone who might write a memoir. Sultans avoided appearing in public; in governmental meetings they would often be hidden behind a screen. With the sultan secreted away, others could establish bases of power within the complex bureaucracy of the palace and the Sublime Porte, the functional Ottoman government, run by the Grand Vizier, who was often the true head of the empire.

At the height of Ottoman power, the palace of the sultan was Topkapi Sarayi (visited today every year by thousands of tourists). The palace housed the royal entourage, including the royal harem, for hundreds of years. Later the royal residence would move to the more European-styled Dolmabahce. Finally, Sultan Abdul Hamid II would move the palace once again, to Yildiz, in an effort to make his residence more secure.

*   *   *

The Islamic view that divided the world into the House of War and the House of Islam made war making a primary function of government. With a permanent state of war as its foundation, the Ottoman culture was defined by a militaristic spirit. In the early years of the empire, the most exalted legions of the Ottoman military were the Janissaries (from *yeni ceri,* meaning in Turkish "new force"). These were crack military units composed mostly of Christian youths harvested from villages of the realm, usually in eastern Europe. In a cycle of three, five, or seven years, emissaries from Constantinople would visit these outlying villages, particularly in Christian Bosnia. The most attractive teenagers were collected under the process of *devshirme,* often with the consent of their families, because to be invited into the sultanic milieu was a great honor and opportunity. These young men were converted to Islam and divided into units for intensive training. Some were sent to work in the countryside to develop their physical strength. Others were transported directly to Constantinople to work in the palace. The most impressive candidates were selected to enter the elite military devoted to the sultan, the Janissaries.

The Renaissance historian Paolo Giovio explained why the Janissaries were a superior fighting force: "Their discipline under arms is due to their justice and severity, which surpasses that of the ancient Romans. They surpass our soldiers for three reasons: they obey their commanders without question; they seem to care nothing at all for lives in battle; they go for a long time without bread or wine, being content with barley and water."[18]

The Janissaries were the first standing army originated in Europe, slave soldiers whose lives were dedicated to war, and who were prepared to fight at any time. In the early years of the empire marriage was forbidden. In fact, they were not supposed to consider any life outside their duties as soldiers. The Janissaries were a primary reason for the Ottomans' success in battle, and they became the germ seed of an elite soldier class that flourished within the empire, until they wielded outsized power in the civilian, commercial, and political spheres. In 1826 the reigning sultan, Mahmud II, after patiently planning the destruction of the Janissaries for some eighteen years, secretly created a new army and, with no warning, trapped the Janissaries and destroyed them. More than ten thousand men perished in one night, gunned down or burned to death in their barracks. The last holdouts died in hand-to-hand combat in a vast murky underground lake, originally built by the Romans, the Cistern of the Thousand and One Columns. The bodies floated down the Bosphorus for days. In Ottoman history, this mass killing of the Janissaries is called "the Auspicious Event."

The history of the Ottoman Empire parallels the history of the royal line. For all intents and purposes, the story begins with Osman and ends with Abdul Hamid II. (The last two sultans following Abdul Hamid were no more than figureheads representing the Young Turks and the British, respectively.) For centuries, the royal line was generated in the royal harem. It was here that the "politics of reproduction" were played out.[19]

"Harem" derives from the Arabic *haram* (h-r-m), with a "root meaning something like 'forbidden' or 'taboo' and evok[ing] constraint and often heightened sanctity as well."[20] In the Muslim household, it refers to the area of the home where the women live and work. The public is not to intrude on these inner rooms. Traditionally, men spend more time in the outer rooms, where the more public aspects of social life take place. In the sultan's household, the imperial harem was located in the inner area of the palace grounds, in the "House of Felicity," where only the closest members of the sultan's personal retinue could enter. Of course, for sexually obsessed Westerners, the area of most interest has always been that part of the harem where the sultan's hundreds of potential sexual partners resided, a warren of small rooms called the seraglio, situated alongside the sultan's quarters, where his complex hierarchy of support staff resided. The seraglio was guarded by black and white eunuchs, who in turn were under the command of the *kizlar agasi,* the chief black eunuch. The *kizlar agasi* was one of the most powerful people in the realm. As overseer of the women of the harem, he was responsible for their care and, if necessary, their disposal.

The denizens of the harem numbered in the hundreds, with about half acting as servants to the other half. The women selected to pleasure the sultan and to bear his children were slaves, acquired for the most part in the outer realms of the empire, particularly Greece, eastern Anatolia, the Balkans, and the Crimean Peninsula. Under Islamic law, Muslims cannot be slaves to other Muslims, so these women were almost entirely Christian. (This rule was fudged with regard to Bosnia.) The earliest sultans *did* marry highborn Islamic women, who could also bear their children, but this practice was eventually abandoned for the more pragmatic selection of young women with no connections to extended families. (The most exceptional case was the concubine Roxana, who married Suleiman and in turn became the most famous of all the slave girls to rise up from the seraglio.) The preferred system of extending the royal lineage was through children born of the concubines. Prisoners of the harem, when concubines were no longer useful they could be put to death, their bodies placed in sacks and thrown into the Bosphorus.

In fact, most of the hundreds of odalisques would never spend even a minute with the sultan. They were under the constant guard and care of the black eunuchs. (Black eunuchs were captured in Africa by traders and, after being subjected to the most extreme form of castration—removal of *all* their genitalia—sold to the wealthy. The royal eunuchs were named after flowers: Hyacinth, Rose, Carnation.)

The imperial harem was no pool of wanton lust. If anything it was a prison filled with bored inmates, a highly formalized institution: "a machine to perpetuate the dynasty, even against the Sultan's will."[21] Over the centuries, the sultan became something like a queen bee, sequestered at the center of a massive hive, protected and pampered and not really in charge of anything. The individual personality of any particular sultan was superseded by the idea and the institution. The sultan could always be replaced. "With the exception of such forceful men as Mehmed the Conqueror, Selim I or Murad IV, the Ottoman sultans were little more than cogs in a machine."[22] In the nineteenth century, sultans continued to lead a cocooned life, with activist Grand Viziers and other ministers actually running the empire. Indeed, there were a number of dissolute, even alcoholic sultans. But for the West to brand the Turkish court as decadent was somewhat disingenuous, given the court of Charles II in England or Louis the XV in France, where hedonism was an established institution in its own right.

When the sultan wished to select a girl, he first had to obtain permission from his mother (his *mother!*), the Valida Sultana, in a long and complicated ritual. The girls were paraded before him, the royal selection was made, and the girl would be separated from the group and, over the next day, prepared for her meeting with destiny. She would be bathed, covered in a mudpack of oil and rice flour, and then scrubbed for hours. Her body would be shaved, her nails would be dyed, her eyelashes brushed with lemon kohl; she would be perfumed and hennaed. Two large candles would be lit, and intimacy would proceed as other women guarded the doors to the sultan's bedchamber.

In the morning, the sultan rose first, accompanied by his usual entourage. A royal secretary would enter the date of the encounter into a register. The girl would return to her cell and, if nine months later she did not produce royal progeny, she would probably never see the sultan again. Concubines who became pregnant with the sultan's child immediately rose in status. Male heirs were prized, of course. Mothers of the princes and princesses had the highest status in the harem. Since the various children usually had different mothers (each concubine was permitted to have only one son by the sultan), this put the mothers in competition with one another. And once the new sultan was firmly enthroned, his mother became Valida Sultana, the most powerful woman in the realm, simply by dint of her ability to control him.

As a result of this competition, there was a very dark side to bearing sons for the sultan. Should a boy find his way onto the throne, all of his brothers were in immediate danger. Beginning with Mehmed the Conqueror, all adult male relatives of the sultan were at risk. This culling would ensure that royal competition could not endanger the dynasty itself. Brothers and cousins were strangled with a silken cord, as it was considered sinful to spill royal blood. It made no difference how old or young the victim was. Babies were smothered; grown men were garroted. It was understood that to leave any other heirs alive would jeopardize the stability of the state. Nothing personal. Murder was an essential part of the smooth running of the empire.

In later centuries the wholesale killing of princes was replaced with a system of sequestering them for their lifetime in "the cage," a suite in the palace which they were never permitted to leave. This confinement transformed some princes into anxious neurotics, cut off from the outside world and in constant fear for their lives. There were instances of caged princes who became sultan but, having been driven mad by their confinement, were unfit to rule and were subsequently removed.

Very few men could enter the most private of the sultan's quarters. Those who did were generally eunuchs or prepubescent pages. In 1566 Selim, the son of Suleiman, ascended the throne. He invited a Hungarian convert to Islam, Gazanfer, to take the job of chief white eunuch and head of the privy chamber. He had to accept castration as the price to be paid for this most lofty position. Gazanfer went on to become one of the most influential persons in the Ottoman Empire, serving for over thirty years.

Militarism and dynastic succession were not the only distinguishing aspects of the Ottoman world. Though it was an Islamic empire, the Ottoman Empire was for much of its history roughly fifty percent non-Muslim, either Christian or Jewish. The millet system, originally developed under Arab-Islamic Sharia law, contrasted sharply with the religious intolerance practiced in Europe, where "heretics" were routinely tortured and executed. Understanding that the non-Muslim minorities had a value in the empire, sultans had for hundreds of years followed the example of the Islamic Arabs before them and invited Christian and Jewish "People of the Book" to live in relative peace in the "House of Islam" as second-class subjects. Under the millet system, Muslims constituted the ruling class, while Christians and Jews were *raya,* the flock, who were tolerated as long as they kept to their place.

Though they were not forced by law to convert, Christian and Jewish subjects were subject to specific restrictions. They paid a tax that Muslims were exempt from. Their men could not marry a Muslim woman. Their church steeples could not be higher than the minarets of the mosques. Loud church bells were not permitted. They were forced to defer to Muslims at all times and had subordinate legal rights in a court of law. A Muslim master could kill or take property from Christians under his command with impunity.

Jews and Christians were "formally forbidden" to dress like Muslims or live near mosques, to build tall houses or buy slaves. "They...were not supposed to wear certain colours;...their houses or places of worship should not be ostentatious; they were excluded from positions of power," with some exceptions.[23] Most important, non-Muslims were forbidden to bear arms.

A millet system of self-governance on the part of each religious group was encouraged and took root, and each group (Greek, Armenian, Jewish) had its religious community leaders or patriarchs. In this way, the millets became political entities within the Ottoman Empire "representing" each community. Different millets were identified by their clothing. "Only Muslims could wear white or green turbans and yellow slippers. Greeks, Armenians and Jews were distinguished respectively by sky blue, dark blue (later red) and yellow hats, and by black, violet and blue slippers."[24] Legal issues that concerned only the millet could be resolved by the millet overseers. The leaders of the millets had power and acted as a conduit between the Sublime Porte and the communities. In time this relationship would evolve, allowing some Armenians to become very powerful within the construct of the Ottoman universe.

In the modern era, the fragmented and dispersed Armenian population existed in areas under Ottoman, Persian, and Russian control. These three antagonistic empires treated their Armenian populations in different ways. Very significantly, Armenians in the Ottoman universe lived as Christians in a Muslim world. In the Russian territories, mainly in the Caucasus (though the border was constantly shifting), Armenians were Christian in a world where the tsar saw himself as a champion of Orthodoxy. Further divisions within the Armenian populations broke along class lines: peasants, artisans, and tradespeople, merchants and wealthy elites moved within their own societies. Over time, the "Turkish" (western) Armenians and the "Russian" (eastern) Armenians would speak very different dialects and become culturally distinct.[25]

The Armenian Genocide was nothing less than the final clash of two civilizations: the ancient Armenian nation and the Ottoman Empire. The centuries-old intersection of two peoples had come to an end. Though the Armenians would continue to be a major presence in the Middle East and the Caucasus, they were no longer living in their homeland. Mere thousands remained of the millions who had dwelled there for millennia. By 1923, with the birth of the Republic of Turkey, the Armenian presence in Asia Minor would effectively be over.

CHAPTER TWO

Rushing Headlong into the Modern Era, 1800–1914

Revolution requires extensive and widespread destruction, a fecund and renovating destruction, since in this way and only this way are new worlds born.

—Mikhail Bakunin, *Statism and Anarchy*

Whether or not they called themselves "modern," from the middle of the nineteenth century onward the citizens of the West understood that the world was changing. Fueled by the Industrial Revolution, the idea that civilization is forever moving forward to new and greater heights caught every thinker's imagination. This, in essence, was modernism. Progress animated all areas of human existence: finance, medicine, education, painting, literature, music, and, ironically, the art of making war. Combat achieved new levels of awesome and unprecedented destructiveness. Technologies combined to foster violence not only between nations but within empires. The Ottoman Empire, like the rest of the world, joined the rush to modernize.

Progress created political turbulence. From the mid-nineteenth century until the conclusion of World War I, assassination, revolution, and war plagued the world. In 1848 revolution broke out in Italy, Germany, Denmark, Hungary, Ireland, Romania, and Moldavia. Civil war and revolution would follow in the United States, Mexico, India, and China. The short-lived socialist regime known as the Paris Commune was born during this period, in 1871, and rebellions arose across the Balkans against Ottoman rule. Successive wars, including the massively destructive Crimean War, broke out between Russia and the Ottomans, leaving hundreds of thousands dead on both sides and further weakening the Turkic empire. No sooner had the Civil War ended before the United States government began an all-out war of extermination against the Plains Indians. The Boer Wars in South Africa, the Boxer Rebellion in China, as well as uprisings in India and the Philippines were all manifestations of a world order in flux. The interplay of modern political institutions and the mechanization of warfare laid waste to human life on a scale never before experienced.

From the killing fields of Gettysburg to the trenches of Alsace, humans now could slaughter one another by the tens of thousands in a matter of days. During World War I, the Battle of Verdun alone left three hundred thousand fatalities, an average of one thousand deaths a day for ten months. New weapons technologies would accelerate and intensify conflict, making possible sudden flashes of mass violence. It was during this period that the machine gun and long-range artillery were developed. Deadly chlorine gas was concocted in German laboratories and deployed by both sides in the Great War. Barbed wire and the simple but deadly fixed bayonet amplified the hell of trench warfare, while land and naval mines intensified the anarchy. The armored tank, the hand grenade, and the long-range carbine were all perfected during this initial era of modern warfare.

The Industrial Revolution accelerated the tempo and scope of war through improvements in transportation and communication. The railroad, the steamship, motorized vehicles, and the telegraph (and later the airplane) allowed military leaders to deploy troops over extensive territory with unprecedented speed. Not only could soldiers and supplies be moved quickly, but so too could local populations. Modern warfare set in motion vast flows of refugees and displaced people, many of whom died for the simple lack of a safe haven.

Information itself became an adjunct to war, as newspapers—the "mass media" of the nineteenth century—proliferated. The journalists of the era endowed nations with personalities and intentions, portraying them as willful actors who were healthy or unhealthy, peaceful or belligerent, who flourished or sickened, had appetites and diseases, made enemies or friends. As World War I began, headlines typically characterized each nation as a sentient being imbued with intention: "Austria Has Chosen War"; "China Fearful of Japan War Moves."[1] Tsar Nicholas I had famously labeled the Ottoman Empire "the sick man of Europe."

At the same time, world conflicts were reported as if they were competitions, not unlike modern sporting events, with the intention of rallying the local fans. Sides were "winning" or "losing." This helped foster nationalism, a new way of thinking that defined a nation by language and culture. When the war in western Europe finally reached its combustion point, many young men (particularly in the West) saw it as an adventure, their appetite for conflict stoked by reports of wars on every continent.

A new breed of assassin appeared on the scene as the deadly accuracy of handguns and explosives improved dramatically. After Samuel Colt's patent of his revolver in 1835, the semiautomatic handgun became easily available thanks to extensive distribution during wartime. Mausers, Brownings, and Colts were the prized possessions of revolutionaries everywhere. When Alfred Nobel invented gelignite in 1875, bomb making became an art, and bombs became a significant part of the revolutionary arsenal. In 1919 anarchists mailed dozens of dynamite bombs to politicians, editors, and businessmen in the United States. One year later Wall Street was bombed; thirty-eight people died. Political agendas could be advanced in seconds as anarchists and other radicals required only a proximity of a few yards to their victims before pulling a trigger or lobbing a bomb.

The half century prior to World War I was open season on world leaders. Three American presidents, Lincoln, Garfield, and McKinley, were shot to death by assassins. A bullet would end the lives of Prime Minister Juan Prim of Spain, King Umberto of Italy, King Carlos of Portugal, King George of Greece, and Naser al-Din Shah Qajar of Persia. Empress Elizabeth of Austria, President Sadi Carnot of France, and Richard Southwell Bourke, sixth Earl of Mayo, were stabbed to death. Gabriel García Moreno, president of Ecuador, was hacked to death by machete. The killing spree against world leaders reached its climax in 1914, when Archduke Franz Ferdinand of Austro-Hungary was gunned down in Sarajevo by Gavrilo Princip, a Serbian nationalist, triggering World War I.

A small cadre of organized revolutionaries could effect broad regime change. And so assassination became an adjunct to revolution. In 1881 the Russian left-wing organization Narodnaya Volya (The People's Will) succeeded in assassinating Tsar Alexander II. Thirty-five years later, the Bolsheviks would tighten their hold on Russia by murdering Nicholas II and his extended family. Between 1919 and 1922, the period of the Nemesis murders, there were over three hundred political killings in the German Reich alone.[2]

In the century before the Armenian Genocide, the Armenian millet consisted of three overlapping groups. In Constantinople and other large cities like Smyrna and Alexandria, the economic and cultural elite flourished. Among these well-to-do were genuinely wealthy families, even men who were addressed as "pasha." The second group consisted of Armenians living throughout Asia Minor who were artisans and merchants, constituting a middle class of sorts, usually clustered in large towns and cities. This was the milieu from which the assassin Soghomon Tehlirian came. And everywhere in the empire, especially in eastern Asia Minor and the Russian Caucasus, lived the rural peasants, who, subject to the predations of armed Kurdish tribes and endless Ottoman taxation, made up the vast majority of Armenians. Their marginal existence only grew more perilous during the Ottoman period of modernization. By the end of the nineteenth century, massacres were common.

The deep poverty of the eastern *vilayets,* or provinces, where most Armenians lived, undermined the stability of the region. The inhabitants of these outlying frontier lands endured a medieval quality of life. Rural peasants shared their mud-walled houses with domestic animals. Farmers tilled their fields with makeshift plows and prayed for rain; blacksmiths hammered red-hot iron into horseshoes just as their fathers had and *their* fathers before them; mothers and sisters worked hand looms, weaving cloth for the home and the market. Shepherds tracked their sheep and goats in the same manner as their ancestors two thousand years earlier. There was no refrigeration, little electricity, and very few motorized vehicles. The brightly colored clothing designating the different millets was washed and beaten on the rocks along streams and rivers, just as it had been washed and beaten for the last twenty generations.

The Industrial Revolution which had radically changed life in Europe barely touched the vilayets beyond the outskirts of Constantinople.[3] The occasional presence of a sewing machine or kerosene lamp gave the only hint of the modern world enjoyed by the West. (Both kerosene and Singer sewing machines were imported from America and usually sold by Armenian merchants.) By World War I, only a few telephones (available since the 1890s in the United States) were in use outside the big cities, not even in the larger towns. Telegraphy provided the only long-distance instant communication. No paved roads connected the cities. In fact, cars and trucks were a rarity and railroads almost nonexistent. When railroad track was laid, most of it consisted of unfinished trunk lines leading nowhere. Municipal services were unknown. The government's main job was to collect taxes and maintain control. No factories existed as the West knew them.

The great cities of the empire—Constantinople, Salonika, Smyrna, Alexandria, and Beirut—all resembled a patchwork quilt of neighborhoods and markets where Muslims, Christians, and Jews commingled and did business. Complex mazes of streets and alleys were crammed with every kind of trade and food production imaginable. Nearby harbors bustled with foreign trade, providing goods for those who could afford them and employment for the poor, who flooded into the great cities. In Constantinople, mansions of the elite rose up along the mighty Bosphorus, itself churning with shipping traffic. Sultans and their families built majestic mosques and rambling parklands, bathhouses and bazaars, often adjacent to the holy institutions. In an era before accurate maps or even comprehensible addresses, these cities were sprawling and mysterious organisms.

Though the territories beyond the great coastal cities could hardly be described as lush, the villages had the potential for natural abundance, especially along the Black Sea and the region known as Cilicia, or "Little Armenia." Fruit orchards and mulberry, fig, walnut, almond, and olive trees supplied seasonal produce as well as leaves for silkworms. Grapevines provided grapes for wine and *bastek* (fruit leather), and of course the blanched leaves for dolma. Honey and wax were harvested from the honeycombs of beehives. When irrigated properly, cotton and tobacco grew easily in the sun-baked volcanic soil. Green tomatoes and raw cauliflower were pickled into *tourshee*. Rose petals were steeped to make rose water. Goats and sheep were milked for yogurt and cheese, then slaughtered for their meat. In every market, piles of apricots, sheaves of mint, cherries, pomegranates, eggplants, and potatoes were piled high alongside overflowing baskets of spices, coffee, and *lokum* candy.

Villages might be exclusively Kurdish, Armenian, or Greek, although sometimes two groups would share a town—Turkish and Armenian, Turkish and Greek. All were "Ottomans," but each group traced a lineage back to a distant and sometimes mythic past. Larger towns were multiethnic, with quarters dedicated to particular groups. In the largest cities, neighborhoods could support a mix of peoples: Turkish and Armenian peasants, Armenian merchants and artisans, as well as Arabs, Jews, Kurds, Tartars, even Roma.

In many rural areas, whoever owned the land owned those who worked it, and when the land was sold, the peasants living on the land came with the property. This system of serfdom was supported by the millet law. Most Christian Armenian peasants had no economic power and no rights. In the east, these vulnerable peasants were surrounded by Muslim tribes, particularly Kurds, whose religion conferred superior social status. Many Kurds were pastoral nomads, not settled in farms and towns as were most Armenians. Over the summer months, Kurds would pasture their animals in the highlands, while the sedentary Armenians tended their crops. But come winter, when the freezing cold and deep snow forced both Kurds and Armenians indoors, it became convention that an Armenian must house any Kurd who demanded it. Not only were the tribesmen allowed to take up residence in Christian homes (along with their animals), but also as Muslims, they were allowed to enjoy all the perks that the head of the household enjoyed, which included, in some cases, the peasant's wife.

When Abdul Hamid II became sultan in 1876, he found himself caught between two conflicting trends. The empire was buckling under the burden of high-interest loans and many felt that the economy had to be modernized. The financial crisis was tearing the empire apart. Outlying territories, inspired by Greek independence in 1829, had been attempting to break away from the empire for decades. At the same time, entrenched power blocs preferred the status quo.

In the years before Abdul Hamid came to power, Ottoman lawmakers, desiring to see the Ottoman Empire become a constitutional monarchy, had pushed through a progressive series of edicts known as the Tanzimat. These efforts led to the establishment of a constitution in 1876 (only months before Abdul Hamid took power) in the hope of bringing the Ottoman Empire in line with the norms of the "Concert of Europe." When Abdul Hamid first became sultan, the empire was struggling to adjust to this new systems of governance. In the same year, 1876, with yet another war with Russia looming and the domestic economy falling apart, Abdul Hamid suspended the new constitution and disbanded parliament, bringing the era of reform to an abrupt end. In contrast to the idealistic "Young Ottomans," moderate precursors to the Young Turks who lobbied for equality amongst all the sultan's subjects, and their European friends, Abdul Hamid saw the constitution, and the system of governance it represented, as untenable. The sultan, a fastidious and bureaucratically oriented man, was afraid of losing his grip on all the outlying regions of the empire. His response was to tug harder on the reins.

In the eastern frontier lands, the uncontrollable power of the Kurdish chieftains diminished the power of the government in the east. The sultan tried to solve the Kurdish problem in two ways: first, by breaking up the most belligerent tribes (either by moving them or arresting or killing their leaders), and second, by co-opting the tribes, incorporating them into a paramilitary called the Hamidiye (named in honor of Abdul Hamid). These Kurdish units were dedicated to the sultan and replicated what the Cossacks had done for the tsar: provide a ferocious advance guard terrorizing problem areas.[4] Because the Turkish army en masse was more powerful than these Kurdish units, the Hamidiye could be disciplined if necessary. If they went rogue, the leader could be captured and either imprisoned or executed.

This, in turn, heightened the danger for Armenians living in the eastern regions of the Ottoman Empire, the areas closest to Russia and Persia. For hundreds of years, the balance of power between the Kurds and the Armenians had been stable, if tense and often violent. But by the middle of the nineteenth century, the fragmented Kurdish tribes became even more lawless. It was impossible for the sultan's troops to be everywhere at once. Besides, restricting what the Kurds did to the Armenians was not a priority for the Sublime Porte.

This bad situation came to a head in 1894, 1895, and 1896, when Sultan Abdul Hamid let the Hamidiye loose on the Armenian villages in a series of bloodbaths, crushing any sign of insurrection, real or fabricated. The violence was terroristic, leading to hundreds of thousands of civilian fatalities. News reports, as well as dozens of books published at the time, describe immolations, flaying, rape, dismemberment, and massacre. Overwhelmingly, the vilayets in the east bore the brunt of the killings. The goal was to undermine Armenian support of the Russians in their perennial war with the Ottomans. This began what Vahakn Dadrian has called "a culture of massacre" in Asia Minor that persisted from that period through World War I.[5]

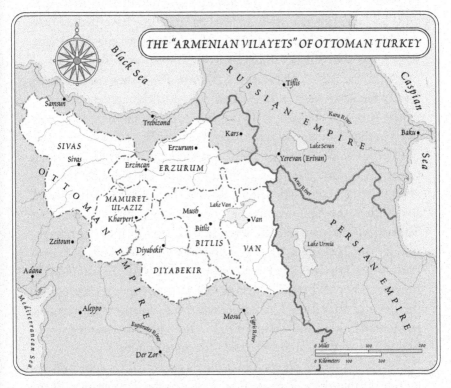

Though Armenians lived throughout the Ottoman Empire, these six vilayets featured major Armenian populations and endured major massacres under Sultan Abdul Hamid's rule.

With no recourse against government-sponsored violence, in the late nineteenth century, Armenians formed revolutionary societies, notably the Armenakan Party, the Hnchag (Bell) Party (or Hnchags), and the Hai Heghapokhakanneri Tashnagtsutiun (the Armenian Revolutionary Federation, or ARF, also known as the Tashnags). Emboldened by revolutionary activity in Russia, these organizations had committed themselves to education of the peasantry, agricultural reform, and the establishment of a constitutional and/or socialist government. They were also, by their own admission, terrorist.[6]

In the end, despite the idealistic goals they outlined in their manifestos, violence as a means to an end would come to define both the Hnchags and the Tashnags. Both revolutionary organizations began their "work" by assassinating small-time Armenian and Turkish officials they viewed as traitors. Bloodied corpses would be dumped in the streets, a note pinned to the jacket lapel describing the offense. Suspected spies were assassinated. In an operation called "The Storm" (*P'ot'orik* in Armenian) in 1900, family members of wealthy Armenians were kidnapped in order to extort funds to support revolutionary activity,[7] a tactic still practiced in the Middle East in the early twenty-first century.

Because non-Muslims were forbidden to carry arms in the Ottoman Empire, Hnchags and Tashnags secretly distributed firearms to villagers for self-defense against the violent Kurdish tribes. In addition, the Armenian revolutionaries sometimes attacked local Turkish officials with the deliberate intention of inciting retribution by the Turkish army. The hope was that the resulting massacres of the innocent local populations would gain the attention of Europe. They did exactly that as Western newspapers trumpeted the news of atrocities. The Armenian revolutionary organizations, particularly the Tashnagtsutiun, or ARF (parent organization to Nemesis), were a real force in the Ottoman Empire.

These Armenian revolutionary groups not only were inspired by the Bolsheviks in Russia (Stalin, one of the early leaders of the Bolshevik Revolution, had been a divinity student in Tiflis) but also looked to the French Revolution and other similar movements that celebrated progress, enlightenment, socialism, nationalism, and social Darwinism. With their headquarters located safely beyond the reach of the sultan and his spies, the Armenian revolutionary groups sent operatives across the borders and back into the empire. Armed teams of fedayeen operated throughout eastern Turkey and the Caucasus. The volunteer fighters adopted an Persian-Arabic name (*fida'i*, or "devotee"), which they took to mean "he who is committed" or "he who is sacrificed." "Field workers for the parties were known as 'apostles'; guerrilla fighters, who had given up comfort to sacrifice their lives for the people, became 'martyrs for the cause'; priests blessed the soldiers on the eve of major battles."[8] Attacks against the Ottoman government were called *surp kordz,* or "holy task."

The Armenian revolutionaries particularly sought the attention of Western leaders. If Europeans could only see how barbaric the Turks were, they might pressure the sultan to ease off on violence aimed at the Armenian peasantry. More than that, external pressure might secure constitutional rights for Ottoman minorities, giving them some relief. The millet system was no longer functional in this modern world. Some Armenians benefited from the new economies and trade with the West, but most were finding life in the eastern parts of the Ottoman Empire barely sustainable.

In the West in the 1890s, every well-read person was familiar with the atrocities committed by the "Bloody Turk" and the "Red Sultan." Every newspaper and monthly magazine featured lurid stories of Muslim violence. The *New York Times* published dozens of accounts. One reported: "A witness hiding in the oak scrub saw soldiers gouge out the eyes of two priests, who in horrible agony implored their tormentors to kill them. But the soldiers compelled them to dance while screaming with pain, presently bayoneted them."[9] Committees were formed by indignant Americans and British insisting that the horrific violence cease immediately. European powers demanded that Abdul Hamid "protect" the indigenous Christian populations living as subjects within the borders of his empire. And if the sultan refused to behave as the West wished, the West would *force* him to behave. The sultan, and Ottoman Turks in general, were developing a very bad rep. As early as 1876, British prime minister William Gladstone summed up the West's opinion of "the Turk":

> Let me endeavor very briefly to sketch, in the rudest outline, what the Turkish race was and what it is. It is not a question of Mahometanism simply, but of Mahometanism compounded with the peculiar character of a race. They are not the mild Mahometans of India, nor the chivalrous Saladins of Syria, nor the cultured Moors of Spain. They were, upon the whole, from the black day when they first entered Europe, the one great anti-human specimen of humanity. Wherever they went, a broad line of blood marked the track behind them; and, as far as their dominion reached, civilisation disappeared from view.[10]

Despite their disdain for the barbarism of the East, Europe and the United States had already written their own bloody histories as overlords of their respective colonies. Utilizing the latest Maxim machine guns and unstoppable "gunboat diplomacy," by the 1800s the major European powers and the upstart United States had used violence to found settlements all over the world. In East Africa (Kenya), the British had forced local Africans onto reservations and turned the natives into a peasant labor force serving the white settlers. When the locals resisted, they were murdered. The peoples of Central and South America had long ago been decimated by Spanish and Portuguese conquistadors. Belgium's King Leopold presided over stunning atrocities as he ran his own personal fiefdom in the Congo. Germany had intentionally destroyed the Herero people of South-West Africa (Namibia). General Lothar von Trotha, who oversaw these massacres, was unequivocal: "It was and remains my policy to apply force by unmitigated terrorism and even cruelty. I shall destroy the rebellious tribes by shedding rivers of blood."[11] British coercion in India (labeled "administrative massacre" by one observer in 1924)[12] and China, the American war against the native people of its frontier lands and its scorched-earth campaign in the Philippines, and the French subjugation of North Africa were all oppressive policies that reached their height during this period.

When the West overpowered native populations, these actions, no matter how violent, were rationalized as manifestations of the natural order of things. "Manifest destiny" and "social Darwinism" laid the foundation for violent improvement of the world. Europeans saw themselves as superior and naturally born to rule. They believed that their domination of faraway lands brought "civilization" to the natives. In return, the rulers of the empires benefited. "The purpose of colonies was to supply the mother country with raw materials and to provide a market for her manufactured goods, all on an exclusive basis."[13] As late as 1943, British home secretary Herbert Morrison, when commenting on the subject of granting African colonies their independence, would be quoted as saying, "It would be like giving a child of ten a latch-key, a bank account, and a shot-gun."[14]

Empires were gradually giving way to a new paradigm, the "nation," an idea that a "people" have a shared history, language, and culture that form the bedrock of a "nationality." As the nineteenth century ended, Europe, and eventually the whole world, became enamored with nationalism. A nation was not a tangible thing; it was an abstract idea, and as such it could be defined to serve different needs. Great Powers like Britain and France included their far-flung colonies in their definition of nation. In theory, the idea of a nation seemed to be an immutable truth, but it was actually a complex ideological fantasy. National "purity," a romantic notion attractive to many, rarely existed in the real world. It would nevertheless be only a matter of time before the idea of "nation" served as a catalyst to war. Nationalism, ethnic cleansing, and genocide are related: they all share mythic notions of a pure and common origin, and they all serve material ambitions.

For the subject peoples of aging empires, "nationhood" became a call to arms, especially with regard to the Ottoman Empire. Egged on by Great Powers like Russia and Great Britain, smaller populations like the Serbs, the Greeks, the Arabs, and the Armenians also began to think of themselves as "nations." Inspired by that idea, they attempted to break away. Some succeeded; others did not. In the case of the clash between Armenians and the Ottoman Empire, nationalism would have tragic consequences.

—⁓—

The Imperial Bank Ottoman in Constantinople served as a "de facto central bank,"[15] so in the eyes of the ARF, it symbolized European economic interests in the Ottoman Empire. Twenty years earlier, the empire had officially gone bankrupt because of lavish spending by Abdul Hamid's predecessors, who were intent on building sumptuous palaces for themselves and their kin while pursuing a debauched lifestyle. That extravagance came to an end when the Ottoman Public Debt Administration was established in 1881. European bankers stepped in and assumed Turkey's debt in exchange for control over how public monies were collected and spent by the Sublime Porte. Britain joined France in picking up a good chunk of the debt. By controlling the economy, the European bankers took over firm control of the state.

The Ottoman Empire had become an economic colony of the West. By World War I, Britain, France, and Germany would own or manage not only the empire's finances but most of its infrastructure and resources as well. Either directly or indirectly, the Great Powers had rights over railroads, shipping, mining, tobacco, cotton, municipal water and lighting, banking, and mineral licenses, including the newly important petroleum reserves. In addition, the Europeans were essentially unregulated when doing business within the jurisdiction of the sultan, because over the centuries they had established a parallel legal system within the empire, especially with regard to business. These "capitulations" were a series of treaties allowing subjects of certain foreign governments to evade harsh Sharia-based law. In the Ottoman Empire, Europeans and Americans had their own courts and their own post offices. In addition, France, Britain, and Germany shipped in numerous military advisors, an easy way to keep a close eye on the Ottoman military.

In 1896, twenty-five years before Talat's assassination, and the year of Soghomon Tehlirian's birth, the ARF established its international reputation by making a spectacular raid on the Imperial Bank Ottoman. The Tashnag attackers hoped that their frenzied attack on the bank would draw attention to the horrific massacres of Armenians at the hands of the sultan's forces and his Kurdish Hamidiye in the eastern provinces.

Two dozen heavily armed fedayeen stormed the bank. They hurled bombs, shot and killed a guard, rounded up hostages, and occupied the building. The Armenian revolutionaries set dynamite charges on every floor and issued a list of demands, threatening to blow up the building if they were not met. In response, Sultan Abdul Hamid surrounded the bank with his troops, rolled in artillery batteries, and prepared to reduce the building to rubble. He seems to have had no qualms about killing the attackers, the employees, or the customers locked inside the bank.

As the sultan's artillerymen primed their guns, foreign warships drifted into the great harbor of Constantinople. British diplomats then contacted Abdul Hamid's Grand Vizier in his offices at the Sublime Porte and explained that if the sultan destroyed the European-owned bank, the sultan's home, Yildiz Palace, would be shelled in turn. Communiqués were quickly exchanged between the sultan's secretaries and the Grand Vizier. Abdul Hamid blinked and stood down his guns. It was a three-way standoff.

One of the leaders of the Bank Ottoman takeover was the twenty-four-year-old firebrand Karekin Pastermadjian, best known by the revolutionary alias "Armen Garo." Before joining the Tashnags,

Garo, an Armenian born into a wealthy Erzurum family, had been studying abroad in Nancy, France. Shocked by the newspaper reports of massacres of Armenians in eastern vilayets, the idealistic young man had traveled to the Geneva ARF headquarters with a group of fellow students in tow to volunteer his services to the cause. Garo and three other students were instructed to move to Constantinople, where they would receive further orders. In Constantinople, Garo joined seventeen-year-old Babken Suni (Bedros Parian), who would lead the attack.

In the spectacular initial raid on the bank, 150 staff members and customers were held hostage. Two employees and four of the young Tashnags, including Suni, were killed. After the day-long stalemate, the British governor of the bank, Sir Edgar Vincent, brokered a truce between Garo and the authorities. The young revolutionaries were safely led out of the bank, past the Turkish troops surrounding the building, and escorted to Vincent's yacht. After escaping Constantinople, they were transferred to a Greek freighter and finally ended up in Marseilles.

Sadly, the sultan's spies had been aware of the Tashnags' plans all along and used the attack as an excuse to punish the Armenian community. As soon as the bank was occupied, hundreds of armed white-turbaned Islamic students (softas) appeared as if on cue in the streets of the city. They had been provided with clubs studded with nails and attacked every Armenian they encountered. Thousands died before British troops entered the city to quell the rioting. Bodies were piled up "like offal in the scavenger carts."[16] The rioting against Armenians spread throughout the provinces, where thousands more died.

Armen Garo and most of his compatriots lived to fight another day (though a number of the Armenian "farm boys" who joined in the attack were deported from France to Argentina, never to be heard of again).[17] Not one of Garo's negotiated demands was met. The resulting deaths of thousands of Armenians were rationalized by the Armenian revolutionaries as collateral damage in the fight for a just cause. The ARF considered the bank raid a success because it put the Armenian conflict with the Ottomans, and the

ARF itself, under an international spotlight. They believed that the world could no longer ignore their plight. Thus was born the revolutionary career of the man who, twenty-five years later, would found the Nemesis conspiracy. Armen Garo would become one of the most prominent and controversial forces within the ARF.

Despite the perceived success of the bank raid, the cause of Armenian rights made little progress in the years immediately following the assault. In 1905, almost ten years later, frustrated at the lack of progress, the Tashnags raised the ante and made plans to assassinate the sultan. Assassination had been a favorite tool of the Armenian Revolutionary Federation since its inception. In the late nineteenth century, spies, snitches, and government officials were routinely shot in the streets. These political assassinations were called *deror,* a word derived from the word "terror." The killings were held sacred, a tool that would "elevate the spirit of the people." In an 1892 publication, the "Program of the Armenian Revolutionary Federation," in which the goals and means of the organization are laid out, it is clearly stated that the organization would strive "to stimulate fighting to terrorize government officials, informers, traitors, usurers, and every kind of exploiter...to expose government establishments to looting and destruction."[18]

Gerard J. Libaridian, the former Tashnag archivist and official of the post-Soviet Armenian Republic, expands on this theme: "Revolutionaries struck down government officials as a show of power. More often than not these officials were the more cruel and unscrupulous; their elimination would provide relief to the populace on the local level. Such actions were also expected to spread fear among remaining functionaries who were thereby warned that their behavior would not go unpunished."[19] The ARF deployed their assassins as virtual weapons, unstoppable once they were set in motion.

The Armenians enlisted the aid of a Belgian anarchist, Edward Joris, to plan the assassination.[20] After considering various options, including sniper fire and launching grenades at the royal entourage, they settled on deploying a time bomb. A custom-built coach was stuffed with the plastic explosive gelignite. The agents carefully monitored the sultan's comings and goings and timed his movements with stopwatches, learning precisely when he would be at any particular point in his routine, and decided to attack during his observance of the Muslim Friday prayer ceremony, something he did every week.[21]

Because of his obsessive focus on security, Sultan Abdul Hamid was not an easy target. A thin, nervous man who chain-smoked, Abdul Hamid rarely drank alcohol and was extremely careful about what he ate, mainly because of his sensitive stomach, but also because he was morbidly afraid of being poisoned. He routinely fed morsels of his dinner to his dogs and cats to test for toxins and reportedly employed a eunuch to take the first puff of every cigarette. Hamid's royal compound, Yildiz Palace, featuring thick twenty-foot-high walls, had been specifically designed and reinforced to withstand attack. Every night he slept in a different room, hoping to confuse potential assassins. He even avoided the use of telephones for fear that his enemies were eavesdropping. Bodyguards were ever present, and the sultan rarely appeared in public. According to James Burrill Angell, the president of the University of Michigan who was appointed minister to the Ottoman Empire by President McKinley in 1897, "The Sultan had suppressed the former mail service because he received so many threatening postal cards and because conspirators could by mail mature dangerous schemes."[22] The sultan's spy network was vast; it was rumored that one person from every major household in the realm was spying for the palace.

Because of his role as caliph, or ceremonial leader of Islam, it was compulsory that the sultan attend the weekly public service at the Hamidiye mosque. He left the palace proper every Friday morning, accompanied by a large entourage of carriages and attendants. To keep his public exposure as brief as possible, Abdul Hamid had built the mosque within the palace grounds. After the assassinations of the king of Italy and an attack on the shah of Persia in Paris, European visitors were forbidden to attend the ceremony without official permission. Unaccompanied Armenians were not allowed onto the grounds at all. To get around these prohibitions, the conspirators pretended to be young couples seeking a blessing for their marriage vows.

Every Friday, surrounded by infantry and cavalry, the sultan would enter the mosque at around eleven thirty with an entourage that included his sons. As his spies circulated among the participants, the sultan would observe the service from a special unseen chamber reserved for him. As soon as the service ended, he would exit the mosque quickly, step up into a two-seat phaeton drawn by two white horses, and drive himself back to the palace.

On Friday, July 21, 1905, Operation Dragon *(Vishab)* went into action. The Tashnag assassins slipped the gelignite-laden carriage into the procession. Because the ceremony followed a specific timetable, the bomb was set to go off within seconds after the sultan emerged from the mosque. On this occasion, however, Abdul Hamid was delayed when the Sheikh ul-Islam, the minister of public worship *(evkif)*, approached him for a short conversation. The two spoke for barely a minute, but the delay was fateful. Lacking a remote control, the timer on the bomb could not be reset. The Tashnag bomb maker and twenty-six members of the sultan's retinue died in the explosion. Another fifty-eight were wounded. The sultan escaped uninjured.[1]

Abdul Hamid had hundreds arrested and tortured in an attempt to root out the conspirators, but to no avail. (Mysteriously, after only two years of confinement, the Belgian coordinator, Edward Joris, was released and allowed to return to his native country.) And again, though the attempt on the sultan's life had been unsuccessful, the Tashnags' reputation as fearless revolutionaries spread all over the empire. With the assault on the Bank Ottoman and now the attempt on Abdul Hamid's life, the Tashnags were establishing themselves as a truly dangerous terrorist organization. In the rural provinces their agrarian principles were blended with armed revolt against the Kurds, but in Constantinople, their goals were specifically anti-sultanic. Either way, they were seen as fearsome, brave, and cunning. For a young Armenian desperately in need of heroes, the Tashnags filled the bill. These were the men young Tehlirian looked up to.

—m—

Around this same time, a clique of young Ottoman military officers chafing at the bit of the sultan's ineffectual rule sought the
reestablishment of the constitution and parliament. These men
would be labeled "les Jeunes Turcs" (the Young Turks). Formally,
they were the Committee of Union and Progress (originally the
Committee of Progress and Union). The Young Turks, with help
from their putative enemies, the ARF, would eventually succeed
in overthrowing the sultan.

The Young Turks needed heroes as much as the revolutionaries
did. For this reason, events halfway around the world made 1905
memorable. In May, Admiral Togo Heihachiro, commanding a
small Japanese fleet, destroyed much of the Russian navy in the
Battle of Tsushima. Japan went on to win the war against Russia.
For the first time in history, a non-European state had defeated one
of the great European powers. In this display of strength the Young
Turks saw a glimmer of hope for the future of the Ottoman Empire.
Japan had embraced constitutionalism in the middle of the nineteenth century, as the Ottomans had also tried to do, and it was in
this "modernism" that the Young Turks saw the possibility of
escaping the clutches of Europe and its relentless absorption of their
nation.

The sultan's days as all-powerful leader of the Ottoman Empire
were numbered. In 1908 the Committee of Union and Progress
(CUP; in Turkish, Ittihad ve Terakki Cemiyeti), with help from
the Armenian Tashnags and other non-CUP Muslims, succeeded
in bringing down the government. (The Hnchags, fearing a double-
cross by these Turkish nationalists, had kept their distance.) Together
the CUP and the ARF pulled off a bloodless coup. Abdul Hamid
was forced to restore the constitution he had shelved back in 1877.
"For the first time in Ottoman history an organized political party
dominated politics."[22]

The revolution of 1908 was embraced by all as momentous. Certain that a new age of equality was dawning, the Armenians and

Greeks of the Ottoman Empire were ecstatic. They believed that something approaching representational government would give them rights like those enjoyed by the citizens of the European constitutional monarchies. Though inexperienced at governing, the leaders of the CUP (who included the future Talat Pasha, Enver Pasha, and Djemal Pasha) were sure that they had saved the country. With the new constitution, the Ottoman Empire could modernize and fend off Europe's plans to parcel out and devour its territories. Muslims and Christians celebrated in the streets and joined together to pray at the graves of those massacred during Abdul Hamid's reign.

A parliament was elected. Among the new deputies who represented the vilayets were a handful of Armenians, including thirty-six-year-old Armen Garo, veteran of the Bank Ottoman takeover fourteen years earlier. The Tashnags had become a legitimate party and as such could participate in running the country. Garo could now have direct dialogue with the CUP leadership, particularly Talat.

But the revolution had not solved the deep-rooted problems facing Turkey. No sooner had the new regime of constitutional government begun than violence broke out in the distant vilayets. "The leaders of the CUP…were unprepared for their sudden accession to power."[24] Maintaining control of an empire was not so easy when entrenched power blocs wanted to preserve the status quo. Warlords in the east, rich *aghas,* even Armenian Church leaders were not ready for a dawning of egalitarianism. The empire was not prepared for democracy. A reactionary counter-coup broke out, designed to put an end to constitutional government and restore Abdul Hamid's powers as absolute monarch. With the quick suppression of the counter-coup, Abdul Hamid was thrown out altogether and replaced with a sultan who would toe the CUP line. A new pragmatic and violent style of governing infected the CUP leadership. Presiding over this new approach to government, one in which assassination and murder would become business as usual, was Mehmet Talat, later Talat Pasha. Over the next four years, Talat, Enver, Djemal, and the Young Turks would tighten their iron grip on the government. Clearly, the CUP "were not constitutionalists."[25]

The new leadership needed to divert attention from its own lack of a clear agenda. Armenian revolutionaries provided an obvious scapegoat. A series of attacks against Armenians erupted in the vilayet of Adana in 1909, leaving some twenty to thirty thousand dead. Many historians now believe that the CUP government was complicit. With these attacks, the specter of massacre across the empire rose up again. Many of the Armenian leaders who had embraced their legal status in the new government became alarmed. Could it be that their "friends" the Young Turks were not to be trusted? Armenian revolutionary activity throughout the empire increased, and on the threshold of World War I, so did violent repression. Most Tashnags and Hnchags could see that the honeymoon with the CUP was over. In response to the violence, pressure from the European powers again increased. An intervention by the Great Powers became imminent, but because the Russians and British would not trust each other, they were unable to put together a plan with any teeth in it. Eventually, European provincial overseers were sent to eastern Turkey to guarantee the civil rights of the Armenians, but it was too little, too late. A few weeks later, World War I broke out and the oversight system was scrapped.

Beginning in 1912, two successive Balkan wars had resulted in defeat for the Ottomans (i.e., the CUP). Major Ottoman territories in eastern Europe were lost. Hundreds of thousands of Balkan Muslim refugees *(muhacirs)* flooded into Constantinople. The Young Turks, squabbling amongst themselves, found their authority slipping away. Finally, in 1913, the more radical members of the CUP completed their takeover of the government. This time the coup was not bloodless. On January 23, 1913, Enver Pasha, accompanied by an entourage of Ittihadists, burst into parliament and gunned down the minister of war, Nazim Pasha. The Grand Vizier, Kamil Pasha, was forced to resign and, fearing for his life, abandoned Constantinople. Other moderates, particularly Prince Sabahaddin, who had lobbied on behalf of the Armenian cause, also chose exile abroad after the takeover. Then CUP opponents assassinated Kamil's successor, Mahmut Sevket Pasha, in June 1913. The Ittihadists (or

Unionists) were now in complete control. Talat, Enver, Djemal, Dr. Behaeddin Shakir, and other members of the CUP Central Committee would from this point on direct the Ottoman Empire. The experiment with democracy was over. The Central Committee was in charge.

These men were the true bosses of the Ottoman Empire during World War I. "The Central Committee would remain until the end of World War I ten years later the centre of power in the Ottoman Empire."[26] The membership of the Central Committee had been secret, evolving over the years. Moderates had been forced out and replaced by ardent racist nationalists. Most histories of the Ottoman Empire during World War I describe the leadership as a "triumvirate" of Talat Pasha, Enver Pasha, and Djemal Pasha, but in fact the Ittihad had many guiding hands.

Mehmet Cavid organized the finances, including large infusions of gold from the Germans. The sociologist and poet Ziya Gokalp provided the Young Turks with a complex nationalist ideology replete with ideas such as "in reality there cannot be a common home and fatherland for different peoples.... The new civilization will be created by the Turkish race."[27] Generals Mustapha Kemal (Ataturk) and Kara Kemal provided military muscle. "The CUP functioned as a strict hierarchy, with the central committee at the top and the periphery totally subordinated to the center whenever it was within its control."[28]

Though Enver and Djemal oversaw the military and were fully versed in the machinations of the central government, it was Talat Pasha, as minister of the interior, who ran the show. Talat was always at the center of things. Clever, strong-willed, and comfortable in his dealings with foreign diplomats, Talat was also a physically imposing man. United States ambassador Henry Morgenthau seemed almost in awe when he described him:

> Physically he was a striking figure. His powerful frame, his huge, sweeping back and his rocky biceps emphasized that natural mental strength and forcefulness which made

possible his career. In discussing matters, Talat liked to sit at his desk, with his shoulders drawn up, his head thrown back, and his wrists, twice the size of an ordinary man's, planted firmly on the table.... Whenever I think of Talat now, I do not primarily recall his rollicking laugh, his uproarious enjoyment of a good story, the mighty stride with which he crossed the room, his fierceness, his determination, his remorselessness—[no], the whole life and nature of the man take form in those gigantic wrists.[29]

Like many Young Turk leaders, Talat was not ethnically Turkish; rather he was of Pomak descent, that is, native Bulgarian Muslim. He was born in 1874, the son of a civil servant. At the time of the Young Turk revolution, he had worked for the post office for ten years. As interior minister, he shared many traits with other leaders of the twentieth century who rose from humble backgrounds. Talat's natural charisma, intelligence, and single-mindedness combined to give birth to a ruthless political pragmatist. Always careful to make strategic moves that enhanced his power, he cooperated with his fellow Central Committee members while never relinquishing control. Unlike his fellow committee members, Talat had neither military training nor an advanced education. Though many of his cohorts were urbane, Talat was flexible and canny, which made him well suited to international politics. He was highly respected by the Kaiser, who in 1917 conferred on him the Prussian Order of the Black Eagle, "one of the highest German decorations... seldom conferred on non-Germans."[30]

Though Enver Pasha lacked Talat's Machiavellian talent for political engagement, his charisma arose in part from his sheer impetuosity. He was well known as a hero to the people and was considered Talat's equal in the Ottoman Empire. Enver was the most prominent military leader in Turkey and, after visiting Germany a few years before the onset of World War I, began to pattern his style of leadership after that of the Prussian military. He had confirmed his reputation as a courageous and resourceful general in the Second Balkan War. (Ironically, he wasn't actually present during the battle for which he is best known.) Brash and cocky, he was famous for his mustache with its upturned twisted ends.

Enver was not only a celebrated general and a snappy dresser; he was also married to the Princess Emine Naciye, making him a member of the royal family. This direct connection to the caliphate lent him an aura of Islamic significance. At the end of the war and later, this special status would give Enver license to lead an "Army of Islam" in Azerbaijan and Central Asia. In contrast to Talat's meat-and-potatoes strongman image, Enver appealed to the public with his dashing exploits and confrontational style. Talat, ever the sly politician, had no problem with Enver's overconfidence, realizing that it actually made his greatest rival for the top leadership position more vulnerable. Nonetheless, Enver, like Talat, would enthusiastically embrace the decision to exterminate the Armenians.

Djemal Pasha, the third member of the triumvirate, was also a military leader. Unlike Enver, he was a Francophile who had trained with the French, and so he lacked Enver's more severe Prussian style. Djemal led the navy and was in charge of the southern flank of the empire, including Syria, the Sinai, and Mesopotamia. Also, as commander of the Syrian region, he oversaw the vast numbers of deportees flooding into the desert around the oasis town of Der Zor and other concentration camps.

The man who later would lead the "Special Organization," the secret paramilitary tasked with some of the most gruesome killings of the genocide, was Dr. Behaeddin Shakir, a former personal physician to the Ottoman crown prince. Shakir kept close tabs on the deportation efforts as he motored from city to city in a large black car, giving personal instructions to commanders and CUP secretaries. In this respect Shakir provided the link between Talat in Constantinople and the local *valis,* or governors, who controlled each vilayet. Shakir, like many of the other leading lights in the CUP, was the son of refugees *(muhacirs)* from Bulgaria. As such he had been witness to the vicious Christian attacks on the Bulgarian Muslim populations. By time World War I began, Shakir had no compunctions about using similar tactics to clear the Armenians out of Turkish Anatolia.

An early indication of the CUP's callous disregard for life presaged its later approach to what it saw as "the Armenian problem." Tens of thousands of stray dogs ran loose on the streets of Constantinople, defecating in the public parks and snapping at people, as packs of wild dogs virtually took over neighborhoods. In 1910, two years after first coming to power, the CUP decided to solve the problem of Constantinople's dogs with an eye toward improving the party's popularity and public image. The dogs, unlike more intractable difficulties, were a problem with an easy solution.

Dogcatchers were dispatched, and the dogs of Constantinople were captured one by one and locked in cages. The cages packed with barking canines were then shipped off to a deserted island, Hayirsiz Ada, one of the Princes' Islands lying just off the coast, a short boat ride from the city and a favorite tourist destination today. The cages were brought ashore and opened, and some eighty thousand dogs were set loose on the rocky island, where, lacking food, the strong cannibalized the weak until those that remained simply starved to death. Supposedly, ships crossing the Sea of Marmara could hear their plaintive howls across the dark waters. Their treatment received so much attention that the Turkish Society for the Prevention of Cruelty to Animals was founded by one Alice Washburn Manning, an American who came to Turkey specifically in response to the plight of the dogs, as well as the horses that had been wounded during the war.[31]

The CUP's approach to the stray dogs was simple and straightforward. A problem had presented itself, and an efficient solution had been found. It's hard not to see a parallel with the fate of the Armenians a mere five years later. Talat and his colleagues were pragmatic and decisive. Without Talat's cold focus on "the problem" and its cold-blooded "answer," the deportation program would never have happened.

CHAPTER THREE

Blood Flows

Genocide, after all, is an exercise in community-building.
—Philip Gourevitch

Many of the best-known histories of World War I have focused on the trench warfare between the Triple Entente (the United Kingdom, France, and Russia) and Germany. World War I was all about aerial dogfights and poison gas, "Tommys" and "doughboys." This was a European war, wasn't it? The events depicted in films like *Gallipoli* and *Lawrence of Arabia* have crept into our consciousness, but most people would probably be hard-pressed to explain how they fit into the big picture of the "Great War."

The southern flank of World War I would hold long-term consequences for the Western world because the prize was nothing less than control of the earth's greatest oil deposits, regions that to this day represent over half the world's known oil reserves. It was on this front that the Ottoman Empire finally fell to pieces, losing its

Arabian territories in the process. And it was under the cloak of this war between the Ottoman Empire and the Allies that the Armenian Genocide proceeded with little detection.

The Ottoman Empire, particularly its war minister, Enver Pasha, admired Germany's might, ambition, and efficiency, but the two nations were not natural allies. In fact, though Kaiser Wilhelm II had professed deep affection for Turkey and Islam, Germany's interest in the Ottoman Empire was above all strategic. Likewise, the Young Turk government could just as easily have found an ally in Great Britain and historically had a genuine affinity for France. The real enemy for both Germany and the Ottoman Empire was Russia, which shared a long, challenging border with both states. For at least a century, Russia had its sights set on controlling the Bosphorus, and that meant Constantinople, which the Russians fondly called "Tsargrad."

Many historians refer to the complicated jockeying for control of this critical intersection of Europe and Asia as "the Great Game." If Russia (or Germany) could gain control of Asia Minor, it would be well positioned to seize the Arab lands, specifically the Levant, the Hejaz (western Saudi Arabia), and Mesopotamia (today's Iraq). As far as Great Britain was concerned, control of Arab lands meant control of the Suez Canal and, by extension, access to Persia and India. For this reason, the central territory of the Ottoman Empire, what we now call Turkey, stood as a massive buffer between the Great Powers. But Germany was unhappy with the status quo for various reasons, lack of oil resources being only one of them. Germany viewed the Ottoman lands, particularly Asia Minor, as fertile ground for development, what would later be called Lebensraum, or "living space," a concept that loomed in the German consciousness long before the Nazi era. At the onset of World War I, the Baghdad Railroad, financed by Deutsche Bank, was slowly but surely penetrating the Turkish hinterlands.

By the summer of 1914, the Young Turk government was exhausted by two wars in the Balkans. Large chunks of Ottoman territory in Europe had broken free. War loomed, and it was easy to see that Russian troops would soon flood into the eastern (Armenian) vilayets, while British forces would be testing the Aegean littoral. The Young Turks tried to stave off a clear decision about joining the war for as long as possible, but by the end of July, Winston Churchill had seized Turkish vessels being built in English shipyards, clearly setting the stage for conflict between the two powers. Secret negotiations led to an alliance between Germany and the Ottoman Empire, and when Ottoman (formerly German) warships fired on Russian ports on the Black Sea, the Turks had finally entered the war.[1]

Six months into the fighting, the Ottomans suffered major setbacks as Russian and Turkish troops fought it out in eastern Turkey. Enver Pasha, in an ill-conceived move, had pushed into Russian Caucasian territory in December, losing more than seventy thousand men in the freezing mountainous heights near Sarikamish. At the other end of Asia Minor, British warships massed in the Mediterranean in preparation for a thrust past Gallipoli and the Dardanelles, through the Sea of Marmara, and into the imperial city. Making provision for the inevitable, the CUP leaders made ready to abandon their home base, planning to pull back from all fronts and consolidate their forces in central Anatolia.

But the collapse of the western (Constantinople) front never materialized. Skittish and under stress, Admiral Sackville Carden could not find a way to move the British fleet past the heavily mined Dardanelles. Over the ensuing months, the Ottoman army held the line at Gallipoli as British, Australian, and New Zealander troops suffered thousands of deaths and tens of thousands of casualties. Both the threat of invasion and the reversal that followed spelled doom for the Armenians, who were viewed by the Young Turk leaders Talat Pasha and Enver Pasha as a potential "fifth column."

To be sure, committed Armenian fedayeen fighters in the east had either stepped up their sabotage against the regime by cutting telegraph wires, working as spies for the Russians, or moving illicit arms. Some drifted across the border and joined the Russian troops as a vanguard of the invading army, working as guides for the Russians through the foreign terrain. The veteran Armenian leaders of these hardened Tashnag and Hnchag troops gathered up and took command of the volunteers migrating toward the war front. The Ottoman parliamentarian and former revolutionary Armen Garo, to the consternation of many Armenians, joined the Russian forces, going so far as to have his picture taken in full Russian battle regalia.[2] But these Armenian fighters, who numbered a few thousand, did not accurately reflect the attitude of the Armenian population of Turkey, at that time estimated at about two million souls.

During the tense weeks prior to the onset of "the war to end all wars," the Ottoman army was desperately in need of men. After two Balkan wars that had dragged on for years, young Ottomans harbored few illusions about what a soldier's life held in store. Before the Balkan wars, a series of conflicts with Russia had decimated generation after generation of peasants. The people had nothing to show for their sacrifice but casualties, famine, and rampant disease. The Ottoman army, unlike the orderly and smartly uniformed European military, was badly outfitted and poorly trained. Conscription was seen as nothing more than a delayed death sentence. Army life meant backbreaking work, near-starvation, and slow death by flea-borne typhus or a fast death by bullet or bayonet. The role of the Turkish soldier was best summed up in General Mustapha Kemal's famous command at Gallipoli: "I'm not ordering you to fight, I'm ordering you to die."

And now, because of the political reforms, even Christians were included in the draft rolls. Young Armenian men, as members of the Christian millet, had traditionally paid the *bedel* tax and were excluded from service. Now, since the restoration of the constitution, they were no longer exempt and were obliged to fight. The first Armenian conscripts were full-fledged soldiers, and as such, armed with rifles. There were even Armenian officers serving in the ranks.[3] But soon after the war officially began, in

February 1915, Enver ordered that the Armenians' weapons be taken from them. Instead of serving on the front, Christian soldiers were collected into "labor battalions" *(inshaat taburu)*. These battalions were little more than slave units in which the soldiers were worked to death like pack animals. The men were exploited until they died, and if they did not die, they were marched to remote areas and murdered outright.

Though many young men, Turkish and Armenian, did serve in the Turkish army, many others avoided military service at any cost. In the countryside, men hid in the mountains where the gendarmes could not find them. In Constantinople, a vast underground network was created to help them elude the authorities. Young men were hidden in cellars, behind walls, in secret rooms. Throughout the city, this "Army of the Attics" *(tavan taburu)* numbered in the thousands. Concealing these young men and maintaining the underground support system became an important function of the urban Armenian revolutionaries.

The Central Committee of the CUP quickly came to believe that the Armenian population represented a mortal threat to the dying Ottoman Empire. Enmeshed in war with Britain and Russia and harassed by small bands of Armenian fedayeen on its eastern front, the Ottoman government decided to solve the "Armenian question" once and for all by eliminating all Armenians residing in Anatolia. This eradication of over a million people would proceed in stages, often disguised as deportations. All would be camouflaged by the fog of war.

Examples of ethnic cleansing can be found at least as far back as biblical times, but the slaughter that was to befall the Armenian people in the Ottoman Empire in 1915 was unprecedented in scope and definition. The intensity of the violence, and the staggering numbers of people murdered in such a short period of time—almost one million people—introduced to the world a new phenomenon: *genocide,* the attempt to eradicate a people, physically and culturally. Equally important, this mass killing was committed by a government against its own subjects. This was not a case of an invading army or a violent colonization of a faraway land. The Armenians were not a rebellious or combative indigenous people settled in conquered territory. Despite the small bands of Armenian guerrillas harassing Ottoman troops during the war, the overwhelming majority of Armenians had steered well clear of politics or rebellion. Rather, they were for the most part peaceful subjects of the sultan who had always lived productively within the borders of the state. The Armenians of the Ottoman Empire paid taxes, obeyed the law, and contributed to the culture and institutions of the empire. Their destruction was a sinister innovation of a society that thought of itself as "modern" and "civilized," and would foreshadow the systematic mass murder of innocents by Nazi and communist governments only a few decades later.

This was not the first time that the Christians in the eastern provinces of the Ottoman Empire had been attacked directly. Twenty years earlier, intensely violent episodes had wiped out over a hundred thousand Armenians under the watch of Sultan Abdul Hamid II. Tens of thousands more had died in the bloodbaths of 1909 after the Young Turks took power. Bloodletting aimed at the Armenians had become commonplace in the eastern Ottoman vilayets, fostering a "culture of massacre." With the advent of World War I in 1914, a vastly more efficient and highly organized wave of terror swelled and broke upon an unsuspecting Christian population, removing the Armenians from their ancestral lands altogether.

The operation to remove and ultimately erase the Armenian population in Anatolia went into effect just as World War I was beginning. It was neither random nor unplanned, but rather systematic and centrally orchestrated by a guiding hand in Constantinople. By the end of the summer of 1915, owing to this program of relocation and massacre, most of the hundreds of thousands of Armenians who had been living in Anatolia no longer resided in their villages. By the end of the war, most of those Armenians of the Ottoman Empire who had not managed to cross the border were either dead or dying in the Syrian desert.

The process began in the regions farthest from Constantinople and closest to Russia, and then, with gruesome efficiency, worked its way westward across Asia Minor. Some Armenians in the western vilayets were forced to pay their own way as they were deported by railway, even if this meant traveling in cattle cars. The sick and dying were mixed in with the healthy. The dead were removed at each station and in some instances thrown down the embankments. Along the Black Sea littoral, victims were taken out in boats and drowned. If local Muslim leaders balked at the deportations because they understood that it was nothing more than thinly disguised mass murder, those leaders were replaced. Sometimes they, too, were executed.

Victims were often forced to undress before being killed, since it was against Sharia law to strip clothing off a corpse and then sell it in the market. Many deportees would arrive at their destination completely naked. In addition to being subjected to organized theft, those in the deportation caravans were attacked continually, and whatever meager possessions they had managed to carry were taken. At one point, in a conversation with Ambassador Morgenthau, Talat Pasha demanded the life insurance proceeds for Armenians the regime had murdered! This real property and treasure would contribute to a program of Turkification, thus subsidizing the cost of the deportations themselves.[4]

The Ottoman campaign against the Armenians of Asia Minor proceeded in the following way:

1) Since the Balkan wars, able-bodied Armenian men faced conscription by the army. Now they were disarmed, segregated from the regular army, and re-formed into "labor battalions" *(inshaat taburu)*. These underfed and ill-clothed young men were worked to death or executed in remote areas.

2) Small villages were surrounded by soldiers or irregulars *(chetes)* and destroyed. All residents were killed on the spot. The village often would be burned to the ground.

In larger villages or towns where the populace was both Christian and Muslim:

3) Male leaders of the Armenian community were arrested, imprisoned, and tortured. Within a few days, they would be "moved" from the prison to another location, farther from the town. These men would not be seen again, having been executed. This group would include those not eligible for the army but who had some capacity as potential leaders: businessmen, merchants, pharmacists, teachers, clergy.

4) Once the leading men of the community had been removed, a proclamation would announce that the remaining Armenians were being moved to another location. A typical posting, quoted in one survivor account, reads:

> Leave all your belongings — your furniture, your beddings, your artifacts. Close your shops and businesses with every-thing inside. Your doors will be sealed with special stamps. On your return, you will get everything you left behind. Do not sell property or any expensive item. Buyers and sellers alike will be liable for legal action. Put your money in a bank in the name of a relative who is out of the country. Make a list of everything you own, including livestock, and give it to the specified official so that all your things can be returned to you later. You have ten days to comply with this ultimatum.[5]

Armenians would be given a few days to get their posses-sions together. Often a "fire sale" would follow, and families would be forced to sell what they couldn't carry at an extreme discount.[6] Large storable possessions — for example, goods in a warehouse or household furniture and carpets—would be confiscated "for safe-keeping" by the government. Deportees were forced to sign over real estate deeds. Bank accounts of those who had been deported were taken. Merchants and farmers and tradesmen lost their stock, including foodstuffs, animals, manufactured goods for sale, and raw materials. Small factories, farms, and mines were seized. Churches and church property were confiscated and converted into mosques.[7]

5) The Muslim population was warned that Armenians who ran away or tried to hide would be executed. Any Muslim who attempted to conceal or in any way aid an Armenian would be punished by death, and his or her family would likewise be executed and their house razed. All Armenians were included in the caravans. No exceptions were allowed for age or disability. The only Armenians permitted to stay behind were those who either had a secure job within a consulate or a hospital or whose skills might benefit the war effort (e.g., working in a flour mill).[8] Eventually every Armenian, whatever his or her value to Turkey, was to be deported. Farmers were killed or exiled before they could harvest their crops, resulting in grain shortages and famine.

6) Guarded by soldiers, police, or *chetes,* the caravans were led into the frontier. Harassment and killings began soon after they left the populated areas. The persecution ranged from small boys throwing stones to theft, beatings, the abduction and rape of young women, and murder. Kurds were allowed to attack the caravan in order to kidnap young women and children or rob those who might have valuables with them; minor infractions were met with whippings, bayoneting, or shooting. Suicides were common. Often the pious would rather die than renounce their Christian faith, as their captors demanded. Others suffered permanent psychological harm.

7) As the caravans continued along the meandering semi-desert tracks, hunger, thirst, and relentless heat would take their

toll. Deportees were often forbidden to drink from springs. The weak, primarily the elderly and very young, were left by the roadside to die. (After numerous reports of corpses cluttering the roads, Talat Pasha sent out strict directives to bury all the dead.) The caravans were quickly transformed into a ragtag collection of starving people dragging their emaciated bodies through the desert. There was little chance that the old, infirm, or very young would survive more than a week of this torture. Young women were kidnapped into households, boys taken as slaves (often as shepherds). The only men who survived were those who escaped and ran.

8) The ultimate destination was a string of outposts in the Syrian desert, particularly the oasis town of Der Zor. Here, with little shelter and no facilities for basic hygiene, the remaining deportees died from hunger and disease. The camps were regularly culled through outright executions in order to make room for new arrivals. Thousands of children were left orphaned.

There were innumerable witnesses. Commissioner Giacomo Gorrini, who was stationed as the Italian consul general in Trebizond in northeastern Anatolia on the Black Sea, wrote:

> There were about 14,000 Armenians at Trebizond— Gregorians, Catholics, and Protestants. They had never caused disorders or given occasion for collective measures of police. When I left Trebizond, not a hundred of them remained. From the 24th June, the date of the publication of the infamous decree, until the 23rd July, the date of my own departure from Trebizond, I no longer slept or ate; I was given over to nerves and nausea, so terrible was the torment of having to look on at the wholesale execution of these defenceless, innocent creatures.
> The passing of the gangs of Armenian exiles beneath the windows and before the door of the Consulate; their prayers for help, when neither I nor any other could do

anything to answer them; the city in a state of siege, guarded at every point by 15,000 troops in complete war equipment, by thousands of police agents, by bands of volunteers and by the members of the "Committee of Union and Progress"; the lamentations, the tears, the abandonments, the imprecations, the many suicides, the instantaneous deaths from sheer terror, the sudden unhingeing of men's reason, the conflagrations, the shooting of victims in the city, the ruthless searches through the houses and in the countryside; the hundreds of corpses found every day along the exile road; the young women converted by force to Islam or exiled like the rest; the children torn away from their families or from the Christian schools, and handed over by force to Moslem families, or else placed by hundreds on board ship in nothing but their shirts, and then capsized and drowned in the Black Sea and the River Deyirmen Deré—these are my last ineffaceable memories of Trebizond, memories which still, at a month's distance, torment my soul and almost drive me frantic.[9]

One group remained dedicated to aiding the Armenians: the Christian missionaries. They pleaded with American diplomats to intercede.[10] Ambassador Morgenthau, in turn, made it his duty to lobby on behalf of the Armenians and wrote long essays on the plight of the Armenians, which eventually became books. *Ambassador Morgenthau's Story* has long been a cornerstone of the case against the Young Turks. Morgenthau knew Talat personally and had many tributaries of reportage finding their way to him. "I now see what was not apparent in those early months," he wrote, "that the Turkish Government was determined to keep the news, as long as possible, from the outside world. It was clearly the intention that Europe and America should hear of the annihilation of the Armenian race only after that annihilation had been accomplished." Though Morgenthau was stationed in Constantinople and did not personally witness the evacuation and slaughter of the Armenian villagers, he was entirely convinced by those on the front lines who reported what they had seen. "For hours, [the missionaries] would sit in my office and, with tears streaming down their faces, they would tell me of the horrors through which they had passed. Many of these, both men and women, were almost broken in health from the scenes they had witnessed."[11]

Missionaries had begun to flood into the region in the last half of the nineteenth century as the dire straits of the Christian population became better publicized. Though the missionaries hailed from several European countries, many were Americans affiliated with the American Board of Commissioners for Foreign Missions. The ABCFM was founded in 1810, part of the wave known as the "Second Great Awakening," which fostered missions, antislavery movements, temperance campaigns, and pacifism around the world. This organization, affiliated with several Protestant churches, had been conceived of by a group of students from Williams College who brought the idea of foreign proselytizing to the Andover Theological Seminary. During the nineteenth century, the ABCFM flourished and had a profound effect on the course of world events. Missions were founded not only in the Ottoman Empire but also in Africa, Siam (Thailand), Ceylon (Sri Lanka), India, and the Sandwich Islands (Hawaii),[12] where the missionaries set in motion forces that would lead the United States to annex the islands in 1898. The ABCFM spread not only the words of Christ but also, infused with a belief in manifest destiny and social Darwinism, a deep commitment to the idea that the American way was superlative. The "object of the missions was moral renovation of the world," wrote Joseph L. Grabill, bringing with them a new way of living embodied in "glass windows, wooden floors, wagons, clocks, sewing machines, organs, cotton gins [and] telegraph instruments."[13]

Beginning in the early nineteenth century, the first waves of American Protestant missionaries met resistance as they arrived to make converts in the Levant. The Jews, having had their fill of Christians in Europe, wanted to be left alone. The Greek patriarch had no use for competition and openly warred with the missions. Some Muslims were curious, but Sharia law dictated that the punishment for apostasy was death. And any Catholics in the region naturally wanted nothing to do with Protestant missionaries.

The "backward" Armenians became a focus of Protestant efforts at conversion. Though the Armenians had been practicing Christianity for over a millennium before Martin Luther nailed his Ninety-Five Theses to the door of All Saints' Church in Wittenberg, the American missionaries saw them as souls in need of saving. Nine hundred years earlier they had aligned themselves with the Crusaders, or "Franks," and this created another link to the West.

Neither as elaborate as Roman Catholicism nor as austere as Protestantism, the ancient Armenian Christianity was nothing like the faith of the earnest preachers arriving in steamships from America. The missionaries wanted to overwhelm this "crusty ritualism" with the undeniable light of their truth. They "hoped that their idea of individual repentance and obedience to God would be more attractive than Gregorian ceremonies."[14] One prominent Protestant writing in 1854 called the Armenian Apostolic Church "a miserable counterfeit of Christianity" and "that degenerate Church," adding the punch line, "There is no essential difference between an Armenian and a Roman mass."[15]

Christians had come to "save" other Christians (including Greeks and Assyrians). "Though they were barely aware of it, American Board personnel were a liberal force in the Ottoman domains, with as much potential for disruption as for renewal."[16] In hindsight, it's easy to blame the fervor of the missionaries for nurturing revolutionary spirit in Christian Anatolia. "They came with arguments, tracts and funds. Their purpose, they said, was to infuse vitality and spirit into the unprogressive and dormant eastern Christian communities."[17] They preached from their pulpits, and, more important, the missionaries built schools and hospitals. Colleges that exist to this day were founded all over the Middle East. The Muslims avoided the Christian schools while the Armenians embraced them. Along the way, they not only became educated in the teachings of Christ but also became exposed to the world beyond their hardscrabble existence. Wealthier students like Armen Garo headed to Europe for higher education and returned full of liberal ideas of progress and even revolution. The missionaries were a full-service institution, bringing not just the Bible to the desperately poor Armenians but literacy, doctors, teachers, and agitation. By teaching the Armenians to read and by disseminating a modern form of Christianity that preached individual salvation rather than deliverance through clerics, the missionaries were not only disruptive but also became a thorn in the side of the established Armenian Church hierarchy.

Because the United States had not yet entered the war (and in fact never declared war on the Ottoman Empire), its diplomats, missionaries, and doctors were allowed to remain in the country, and were able to bear witness to what was going on. Their accounts have appeared in various forms: in Viscount Bryce's volume *The Treatment of Armenians in the Ottoman Empire, 1915–16* (known as the Bryce "Blue Book"), the Reverend James L. Barton's compilation of missionary reports, and individual memoirs by others stationed all over Turkey.

Myrtle O. Shane, a missionary, attested:

During the first two days after leaving Diyarbakir we quite frequently saw bodies on or near the road. Some of these had apparently been killed while trying to escape. Others had been stripped of their clothing. In many cases the bodies were terribly mutilated. In one place we passed three lying near together. The faces had been so mutilated that no features were discernible and the bodies were one mass of gashes. Once our driver had to turn the horses aside in order to avoid running over a body which lay across the road. We saw a dog standing over one corpse and as we drew nearer could see that it had already gnawed a part of the flesh from the bones.

Another witness told the Reverend George P. Knapp that "she saw fifty men near the road forced to lie down on their backs in a row, their hands and feet bound. Then a butcher proceeded to cut their throats one after another, each man knowing when his turn would come."[18]

Missionaries from different countries would often work together toward a common Christian goal of helping the unfortunate. A Danish missionary, Maria Jacobsen, a member of the Women Missionary Workers (Kvindelige Missions Arbejdere), kept a diary while in Kharpert. On May 30, 1915, she reports: "From other places we hear of terrible ill-treatment. It is said that in one place 13 Armenians have been crucified, nails being driven through hands, feet and chest. In Severek the old minister has been crucified." On July 29: "Last night about 100 Armenians were sent away from Harpoot, but they reached no further than the spring, two hours walk from the town. Here the soldiers started shooting." On August 7: "They do not make such great efforts now. They just take them outside the town and kill them. It would be more merciful if they took them as far as the river to drown, instead of torturing and flogging them to death." On August 14, 1915, Jacobsen visited the local Armenian cemetery, where the dead and dying were dumped. As she entered the grounds, Turkish soldiers standing guard outside told her, "You cannot stand this." She entered with the American missionary Henry H. Riggs and the American consul.

> The large area was filled with the sick, but these poor ones no longer looked human. Not even animals could be found in such a condition. People would have had mercy on them and killed them, but these were the hated Christians— now in the hands of their enemies—who intended to make it as difficult as possible for them. As soon as we entered the gate a crowd gathered around us. All who could move jostled each other to come close enough to beg for money— ten paras for bread. . . . They were dirty, with unkempt hair,

and as thin as the people who died of starvation in India. Beside this, they were ill and black with flies. Many were too ill to rise and follow us, but they tried to sit up and they cried for help. Others were even too weak to cry after us, only raising their heads to see what all the stir was about them. Half naked women lay around and one could not tell if they were alive or dead. Two little girls nine or ten years old, were dragging away the corpse of a six year old boy.

On the same day she wrote: "In Hooiloo all women were gathered together and killed. The men had been killed earlier. The women were ordered to remove their best clothes, and they were laid on top of each other, two by two, and beheaded." On October 2 she wrote: "The Consul went to Kezin Khan and said that the corpses of Armenians are lying so thick on the main road that there are too many for the animals to eat. How frightful it must be for those now being sent away, to see their brothers and sisters lying dead on the road."[19]

Leslie Davis was the American consul stationed in Kharpert. In the 1980s Susan K. Blair, a diligent American researcher working in the United States National Archives, managed to retrieve his misplaced report after much digging. The report, which has since been published under the title *The Slaughterhouse Province,*[20] is a horrific indictment of the Ottoman government. In a letter to Ambassador Morgenthau, Davis states: "The term of 'Slaughterhouse Vilayet' which I applied to this Vilayet [Kharpert] in my last report...has been fully justified by what I have learned and actually seen since that time." Davis, an athletic and deeply ethical man, rode on horseback for five hours to Lake Guljuk to see for himself what others had described. His descriptions and photographs of corpses and killing fields are like scenes from the most gruesome horror film. According to Davis, caravans of deportees were led into the remote valleys and dispatched in the thousands.

In almost every valley there were some bodies and in several of them a great many,—in one, at least a thousand; in

another I estimated that there were more than fifteen hundred, but the stench from them was so great that, although
I tried to go up in the end of the valley, I was unable to do
so at the time. I explored it more carefully a month later.
This valley, like many of the others, was triangular in shape
and shut in on two sides by high precipitous banks which
the people when attacked were not able to climb. Two or
three gendarmes stationed on each side could prevent a
multitude from escaping in that way. Many bodies lay
wedged among the rocks at the extreme end of the valley,
showing that some had tried in vain to scale them in their
attempt to escape and had been killed there.... Thus the
victims were literally penned in and butchered in cold
blood. The bodies were piled on top of one another and
had apparently been there between two and three weeks.

A collection of American consular reports runs to over six hundred
pages.[21] These reports are congruent with the reports by German,
British, and French observers. Turkish deniers of the genocide
argue that the reports were made by American missionaries and
diplomats and so are unreliable. The implication is that Americans
were on the "other side" by the end of the war (although the
United States never declared war on Turkey), so the reports must
be biased. Reports by the Turks' German allies, however, confirm
rather than refute the missionary and consular reports.

The Ottoman Empire threw its lot in with Germany during the
war. Hundreds of German officers were stationed in Anatolia. The
asymmetric relationship between Germany and the Ottoman Empire
as allies was complex and was not always fully embraced by either
high-level Germans or Turks. Nevertheless, owing to the machinations of hawks on both sides, the alliance thrived. This meant
that Germany and German officers must have been aware of, or in
some way a party to, Muslim actions against Christians in the

Ottoman Empire. How Germany aided and abetted the genocide has been debated for years. But without doubt, German diplomats knew that bad things were happening to the Armenians.

Wolfgang Gust has collected a massive archive of German documents in his *Volkermord an den Armeniern 1915/16 (The Armenian Genocide: Evidence from the German Foreign Office Archives, 1915–1916).* The archive consists of six hundred pages of German testimony regarding the genocide. General Otto Liman von Sanders, who testified at Tehlirian's trial, addresses the deportation of the Armenians in Smyrna: "It was confirmed to me that several hundred Armenians had been arrested by the police—partly in the roughest manner, by fetching old women and sick children out of their beds in the night—and had been taken straight to the train station. Two trains full of Armenians had been transported away."[22]

Heinrich Vierbucher, who was Liman von Sanders's interpreter during the war, visited much of the territory and was able to make objective observations. In the book *Armenia 1915,* this German national reports on what he learned through official sources:

> The teachers of the American school in Kharpert were gruesomely tortured before they were killed. Professors Tenekejian and Bujiganian had their hair and beards ripped out while in prison in order to extort confessions, and were hung by their hands for days at a time. Another professor went insane when he was forced to watch Armenians being beaten to death. The vali himself took part in the torture of Professor Lulejian. The senior executive president beat him until he was exhausted and said, "Whoever loves his religion and his people, may he continue beating."
>
> In Diyabekir the same procedure was followed as in Trabizond. Twenty-six prominent Armenians, among them the priest of Alpiar, were first murdered in prison; the priest's young wife was raped by ten policemen and almost humiliated to death. Then 674 men were loaded onto rafts,

and thrown overboard in the Euphrates and shot by the policemen. Five priests were stripped and tarred, and led through the streets of Diyarbakir. A noncommissioned officer boasted that along with five policemen he had shot to death seven hundred defenseless Armenians on the road from Diyarbakir to Urfa. The district administrator of Lijeh, who did not comply with a verbal order from the vali to mow down the Armenians, was removed from office and murdered on the way to Diyarbakir.

In the vicinity of Sasun three thousand men were deported to Kharpert and with the exception of three persons, were slaughtered.[23]

Lieutenant Colonel Stange, a German officer stationed in Erzerum, states: "The Armenians from Erzindjan were all driven together into the Kamakh gorge (Euphrates) and massacred there. There are fairly credible reports that the bodies were loaded onto carts which had already been placed there in preparation, and driven to the Euphrates and then thrown into the river."[24] Vice Consul Walter Holstein reports from Der Zor, "The misery of these people is indescribable; women and children are dying of hunger every day; their clothes decay on their bodies."[25]

The German consul, Wilhelm Litten, traveled from Baghdad to Aleppo, in the direction opposite to the deportation trains. He describes the scene along the route:

Beyond Der Zor began the Trail of Horror....I no longer needed to guess the individual fates but had to behold the misery with my own eyes: a large transport of Armenians passed me by just beyond Sabha, driven by the gendarmerie guards to walk faster and faster, and then the whole misery of the stragglers became apparent in live form. I saw by the wayside hungry, thirsting, sick, dying, freshly deceased, mourning beside fresh bodies, and those who could not part quickly enough from their relatives endangered their own lives, because the next station or oasis was three days march away for those on foot. Weakened by hunger, disease, pain they staggered on, fell, and lay still on the ground.... Not until I was between Meskene and Aleppo did I see no more Armenians and no more bodies since the transports did not touch Aleppo at all, but were re-routed via Bab.[26]

The issue of German complicity is one that is argued to this day. Liman von Sanders was explicit in his court testimony that Germany did not take orders from Turkey and committed no atrocities or massacres. More recently, in a 2005 interview, Hilmar Kaiser, a German historian who specializes in the Armenian Genocide, stated, "The complicity of the Germans in the Armenian Genocide is a political invention and does not withstand scrutiny."[27]

Yet historian Vahakn Dadrian insists: "By explicit and strict orders from the German High Command in Berlin, the multitudes of German officers affiliated with the Germany Military Mission to Turkey were forbidden to intervene in the process of the extermination of the Armenian population of the empire."[28] (A footnote to the topic of German complicity: hundreds of Germans fought in the Ottoman Empire during World War I, including a man who would become one of Adolf Hitler's best friends, Max Erwin von Scheubner-Richter. Many of these German soldiers would later serve as SS officers during World War II.)

Dadrian quotes one soldier: "Turkish officers and gendarmes each evening were picking out dozens of Armenian men from the ranks of the deportees and were using them as targets for practice games." As a Turk who served in the army explained after the war, "They were going to die anyway."[29] Among the many German witnesses was Armin Wegner, who backed up his reporting with photography. He would become an ardent friend of the Armenians after the war, as would a number of fellow Germans who witnessed the atrocities.

There are several collections of survivor interviews as well. The following is from Verjiné Svazlian's vast volume of testimony. Svazlian spent fifty-five years compiling testimony by Armenian survivors, most of whom were small children at the time of the genocide. They are damning in their details.

Smbyul Berberian was seven years old when he was deported from Afion-Garahissar:

> We heard afterwards that, together with seventeen other Armenian young men, they had massacred them by night and had thrown them under the bridge. Thus, when we were deported, there were no males left in our family. They took away my five aunts in Der Zor, later they cut off their heads, impaled their heads with their bayonets to show them to us and then they threw their corpses in the Euphrates. We found only half of the body of my mother's aunt. My mother buried her in the earth. They massacred everyone. My mother wept so much that she lost her eyesight.

Eva Choulian, the sole survivor of her village near Zeitoun, was thirteen:

> The Turks came and drove us all out of the village. They were forcing us to march with whip strokes. They tied our hands behind.... They disrobed us totally and we stood naked as the day we were born. Then they broke one's hand, another's arm, still another's leg with axes and daggers. Behind us a little boy, whose arm was broken, was crying and calling for his mother, but the mother had already died by an axe....[T]hey came in the morning,

assembled us and started once more to kill and drop the bodies in water. Below the cave, the River Khabur was flowing. They cut someone's head, another's leg, still another's hand and all these human parts were piled one upon another on the ground. Some were not yet dead, but had their bones shattered or their hand severed. Some were crying, others squeaking. There was the odor of blood on the one hand and hunger on the other. People who were alive started to eat the flesh of the dead.

Trvanda Mouradian, born in Kharpert in 1905, was ten years old:

They confined all the young people in a cave-like place, poured kerosene from an opening in the roof and set fire to them. Then they gathered all the women and smashed their heads with stones. They killed my mother and grandmother with stones too. They separated the children like lambs from their mother-sheep. I had a three-year-old sister; they took her also, together with other children near the Euphrates River bridge, cut their throats and threw them in the river.

Megerdich Karapetian, born in Diyabekir in 1910, was six years old:

They separated us, the children, and took the adults towards the valley and made them stand in a line. There were about three to four hundred adults and we, the children, were nearly as many. They made us sit on the green grass, and we didn't know what was going to happen. Breaking from the line, my mother came several times to us, she kissed and kissed us and went back. We, my elder brother, I and my one-year-old brother, saw from afar a line of women moving forward; our mother was among them. On coming out of our house, mother was dressed in her national costume — a velvet dress, embroidered in gold thread; her head was adorned with gold coins; on her neck was a gold chain; twenty-five gold coins were secretly sewn inside her dress on both sides. When mother came for the last time and kissed us madly, I remember she was clad only in her under-wear; there were no ornaments, no gold and no velvet clothes. We, the children, were unaware of the events happening there.[30]

Ottoman authorities forbade Germans and missionaries to photograph the victims. To reinforce this edict, when passenger trains traveled through the worst regions, the windows were blacked out. Any shop or studio that developed photographs was ordered to confiscate and report photos of the deportees or the corpses.

Although my grandfather blamed the killings on "the Turks," this is an oversimplification. While governmental entities organized most of the killing, many of the attacks on Armenians were also fueled by a combination of tribal hegemony, religious antipathy, and desperate poverty. Kurds, gendarmes, soldiers, and local Muslims were all encouraged to take part in the slaughter.

There was, however, one group that had no such larger motivation, and whose participation in the genocide was utterly malicious and mercenary. In fact, its ranks were fortified with convicted felons released from prison specifically for the purpose of intensifying the sadistic terror of the killings. This group, which took orders directly from the Committee of Union and Progress, was the "Special Organization" (Teshkilati Mahsusa), a paramilitary network under the direct command of Dr. Behaeddin Shakir. The local populations knew them as *chetes*.

The Special Organization was formed during the Balkan Wars of 1912 and 1913 to carry out secret operations, like committing sabotage and fostering terror. These *chetes* were guerrilla fighters, dedicated to doing whatever was necessary to force populations to abandon territory. As the genocide commenced, the Special

Organization was expanded to include in its duties the rounding up and destruction of the Armenian population. Toward these ends, some thirty thousand prisoners were released from custody specifically to boost the violent capacity of these outfits. Many of these men relished fearsome, brutal sadism. Working in tandem with the Kurdish militia, the Special Organization was responsible for much of the dirty work of the genocide.

Slitting throats, gouging out eyes, beheading, and torture — these were hallmarks of the *chetes*. They tore out teeth, hair, beards, and fingernails, and sliced off noses and ears. Victims were whipped raw with animal-hide whips. Locked into barns or churches, many victims were burned alive. Rape was followed by rudimentary crucifixion and impalement. Young women were stripped, doused with kerosene, and forced to dance as they burned.

In addition to the horrors perpetrated by the Special Organization, much of the worst violence against the Armenians was dealt out by Kurds, a Muslim people who shared parts of the Armenian homeland in eastern Anatolia. When the Armenians were uprooted and forced on long marches through Kurdish territory, it served the purposes of the Turkish government in Constantinople to encourage the nomadic Kurds to harass, rob, and injure, and often kill, the hapless Armenians passing through.[31] The population of eastern Anatolia, whether Muslim or Christian, was extremely impoverished at this time. The Muslims were told again and again that the Armenians were terrorists, that they were infidels. That they were the root cause of their poverty. Muslims were encouraged to steal from or murder those Armenians, especially those who came from distant towns. They would be doing God's work. Among these intensely poor populations, some were bound to avail themselves of virtually free household goods, clothing, and even small children taken as "servants."

Muslim refugees from the former Ottoman territories which had recently been "freed" from the empire — the *muhacirs* — also participated in tormenting the deported Armenians. Originally from Serbia, Bulgaria, and the Crimea, they had been terrorized and forced to flee from their provinces to avoid the massacres of the 1850s and the Balkan wars. Having lost everything, in some instances having seen their families murdered, the *muhacirs* migrated to Muslim Turkey. They felt they had a right to whatever they could get their hands on, whether it be possessions or homes, because they were refugees themselves. From the government's point of view, these returning "Turks" could be put to good use. They could help unify the country, "Turkify" the country, make the nation "one," and end the everlasting problem of the restless minority population. They could assume ownership of property, housing, and land that had formerly belonged to the missing Armenians. This substitution of Muslims for Christians in Anatolia was integral to the CUP solution to the Armenian problem.

Despite the relative indifference to religion on the part of the Young Turks (an attitude that evolved into genuine animosity toward the religious establishment when Kemal Ataturk "founded" the Turkish Republic), the CUP was happy to enlist the cooperation of the Islamic leadership in its attack on the Christian millets. As Peter Balakian writes: "On November 14 [1914], less than two weeks after the Ottoman Empire entered the war, the Sheikh ul-Islam (the chief Sunni Muslim religious authority in the Ottoman world), Mustafa Hayri Bey—who was a CUP appointment and not, as it was traditionally, the sultan's choice—made a formal declaration of jihad in Constantinople, followed by well-organized demonstrations on the streets."[32] Proclamations and pamphlets were distributed. Ambassador Morgenthau quotes extensively from one such pamphlet: "He who kills even one unbeliever of those who rule over us, whether he does it secretly or openly, shall be rewarded by God."[33] There had been many clashes between religious Muslims and Christians in the streets over the years, but this fatwa gave license to wholesale slaughter. In a bizarre twist, Morgenthau was assured by Enver Pasha that no harm would come to American Christians in the empire. And the Germans—allies of the Ottomans but Christians as well—were also exempt from harm. This left only the Armenians, Greeks, and Nestorians as the targets of the jihad. It's true that many devout Muslims, particularly in the east, understood that attacking helpless people, nonbelievers or not, was contrary to the tenets of Islam. Still, a vast number of Muslims saw the pronouncement of jihad as an endorsement for killing and looting.

The planning of the genocide included a program of cover-up to follow the process of carving out and killing off population groups. Though the Allies, particularly Ambassador Morgenthau, were aware of the massacres of Armenians, the organization behind the effort was very difficult to uncover. After the war, it became almost impossible.[34]

The cover-up was designed to confuse and obfuscate. To this day, the Turkish government refuses to admit that the actions against the Armenians were centrally planned. The cover-up included:

1) Saying one thing while doing another. When diplomats complained of the killings, the Sublime Porte replied that it would look into the allegations, or that the diplomats were misinformed.

2) Blaming the violence on the Armenian insurgents.

3) Making hollow public pronouncements that the Armenians in the caravans must be protected, or that seized property must be carefully inventoried, orders that were later presented as evidence that the Ottoman government had only the deportees' best interests at heart.

4) Sending double telegrams. One telegram gave the actual order; the second was contrary to it. The actual order was destroyed, the second saved to support the cover story during the inevitable trials to come.[35]

5) As the war came to a close, ordering the destruction of relevant CUP files and other pertinent documents.

6) Continuous destruction of relevant files by the Turkish government to the present day.

7) Restricting or banning access to archives.

Finally, denial itself was institutionalized as a government function. Since 1923, the Turkish government has spent tens of millions of dollars in a concerted disinformation campaign to delude the world at large and, perhaps more important, its own people.

PART II

PART II

CHAPTER FOUR

Tehlirian Goes to War

A nation is a group of people, united by a mistaken view of their past and hostility toward their neighbors.

—Karl Deutsch

Soghomon Tehlirian, the young man who would gun down Talat Pasha on a placid Berlin street, was born in a small village in the Anatolian province of Erzurum in 1896. The village was usually peaceful, but violence could break out at any time. By the end of the nineteenth century, massacre and famine had transformed eastern Turkey into something not unlike America's "wild West," rife with famine, disease, and lawlessness. In a region where the meager economy depended on subsistence farming and sheepherding, revolutionaries, hard to distinguish from the bandits who roamed the countryside with impunity, made it their life's work to pester the local authorities. This was the world that young Tehlirian grew up in, a desperate world interrupted every few years by massacre.

Around the time of the raid on the Bank Ottoman in Constantinople, the weak economy obliged Tehlirian's father to leave his family and head for Serbia. Khatchadur Tehlirian was typical of thousands of Armenian men who (like my great-grandfathers on both sides) emigrated during this same period. Mired in poverty, unable to feed their families, these men covered great distances to find profitable work, hoping to send some money home. Emigration to outlying parts of the Ottoman Empire was typical. In Valjevo, Serbia, Khatchadur joined other men from the Kemah region of Erzurum, establishing himself as a "coffee merchant." Though he made promises to return to visit his family, he never made it back before what the Armenians would later call the *Medz Yeghern,* or "Great Crime." During the war, crossing borders was almost impossible. Once the war was over, there was no home to return to.

With the head of the household gone, Soghomon's mother moved the family to the larger town of Erzincan. With 26,000 Armenian residents, Erzincan (or Erzinga) was a provincial center where rural folk could come to buy dry goods, have their horses shod, see a doctor. It was a more sophisticated place than the Tehlirians' home village of Pekarich. The boy was exposed for the first time to the corrupt practices of Ottoman government "tax farmers," the proselytizing of Protestant missionaries, and the exciting and brave revolutionary actions of the Tashnag fedayeen.

In 1913, with the Balkan wars winding down, and with the hope of eventually making his way to Germany to study engineering, Tehlirian emigrated to Serbia to join his father. In the late summer of 1914, on the eve of World War I, eighteen-year-old Soghomon heard that Armenians were volunteering to join the Russian forces massing along the border on the brink of war with the Ottoman Empire. Thrilled by the news, the young man was determined to enlist, although his father, with whom he was now living, had forbidden it. In this way he was no different from the millions of idealistic young men in Britain, France, Italy, Greece, Russia, and Germany lining up to volunteer for their respective armies, inflamed by romantic notions of war.

Defying his father, Tehlirian slipped out of Serbia in the fall of 1914 and traveled for twenty-four hours by train to Sofia, Bulgaria, where he found a gathering of Armenian volunteers. Telegrams flew back and forth between the teenager and his father. Khatchadur finally relented and gave Soghomon the permission he needed as a minor, whereupon he formally signed up. Tehlirian and his comrades covered hundreds of miles by rail, crossing eastward through the Crimea and Rostov-on-Don deep within Russian territory. After days of travel, the group of volunteers finally arrived at the northern foothills of the Caucasus Mountains. Here in the capital city of Georgia, Tiflis (Tblisi), Tehlirian officially became a soldier. Barely eighteen, too young to carry a rifle, he insisted on joining the troops headed for the front. In October he was inducted into the medical corps as a *gamavor* (volunteer).

The volunteer Armenian battalion was led by General Antranig Ozanian, a veteran fedayee, known by all simply as Antranig. Antranig had the look of a storybook Caucasian paramilitary soldier, with a dramatic black mustache, his chest crisscrossed with bandoliers of bullets, his head topped with an astrakhan hat adding an extra few inches of height. By World War I, Antranig was legendary, having thrown himself into violent confrontations with Muslims since the 1890s, both as an insurgent against Ottoman forces in Asia Minor and Bulgaria and, some say, as an ARF assassin. He had squabbled with the ARF leadership, never trusting their affiliation with the Committee of Union and Progress, and for this reason had always been considered a maverick. (In his later years he would distance himself from the ARF altogether.) Antranig's total commitment made him invaluable to the cause. He fiercely refused to retreat from any battle zone, and he was nothing short of brutal when it came to dealing with Muslims. (When World War I fighting was over, he would be accused of war crimes by the Ottomans.) He was typical of the non–intellectual component of the ARF forces. According to the biographer of another renowned fedayee fighter, Murad, both men were "almost illiterate."[1] A large monument of Antranig astride a rearing horse stands at his gravesite at the Père Lachaise cemetery in Paris.

In Tiflis, the tsar's commanders had set up dormitories for the volunteers, and it was here that Tehlirian bunked while waiting for deployment. Every morning after a quick breakfast of bread and tea, commanders would gather up the young recruits, march them to the parade grounds, and instruct them in the fundamentals of warfare. Under his Russian trainers, Tehlirian learned how to handle a weapon and how to survive by his wits. Thus began his transformation from country boy to disciplined soldier.

Tehlirian loved spending his off-hours in the sophisticated and populous Georgian capital city, very different from his small hometown. In 1914, a greater concentration of Armenians lived in Tiflis than anywhere else in the world. Georgia, primarily a Christian country, had embraced these Christian Ottomans who had roamed beyond the borders of the empire. The flourishing Armenian culture and society in the city supported a growing Armenian merchant class. In the Anatoli Restaurant, famous for its shish kebab and Georgian wines, Tehlirian found plenty of friends from his home vilayet.

Tehlirian would trudge the snowy streets toward Yerevan Square, the center of Armenian life in Tiflis. Here he would hang out in the Russian coffeehouses where the artistic types and his fellow volunteers gathered to argue politics. Influenced by the intellectual traditions of Russia, the Armenian intelligentsia residing in Georgia were deeply literate. These young men who gathered to drink and eat and trade stories were for the most part poor country boys with more passion than insight. They were like the emaciated young antiheroes of Dostoyevsky and Chekhov, too full of idealism for their own good. Though the elders of the Armenian diaspora were effective and industrious capitalists, many of their progeny were more interested in confrontation.

The Hamidian massacres of 1895–96 had taken the lives of thousands of Ottoman Armenians when most of Tehlirian's new young friends were only infants. These young Armenians had grown up hearing the stories of Kurdish atrocities, but they had not experienced the terror firsthand. Intoxicated with the patriotic promise of a national homeland, they did not fear the prospect of violence. In fact they welcomed it. They were eager to test their mettle against the hated enemy, "the Turk." They were ready to throw off the "yoke of servitude" (as Tashnag rhetoric had it) forced upon the Armenians by their Muslim masters.

One day, in the Aramiants café, a popular spot for Armenians in Tiflis, Tehlirian ran into Nishan Tatigian, a grizzled former ARF fighter who hailed from Tehlirian's hometown of Erzincan. The meeting sparked feelings of nostalgia and even homesickness. Tatigian insisted that the young soldier join him for dinner at his home. Upon his arrival, Nishan's wife pumped the young man for gossip about her former neighbors. It had been eighteen months since Tehlirian had left the town, even longer for the Tatigians. Their bond of homeland and politics was deep and genuine.

Living with the Tatigians was their teenaged daughter Anahid. This was an era when Armenian women rarely left the confines of home. Over dinner, shy Anahid found the teenaged would-be rebel spellbinding as he described his life as a volunteer fighter. As she laughed at his stories, Tehlirian was stirred by her interest in him. Years later he would write in his autobiography that he felt like he "was drunk." Tehlirian's romantic feelings for Anahid tested his commitment to the Tashnag cause. In his autobiography he added that he hadn't intended to be "in love." But, he said, "I felt like I'd always known her." The fedayee was a holy warrior, saintly in his devotion, pure. Fighters were expected to keep their desires in check until completion of the mission. To volunteer as a revolutionary was to make a commitment as serious as one's commitment to God. Nothing should stand in the way of one's dedication. Soldiers had no time for a love life.[2]

When the call came for the troops to move out, Tehlirian opted against seeing Anahid one last time. He was going away, perhaps forever, to lay his life on the altar of the cause. This was no time to be distracted. Filled with emotion, torn between love and honor, he wandered the narrow winding streets of old Tiflis in a dreamlike state. He passed a boy standing alone on a bridge. Impulsively, like some kind of Armenian Raskolnikov, Tehlirian emptied his pockets of rubles and dumped the money into the boy's hands.

Then in a trance he resumed his wandering. He found himself standing before the Tatigians' shop, not quite sure how he got there. He interpreted this serendipitous moment as proof that Anahid was his destiny. Tehlirian went inside and spent a few precious moments with his beloved until, moved to tears, he finally tore himself away and joined his comrades. At least this is how he tells the story in his intensely lyrical autobiography.

A National Bureau run by the ARF coordinated incorporation of the hastily trained and outfitted Armenian volunteers into the greater Russian forces. In the early spring of 1915 the decision was made to move out, and on March 28 Antranig's sub-commander, General Sebouh, and his legion of two hundred Armenian fighters were sent by train toward the front, where sporadic clashes had broken out between Ottomans and Russians. The first stop for the recruits was Alexandropol (Gyumri), situated in the midst of historic Armenia. According to Tehlirian, thousands surrounded the carriages, cheering and waving handkerchiefs. The young men stood at the railings of the open cars and gazed down at the enthusiastic well-wishers, already feeling like heroes.

Moving through Alexandropol, Tehlirian and his two hundred comrades rode the last link of the railroad to the ancient city of Julfa, just north of Persia. (Founded by an Armenian king in the Middle Ages, Julfa was later destroyed by the Persian Shah Abbas I, who then moved over 150,000 Armenians across the border and resettled them in what would become "New Julfa.") This was the wildest and most difficult terrain of the empire, mountainous and inhabited by tough Kurdish tribesmen. The region had at various times been Armenian, Persian, Russian, and Turkish. Crossing the border between Persia and Turkey, Tehlirian met veteran Russian fighters face-to-face for the first time.

Over the next few years Tehlirian would learn the heartbreaking lessons of war, but in the late fall of 1914, as he first stepped onto Persian soil, he was still a freshly trained recruit, in love and ready to fight, surrounded by fellow Armenians hungry to confront Ottoman troops. The eager Tehlirian could not know how gruesome the next four years would be, but what was truly beyond his imagination was the tragedy about to befall his family back home in Erzurum and how that event would shape his destiny.

Tehlirian's first assignment was as an unarmed medical orderly, attached to troops equipped with German Mauser or British Lee-Enfield rifles, always fitted with bayonets. In addition, the seasoned fedayeen draped bandoliers over their shoulders and kept pistols and fighting knives thrust into their belts. The Russian troops were further supported by horse-drawn artillery guns—provided there were any horses available and the roads passable. Cumbersome machine guns weighing sixty pounds or more were rare but, when brought to bear on the enemy, terribly effective. These self-loading weapons evolved from the original Gatlings and Maxims, the fierce rapid-fire killing machines that had opened the colonies in Africa and China. One gunner with a Gatling gun could make mince-meat of any conventional formation of troops.

Horses were in short supply, giving the Turks, Germans, Kurds, and Cossacks an edge over the irregulars. Motorized vehicles, unusual in the east, weren't of much use because of the exceptionally rugged roadways. Though airplanes fitted for battle were being employed for the first time on the European front, they played no part near the Caucasian front. Tanks were also absent since it was impossible to transport them into the battle zone. Artillery, mortars, and machine guns gave the Russians and Armenians some advantage over the Kurds, who were equipped with nineteenth-century weaponry and carried little more than swords, clubs, and hatchets alongside their rifles.

Most of the fighting took place in landlocked or mountainous no-man's-lands. During the winter months, the snow would drift so deep that horses were mired in their tracks, dying where they stood. Stranded on treacherous heights, the thinly dressed soldiers froze by the thousands. Supply lines were easily cut, adding to the distress of the troops. Surrounded by weak and diseased men, the commanders had no choice but to abandon the wounded to die where they lay. Typhus (spread by fleas), cholera, and famine killed thousands more.

During their first months on the ground, Tehlirian's company roamed northern Persia spoiling for a fight. The bitter winter winds brought sleet and snow, slowing the action and making confrontation infrequent. Even as the Russians pushed forward, the Ottoman troops simply melted away, abandoning the region and retreating westward. Combat was confined primarily to skirmishes with the local Kurdish tribesmen.

Tehlirian and his cohorts had no idea that the cataclysm of the Armenian Genocide had begun. Virtually overnight in the spring of 1915, on the evening of April 24–25, prominent Armenians throughout the Ottoman Empire had been swiftly rounded up as a prelude to what was to come. In the first series of arrests in Constantinople, gendarmes roused over two hundred doctors, editors, pharmacists, teachers, authors, and statesmen in the middle of the night, usually under the pretext of some minor violation, and ordered them to report to the local police station. These important members of the Armenian community dutifully arrived at their respective precinct houses, whereupon each was placed under arrest. In effect, each police station acted as a collection point for its precinct. In the early morning hours of April 25, the arrested men from all over Constantinople were marched through the streets to the "new prison" near Topkapi Palace. (Another nearby prison has been refurbished with a fancy hotel and restaurant. You can enjoy a four-star meal not far from the location where the genocide began in the capital.) The men remained imprisoned for a few days, confused as to why they had been arrested in the first place. Families were allowed to pass food and bedding to the inmates through the barred windows.

Two nights later, the entire group was woken a few hours before dawn and again marched through the old city down to the docks, where a small steamer lay anchored. It was becoming clear to all the men, Constantinople's Armenian elite, that this was more than simple harassment. The men were hustled aboard, and within the hour the steamer was ferrying them across the Bosphorus to the Asiatic side of the city, where they were herded onto passenger trains. The journey from the city was broken only once, when the prisoners with political affiliations were segregated, removed from the carriages, shackled, and taken away on carts. These men would receive special torture. The end of the line was the fortress town of Cankiri.[3]

In Constantinople, arrests continued as the authorities sought every Armenian man with an education or who had the potential for any kind of leadership. This pattern of arrests was repeated in all the major cities of the empire where large Armenian communities existed. In the end, thousands of "notables" were collected up. Some were held as prisoners for months before being deported in the death caravans, others were tortured and killed on the spot, and others, in a confusing but relentless pattern, were moved from prison to prison before being murdered. Some of the most politically sensitive prisoners (former parliamentarians) were transferred far to the east "for trial" and, while in transit, killed "by bandits" on the open road.

The CUP had achieved a major goal: the destruction of the Armenian leadership at the outset of the larger genocide. Some of the men were spared death but were left so traumatized that they went mad. A prime example was the composer Gomidas Vartabed. Internationally known, Gomidas, a priest and creator of haunting liturgical music, was the greatest Armenian composer of the modern era. His composition for the Armenian liturgy is considered a masterwork. After Gomidas was arrested and deported on April 24, pressure by Turkish and American VIPs forced his return. But the damage had been done; no longer capable of caring for himself, Gomidas, one of the most brilliant minds of the late Ottoman period, spent the remainder of his life institutionalized.[4]

The German humanitarian and Armenophile Johannes Lepsius testified: "The Young Turks and the Armenians made the revolution together. The leaders were friends and supported one another's election. During the first months of the war, relations between them seemed amicable. Suddenly on the evenings of April 24 and 25, 1915, to the complete surprise of everyone in Constantinople, 235 Armenian intellectuals [*meilleure société*] were arrested, jailed, and then sent to Asia Minor.... Practically all of the Armenian intellectual leaders in Constantinople were wiped out in this manner."[5]

Among those not immediately arrested were author and parliamentarian Krikor Zohrab and another deputy, Hovhannes Seringiulian (known as Vartkes). Both had been on friendly terms with Talat before the roundups, so they believed they could persuade the interior minister to release their cohorts. Visiting Talat at home, Zohrab engaged him in a friendly game of cards. When queried about the whereabouts of the arrested men, Talat answered, "During our time of weakness, your people pushed for reforms and were a thorn in our side; now we are going to take advantage of our favorable situation and disperse your people so that it will take you fifty years before you talk again about reforms."[6] To Zohrab, perhaps the most sensitive and intelligent leader of the Armenian community (and not a member of the ARF), the message was clear. The CUP was in the process of "solving" the Armenian question.

About a month after the first arrests, Zohrab was detained. At the end of the summer, Zohrab, poet Daniel Varoujan, and three others were moved to another location "for trial." While in transit, the group was stopped by orders from the CUP. When Varoujan resisted, his eyes were gouged out and he was disemboweled. The parliamentarian Krikor Zohrab was shot once in the chest and died on the spot.[7] Around this same time (the summer of 1915), twenty Hnchagian activists who had been imprisoned for almost a year were hanged in Sultan Bayazid Square in Constantinople. The Armenian leadership had been nullified.

Harassment and massacre of Armenians had become commonplace, but during the momentous spring of 1915, as Tehlirian's battle group moved through the Turkish provinces six hundred miles east of his hometown of Erzincan, it still was not clear to them that an all-out eradication program had begun. The confusion of war interrupted communications and obscured the grave intent of the deportations. Tehlirian was overwhelmed by the experience of war nonetheless. Caught between the Cossack advance guard of the Russian army and the Kurdish tribesmen, the civilian populations in the region had been decimated. Towns had been razed, wells poisoned, stores looted. Anyone unlucky enough to have been born on the wrong side of the religious fence had been massacred.

As Tehlirian's battalion chased the Ottoman army, the empire's fighters became "bestialized," to use the jargon of the period, wreaking death as they passed through the defenseless villages. The Muslim fighters were well aware of acts of atrocity that the Russian army had committed against their Bulgarian brethren during the Balkan wars only a few years before. Attacks on civilians were nothing new. The legacy traced back almost a thousand years to the Mongols, the brutality of the Christian Crusaders, and even further back to the Romans. The chain of terror had been forged link by link over centuries and had come to define normal warfare. Atrocity was a means of terrorizing the population and breaking their will to resist. Each side blamed the other, while the civilians paid the price.

In his autobiography, Tehlirian describes the stench of burnt wood and unburied corpses, the plagues of flies. What had begun as an adventure had become an excursion through hell. His psychic torment found no relief in the excitement of battle because the Ottoman army was not there to be confronted. The young Armenian had come to fight the Turks; instead, he buried the dead. Not yet twenty years old, in six short months Tehlirian had traveled a long way, both geographically and psychically.

One evening as dusk fell, after a long day of marching, Tehlirian and his group discovered a cluster of twenty young female corpses, their "eyes glassy with fear."[8] His mind reeled. Was this happening everywhere? Was this going on in Erzincan? What about his own family? Were they safe? Violence was dismantling Tehlirian's sense of self. Fainting spells plagued him. He suffered from graphic nightmares in which cadavers burst from their graves, shook off their dirty shrouds, and morphed into armies of vengeful skeletons.

Tehlirian was finally issued a weapon and saw sporadic action. Untested and unreliable, he was not a natural-born fighter. He prayed for his life as bullets whizzed past his head while, mortally wounded, his friends fell all around him. He was not a coward, but he was too agitated to throw himself into the battle with unthinking energy. At one point the fighting built to such intensity that he passed out in the midst of a firefight.

In May of 1915, the Russian and Armenian forces had finally entered what remained of Van, a major fortress city on the eastern edge of the empire. Before the war, Armenian Christians had represented a majority of the population in Van. Over the decades, along with Zeitoun, another mountainous enclave in the middle of Anatolia, Van had become one of the most independent-minded of Christian provinces. As such it attracted revolutionaries, not to mention the attention of the Ottoman government. Earlier that winter, certain they were about to be attacked by the Ottoman army, the local Christians fortified their city and prepared for battle. These preparations incited the military to attack, and soon a full-scale battle for the city was under way. The Turks called it a "revolt" and brought in the artillery regiments. The Armenians stood their ground and a bloodbath ensued.[9] Tehlirian was seeing for the first time the destructive force of full artillery regiments. He was seeing for the first time the complete destruction of a major Armenian population center.

By August 1915, Tehlirian had ended up back in the Armenian city of Yerevan, well behind the Russian-Ottoman lines. Refugees, terrified of what might befall them should the Ottoman army catch up, had trailed the Russian troops, now unexpectedly in retreat, as they relinquished territory. Thousands of starving refugees poured into the city. Bit by bit, Tehlirian discovered the fate of the Armenians back in Erzurum vilayet. He devoured an Armenian newspaper from Tiflis that described a ragged caravan of deportees arriving in Kharpert after having traveled for two months, deprived of adequate food and water. The caravan had been deported from his hometown of Erzincan.

Tehlirian also set a task for himself: collecting up orphans. Some of the children had seen their parents murdered. Some had escaped the caravans. Starving mothers, no longer able to care for their children, would arrive from distant villages and abandon their young ones in the streets of Yerevan, hoping for the best. The children had "gone crazy, gone wild," and clung together in packs, having learned to avoid adults. They were always on the move, begging for scraps of bread as they scratched at the lice infesting their rags. Tehlirian recounts, "Such [children] could only be caught at dawn, asleep in the doorways of stores, under tree trunks, at corners of deserted streets, or among the ruins of destroyed buildings, because as soon as they awoke, they could not be caught." The most difficult children were the little boys who had escaped the Kurds and were trying to find their way back to their villages. These traumatized boys, eight to twelve years old, were quiet and defensive. When queried about the whereabouts of their parents, they had a standard response: "They all killed." Tehlirian, confused and frightened himself, sought solace by soothing the anxious children. He tells the story of one boy bursting into tears as he described how his parents were "killed in an oven."[10]

Collecting the children became Tehlirian's single focus. Tashnags believed that each child was precious, essential to the future of the Armenian people. They were symbols of hope. Soghomon needed these children to live and to thrive so he could believe that there was a future, any future. He knew that with most adults gone, these small boys needed men in their lives to act as father figures. He would take on that role, even though he was not yet twenty himself. Tehlirian's work had doubly changed him: it had sickened him physically and it hardened his will to fight.

In early 1916 the Armenians had grown increasingly demoralized. The British general Ian Hamilton had abandoned the overland campaign to take Gallipoli, and thus any attempt to invade Constantinople. This was a significant turn: if the British could not take Turkey proper, the killings of Armenians would continue until the war was over. Tehlirian and his cohorts also understood that Russia and Great Britain had never formed a true coalition, that the so-called Allies were fighting two separate wars.

In March 1916 the Russians made one last push into Asia Minor. The thrust got as far as Erzurum and Tehlirian's town of Erzincan. Entering the ruined streets, Tehlirian could see that the Turkish sector had been left intact, although Russian flags now flew over the buildings. But when he entered the Armenian district, he found that "everything was gone." Portions of walls were all that remained of the burned-out buildings. Only the Armenian church, the center of the neighborhood, remained. In his words, Soorp Sarkis Church had become "orphaned." Even the fruit orchards had been chopped down. "Everything was wrecked." Directly opposite the church stood Tehlirian's former home. He approached it with trepidation. A Russian officer stopped him and asked him to state his business. Tehlirian replied, "This is our house. I want to see it." The officer asked him where his family was now. He answered, "I don't know." The Russian took out tobacco and offered it to him in sympathy. The house had been turned into a barracks for Russian soldiers.[11]

Alone, Tehlirian wandered into the garden running alongside the house. Dread welled up in his chest, the stench of blood filled his nostrils, and before he knew what was happening, he had collapsed onto the moist spring earth. He woke to the sound of cawing crows perched in the bare branches above as darkness gathered. Trembling uncontrollably, unsure of how he had ended up in his childhood garden, Tehlirian found his way out to the square. Disoriented, lost, and hollow with fear, he staggered toward the household of former neighbors.

A vision materialized before him. His older brother was standing in the yard. But this was not a hallucination; it was Misak in flesh and blood! The siblings fell into each other's arms. Tehlirian's brother had just arrived from Serbia and was also looking for the family. Aware that Soghomon was ill, Misak led him into the neighbor's home.

After conversion to Islam, the neighbors had been allowed to remain behind in Erzincan unmolested. In the early days of the killings, this was policy. Conversion meant real salvation — literally, a means of saving one's neck. "In order to sidestep the clutches of the CUP dictatorship, many Armenians saw themselves obliged to convert."[12] The focus was primarily on the children: "While the Ottoman authorities were intent on murdering all adult male Armenians, they occasionally presented women and children with the option of becoming Muslims."[13] At first there was also some leeway given to Catholic Armenians, clearly a political move on the part of the Sublime Porte. Over time, though, the option of conversion as a means to avoid a death sentence was retracted, and even those who had converted were ordered away.

With the publication of the best-seller *My Grandmother* in Turkey in 2004, more light was shed on the fate of the children who were converted and absorbed into Turkish society almost one hundred years earlier.[14] *My Grandmother* is the story of Seher, the matriarch of author Fethiye Cetin's extended Turkish family. In 1975 Seher summoned her twenty-five-year-old granddaughter to join her for a chat. Seher told her, "My name was Heranush." This made no sense to Fethiye, as it was a Christian Armenian name. How could her Muslim grandmother have had a name like that? The old lady explained that when she was very small, she and her brother were adopted by separate Turkish families to save them from deportation. Her brother Horen worked in a nearby town as a shepherd. Heranush had been taken in as a household servant girl. Life was not easy, but the deportation caravan left without her, possibly sparing her life. Fethiye slowly came to realize what her grandmother was telling her: she, a Turk, had Armenian ancestry.

After the war, Heranush's father, who was working in America at the time of the deportations, traveled to Aleppo. There he hired a smuggler who worked the Turkish-Syrian border. The plan was for the smuggler to find the children and slip them out of the country to Syria. The plan was only half-successful. Horen made it; Heranush didn't. The little girl grew up Muslim, as a member of a Turkish family. As far as everyone was concerned, she was a Muslim Turk. Now, near the end of her life, she was letting her granddaughter in on the secret because before she died, she wanted to make contact with her brother. She believed he had been living in America all this time, and knowing that Fethiye had friends in academia, she concocted a plan to have her granddaughter find him. In fact, on a trip to Chicago, one of Fethiye's fellow academics checked a phone book and discovered the family of Horen Gadarian, Heranush's brother.

Sadly, Horen died soon after, and brother and sister were never reunited. Still, the connection had been made. Fethiye's grandmother lived to be ninety-five years old, dying in 2000. She never met her extended American family. But Fethiye, the granddaughter, did make it to New York City and visited her great-aunt's family, the Bedrosians, who embraced her as the long-lost family member she was.

The publication of *My Grandmother* shook Turkish society. The memoir suggested that thousands of formerly Christian "grandmothers" had survived in Turkey, maybe tens of thousands. If this were true, what did this say about "Turkishness"? Pure-bloodedness? As the introduction to the book declares, "There are, by some estimates, as many as two million Turks who have at least one grandparent of Armenian extraction."[15]

In a grotesque twist on the question of faith, foreign missionaries would sometimes give thanks to God for the steadfastness of their Armenian disciples even though they were being led to a certain death. Maria Jacobsen, a Danish missionary, writes in her journal for 1915 (July 10): "Now we have heard that anyone becoming a Mohammedan will be allowed to remain here in peace, and they come one after the other, to ask for our advice. Of course, we cannot advise anyone to let their faith down." On October 24 she writes of one man who exclaimed, "They will try to make us Moslems, but I have taken my stand. I cannot do it. I would rather be killed." Jacobsen follows with her blessing: "God help him to hold out to the end." By 1917, as she watches the last remaining survivors starve to death before her eyes, Jacobsen writes, "Here there are still people who belong to the Lord and who have not soiled their garments with sin."[16]

Tehlirian sat quietly in the dining room of the neighbors' half-ruined house as survivors told stories from their travels and a feast of sweet *choereg* bread, eggs, cheese, and pickles was laid out. Gossip was shared. Misak and Soghomon were hailed as brave soldiers.

But Soghomon found himself unable to smile. Of the 25,000 Armenians who had been living peacefully in Erzincan, little could be said. The truth was too horrible to face.

Five years later, when Soghomon Tehlirian took the stand at his trial, he knew that the people of his hometown had been rounded up and killed, but he still didn't know the details of the killings. Historians have since pieced together how the Armenians of Erzincan were disposed of. [17]

As usual, the first act of the deportation was to round up the politically oriented notables. After their arrest, these men were tortured and summarily executed. Then, on Sunday May 16, 1915, the local priest of Erzincan, Father Mesrob, was ordered by the local Turkish authorities to alert his people to a deportation. On May 18, the sixteen most affluent families of the town were deported to Konya, a dry, inhospitable town, deeply Islamic, some five hundred miles from Erzincan. (It is doubtful that the families actually ever made it there.) On May 23, a force of twelve thousand gendarmes (Turkish police), Special Organization *chetes,* and Muslim peasants arrived and began the process of herding Armenians from the town and the neighboring villages. Able-bodied men were separated and "either shot or had their throats cut in trenches which had been dug in advance." Women and children were sent to the Erzincan Armenian cemetery to be concentrated in preparation for transfer to the killing areas. On May 28, deportees were dispatched from town in groups at one-hour intervals. They followed a road that ran along the top of the Kemah Gorge (actually a series of gorges) approximately three hours from the city. Here the cliffs along the Euphrates River are hundreds of feet high. According to the French historian Raymond Kévorkian, "the Armenians were caught in a trap from which there was no escape: on the one side was the turbulent Euphrates and, on the other, the cliffs of the Mt. Sebuh mountain chain." The victims were stripped of their belongings by squadrons of the Teskilat-I Mahsusa (Special Organization). "Veritable slaughterhouses had been set up, in which some 25,000 people were exterminated in one day. Hundreds of young women and children joined hands and leaped into the void together."

Back in the town, in the Armenians' municipal park, "200 to 300 children between the ages of two and four had been gathered; they had been given neither food nor water, and some were already dead." Another witness reported that "six-month-old and seven-month-old babies . . . were being collected in sacks in the villages of the plain and thrown into the Euphrates." Anyone who attempted to run or hide was hunted down and killed. Thousands of Armenian army conscripts from the region who had been working in labor battalions were summarily slaughtered, their bodies thrown into mass graves. The few women who survived the killings were "taken into the households of the gendarmes and the dignitaries with the heaviest responsibility for the massacres, now having finally been given permission to 'marry' Armenian women."

The full truth of what had happened in Erzincan was not known to Tehlirian upon his return to his hometown. Still, it was impossible not to see and understand that something tragic had happened there. He could not escape his surging emotions. Feeling another attack coming on of what would later be termed epilepsy, Soghomon left his brother and the others and wandered upstairs, found a bed, and lay down. He was overwhelmed by a sense of impotence compounded with disgust. Why couldn't he focus on the problem? "People who have the goal of survival and determination are not like me," he thought. As he lay there, a vision of Talat Pasha appeared before his eyes. The minister of the interior raised his hand and Tehlirian imagined cutting it off. In his autobiography (written more than thirty years after the assassination), he describes this as a moment of revelation. "Is it possible to believe that one day, whenever it may be, a just judgement could occur?"[18]

As he fell into a tortured sleep, vivid dreams danced in Tehlirian's head. They began as his waking day had begun, with his arrival in Erzincan after a long journey. As he made his way down the road, he was surprised to see a head rolling on the ground toward him, coming to rest at his feet. It was his mother's head and it was speaking to him: "Go there! So that they don't see you, my child!" The head rolled off, and when he followed it into the garden, Tehlirian found his lost family waiting for him. "My brother Avedis with open eyes is looking up at the sky. My mother's head has gone to sleep next to her body. I see my sisters. Suddenly, my brother looks at me and asks, 'Who are you and what do you want from us?'" Tehlirian screamed, "Don't you remember me?" Avedis answered, "No!" "Suddenly the moon comes out from behind the clouds... and I now see that my brother's skull has been smashed. 'I am Soghomon, Avedis,' I say. Bending down, I want to embrace the head but suddenly his face darkens and a cold smile appears on his lips. 'Yes you resemble him. Where were you when we fled here? Why are you not lying here with us and why have you come back to caress me like a thief in the night? Go, go, I do not know you.'" Tehlirian broke from his fever dream to find his brother Misak standing over him.[19]

In the fall of 1916, the Armenians attempted to resettle their devastated towns. As the Russians consolidated their advance, they began to rethink their attitude toward their Armenian comrades. The official Russian position no longer promised an autonomous Armenian territory—no longer promised any territory at all. The tsar was offering only religious and educational aid to the beleaguered Armenians. Tehlirian reports: "[Russian overlords] filled the region with Armenian-hating officials. Turkish spies, who remained in the guise of civil officials in Erzinga after the retreat of the Turks, swarmed about everywhere."[20]

As a "nation" physically caught between two empires, Russian and Ottoman, the Armenians were at the mercy of geopolitics. The Armenian vilayets of the Ottoman Empire (as well as the Caucasian-Russian provinces) were a buffer zone dotted with hundreds of villages, a vast unprotected area that was now a contested battleground. In the end, the tsar and the Ottomans saw the

Armenians as little more than pawns in a much larger game. Besides, the tsar had an imminent and serious problem on his hands. The Ottomans had closed off shipping through the Bosphorus, past Constantinople. Russia was boxed in, no longer able to move grain from its warm-water ports. A swooning economy and massive loss of life on the eastern front had weakened the tsar's hold on power.

In the early months of 1917, the Bolshevik Revolution gathered momentum in Russia. Civil war broke out. By March and April, the Russian army itself had split into two camps mirroring the Red (Bolshevik) and White (tsarist) sides of the conflict. Soldiers deserted the front and headed home to join the domestic fighting. The tsar abdicated in March, clearing a path for the communist takeover. The Bolsheviks couldn't afford the distraction of an external war as they struggled to secure their hold on power. They decided to abandon the conflict. Armistice was declared between revolutionary Russia and the Ottoman Empire on November 7, 1917, removing Russia as a threat on the Caucasian flank of the empire. Upon the signing of the treaty, Russian troops abandoned eastern Anatolia altogether, including the Armenian provinces of Erzurum, Bitlis, and Van. By the end of the year, the Bolsheviks had pulled every soldier out of the Ottoman occupation. The Armenians were left on their own to continue what would be a futile struggle to hold the territory.

While the Russians were preoccupied by the civil war between the "Reds" and the "Whites" that followed the revolution, the Caucasian nations of Georgia, Azerbaijan, and a newly independent Republic of Armenia began a shaky attempt to form a "Trans-Caucasian" confederation. Georgia and Armenia, both Christian countries, seemed to be natural allies. Muslim Azerbaijan's leaders saw their counterparts in Ottoman Turkey as their cousins. Yet Georgia and Azerbaijan had reasons to strike an alliance, in spite of the fact that neither the Russians nor the Allies were going to allow Baku (in Azerbaijan) and its vast oil fields to break away. Ottoman,

German, and British armies flooded into the region from all directions in an attempt to secure Baku, the prize.

In February 1918, around Erzincan, an epic battle between the Armenians and the Ottoman troops began. Despite the overwhelming odds against them, the Armenians managed to slow the eastward Ottoman advance, opening a tiny window of opportunity for the terrified populace to abandon the region with their lives. The civilians, wearing "worn-out coats, blankets, even tablecloths,"[21] were unprepared for the exodus. Women trudged and stumbled along, clutching crying children to their bosoms. The crowds of civilians hampered the movements of the Armenian military, the main target of the Ottoman forces. When the Kurds charged the columns, the refugees would panic and scatter, sowing chaos.

As they struggled through the rocky mountain passes, hundreds of soldiers and civilians froze to death. Corpses lay jumbled amidst the discarded artillery and crates of supplies too heavy to move. Munitions stores were blown up to prevent them from falling into the hands of the pursuing Turks. People staggered through the deep snow until they could go no farther and simply gave up. Tehlirian reports finding the icy cadavers of officers lying in the middle of the road, abandoned, impossible to bury in the frozen ground. He describes weather "cold enough to break stone," the air "like ice cream melted in a man's mouth."[22] No matter how many died alongside them, the troops had no choice but to push eastward toward Armenia. Certain death was the alternative.

The major players in the war wanted much more than to simply secure the region militarily. Each wanted to guarantee that any postwar decisions by the Great Powers would not be affected by any lingering presence of the opposing side. In January 1918, President Woodrow Wilson had presented his "Fourteen Points" to Congress. Among his recommendations was a guarantee that "a people" have a right to their own representation. The twelfth point applied to the Armenians: "The Turkish portion of the present

Ottoman Empire should be assured a secure sovereignty, but the other nationalities which are now under Turkish rule should be assured an undoubted security of life and an absolutely unmolested opportunity of autonomous development."[23]

Wilson defined "a people" as the ethnic group constituting the majority in a region, without taking into account that "ethnicity" was likely to come down to religion—Muslim or Christian. Such a vague definition only guaranteed more ethnic cleansing. The Ottoman government wanted to be very sure that the Great Powers could not claim a Christian "majority" anywhere in Anatolia. Talat, having assumed the role of of Grand Vizier in February 1917, had made it clear through his directives that no vilayet should be left with more than ten percent non-Muslim population. This program of Turkification had been an underlying rationale for the genocide. But now, each side bent to the task of killing as many from the opposing side as possible. This was true of both Muslims and Christians.

In March 1918 the Treaty of Brest-Litovsk was concluded, formalizing Russia's exit from the war. As part of the treaty, the new Soviet government conceded the key cities of Ardahan, Kars, and Batumi to the Ottomans. This freed up Russian troops to deal with the civil war at home in the Russian Soviet Federative Socialist Republic.[24] Many sectors that Russia had conceded to the Turks lay within the newly established Georgian and Armenian states. Worse, the Russians committed to "utilize every available means to disperse and destroy the Armenian bands operating in Russia and the occupied provinces of Turkey."[25]

Moving eastward, with Russian troops abandoning the region, the Ottoman army took Erzurum on March 11. The Armenians, left with no options, retreated. As they moved, so did the bloody fighting. Twelve hundred Armenian soldiers were attempting to hold off over a hundred thousand Turkish soldiers. After receiving a severe wound to his right arm, Tehlirian was removed from the ranks of fighters in order to seek hospitalization behind the lines in Yerevan. Surrounded by the chaos of refugees streaming out of the territory, Tehlirian's train once again passed through Kars, and by noon of his day's long journey, the young soldier had returned to Alexandropol in Armenia. Three years earlier he had passed this way en route to the front. Crowds of fearful relatives searching frantically for lost family members had replaced the cheering throngs applauding the troop transport trains heading for the front. By evening Tehlirian was back in Tiflis, Georgia, where he was sent to Hospital Number Four.

Upon his release from the hospital Tehlirian found his favorite coffeehouses deserted. The massive deportations and killings back in Turkey were no longer a secret, and a depressing pall hung over the Armenian quarter of the city. Every Armenian in Tiflis had relatives who had vanished without a trace. Many expats hailed from towns and villages that no longer existed. Nishan Tatigian, Anahid's father, sought out Tehlirian and brought the quiet young man home to the only refuge that remained for him.

Three years had passed since Tehlirian had said farewell to Anahid. In his usual earnest style, his autobiography recounts how surprised he was to find the girl had grown into a young woman of great beauty. Soghomon and Anahid shared their worries about her brother in the army and what had happened to friends back home. They dared to discuss the notorious labor battalions and the cold-blooded executions of the Armenian soldiers in the Ottoman army. But their relationship had changed. They were no longer teenagers. Tehlirian was a seasoned soldier now, potentially dangerous, not to be trusted. Anahid kept her distance.

On April 22, 1918, Transcaucasia was declared an independent state. But the fragile coalition of the three new "nations," Georgia, Armenia, and Azerbaijan, was already dissolving as each one tended to its own needs. The Turkish army took advantage of this instability to advance deep into the disputed Armenian territory. Then, on April 24, 1918, Akaki Ivanovich Chkhenkeli, the Georgian premier-designate of the Transcaucasian Federation, surrendered Kars to the Ottomans.

Within weeks, Turkish forces surged forward, invading the new democratic Republic of Armenia, no longer protected by any kind of Transcaucasian alliance or by the tsar's army. The Georgians brokered a deal with the Germans, hoping for their support against the looming threat of the new Soviet Republic. At the same time, Azeris intent on connecting with their Turkish Muslim brothers attacked Armenians in Baku. All efforts to save an independent Armenia came to naught. The little nation was doomed.

Furious and unfettered, Armenian troops roamed the countryside, sporadically attacking both Turkish troops and Muslim civilians. The Ottoman government protested publicly. Tehlirian claims that reports of atrocities were "baseless," stating, "Supposedly Turks and mosques were burned." The Turkish command began to use Armenian-Kurdish clashes which it was encouraging (and in which both Armenians and Kurds were killed) as grounds for complaint against Armenian actions. Tehlirian gives an example: "Supposedly, we on January 12 burned the Turkish village of Zeggiz 18 kilometers to the southeast of Erznga. Supposedly, we raped the women of the Turkish villages of Kesg southeast of Ardas, and massacred the men; supposedly, after the Russian troops of Erznga withdrew, partial massacres were conducted in the region." He admits that Turkish troops were killed but insists that no violence against civilians occurred.[26] The atrocities committed by these troops were nevertheless recorded and publicized. They would become an important weapon in the denialists' arsenal of counter-history to the genocide.

By mid-May 1918, Ottoman troops had entered Alexandropol, seventy-five miles from the Armenian capital of Yerevan. In a final, hopeless battle against the Turkish nationalists, the Armenians drew a line in the sand at Karakilisa, Bash Abaran, and Sardarabad, managing to stop the advance only twenty or so miles from the capital city. Invasion was imminent.

Back on his feet, Tehlirian ran into friends who had served as volunteer fighters just as he had. The war-wracked veterans harbored feelings of bitterness and resignation. Some Armenian fighters in Georgia wanted to fight on, to head for Baku as the British and Turkish forces converged on the oil city. But as the Turkish armies moved northward through Armenian territory, it became clear that a battle on Muslim territory could not be won.

Tehlirian and Anahid's family, trying to put as much distance as possible between themselves and the war front, migrated northward and deeper into Russian territory along the Black Sea coast. Along the way, Tehlirian ran into the grizzled Armenian General Torkum (Arsen Arshag Harutiwn Nakashian, 1878–1953), who urged him to travel to London, where Armenian fighters were gathering to join the still active British and French armies to attack the Turkish Mediterranean littoral. Tehlirian decided against joining these men, claiming in his autobiography that he replied, "Colonel, forgive me, but I have no capacity for diplomatic activities. This is not my work."[27] Perhaps he was also prescient, as the French-Armenian invasions of Anatolia would lead to disaster.

Now that he was reasonably healthy, Tehlirian needed to come to some kind of understanding with his beloved, Anahid. Was it time to propose marriage, break off from the fighting and settle down? Have children? Wasn't the war almost over? Hadn't the Armenians been soundly defeated? But what about his mother, his little brother Avedis? Tehlirian knew he could never settle into a normal life as long as their faces haunted him. Until he made some kind of peace with his guilt over "abandoning" his family, he could never start one of his own.

On October 30, 1918, the Armistice of Mudros was signed and World War I officially ended for Turkey. Constantinople, now occupied by British and French forces, became a safe haven for the likes of Tehlirian, a former enemy combatant. In the Ottoman capital city, the British were arresting members of the CUP in preparation for war crimes tribunals. The time seemed right for Tehlirian to head for Constantinople to see if he could discover what had happened to his mother, his sisters-in-law, and his younger brother.

Concurrent with this plan, another scheme was beginning to take shape. If he could not find his mother or his family, Tehlirian would find revenge. He wasn't sure what he was going to do exactly, but if it was something consequential, perhaps he could gain some sort of peace. Perhaps he could move on with his life.

Tehlirian said good-bye to Anahid and the Tatigian family in the port of Novorossiysk on the Black Sea and headed for Odessa, where he caught a passenger ship to Constantinople. As the steamer *Euphrates* churned down the Bosphorus and entered the harbor of the imperial city, the great mosques came into view. Tehlirian was twenty-two years old and only weeks away from his first kill.

CHAPTER FIVE

The Debt

"War crimes" are defined by the winners. I'm a winner. So I can make my own definition.
   —Adi Zulkadry, Indonesian executioner in the documentary film *The Act of Killing*

Soghomon Tehlirian arrived in Constantinople a twenty-two-year-old burnout on December 15, 1918, having spent the previous four years camping on the bare ground of deserted villages, rescuing refugee orphans, and burying mutilated corpses. He had covered thousands of miles, crossed many borders, survived a war zone, and wandered the ruined streets of his hometown. In the heat of battle, and while trudging across frozen wastes, he had watched as friends and strangers died. Now, although the fighting was over and an armistice had been declared, Tehlirian could not wake from the nightmare. He was lost in a haunted landscape of grief and pain.

In a state of shock, he wandered along the quays and crossed the teeming plazas, through the Grand Bazaar and past the *hammams,* the centuries-old bathhouses. He gazed up at historic façades he had only read about in books. Here was Constantine's venerable Saint Sophia Cathedral, there the imposing gates of Topkapi Palace, where sultans had lived during the heyday of the empire. The famous Blue Mosque. The Hippodrome. He heard the muezzin's call to prayer from the minaret of the awesome Suleymaniye Mosque, built on the orders of Suleiman the Magnificent four centuries earlier. Following the throngs, Tehlirian descended back down to the wharves and crossed the new Galata Bridge, where fishermen stood shoulder to shoulder. He climbed the hill past the medieval Genoese tower and entered the European neighborhood of Pera, where foreign soldiers mingled with desperate refugees. The British and the French recruits sauntered through the streets, all but oblivious to the hurly-burly surrounding them. It struck Tehlirian that the foreigners seemed amused by the neediness of the populace everywhere on display. Tehlirian cautiously stepped past decommissioned Ottoman soldiers in tattered uniforms lying on benches or crouched in doorways. These had been his enemy; now they slept in the parks or sold lemons outside the bazaar, destitute yet happy to have survived hell on earth. Tehlirian cursed them under his breath. These were the dogs who had killed his fellow Armenians, killed his friends and family. The young soldier had entered the belly of the beast.

Tehlirian had come to Constantinople to discover the fate of his missing mother and sisters-in-law. Fearing that they were dead, he needed to believe there was a possibility, no matter how slim, that they had survived. Perhaps they had been moved to some distant refugee camp or had emigrated to Greece or to France. There was little chance that they had returned to Erzincan, because going home was a dangerous option for any Armenian. Though armistice had been declared and British and French troops had secured Constantinople, eastern Anatolia was caught up in an anarchic civil war as nationalist troops, loyal to the CUP's Ittihad regime, skirmished with Armenians and Greeks in the countryside.

Months earlier, in the fall of 1918, the Great War between

Germany and the nations of the Triple Entente had officially ended. In anticipation of the arrival of British and French occupying forces, Talat and most of the top CUP officials had resigned on October 8. On November 1, with the "approval" of German diplomats, the key Central Committee members of the CUP had boarded a German torpedo boat, the *Lorelei,* and slipped out of town. With Talat were the remaining two thirds of the triumvirate, Djemal Pasha and Enver Pasha, as well as Dr. Bahaeddin Shakir, Dr. Mehmet Nazim, former Trebizond governor Djemal Azmi, and the notorious Bedri Bey, police chief of Constantinople. The *Lorelei* had steamed up the Bosphorus to the Russian port of Sevastopol in the Crimea. Safely beyond the reach of the British and French occupiers, the fugitives split up. Some headed for Berlin, others to Moscow or Rome.[1]

Lacking a legal government, the empire drifted like a ghost ship. The pro-British Sultan Mehmed VI, who had inherited the figurehead position from his half brother Mehmed V, who in turn had picked up the reins of power after Abdul Hamid abdicated in 1909, held no real power and so ingratiated himself with his British and French overseers. Sultan Mehmed hoped for reasonable terms for the last days of the Ottoman Empire as treaties of surrender were hammered out. And perhaps he could also hold on to some small piece of the sultanic treasure. Everyone could see that the empire was finished. The "sick man" was on life support.

With the dreaded Ittihadist leaders gone, the Greek patriarch took it upon himself to step into the power vacuum and enthusiastically declared independence for Greek subjects living in Constantinople, granting them independence from Ottoman law. Blue-and-white flags hung from windows throughout the Greek quarter. The Greek Christians of Turkey, subjects of the sultan for centuries, aspired to more than freedom from Muslim oppression. They dreamt of a "Great Idea" *(Megali Idea),* in which the neighboring country of Greece would invade and occupy the Turkish-Aegean coastal regions surrounding Smyrna, a territory historically populated with a majority of Turkish-speaking Christians who traced their lineage back to the Byzantines. Britain's prime minister, David Lloyd George (a great friend of Greece's King Alexander, who would famously die in 1920 from an infected monkey bite), supported a Greek troop invasion of the Turkish mainland. France did its part by training Armenian volunteers to bolster this post-armistice military occupation. Italy, too, wanted its piece of the pie and sent troops. Britain, having already occupied Mesopotamia (Iraq), was happy with the status quo. The British had also secretly agreed with France to share the conquered Arab lands. With the secret Sykes-Picot accord of 1916, France would gain control of Syria and the Levant.

Constantinople itself was divided into zones governed by the British, Italian, French, and Greek contingents. Non-Muslim high commissioners enjoyed powers that superseded even those of the sultan. The Allies had left thousands of dead behind on the beaches and bluffs of Gallipoli and suffered a grotesque defeat in the desert city of Kut. They memorialized their thousands of fallen brethren by stomping on Ottoman pride.

Marshal Louis Franchet d'Espèrey of France entered the capital city riding a white horse, a symbolic gesture of victory harking back to the Crusades. Greeted by cheering crowds of Armenians and Greeks, d'Espèrey occupied Enver Pasha's mansion at Kuru Chesme. An armada of hundreds of British, French, and Italian ships lay anchored in the Bosphorus and the Sea of Marmara. The streets of Constantinople were crowded with thousands of foreign troops, Muslim refugees from Christian lands, Turkish refugees from Arab lands, Armenians, even Russians escaping their civil war. There was no room for optimism; the good old days, if they had ever existed, were surely gone forever. "The only Turks who prospered were black marketers and criminals."[2]

At the offices of the ARF newspaper *Jagadamard* (Battlefront),[3] Tehlirian placed a notice of inquiry listing the names of his mother, his younger brother Avedis (the one he had met in his dream), and his older brothers' wives and children. After chewing the fat with the editor about what he had seen in the east, Tehlirian was approached by a woman, Yeranuhi Danielian, who introduced herself as a friend of friends, a teacher who lived with her mother nearby. She invited the young soldier to dinner. At least, that is the way the story has been told many times. In fact, Danielian was an Armenian activist and her mother's home was well known to politically minded Armenians in Constantinople. However it came to pass, the meeting was propitious.

Danielian was a Hnchag, not a Tashnag like Tehlirian. In the world of Armenian politics, the Hnchags were rivals to the Tashnags, espousing a more Marxist revolutionary agenda. The Hnchags, like the Tashnags, embraced violence to draw attention to their cause. The schism between the Hnchags and the Tashnags had worsened after the latter chose to ally themselves with the Committee of Union and Progress in 1908. But both Tashnags and Hnchags had been targeted by the CUP, and now, ten years later, all surviving Armenians were fighting on the same side.

On their way to supper, Tehlirian learned for the first time that Talat, Enver, Djemal, and the leaders of the Special Organization had fled and were hiding out in Europe. The young soldier also learned that the arrests and murders that had begun on April 24, 1915, in Constantinople had eviscerated the Armenian political elite. Armenians needed to take action on many fronts, particularly getting aid to survivors and caring for orphans, and yet with most of the leadership dead, the community was effectively paralyzed. What was worse, many Ottoman leaders and their allies who had planned and executed the destruction of the Armenian community were still at large, in many cases securely tucked away in what was left of the Ottoman bureaucracy. For example, the *muhtar* of Danielian's district, Harutiun Megerdichian, an Armenian who had helped compile the lists of names used for the April 24 arrests, was now residing comfortably only a few blocks away.

This last piece of news shocked Tehlirian. He demanded, "Why don't they take vengeance?"[4] Danielian explained that the surviving Armenians of Constantinople no longer had the stomach for violent retribution. Many who had remained hidden during the war had not seen what Tehlirian had seen, had not lived through what he had lived through. These were city folk, accustomed to hanging out in coffeehouses and debating politics, not soldiers trained for action. Anyone with the guts to stand up to the authorities had been arrested and killed. Tehlirian made note of the name: Megerdichian.

While Tehlirian was making connections in Constantinople, peace negotiations had stalled in Paris. In a last-ditch attempt to create headaches for Russia, Britain had recommended that the United States assume a "mandate" over Armenia. "Mandates" and "protectorates," terms that rang with a benevolent air, were the new way to describe the links between stronger and weaker states. In the post–World War I era, all the major powers would "protect" weaker nations once thought of as "colonies." But this greater "Armenia" (not to be confused with the tiny Republic of Armenia) was unusual because it had no natural borders, and in fact the Armenians themselves did not constitute a majority in most of the territory considered a potential homeland for them.

Though the president of the United States had sponsored this plan at first, it was an untenable concept. Any mandate would require stationing American troops in Anatolia, an unstable and foreign territory with no port to protect it. The British then went further and suggested that the United States "protect" all of Asia Minor (Turkey). Their motives were transparent. If the United States, under the guiding hand of Woodrow Wilson, occupied the eastern half of Asia Minor, it would in effect create an impregnable wall between Russia and Britain's significant oil-rich territorial possessions in Persia and Mesopotamia. If Russia were to make any attempt to invade southward, it would be forced to engage the Americans. This was an appealing scenario for British leaders, who thought they could sell such a plan to the idealistic and inexperienced American leadership.

As for the nationalistic Tashnags and Hnchags, although in the past they had never specifically lobbied for an independent territory carved from the Ottoman Empire, a mandate would solve many problems. It even suggested a rebirth of the ancient Armenian kingdom. Also, a mandate would immediately end the ongoing conflict between the tiny embattled Republic of Armenia and what remained of the Turkish troops in the eastern end of the Ottoman Empire. Those hostilities had persisted while talk of a mandate had only served to inflame Turkish nationalism.

Despite Wilson's seemingly good intentions, the United States had little will to enter into such a deal, let alone enforce it. A mandate for Armenia could not be sold to Congress, where the proposal died, along with Wilson's celebrated League of Nations and his famous Fourteen Points. The Wilsonian era was at its end. By the fall of 1919, the president could no longer lobby for his agenda. He had suffered a stroke from which he would never fully recover. Moreover, now that the war was technically over, powerful men in the United States like Cleveland Hoadley Dodge, who publicly supported the Armenian cause and had helped raise millions for Near East relief, were now thinking of Turkey not so much as an antagonist than as a future partner. To further complicate matters, the Americans were not allowed to participate directly in the Turkish component of the Paris peace talks because the United States had never officially declared war on the Ottoman Empire.

Likewise, the Armenians had hoped for inclusion in treaty negotiations in Paris. Instead they were barred from the room because the infant Republic of Armenia had not been a party to the war proper. Two Armenian delegates had arrived in Paris nevertheless: Avedis Aharonian and Boghos Nubar, representing the two distinct aspects of the embattled Armenian nation. Nubar was the Armenian son of Egyptian aristocracy and a former member of the Ottoman elite. He represented what remained of the former Armenian Ottoman establishment, in which church and business leaders tried to work with the authorities. He lobbied for the conservative upper crust of the Armenian diaspora. Aharonian was a Tashnag who had been imprisoned by the Russians, and was now an active leader in the new Armenian state. He represented a stubborn nationalism, as well as socialist ideals.

Boghos Nubar complained in a letter to the *New York Times:*

> Our volunteers fought in the French Foreign Legion and covered themselves with glory. In the Legion d'Orient they numbered over 5,000 and made up more than half of the French contingent in Syria and Palestine, which took part in General Allenby's decisive victory. In the Caucasus, without mentioning the 150,000 Armenians in the Russian Armies, about 50,000 Armenian volunteers under Andranik, Nazarbekoff and others, not only fought for four years for the Entente, but after the breakdown of Russia, they were the only forces in the Caucasus to resist the advance of the Ottoman Empire, whom they held in check until the Armistice was signed. They helped the British in Mesopotamia by preventing the Germano-Turks from attacking elsewhere.[5]

Two years earlier, as the Bolsheviks abandoned the war, they had upset the international applecart by publicizing the secret Sykes-Picot agreement, which would partition out Turkey's territories and resources to the predicted "winners," Britain and France. The plan was amended after the Bolsheviks made it public, because Woodrow Wilson (who had been ignorant of the secret accord) had expected the United States to share in any divvying up of the Ottoman Empire. The Americans entered the war late, but their men and matériel had saved the day, so they felt they had a right to any spoils.

The Ottoman prize consisted of three parts. The first was control of the highly strategic port of Constantinople and the Bosphorus straits, of vital importance to the Russians. Second were the regional territories: France wanted the Lebanon-Syria-Cilicia region; Greece desired the Aegean Islands, the adjacent littoral, and Smyrna; and the Armenians wanted eastern Anatolia, the so-called "six vilayets" constituting an Armenian "homeland" as well as Cilicia on the Mediterranean coast. The third piece was control of raw materials, particularly the Mesopotamian and Arabian oil reserves. These were claimed by Britain along with a pipeline partnership with France. The remaining portions of the empire — the Balkans, Thrace, Egypt, Libya — had already broken free of the Ottoman orbit.

As the war was winding down, Prime Minister Lloyd George, a great champion of the Greek nation, encouraged the former Ottoman possession, which had been independent from Turkey since the early nineteenth century, to invade the Turkish lands along the coast in an attempt to "reclaim" its ancient littoral. To the Greeks this made sense, because there still existed large Greek populations in the city of Smyrna, in villages along the coast, and in the Aegean Islands. This ill-considered move would result in the tragic destruction of the city of Smyrna in a devastating fire.

In addition, the war crimes trials gearing up in Constantinople added insult to the injury of defeat. In the spring of 1915, Britain and its allies had promised that when the war ended, those Turks guilty of "crimes against humanity" would be severely punished. Though the newly constituted Ottoman government under Sultan Mehmed had little real power, it objected to foreigners standing in judgment of Turkish nationals and so insisted on holding its own trials. A tug-of-war began between the Ottoman government and the occupying forces. Delays in the trials, and later in the peace talks, gave the Turkish nationalists, most of whom were former members of the CUP, time to regroup. Foot-dragging on every level of the bureaucracy held back any real response to the war crimes, while ex-CUP military leaders led by Kemal strengthened their forces in the east.[6]

And so the new sultan's government began its own lengthy series of trials to ascertain the guilt or innocence of the arrested CUP members. Many of the key players (like Talat and Shakir) had to be tried in absentia, as they had fled Constantinople. Others had been arrested by the British and locked up on the island of Malta to prevent their escape. The trials were further hampered by the fact that most evidence of the CUP's wrongdoing had been either destroyed or hidden by CUP officials in the fall of 1918. (Rumor is that there exists to this day a trunk of evidence secreted in a Swiss bank vault.) The trials relied on the damning witness testimony almost exclusively. Transcripts were published daily in official government newspapers. These clearly indicate that in 1919 and 1920, many members of the non-CUP Turkish elite were highly critical of the CUP, its alliance with Germany, its thuggish tactics, and the destruction of the Armenians. Records of those proceedings would be assiduously hidden and denied by future Turkish governments. All the same, Talat Pasha, Enver Pasha, Djemal Pasha, Dr. Nazim, and Dr. Behaeddin Shakir were sentenced to death in absentia.[7]

As tensions rose in Constantinople, Tehlirian grew increasingly obsessed with Megerdichian, the quisling who had provided Turkish authorities with the names of Armenians leading to the arrests of April 24, 1915. Hanging out in the neighborhood for weeks at a time, staking out the *muhtar*'s house, the young Armenian had become a fixture in a small café in the neighborhood by March 1919, even trying to get a job there. Though the locals had no interest in taking action against "the traitor," they were perfectly happy to gossip about his social life and his family. The general understanding was that he was untouchable, protected by the authorities.

According to his autobiography, one night, Tehlirian stationed himself outside Megerdichian's home and observed a gathering through a large window. He identified Megerdichian as the man leading toasts in the midst of his guests. After debating with himself whether a shot to the heart or the head would be more effective, Tehlirian fired his pistol through the window and watched Megerdichian fall.

Wildly agitated, Tehlirian raced back to his room and lay low. When he emerged hours later, the news of the shooting was on the lips of every Armenian in the community. Apparently Megerdichian had not died on the spot but had been gravely wounded and rushed to a hospital. Tehlirian berated himself for not attempting a head shot. His funk evaporated the following morning when Danielian arrived, shook his hand, and whispered in his ear, "I congratulate you, my brother." She had visited the hospital where Megerdichian had been taken, and a Greek doctor working there informed her that his days were numbered. The *muhtar* died the next day.[8]

Tehlirian had crossed his Rubicon, from anonymous insurgent to assassin. He was twenty-three years old.

In the spring of 1919, as Soghomon Tehlirian was stalking Megerdichian, Turkish nationalists began to push back at the postwar Allied invasion of Asia Minor. Allied forces had failed to secure vast remote territories of Turkey. The Allies never understood that although the CUP leadership had fled Constantinople, the key members were alive and well in every corner of Turkey. Perhaps even more important, the Central Committee—safely in hiding in Berlin, Rome, and Moscow—continued to communicate with mid-level bureaucrats in Constantinople, particularly those who were still free because they could not be linked to the destruction of the Armenians. The British had even tasked some of these hidden CUP sympathizers with creating the successor government to the CUP's regime. So it was easy to mislead the occupation high commissioners while nationalist forces gathered strength in the hinterlands in order to commence what Enver Pasha would call "the second phase of the war."[9]

The nationalists had the will, the manpower, the strategic high ground, and they had resources. In the challenging terrain east of Constantinople, reassembled Turkish military units exhumed caches of weapons that had been hidden years earlier with the specific intention of fostering insurgency should the war be lost. Armenian and Greek financial assets seized during the war had been converted to foreign currencies in Switzerland and the Netherlands and were used to purchase fresh arms for the resistance. The Bolsheviks, hoping to nurture a profitable alliance, had also made big contributions to the Turkish nationalists.

The Young Turks were committed to resuscitating the "sick

man," whatever it took. Rearmed, the nationalists began a guerrilla war against the invading Greeks and whatever remnants were left of the Armenian army, securing as much Turkish territory as possible and creating a vast base from which to operate. These rebel Turkish units were now fighting under several former Ottoman generals. One general in particular, Mustapha Kemal, would in time take command of all the forces and coordinate an unrelenting series of victories. Already famous for successfully leading his men against the British at Gallipoli, Kemal, later known as Ataturk (Father of the Turks), was a born leader of rare genius. His confidence was infectious. Referring to the Greeks, French, and Armenians, General Mustapha Kemal disdainfully predicted, "Just as they have come, so too they will go."[10]

The British had underestimated General Kemal, believing he was a supporter of the occupation-sponsored regime. In May 1919, when the British-controlled Ottoman government sent him to quell disturbances in the Samsun region near the Black Sea, the thirty-eight-year-old general switched sides upon arrival and joined the rebel forces. Once he was safely beyond the reach of the British military, Kemal commenced reorganizing the army, throwing what was left of the Turkish forces against multiple fronts: the Armenians in the Caucasus, the Greek army invading the southwest, and the French-Armenian forces invading Cilicia, just north of Syria. The occupation government in Constantinople responded by issuing a warrant for Kemal's arrest, but it was too late. Kemal and his allies declared that the government in Constantinople was bankrupt, that it no longer represented the Turkish people. They established a new capital, Ankara, and a new government. Furthermore, Kemal declared that the sultan was being held hostage by the West, and because "the shadow of God on earth" represented Islam to millions, he had to be rescued!

By the fall of 1919, it had become clear that the postwar punishments against the Ittihad could never be fully implemented. Most of those who had organized or prosecuted the annihilation of the Armenian population had either evaded arrest altogether or been granted their freedom in exchange for the release of British prisoners kidnapped in the east by Kemal's nationalists. To make matters worse, the few executions of war criminals that did take place were immediately met with an enormous negative backlash from the Muslim population. Former CUP members were emboldened to speak out against the British occupation and fire up the popular resistance.

The nationalist Turks under Kemal were winning the war of attrition against the Allied occupiers. The British were essentially on their own; the Americans could not establish a mandate, a protectorate, or anything like it. Russia would no longer support the Armenians in the east while the Turkish National Movement's General Kazim Karabekir had Yerevan surrounded. *Medz Yeghern*— the Great Crime—was going unpunished, unanswered, even as massive numbers of refugees continued to perish on the outskirts of and within the Republic of Armenia.

Certain prominent ARF members demanded that action be taken to "clear the debt." Assassination was one answer, but the ARF "Bureau," as the official Tashnag leadership was known, were not enthusiastic about such a scheme. Armen Garo, of Bank Ottoman fame, now the special ambassador for the new Armenian Republic, and his fellow Bureau member Shahan Natali were persistent, and presented the plan before the Armenian Revolutionary Federation's Ninth General Congress in Yerevan in September– October 1919. A heated debate arose concerning reprisals. Many were not so keen on violent retribution, believing that the best revenge would be to strengthen the young nation and find an answer to the massive influx of refugees there. Vast numbers of starving, diseased refugees were crowding into the tiny state, which had neither enough food nor adequate health facilities for them. Even as the Armenian soldiers continued to fight, thousands died in the streets, victims of rampaging typhus and desperate food shortages. In what remained of the deportation camps in Syria, a parallel universe of illness and starvation was destroying what was left of the survivors there. Indeed, many saw the very survival of the Armenian people as itself a kind of revenge. For these Armenian nationalists, preserving the beleaguered nation was the first and only concern. Nonetheless, Garo and Natali prevailed upon the General Congress to approve a secret resolution titled the "Special Mission" *(Hadug Kordz)*. Garo would be the executive in charge.

The first step in the creation of "Operation Nemesis" was the compilation of a list of the former Ittihadists and Ottoman leaders responsible for the deportations and massacres. In fact, lists had already been compiled for the tribunals in Constantinople; these lists were reviewed and became prioritized for the meting out of lethal punishment. The men on the final list would become the targets of specially assembled assassination squads. The actual lists are buried in Tashnag archives, but some are said to be as long as two hundred names. They would include Enver Pasha, Mustapha Kemal Pasha, and Djemal Pasha; notorious governors like Cevdet Bey (Van), Muamar Bey (Sivas), and Djemal Azmi Bey (Trebizond); police chiefs Bedri Bey and Azmi Bey; ruthless commanders like Topal Atif and Kara Kemal; and leaders of the Special Organization, Dr. Behaeddin Shakir and Dr. Mehmet Nazim. At the top of the list was Talat Pasha, minister of the interior and finance and, during the last months of the war, Grand Vizier. For the Nemesis conspirators, Talat would be known as "Number One."[11]

The highest level of secrecy was maintained, while almost a year went by as the logistics were ironed out. Operation Nemesis was christened on July 8, 1920, in Boston, at the twenty-seventh regional conference of the Armenian Revolutionary Federation.[12] It would operate out of Watertown, Massachusetts, with Shahan Natali (Hagop Der Hagopian), former editor of *Hairenik* newspaper, as operational coordinator. Natali had become an American citizen in 1915 and was living in Watertown under an assumed name, "John Mahy." CPA Aaron Sachaklian, a man Armen Garo trusted totally, then residing in Syracuse, New York, would act as bursar and logistical leader. Later, General Sebouh (Arshag Nersesian) would immigrate to the United States to replace the ailing Garo. A protégé of General Antranig, Sebouh had seen almost twenty years of continuous fighting and had been Tehlirian's commanding officer in northern Persia. The assassination team's efforts would be financed by the *Hadug Kumar,* or "Special Fund," which in turn would be fed by a stream of donations from wealthy (mostly American) Armenians who may or may not have suspected where their donations were going. The teams of "avengers" volunteering to "service the debt" were called the *Hadug Marmin,* or "Special Corps." There would be no shortage of volunteers.

Tehlirian, having decided on his own to find and kill Talat, was ignorant of the ARF's decision to sanction this plot to avenge the genocide. For months he had knocked around Constantinople, seeking sponsorship for his own one-man crusade. He had even approached the Armenian patriarch Zaven Der Yeghiayan, seeking funds to underwrite his mission of revenge. The former leader of the Armenian millet in Constantinople, like the entire Armenian community, was aware that this youthful soldier had gunned down Megerdichian. Zaven blessed the young man but, as a man of the cloth, would not help Tehlirian.

Hiding out in Constantinople, Tehlirian became distraught. His mother haunted him in his dreams. He saw himself as having little worth, as he had not been able to avenge his family's murder. Frustrated that he could not find a sponsor, and in the hopes of running into Danielian, Tehlirian moved to Paris in November 1919. He had received a postcard from her inscribed with a poem. He believed he was being sent a cryptic message and that he would soon be called to action.

Tehlirian arrived in Paris restless and adrift, annoyed by the hustle and bustle of the big city. The streams of speeding automobiles reminded him of flocks of crows. Unsuccessful in locating Danielian, he dropped in on Avedis Aharonian, the Armenian diplomat in Paris who was lobbying on behalf of Armenia in the peace talks. Tehlirian was received politely but then quickly shown the door. Aharonian could not jeopardize his position by being linked directly to a man who might be an assassin. His primary concern, as Turkish troops moved closer and closer to Yerevan, was survival of his fledgling republic.

Tehlirian bided his time in the French capital, finding work as a cobbler. As the months dragged on, his obsession with Talat grew, as had his obsession with Megerdichian. While he mended shoes, he fantasized about the various ways he might kill the ex-leader, revisiting the problem over and over in his mind, breaking it down into steps. The first step was obvious: to find the man hiding somewhere in Europe. This would require funds as well as the proper passports and visas to travel freely. He would need access to the kind of privileged information to which only government agencies were privy. He would need a weapon. Where could he obtain a pistol? What sort of pistol would be most effective? And, assuming he found him, what if the burly Talat somehow fought back? Or what if Talat were surrounded by bodyguards? Would Soghomon lose his nerve? Would he be willing to die in his effort? And what if he succeeded? How would he escape? What if he couldn't escape? Could he face execution? It would be worth it. He pictured Talat's face as "the monster" died. The fantasy sustained the nervous young man.

Bound by the shackles of guilt and hatred, Tehlirian found himself both energized and disgusted by his daydreams. He was a prisoner of destiny. He now believed he could travel no other path than the one that led directly toward a confrontation with Talat. He loved Anahid, he loved life itself, but all his passions faded before his one overweening obsession: revenge. Disciplined by his budget and his self-appointed role as Talat's executioner, he ate little and led the life of a monk. He rarely socialized, and when he did, he avoided discussion of the massacres. He preferred to live in isolation, with but one thought in mind: his target.

It was during this period that a brief glimmer of optimism appeared for the Armenians. In January 1920, the Allied Supreme Council, the British command tasked with coordinating war efforts, formally recognized the new Democratic Republic of Armenia. Though no borders had been set, it now seemed possible that Armenia could achieve a foothold in eastern Anatolia. A few months later, at the Allied conference in San Remo, a division of territories was postulated. The Arabs would get Mesopotamia. A "Kurdistan" would be established for the Kurds. The Aegean would go to the Greeks. By August 1920, the Treaty of Sèvres had been finalized. This agreement proposed ceding major territory to the Armenians and the Greeks while making Constantinople (Istanbul) an international zone. Had such a plan gone into effect, there would have been little left of the Ottoman Empire but a fraction of its former self.

In late summer 1920, Tehlirian learned that Danielian was trying to find him. An intermediary instructed him to pick up a letter at the Armenian delegation in Paris. According to Jacques Derogy: "It was a letter from the secretary of the Tashnag Central Committee in Boston, Hamo Paraghamian, a member of the editorial team of *Hairenik,* the party's paper in America: 'Your ticket for New York will be collected by Mr. Hanemian, who has received instructions from Armen Garo for the financing of your trip.'"[13] No other details were given. Tehlirian understood that he was being ordered to head to Boston and assumed that the trip had something to do with Talat. But why was he being asked to travel to the United States? Was "the monster" there? What Tehlirian couldn't know was that because of his success in dispatching Megerdichian, he had been nominated by Danielian to spearhead the "Special Mission."

Tehlirian was being summoned to Boston not only to be recruited as the Berlin assassin but also to be vetted as to his presentability to the public. A key element in Garo and Natali's plan would be the intentional surrender by the assassin in Berlin, followed by a well-publicized trial. This trial would offer a unique opportunity for the Armenians to make their case—to present the facts of the genocide and decry the lack of justice—before the eyes of the world. Shahan Natali, the coordinator of the team, explained in an article published in 1964 that when Tehlirian received his final instruction, he was clear:

> Understand, dear Soghomon, why Berlin has been chosen first, [because this is] where the Armenian-murdering criminals have taken refuge.
>
> And why no matter if it is day or night, in the street or in a store, whether he is alone or before the eyes of the police, you will explode the skull of the number one nation-murderer. You will stay at your place with your foot on the dead body and you will surrender to the policemen who come, who arrest you.
>
> And in the Berlin court you will become the prosecutor also against Germany in the name of our millions of victims.
>
> Only in this way will the judgment be fully just.[14]

With that plan in mind, Garo had to make certain that the future representative of the Armenian people would cut a sympathetic figure. He had to meet Tehlirian face-to-face.

Though Tehlirian had neither the necessary paperwork nor the funds to pay for his trip to the United States, within a few days his contact at the delegation arranged a fresh passport with visa attached and a third-class steamship ticket to New York City (costing about a hundred dollars). He would enter the United States as an ordinary southern European immigrant, one among the thousands who were arriving weekly. Departing from Cherbourg on August 19, Tehlirian crossed the Atlantic to New York in seven days aboard the *Olympic,* the "twin sister" of the ill-fated *Titanic.* (The *Olympic* had been part of the massive rescue effort eight years earlier.) Like the *Titanic,* it was a huge ship, fitted out as a troop carrier in 1915 and now totally refurbished as one of a new class of luxury liners servicing the burgeoning traffic between the continents.

Tehlirian's travel arrangements were modest but not spartan.

The White Star Line's third class was equivalent to second class on most other lines. The cabin he shared with three other immigrants was supplied with bunks, electric lighting, and a washbasin. One bath down the hall was sufficient for all the men in steerage, as most avoided bathing. (A common belief at the time was that taking baths resulted in lung disease.) Meals were simple but nourishing, with typical menus including oatmeal, coffee, canned herring, boiled beef and cabbage, biscuits, and canned peaches.

For the first time in his life, Tehlirian experienced the vastness of the ocean. Losing sight of land and gazing out at the rolling Atlantic for hours at a stretch gave him time to think deeply on the difficult mission before him. He lost himself in his meditations and, unlike his fellow passengers, was neither fascinated by the massive ship nor bored by the long voyage. The transatlantic crossing was merely prelude; his adventure would begin only after the ship docked. After waiting patiently for two years, Tehlirian was finally moving forward.

As the ship steamed into port, the twenty-four-year-old stared in wonder at the skyscrapers towering over New York Harbor. This was neither frantic Paris nor crumbling Constantinople. This was the city of the future, of new beginnings. This was where he would find a new beginning. According to Ellis Island records, Tehlirian entered the United States on August 25, 1920, as "Solomon Telarian" and used his shaky command of the French language to report his ethnicity as Armenian with a residence in Paris.

After processing through immigration and a short ferry ride across the Hudson, Tehlirian hailed a taxi and handed the driver a slip of paper on which was written the address of the New York Tashnag "clubhouse," 53 Lexington Avenue at Twenty-fifth Street, just south of the Armory. As he traversed Manhattan, he marveled at the energy of the city "bubbling like a furnace everywhere."[15] Inside the club, fellow countrymen surrounded him and peppered him with queries in the mother tongue. Tehlirian tried at first to satisfy the interest of his peers, then found the enthusiastic curiosity repellent. He grew silent. Soghomon could not bear casual discussion of what Armenians were now calling *Medz Yeghern* (the Great Crime).

Tired and angry, Tehlirian made a move to leave. One of the older boys collared him and asked him what he was upset about. Frustrated, he blurted out that he was on a mission under the direction of the Tashnagtsutiun, that he didn't have time for gossip. The mood in the room shifted. The young men surrounding him finally understood: this skinny war veteran was not just one more newcomer to America, peripherally associated with the Tashnag organization, but a genuine fedayee who was part of something deeper and much darker. He was quickly escorted to the recently refurbished Grand Central Station, where he caught a train to Boston.

Tashnag operatives picked up the fiery young man at Boston's South Station and drove him to the editorial offices of the *Hairenik* newspaper. The newspaper's offices, like those in Geneva and Constantinople, provided a safe haven for revolutionaries. Newspapers factored greatly in the dissemination of radical ideas and provided a natural cover for those who organized the intellectual superstructure of revolution. All over the world, newspapers had become the first real mass media. They were cheap to print and circulate, and could target specific ethnic minorities, consolidating their agenda. Newspapers created a sense of unity for factions, political parties, and revolutionaries.

Stepping into the offices, Tehlirian found himself shaking the hand of the Armenian Revolutionary Federation's Central Committee secretary, "Hamo" Paraghamian. Paraghamian, an insurance salesman by trade, was an extrovert, a man with great appetites, evidenced by his large girth. His jolly demeanor disguised an intense commitment to the assassination effort. It would be Hamo's job to transfer the funds that Aaron Sachaklian collected through charitable contributions and wire them to the Nemesis operatives in Europe.

Tehlirian did not understand that in the world of spies, appearances are deceiving. He had crossed an ocean to do whatever was asked of him, yet once again found himself surrounded by people who spoke casually about the task at hand. This angered the young fedayeen. As Hamo made small talk, Tehlirian felt distant, ill at ease with this "Armenian American" with his tailored suit and chubby cheeks. This man was nothing like the fierce fighters Soghomon had known and loved on the front. Everywhere he went, the Armenians here used big words, had soft hands, soft eyes. They were not to be trusted. Tehlirian found it hard to focus.

Hamo explained to Tehlirian that Talat and his confederates were working with European associates to resuscitate the Turkish state as a prelude to the return of the former leadership. A big part of that effort would be to improve the reputation of Turkey with the West. The former Ittihadists had met with Italians to broker loans and foster military assistance for General Mustapha Kemal's rebel army. In addition, the Turkish nationalists had been receiving funds from the Soviet Union and had used this cash to order fresh weapons. In Baku, Enver Pasha had made an appearance at the first Soviet-sponsored Congress of the Peoples of the East, claiming to represent the North African Islamic nations. The former CUP bosses were playing a complex game, testing the waters with the Russians, the British, and the Germans, all at the same time, as they sought to build new alliances. The former Ottoman leadership, though chased out of Turkey, was regaining its strength and poised to rise again.

Tehlirian was overwhelmed by what he was hearing.[16] He wanted to grab this fat man's lapels and shout in his face, "Just tell me where the monster is! Is he here in the States? Where is Talat? And how can I get at him? I am a weapon, aim me." But he bit his tongue and waited. It was important to remain calm. A familiar feeling was stirring in his chest, the illness that had felled him on the front and in Erzincan. It would be very bad if he fainted here in front of these people after coming so far. Another man entered the room.

Tehlirian instantly recognized Armen Garo of the Bank Ottoman attack, Garo who had served in parliament with the murdered
Zohrab, Garo who was ambassador for the government of the new
Armenian Republic. According to Tehlirian's memoir, his mood
lifted instantly as he realized he was in the presence of a genuine
hero of the Armenian nation. Clearly the affinity was reciprocated.
Garo shook Tehlirian's hands "with paternal love and fraternal
warmth."

The horrific killings in Asia Minor had eroded Garo's spirit,
and to Tehlirian he seemed worn. Garo had fought the good fight,
had done everything he could, had been a leader during a time
when the Tashnags were working with the CUP to overthrow the
sultan. When the war began, he had joined the military, he had
traveled thousands and thousands of miles. Yet despite all his
efforts, a tragedy of epic proportions had transpired during his
watch. Garo understood the full dimensions of the debacle more
than most. He was soul sick.

The older man outlined all the work that needed to be done,
and Tehlirian felt himself growing buoyant with purpose. He was
being invited to join the front lines, to make a difference. "We
were like members of a family," said Tehlirian, the man who had
grown up barely knowing his father. Now he had found one. And
Garo, who wanted to believe that all his efforts on behalf of his
people had not been futile, needed someone who would have
complete faith in him and who could bravely pick up the torch
he himself had carried for so long. He needed someone whose
passion equaled his own. Garo suggested they get something to
eat. They ended up at the Koko Restaurant,[17] only a short walk
down the hill.

As the two men became more comfortable with each other,
Garo regaled Tehlirian with stories from his glory days as gadfly to
the powerful Talat. He recounted how in June 1914, only a few
months before the war began, Garo, as a member of the Turkish
Assembly, had visited Talat in his office. Talat had complained that
the Armenians were once again seeking outside help from Europe

for their grievances. The minister of the interior fixed his glare on the Armenian parliamentarian. "Why do you not come to us for help? Why do you have to bring the British in on this?"

Garo had replied that the CUP leaders were not abiding by the spirit of the reforms. As Garo laid it out to his new protégé, he knew he was in the right and had refused to give in to Talat's bullying. The age of the subservient Armenian was over. As far as Garo was concerned, Armenians and Turks were all Ottomans, equal citizens within the empire. It said so in the constitution.

As the argument wore on, Garo could see that Talat was toying with him, "smiling satanically." Garo realized that there was no point in continuing the debate. But Talat wouldn't let the matter drop. He insisted on an answer. Garo knew he was being patronized; the time for argument was past. And then, in his next breath, Garo warned Talat that he and the Ittihad were leading the empire down a road to ruin.

Talat replied, "You've changed."

Garo's last words to Talat were: "We will bring down the great edifice of the Ottoman Empire. It's only a matter of time." By relating this dialogue, Garo was painting a picture for the young soldier. He meant to inspire him just as he had been in the Geneva ARF offices almost twenty-five years before. This effort, this "Nemesis," was not only about revenge. It was about one nation pitted against another. It represented a historic battle. And Garo was inviting Tehlirian to be part of it.

What Tehlirian could not see was that for Garo, probably more than any of the other Nemesis conspirators, the attack on the former Turkish leadership was both political and personal. Garo had watched Talat gloat as he made plans to destroy the Armenians. Nemesis had become necessary not only as a vendetta but also as a way to restore some vestige of dignity to a people who had been crushed so mercilessly. Nemesis was about pride as much as it was about vengeance. Tehlirian was ready to die for his family. Garo was already dying, even as he spoke, of heartbreak.

Garo handed Tehlirian photographs of Talat Pasha, Enver Pasha,

Djemal Pasha, and their spouses clipped from newspapers and journals. Three copies of each man's photograph had been prepared. Since Tehlirian viewed these Turkish leaders as monsters, he was surprised by how appealing their wives were. In his autobiography he asks himself how these women with faces like angels could live with such murderous men, again revealing his naïveté.

Focusing on the photo of Talat, Tehlirian made note of the man's muscular arms and square shoulders. The former interior minister cut an imposing figure. What if something went wrong and he had to attack Talat with his bare hands. Would he have the strength to be able to overcome such a bull? It made no difference; he would welcome the opportunity to grapple with Talat.

Tehlirian then examined the photographs of Enver and Djemal. The twisted points of Enver's mustache and the young general's ramrod posture revealed the arrogance of a peacock. That would make him a more vulnerable target in the end. Turning to Djemal, he saw in his eyes a cunning and an appetite for barbarity. Tehlirian stared at the photographs until they swam before his eyes. These men had killed so many. Hundreds of thousands of mothers and children. Innocent people like his own kin had died because of these men. Garo broke the silence. "You know that after 1909, Djemal was governor of Cilicia. After the massacres in Adana. He wanted to break away, form a kingdom of his own."

Garo handed Tehlirian a new photograph. "This is Bedri Bey. He was head of the police in Constantinople who rounded up our brothers in April 1915. He supervised the tortures, the killing of Zohrab. He escaped with the rest of them in November 1918." Soghomon knew Bedri Bey because he was an associate of his first victim, Megerdichian. "Also Doctor Shakir and Djemal Azmi. These men are in communication with one another, we are fairly sure of it. Naji Bey, Said Halim Pasha, the Grand Vizier before Talat...they are all preparing to return, only waiting for the right moment to re-enter Turkey. You know who Azmi is, right?" Yes, Tehlirian had heard of Azmi's crimes. This was the governor of Trebizond who had executed hundreds of young Armenian men serving in the labor battalions. In addition, Azmi had emptied his vilayet of its Armenian civilians, sending them out into the Black Sea on fishing boats to be drowned. Tehlirian quietly murmured, "Yes, I know."

Garo continued, "Azmi ended up in Baku where he continued his massacres." Tehlirian felt the familiar floating sensation about to overwhelm him as he concentrated on Garo's words. He must not faint at this important moment. Soghomon was prepared to do anything for this man whose face reminded him of his uncles in Serbia. Whatever was asked of him. He refused to squander this opportunity.

It was after midnight when the two finally finished. Garo left the restaurant and did not return. Hamo walked Tehlirian back to the offices of *Hairenik,* where a room with a bed had been prepared. He was alone for the first time in weeks. In the dark, Tehlirian closed his eyes but could not find sleep. He tried to conjure his beloved Anahid, but instead the photographs of the villainous Turks crowded his mind. "The monstrous faces jumped up and down before my eyes," he recalled.[18]

Tehlirian returned to Europe on a steamship to Le Havre. There he boarded a train and went directly to Paris, where he was handed a fresh passport, issued on November 18, 1920, by the Persian consulate. This new paperwork would identify him as a subject of Persia rather than of the Ottoman Empire. Once he reached Germany, it would be important for the young Armenian to mask his nationality as thoroughly as possible. Turkish agents would be on the lookout for Armenian spies and killers.

From Paris, Tehlirian traveled to Geneva, where he visited the editorial offices of *Troshag* (The Flag), the official newspaper of the ARF. These were the offices that doubled as ARF headquarters, the same headquarters Armen Garo had visited as a student. Here Tehlirian met with the editor, "Mr. Anton," who explained to Tehlirian that "our representative" (Shahan Natali), who had passed through a few days earlier, was certain that Talat was in Berlin.[19] Anton arranged for Tehlirian to obtain a Swiss student visa, which would allow him to enter Germany without any difficulty. He urged Tehlirian to get to Berlin as soon as possible so that he could sign up as an engineering student before the schools closed registration for the next period. Tehlirian left Geneva on December 3 and arrived in Berlin the same day. The agents in Geneva reported back to Boston that "Simon Tavitian," the code name Tehlirian had been given, had moved on to Berlin.[20]

CHAPTER SIX

The Hunt

I am the son of peasants and I know what is happening in the villages. That is why I wanted to take revenge, and I regret nothing.
— Gavrilo Princip

Assassination has had a very long tradition in the Ottoman Empire. The murderous competition between heirs for the royal throne was key to the sultanic succession. Should a prince ascend to the throne, all of his brothers and male cousins, regardless of age, were smothered or garroted to ensure that royal competition would not endanger the dynasty itself. Murder was an essential ingredient to the successful management of the state.

Murder wasn't always preemptive. Sultans were routinely dispatched by rivals. In the most famous case of sultanicide, the mother of Sultan Ibrahim, Valida Sultana Kiusem, ordered her son to be murdered and replaced by his eight-year-old brother in order to maintain her own control over the empire. On the eve of World War I, the CUP secured its shaky hold on power by gunning down the minister of war and then, six months later, the new Grand Vizier.

The term "assassin" dates back almost a thousand years, rooted in medieval Islamic power struggles. It refers to the followers of Hassan-i Sabbah, a rebellious eleventh-century Ismaili Shi'a who vengefully sent out his followers to murder his enemies. Holed up in a remote and impregnable castle in the mountains of northern Persia, Hassan would extort protection money from potential targets, terrorizing rulers hundreds of miles from his base.

The psychological impact of terror was an essential ingredient in Hassan's modus operandi. His assassins always killed with daggers, forcing a bloody face-to-face confrontation. Ironically, Hassan's first successful assassination was that of the Grand Vizier of the Seljuk Turks, Nizam al-Mulk. Nineteen hundred years later, Soghomon Tehlirian would follow in the footsteps of the first assassins when he murdered one of the last of a long line of powerful Ottoman Grand Viziers, Talat Pasha.

—⁂—

On December 3, 1920, the very day when Tehlirian arrived in Berlin to begin hunting for Talat, General Mustapha Kemal's Grand National Assembly of Turkey signed the Treaty of Alexandropol with the tiny Democratic Republic of Armenia. With the stroke of a pen, Armenia formally recognized the new Kemalist Republic of Turkey (something the Allies were not willing to do just yet). This paradoxical treaty, an act of desperation on the part of the Armenians, was meant to mollify the Turkish forces that were on the brink of finishing off the fledgling nation. This recognition of the new Turkish state outraged those Armenians who had fought for the homeland vilayets, and some, like General Antranig, refused to stop fighting. The dream of a "Wilsonian" Armenia was dead.

Kemal's role in the destruction of the Armenians has never been completely explored. As Christopher J. Walker noted in his book on Armenia, "Mustafa Kemal was known personally to hate fanaticism and to despise religious extremism, and to be devoid of anti-minority sentiments that had characterized Turkish leaders in the past."[1] But Kemal was also a pragmatist, a master of survival, and for that reason his government, and those governments that carried on his legacy, would continue to pursue and destroy Christians in Turkey, as well as Kurds.

The Treaty of Alexandropol kept Kemal's forces at bay, but it did not stop the Russians. Concurrently with this futile maneuver of recognition, the Soviet Union completed its annexation of the Armenian state. From check to checkmate. Despite the treaty with the Turkish nationalists, it was only a matter of time before Kemal's armies would invade Armenia. To fight on against the Turks without an alliance with the Soviet Union would mean total destruction of what little there remained of the Armenian people in the Caucasus. Thus, on virtually the same date as the signing of the Treaty of Alexandropol, the Armenian Soviet Socialist Republic was born.

On that dark day for what was left of any independent Armenian state, Soghomon Tehlirian arrived in Berlin. A stranger to the city, unable to speak a word of German, he did not know one face in this vast and hectic cosmopolis. His tiny support network was ragtag and diffuse. In contrast, Talat and his comrades had surrounded themselves with a well-organized underground network of former police, spies, and diplomats as well as the full, if unacknowledged, support of the German government. Swiss and German bank accounts holding millions in gold would sustain the Ittihad exiles, while the Nemesis conspirators relied on an austere budget of thousands of dollars. While Talat's cohorts enjoyed the freedom of unrestricted funds, Shahan Natali would have to argue for every penny spent, down to the smallest purchase.

After a full day on the train from Geneva, followed by an apprehensive cab ride across Berlin, Tehlirian arrived cold and hungry at the Tiergarten Hotel around ten p.m. on December 3. He found his contact hunched over a Turkish-language newspaper. The man did not look up. Instead he pointed to a newspaper article reporting on the various Turkish expat factions squabbling amongst themselves in Berlin. He whispered, "The big game is indeed here."[2]

The Armenians would be trying to find one man among a population of four million. To make the pursuit more difficult, the city these men had entered to hunt their "big game" was teetering on the brink of chaos. This was Weimar Berlin, the metropolitan center of a country still reeling from years of pointless war. Two million German soldiers had died, while the surviving demobilized veterans had little to show for their service. Unemployment was soaring. Soon, hyperinflation would reduce the German mark to worthless paper. What was worse, the punitive treaties about to be signed with the French would further humiliate the defeated nation and hobble the economy for years to come. In January, Germany would be ordered to pay 226 billion gold marks.[3] Vast border territories had been partitioned and handed off to Poland and France. The war had left a sour taste in everyone's mouth.

Enraged at the Kaiser, German citizens had abandoned the monarchy altogether and embraced what would become known as the Weimar Republic. This new parliamentary government was an unstable mess, allowing dozens of extremist political parties to rise up and flourish. These armed factions literally fought each other in the streets. Among them were the "Freikorps" reactionaries, mostly disaffected veterans who would later morph into the SA (Sturmabteilung), or "Brownshirts," of the Nationalsozialistische Deutsche Arbeiterpartei—the Nazi Party. In early February, the NSDAP would hold its biggest rally yet, at Circus Krone.[4]

Extremism radicalized every aspect of German life. A heady mix of modernism and postwar euphoria gave way to a permissive and lawless underground. "The streets became ravines of manslaughter and cocaine traffic, marked by steel rods and bloody, broken chair legs."[5] Friedrich Bayer & Company had invented a new wonder drug called heroin, which joined alcohol and tobacco as a scourge of the masses. Only a few years earlier, Stravinsky, Schoenberg, Picasso, and Duchamp had tossed realism out the window; now reality itself had become surreal. The decadence and near-anarchy of the Weimar Republic provided a perfect backdrop for the rise of Hitler's thugs, men who would soon sweep away an inconvenient legal system and usher in the Third Reich. This was the anarchic atmosphere in which the Nemesis conspiracy found itself in Berlin.

The circle of Armenian conspirators was led by the deeply committed Shahan Natali (born Hagop Der Hagopian in 1884 in Kharpert), a histrionic man whose short stature and idiosyncrasies were offset by his intensity and dedication. Natali had lost both his father and an uncle during the Hamidian massacres twenty-five years earlier, and he remained burdened by memories of helping his tearful mother bury his murdered father. In 1904, twenty-year-old Natali had joined the ARF, then immigrated to Watertown, Massachusetts, where he found employment at a shoe factory. In 1908, after the Young Turk revolution brought the CUP to power, Natali returned to Turkey; like many, he believed that a new day had dawned in the Ottoman Empire. After the Adana massacres chilled Armenian-Turkish relations, Natali returned to the United States to study philosophy and theater at Boston University. By 1912, eager to reenter Turkey, he traveled first to Greece, but as an Ottoman citizen, he was prevented from crossing the border at passport control. Returning to Boston one more time, where he would become an editor of the ARF newspaper, *Hairenik,* Natali was consumed with rage as he tracked the wartime action from thousands of miles away. Nothing about Natali's feelings regarding "the Turk" was moderate. His hatred was deep and his focus absolute.

While logistical support and financing were run by Aaron Sachaklian,[6] a CPA living in Syracuse, New York, Natali remained in Europe and kept close watch over the agents in Berlin. In addition to Tehlirian, the group included "Hrap" (Hrach Papazian, going by the alias "Mehmed Ali"),[7] "Vaza" (Vahan Zakarian),[8] "Hazor" (Hagop Zorian),[9] and "Haigo" (Haig Ter-Ohanian).[10] Code names were consistent with a system used to befuddle the sultan's spies going back to the 1890s. (In correspondence between the conspirators, Tehlirian would be referred to as "Simon

Tavitian" or "the engineering student.") Assisting this core group were expat Armenian artists and writers living in Berlin.[11] Armenian diplomats based in Europe who had been associated with the republic facilitated passport and visa paperwork. Newspaper offices and embassies provided enough middlemen to handle communications and logistics. According to Marian Mesrobian MacCurdy in her book, *Sacred Justice,* Shahan Natali bribed border guards and police in Berlin to alert him to the comings and goings of Turkish nationals in Germany.[12]

Oblivious to the politically unstable world of the Weimar Republic surrounding him, Tehlirian saw the city of Berlin as nothing more than a vast and complex maze in which to track his quarry. Upon his arrival, he learned that his fellow agents had already deduced that a small tobacco and carpet shop near the Tiergarten was owned and operated by Djemal Azmi, the infamous former governor of Trebizond. The shop, visited only by Turks, existed as a kind of nerve center for the Ittihadists living in the city. Publicly, Azmi presented himself as an immigrant merchant, but the Armenian spies knew his résumé well. His list of war crimes was long. The tribunal in Constantinople had sentenced Azmi to death in 1919. Like Talat, Azmi had eluded capture by both the current Turkish government and the British. His name was high on the Nemesis hit list.

Tehlirian wanted to storm the shop and "shoot the dog." But Azmi was not "Number One," and Tehlirian opted to stand down. "It was important to act cautiously and not allow the prey [Talat] to escape." Natali had warned Tehlirian that although there were many who deserved to die, he must not forget that Talat was unique in the eyes of the world. In other words, this operation needed resonance beyond revenge. The killing would have to appeal to the sympathies of a world outraged by the Armenian massacres.

Joining the stakeout was twenty-seven-year-old Hazor, who, unlike the sorrowful Tehlirian, was easygoing and affable. Once again Tehlirian was put off by an Armenian's apparent lack of grief. He felt the same confusion he'd experienced when meeting with the organizers in Massachusetts. How could this man smile and tell jokes? How could anyone from back home ever smile again? In fact, Tehlirian's brooding nature set him apart from his fellow commandos. His motivation to find and kill Talat was born out of something deeper than anger or the need for revenge. Something deeply mournful that sought to appease the need of those who were no longer alive. In this respect he was different from the others with a more straightforward determination.

Some of the fedayeen found the hunt for the Ittihad criminals to be an adventure, a thrilling game of cat and mouse. Others, like the politically violent everywhere, had always been tough characters, inured to bloodshed. They had always been at war with the Turks. Their reflexive response to the crimes of the CUP was to push back, hard. All were men who lived through action, obeying a simple code: an eye for an eye. If Turks committed atrocities against Armenians, they, as Armenians, would commit atrocities against Turks. It was that simple.

Or not. As individuals, these men were avenging the deaths of hundreds of thousands, but there was also an institutional aspect to their actions. Both the ARF and the CUP were underground organizations with no compunctions about deploying violence in order to achieve their goals. They were neither democratic nor entirely legal, dependent on secrecy and hierarchy for smooth operations. As a result, each recognized in the opposing party a shared code of violence and clandestine methodology. Raymond Kévorkian, the venerable historian of the Armenian Genocide, put it this way when he spoke with me in Paris: "You must understand. The Tashnags and the Ittihad, they were like lovers who now hated one another."[13]

Tehlirian was different. He had no taste for violence, nor did he want to deal in payback. Rather, he was an idealist who had volunteered to fight in a patriotic war and been transformed by the experience. After the disappearance of his family, the fight had become nothing less than an existential mission. Without it, he feared he might lose his sanity. This deep resolution, founded on the sanctity of his objectives, made his discipline absolute. He constrained himself, through illness and depression, to focus on his objective, no matter what he had to do to reach it. Manifesting such singleness of purpose, Tehlirian himself became exactly what the Tashnag organization wanted: a virtual weapon that would get the job done.

Though he had no aptitude for languages, he did the best he could to learn German. He familiarized himself with the *Stadtplan* of Berlin, memorizing the location and layout of all major train stations. He ignored his own poor health. Finally, he forced himself to remain as patient as a stone. Tehlirian understood that allowing his passions to get the better of him could endanger the ultimate goal of killing the man who had murdered his mother. Tehlirian removed every aspect of himself that in any way hampered his mission. His personal needs were the last thing on his mind. Unlike Garo, Natali, Shiragian, and the others, Tehlirian seems to have been almost egoless. In this respect, Tehlirian was unique.

The hunt began in earnest while Berlin, wrapped in a damp, penetrating cold, was relatively quiet. During the stakeout one day, the Nemesis team noticed a striking woman wrapped in a black astrakhan coat entering Azmi's shop. Hazor wandered inside and eavesdropped as she conversed with Azmi. All he could make out were her words "Yes, if he agrees." As the mysterious woman departed the shop, Tehlirian insisted on following her despite the group's misgivings. She stopped at number 165 Wilhelmstrasse. Beyond a snow-encrusted garden door, the woman in black ascended the stone steps, produced a key, and entered the building. This house became a new spot to watch.

It was dusk by the time Tehlirian returned to the Tiergarten Hotel. He found Hazor with two new "friends": Vaza and Haigo. The young men traded notes, and it was revealed for the first time that Dr. Behaeddin Shakir, the notorious former head of the Special Organization, was also in Berlin. Perhaps Enver was here as well? Was it possible that the woman Tehlirian had followed was Enver's wife? The two locations were kept under surveillance for a full two weeks, but the woman was not seen again. Servants came and went; nothing more. The lead had gone nowhere.

Enver Pasha's presence in Berlin was significant because Enver represented the wing of the Ittihad that was seeking solidarity with Islamic rebels in Central Asia. This subgroup of Turkish nationalists envisioned a pan-Turkic or even a fabulous "pan-Turanist" empire that would include those "homeland" regions of Central Asia where Turkic peoples represented a majority. "Pan-Turania" was a nationalist dream, a chain of revived Turkic/Muslim khanates extending from the Mediterranean to China. In the pan-Turanist scenario, Turkey would link up with Azerbaijan, Uzbekistan, and Kazakhstan to establish an Islamic/Turkic empire running along the entire southern flank of Russia.

The pan-Turanist ambition was a variant of the "pan-Islamic" dream in which every Muslim-majority nation would unify to form a vast multinational Islamic empire. That scenario had never been popular with Turkish leaders because they viewed Arabs as subordinates and adversaries, not confederates. Still, Islamic unity in either a pan-Turanist or pan-Islamist scenario was appealing to the former CUP leadership. First of all, such ideas would be attractive to Muslims all over Europe and Asia, building a populist base. Second, Islamic or Turkic revolution threatened British and Russian interests, providing Enver and his cronies leverage when dealing with the major powers.

Talat and Enver disagreed in their opinion of these pan-Islamic and pan-Turkic alliances. Enver wanted the pan-Turkist movement to be coordinated from Moscow, where he had begun to set up a base of operations. Enver had ingratiated himself with the Soviet leadership, claiming that he could be the man to resolve the friction with their Muslim territories. He had even attended the Soviet-sponsored First Congress of Peoples of the East in Baku in September 1920, claiming to represent the Islamic nations of the Maghreb (Morocco, Algeria, Tunisia, and Libya). Enver's courting of the Soviets was in line with the Turkish nationalists who wanted to preserve good relations with this powerful neighbor. Kemal's forces fighting in Anatolia desperately needed the hard cash and weapons the Soviets were, for the time being, supplying.

Talat, by contrast, never trusted Lenin or Stalin as true allies. As Talat would explain in an interview only days before his death, "The Turk and the Bolshevik [have] nothing in common but a temporary alliance, a convenience from the point of view of Russia that answered a need from the point of view of Turkey."[14] Talat envisioned a completely different scenario. Unbeknownst to Enver, he was testing the waters for an alliance with the British, a relationship that Enver would never have agreed to.

Because Talat did not see an upside to a partnership with Moscow, he wanted any secret pan-Turkic organization to be based in Berlin. Once things settled down in the heartland of Turkey proper, Talat hoped to return home and join Mustapha Kemal, planning to share in the supervision of the reconstituted nation. As far as the exiled CUP leadership was concerned, the war with Great Britain and France was not over. There was much unfinished business, particularly in the form of any peace treaties. Talat, Enver, and their cohorts understood that they should bide their time until these treaties were settled in a way that was favorable to Turkey. After that, it would be safe to return to Turkey and continue business as usual.

But Talat and Enver had to wait for Mustapha Kemal to decide it was time to allow them reentry into the territories he controlled. (They could not return via Constantinople because they had been condemned to death in absentia and would be arrested by the British authorities there.) To Talat's consternation, Kemal was biding his time. He explained to his fellow Ittihadists that before the former CUP leaders could return, a beachhead for the new Republic of Turkey had to be firmly established. Grudgingly, Talat, Enver, and the others busied themselves beyond the borders, trying to build unity among the non-Ottoman Soviet Islamic/Turkic republics.

In other words, Talat, Enver, and the former CUP leadership

needed Mustapha Kemal, but with every passing month of conflict, Kemal needed them less. If he succeeded in chasing the Greeks, French, and British out of Asia Minor, he wouldn't need them at all. "The Young Turks, anxious for restoration of their power, were the rivals of Kemal, and he prudently kept them from gaining control of his movement."[15]

Around this time, the Nemesis agents in Berlin would meet regularly at the home of a diplomat named Libarit Nazarian, an old friend of the German humanitarian Johannes Lepsius. Nazarian was vice consul of the Republic of Armenia in Berlin. Without being privy to operational details, Nazarian and his secretary, Yervant Apelian, assisted Shahan Natali in pursuing the exiled Turkish leaders. Utilizing diplomatic prerogative, Nazarian was able to act as a conduit for communications from Geneva, Boston, and Yerevan. (The conspirators communicated chiefly through letters written in Armenian and utilizing code words, usually with reference to a metaphorical "wedding.") In addition, he could counsel the team with his own political insight. For example, Nazarian believed that Enver was intentionally spreading false rumors about his whereabouts in order to confuse those who were trying to find him. In Nazarian's opinion, it was pointless to wait for Enver in Berlin.

At the same time, Hrap (Hrach Papazian) was passing himself off as "Mehmed Ali," a rich expatriate Turk. The handsome young Armenian moved easily through Ottoman society in Berlin. Fluent in Turkish without a trace of an accent, he had attended law school in Turkey and had gone so far as to have himself circumcised so that he might pass as Muslim without suspicion. With his particular talents, Hrap easily picked up snippets of news from the Turkish students with whom he socialized.

Hrap reported to Shahan Natali that the Turkish underground had met with Egyptian sheik Abdul Aziz and a Druze emir, Shakib Arslan, as well as several Muslims from India. Arslan, who was an ardent pan-Islamist, wanted to bring the Turks and Arabs together in an alliance. An Arab contingent, headed by Amir Faisal (who also represented the Arabs at the Paris peace conference), had reached out to Talat with the hopes that a coalition of some sort could be formed. These were the actors the British were hoping to motivate against the Ottomans during the war. Thus the pan-Islamic circles with which T. E. Lawrence (Lawrence of Arabia) had been involved had a relationship with the exiled Ittihadists. Though the young Armenian fedayeen could not fully parse this information, it clearly indicated that the Ittihadists were regrouping, finding allies, and preparing for anything but concession to Allied desires.

Also, though the Nemesis operatives did not know it at the time, in a classic case of "the enemy of my enemy is my friend," the British viewed the Tashnag agents as allies. The British were keeping an eye on Talat (they knew just where he was but claimed otherwise) and were following the Armenians as best they could. Old hands at spycraft, the British had no compunctions about employing or abetting assassination if necessary. Not only Talat, but Enver, too, was in their sights.

The British were determined to counterbalance any moves that might threaten their hegemony in the east (Mesopotamia, Persia, and India). They were well aware of the pan-Islamists' intentions, and had even encouraged them when they were at war with the Ottoman Empire. But now they were alarmed by the continued attempts at alliance among Muslims in Egypt, the Levant, and India. T. E. Lawrence warned the Foreign Office "of the mischief which might follow a pact between Faisal and Ataturk or Russian penetration of the region [as] Faisal fruitlessly sought a common front with Turkish, Kurdish and Egyptian nationalists."[16] Secret British documents from the period report at length on these potential dangers and alliances and Britain's fears reminiscent of the "Great Game." The Armenians could not possibly have been aware of all the particulars of the deals being proposed by the Turks, Arabs, and Muslims amongst themselves. But what they did understand was that if Enver Pasha prevailed and received endorsement for an alliance with the Russians, Talat—if he was actually in Berlin—might depart the city altogether, and they would lose him.

Why had Talat settled in Berlin in the first place? The primary reason was probably the fortune in gold that the CUP had stashed outside the empire. Berlin provided easy access to these funds, which were located in Swiss and German banks. Moreover, Germany was the safest place for an exiled Ittihadist to reside. France was swarming with Armenians who would be happy to seek vengeance. Britain could never harbor a man it had repeatedly labeled a war criminal. Likewise, any of the Balkan regions would be very dangerous for a Muslim seeking safe harbor. The United States was out of the question. This left Germany, which was tolerant of its former ally's presence. German authorities also liked the fact that as long as Talat stayed in Berlin, they could keep an eye on him.

The British certainly knew that Talat was hiding out in Germany. Intelligence officer Sir Andrew Ryan had personally demanded that Germany return Talat and his associates to Turkey for trial. Ryan was "the last of the Dragomans" stationed in Constantinople before the war.[17] (A "dragoman" was an enhanced translator, stationed at each embassy, who would interpret what was being said in negotiations and act as a mediator as well, and thus held a position of power.) German officials answered Ryan with coy stubbornness, demanding to see papers showing that these persons had been found guilty. Only then would they cooperate, but even if they did decide to do so, they claimed to have no idea where these persons were. This attitude enraged the British, who had suffered huge losses at the hands of Ottoman armies at Gallipoli and in the Mesopotamian desert. Documents show clearly that, unable to extricate Talat from Germany, British spies kept tabs on him and knew exactly where he was living.[18]

While deep currents of international intrigue flowed around them, the Nemesis squad had lost the scent of their quarry. All leads had gone nowhere. In fact, rather than moving toward their goal, they were losing ground. Long hours of surveillance in Berlin's cold, damp weather were wearing Tehlirian down. And the fainting spells continued to plague him. Would he be able to rise to the occasion should Talat suddenly appear? He had no choice but to lie low and recuperate.

When Tehlirian finally got back on his feet, Apelian moved him out of the hotel to a room in his own apartment building on Augsburgstrasse in an effort to settle him closer to Azmi's tobacco shop, where most of the surveillance was going on. Despite the scarcity of apartments in Berlin, "the secretary of the Armenian legation, Yervant Apelian, arranged with the landlady of his flat, an elderly spinster, Elisabeth Stellbaum, to rent him a student room in the same building, 51 Augsburgstrasse, where there was another student, Levon Eftian."[19]

Over these months Tehlirian had met many Armenians, none of whom knew his real reason for being in Berlin. For them, he was nothing more than a melancholy fellow immigrant. Most of them felt sympathy for Soghomon because they knew he had seen the worst of it, and they made every effort to gather him into the fold of the growing Armenian German society. Tehlirian's first instinct was to keep his head down and avoid interaction. But with his move to the new apartment and his growing friendship with Eftian, socializing was unavoidable.

Levon Eftian, who had first met Soghomon in Paris, was unaware of his friend's true mission in Berlin, and so was particularly critical of Tehlirian's poor command of German. He was concerned that Tehlirian would never succeed at the university without mastering the language. Eftian's plan was for Tehlirian to work with his girlfriend, a lovely German fräulein named Lola Beilinson, who would dedicate herself to improving Soghomon's language skills. Despite Tehlirian's resistance, Eftian persuaded him to take weekly lessons, arguing that doing so would be "a favor" to Lola, since she so ardently wanted to help the sad-eyed foreigner.

Tehlirian cautiously widened his circle of young Armenian friends through the oblivious Eftian. As he met more and more young Armenians in Berlin, he was dismayed to find that most were not incapacitated with mourning. In his memoirs, he notes with amazement that these Armenians had, after only a short five years, begun to move on and live full and successful lives in Germany. To be sure, most of them had not been as engaged with the violence as Tehlirian had. Some had simply packed up and left Turkey as trouble loomed. Some were from Constantinople, where the deportations had not been so thorough. All were fluent in German. All had jobs. And like young people everywhere, they socialized as often as they could.

One such occasion was a birthday party for Eftian. Upon arriving, Tehlirian found himself wrapped in a bear hug by a former muleteer named Karekin. Karekin was from Mush, a town west of Van that had been particularly hard hit. Over a hundred thousand Armenians had died there when the Special Organization in concert with Kurdish Hamidiye emptied the town and the surrounding villages of Christians. Tens of thousands were deported, but just as many were killed on the spot. In 1915 Mush had been hell on earth.

In contrast to Tehlirian's persistent and indelible grief, Karekin seemed to revel in his status as a survivor. In Tehlirian's words, for Karekin, "the days of misfortune appeared as a desirable past."[20] The muleteer of the desert, having established himself as a manual laborer in Berlin, replaced mournfulness with a bittersweet nostalgia for the harsh life he had endured in Anatolia.

Happy to see a familiar face, Karekin peppered Tehlirian with questions about old friends and allies. Soon everyone at the party was trading stories about what had happened to their respective families. Karekin launched into a long story about how all three of his sisters had been kidnapped before reaching the Euphrates. He added that the smaller children had hidden in the fields with his mother, but the dry grass was set on fire. Snatched up by the gendarmes as they tried to run, the children were corralled into nearby stables, where they were forced to accept Islam or die.

Tehlirian begged Karekin to stop. Karekin's lined face broke into a wincing grin. "Why, did I strike a nerve?" Tehlirian replied that he himself was overflowing with stories and had no room in his heart for more. Levon Eftian, in an attempt to break the tension between the two men and redirect the conversation, cursed Talat's name. Others repeated the oath. But this was exactly the sort of ineffectual demonstration that Tehlirian hated: people histrionically ranting against the "bloody Turks" but doing nothing, taking no action. Bottling up emotions he could not express, Tehlirian felt a black mood building. "It was our own fault," he muttered. "We are the guilty ones and not Talat, for having trusted him after the Adana massacre."[21] He glowered at Karekin. The muleteer struck his table with his fist and shouted, "What is this person who calls himself Armenian, he is defending Talat!" and stormed out of the party.

The encounter left Tehlirian upset and at loose ends. Memories of his family, and of their anguish, flooded into him. A deep anxiety seized him. What if he slipped up while in the company of these silly people and inadvertently exposed the plot to hunt down Talat? But what choice did he have? He had to stay the course; he had to continue to interact with these impotent complainers, pretending to be one of them. He would try to avoid debating the pros and cons of the tragedy, but these conversations were inevitable. These happy Armenians were, in Tehlirian's view, consciously shirking their duty to the dead by living their lives as if nothing had happened. Something *had* happened. And someone must answer for it. Someday they would see what people with a conscience could do.

One afternoon Eftian and Apelian arrived at Tehlirian's room unannounced. "You are coming with us to take dancing lessons."[22] Tehlirian didn't understand. Learn to dance? He knew how to dance! Apelian slipped an arm around his waist and whirled Tehlirian around his room. "Like this! The way they dance here!"

Tehlirian, immersed in his sunless world where dancing was unthinkable, replied, "Are you crazy? Is this a time to dance?"

Apelian didn't hesitate. "Of course! Spring is here. It is the time for dance and love! And you will improve your German as well. You've been here for over a month and you can't speak two words!"

"I'm not a dancer," Tehlirian protested simply.

Levon chimed in, "You have no choice. We've already spent the money!"

At the dancehall, the robust and glowing young students were greeted by the dance instructor, Professor Friedrich. The Victrola was cranked, the turntable was set spinning, Herr Professor blew into a tiny whistle, and everyone launched into a whirling polka. Tehlirian was lost. He knew only one sort of dance, the traditional circle dance of Anatolian weddings and baptisms. The strange set of movements spinning all around him only thrust him deeper into his misery. He began to fantasize about the way they used to dance back in Erzincan, in the days when everyone was happy, when everyone... The scent of blood flooded his senses, his knees grew weak, and Tehlirian collapsed onto the dance floor.

The incident saved young Soghomon from dance instruction that day. It also served to remind him that the seizures were not abating. What if at the moment of truth he was not able to execute the order? What if all this effort was leading up to a colossal failure? The "sickness" was not as serious as it had been in Yerevan, but it was active nonetheless. The next day, when he attended his language lesson with Lola, he couldn't focus. His "Fräulein Lehrer" would testify six months later that he was "preoccupied."

In the first days of 1921, Tehlirian, despite his erratic health, resumed his surveillance. The work was both tedious and agonizing as the winter weather grew bitter. Eyes drooping with fatigue while standing at his post one day, Tehlirian realized he was watching the approach of two familiar-looking men. It was Drs. Shakir and Nazim, the notorious leaders of the Special Organization. They entered 47 Uhlandstrasse. Fifteen minutes later, Shakir exited the building and Tehlirian followed him, leaving a man behind to cover Nazim.

Fighting the Berlin cold, Tehlirian trailed Shakir block after block while the former head of the Special Organization maintained a feverish pace—"like fire," in Tehlirian's words. Exiting the neighborhood, they rounded the sprawling Tiergarten park, which covered the center of old Berlin. Hurrying along for over half an hour, Tehlirian wondered why Shakir had not taken a car. Did he suspect that he was being followed?

Shakir made his way from one end of the Tiergarten to the other, eventually arriving at the old British embassy on Wilhelmstrasse. The former SO leader entered the building. Lacking the credentials to follow him in, Tehlirian waited outside, stamping his feet, blowing on his frozen hands, his head aching from fatigue. Suddenly the doctor appeared between the columns of the front portico and raced down the steps. He immediately resumed his rapid pace. Tehlirian followed for a few steps then felt the peculiar sensations that always preceded a fainting spell. His slowed to a standstill, his eyesight dimmed. Shakir slipped into the crowd as Tehlirian collapsed onto the pavement. He awoke to find himself surrounded by curious onlookers peering down at him. Tehlirian rose weakly to his feet, only to find that his man was gone. But perhaps a new piece of the puzzle had been discovered. Why was Shakir visiting the British? Brushing himself off, Tehlirian pushed through the onlookers and staggered back to his room. The next day, Vaza took him to the doctor.[23]

By the end of January, Tehlirian was consumed with nerves and frustration. It was time to act! Why were they waiting? He was obviously running out of strength and out of time. If he could not discover Talat's whereabouts, then at least he could attack Shakir and Nazim, two mass murderers. Tehlirian lobbied his co-conspirators. "Let's just kill them. They are as bad as Talat." Shahan Natali refused to give the go-ahead. It had to be Talat, because killing Talat assured a highly publicized trial, and such a trial would reveal to the world what the Turks had done.

Around this time, Hrap heard rumors that a meeting of the former CUP leaders would soon be taking place in Rome. If the rumors were true, Talat would be forced to emerge from hiding and reveal himself when he boarded the train for Italy. The gathering of the Ittihad leadership-in-exile was confirmed in an article in an Italian Fascist newspaper. Shahan Natali prepared to go to

Rome but had trouble getting his paperwork together. He missed the train that would have gotten him to Italy in time to stake out the meeting. Boarding a train two days later, Natali found himself seated in a coach with Turks who had no notion that this man in Western dress could comprehend their every word. He understood that others would come to see these Turks off before the train left the station.

Natali's and Tehlirian's accounts of what happened in that train station do not jibe perfectly, but they do agree on the central point.[24] A man arrived at the train platform to see the others off (one of whom Natali would later identify as Bedri Bey, the notorious former police chief of Constantinople and cohort of the assassinated Megerdichian). This man, the "Man of the Station," as Natali labels him, was heavyset and carried a cane. But more important was this man's obvious superior status relative to the men surrounding him.

Tehlirian, who was at the station to see Natali off, observed the heavyset man carefully. Who was he? Could this be our man? Could this be Talat? But he was clean-shaven; he lacked Talat's signature thick black mustache. As the round-faced man approached several "students" on the sidewalk, the group sprang to life, arranging themselves like soldiers in an honor line. One kissed the large man's hand and said, "They are already inside, pasha." The heavyset man stepped up to the train and, with his cane, rapped on Bedri Bey's window in a farewell gesture. He then rejoined the others, and they all backed away as the train slowly chugged out of the station. The group moved toward the exit, allowing the man they called "pasha" to take the lead.

Hazor and Haigo appeared. "Is that him? Who is that?"

"They called him 'pasha' "

"Every dog of the days of the deportations is called 'pasha' now."

The Nemesis agents trailed the group and noticed that the entourage lagged a few steps behind two "leaders," the heavyset man with cane and "a dark-faced one." Tehlirian tried to make sense of what he was seeing. The one they called "pasha" was large and powerfully built. His thick trunk was right for Talat. But the face...Collecting his thoughts, Tehlirian let his fellow spies walk ahead. The route passed the Tiergarten, now a familiar neighborhood, one that the agents had traversed several times while following their targets. The three "students" accompanying their superiors bowed deeply, said their good-byes, and moved off.

The two men, "heavyset" and "dark face," were standing before a comfortable apartment building: number 4 Hardenbergstrasse. Hazor and Haigo sidled up alongside Tehlirian. "We've been here before. On this street!"[25]

"Yes." The young Armenians shrank back into the shadows of the leafy boulevard and watched the building for over an hour. Neither suspicious individual reappeared. Tehlirian was excited. He had not felt this way since the retreat from Erzinga.

Was the man living at 4 Hardenbergstrasse Talat Pasha? It must be! How could they determine the truth? As a foreign national, Talat would have had to register with the police, but any visit to the local precinct house to make inquiries would bring suspicion upon the Nemesis gang. Besides, how likely was it that Talat was living in Berlin under his real name? One of the men ran up to the door to take a peek at the brass plate affixed there. In Arabic script was written the name *Ali Salih Bey*.

The following day, Vaza rang the doorbell at number 4 Hardenbergstrasse and introduced himself as the representative of a Swiss insurance company looking for a room to rent. The bored landlady, welcoming the distraction, invited the young Armenian in. "How many rooms do you need?"

"Only one."

The landlady replied that the current tenant still had three months on his lease, then cheerfully explained that three people were living there: a merchant, his beautiful wife, and a third man. The merchant was a Turkish businessman by the name of Ali Salih Bey. She explained that "Salih" had not signed the rental contract himself. Rather, the arrangements had been taken care of by the secretary at the Turkish embassy. Vaza smiled. "He must be an important man."

"Oh yes. He is very well off. But perhaps you can come to an agreement with my tenant? He has a lot of room."

Vaza demurred. "That would be impossible. I cannot rent in the building in which a Muslim keeps his wife." Anxious to return to his cohorts, Vaza thanked the chatty landlady and departed.

When Vaza delivered the new information, it threw Tehlirian into a funk. This news was tantalizing but inconclusive. No businessman would have had a room rented for him by the consulate. If this was indeed Talat, it was vital that they act quickly, before he could escape. But then where could Talat escape to? Another city? If he had not joined the others in Rome, that must mean that his presence was needed here. His thoughts chased one another. Talat must be planning something. It was necessary that he be present here as a leader. His collaborators could not be brought from place to place...But could he not change his residence? He could, especially if he was suspicious. Did we make him suspicious?

In his memoirs Tehlirian clearly states that he was ready to kill the man living at 4 Hardenbergstrasse. He was possessed, plagued by morbid dreams in which he wandered landscapes littered with bodies or in which his mother appeared carrying her head in her hands. He fantasized enormous armies of skeletons being led by famous dead Armenian heroes like Murad of Sepasdia, the legendary Tashnag fighter who had also fought in the Caucasus and western Armenia with Tehlirian, and was killed in Baku in 1918.

Tehlirian would wake early every morning and stake out the house on Hardenbergstrasse. He would follow the heavyset man as he traveled from one residence to another, one appointment to another. It soon became clear to Tehlirian that "Salih" stuck to a consistent schedule, routinely leaving his house between ten and eleven in the morning every day. Tehlirian studied the photographs of Talat that Armen Garo had handed him in Boston. He would stare at the photos until his head ached.

In frustration, Tehlirian scratched off the prominent mustache in Talat's portrait. Lacking the mustache, the face was transformed into an entirely different visage. This was the man they had seen at the train station. This was the man Tehlirian had been following. *This was Talat Pasha.* Yet when he presented his evidence to his comrades, they remained unconvinced. This was not proof, and murdering an innocent man would be unconscionable. "We might lose him by delaying, but it would be worse if we are wrong."

Tehlirian and his band had no way of knowing that British intelligence knew exactly where Talat Pasha was living. Eighteen months earlier, in September 1919, Aubrey Herbert, a former diplomat (and as such connected to intelligence operations), had received a letter from Talat. Talat had known Herbert when he had been a member of the British delegation stationed in prewar Constantinople, and the two men had become friendly while attending the obligatory social functions. After the war, when Talat wanted to send a message to British policy makers, he thought of Herbert as someone he could trust. In a September 1919 letter (written in French), Talat requested an opportunity to meet with Herbert so that he could explain Turkey's position vis-à-vis Britain, adding that he also wanted to explain any supposed wrongdoing against the Armenians.

Aubrey Nigel Henry Molyneux Herbert (1880–1923), second son of Henry Herbert, fourth Earl of Carnarvon (the "second sons" of the British aristocracy had traditionally been the great reservoir of manpower for overseas service), was born with a silver spoon in his mouth. Herbert's family estate was the impressive Highclere Castle (now famous as the setting for the popular television show *Downton Abbey*). He was educated at Eton. His half brother George Herbert was one of the discoverers of the tomb of Tutankhamen. Aubrey Herbert was father-in-law to novelist Evelyn Waugh. Herbert possessed all the essential features of a man who came from the British ruling class.

In addition, Herbert was a part of that small subset who thought of themselves as "Orientalists," men fluent in Turkish and with a great fondness for, and curiosity about, things Middle Eastern. As

Britain became more and more involved in Middle Eastern affairs, first in Egypt, then Persia, and then Mesopotamia and Palestine, these specialists (T. E. Lawrence being the most famous of the bunch), with their wide-ranging if disorganized knowledge of all things Arabic and "Oriental," became integral to British foreign policy. These men and women loved the exoticism and visceral excitement of exploring Muslim lands and society.[26]

After the war, with the rise of fascism in Italy and Germany and the success of the Bolsheviks in Russia, the political scene in Europe became highly dynamic. Scotland Yard had its hands full tracking and reporting on the multitude of political factions vying for power in Europe, the Middle East, and India. Perhaps Aubrey Herbert was not a spy per se, but he was often where the action was, and he was trusted by those in the highest positions. Herbert had proven himself in World War I by negotiating an armistice in Gallipoli and attempting to secure the release of British prisoners in Kut (Mesopotamia). He had strong bonds with a number of significant players in the Middle East of the early twentieth century, specifically Gertrude Bell (who had a hand in the creation of Iraq in 1921), Mark Sykes (who negotiated the Sykes-Picot agreement), and T. E. Lawrence. Although historians have barely focused on Herbert, he was a key actor behind the scenes in the acquisition of oil territories.

In 1919, when Herbert received the letter from Talat, the war had been over for barely one year. Tensions between Great Britain and Turkey were still running high. Not only was the former minister of the interior a onetime enemy leader; he was also a fugitive from justice. In his letter, Talat proposed that he and Herbert meet in any "neutral country of his choosing." Talat wanted an opportunity to convince Herbert that "good relations between Britain and Turkey were essential to the welfare of both peoples" and that "he was not responsible for the Armenian massacres. That he could prove it and was anxious to do so."[27]

Unsure of how he should reply, Herbert contacted a good friend described in his memoirs as "a distinguished man who is

famous for his spotless integrity." This man was Viscount Cecil of
Chelwood (Lord Edgar Algernon Robert Gascoyne Cecil), who
would be awarded the Nobel Peace Prize in 1937 for his role as a
founder and supporter of the League of Nations. (Cecil was also a
patron of the Bryce report on the Armenian Genocide.) According
to Herbert, upon reading the letter, the viscount leaped to his feet
"as if he'd been stung."

"What did you want to bring me into this for? Couldn't you
have left me out? It's illegal to correspond with the enemy!" Cha-
grined, Herbert wrote back to Talat to say, "I was very glad to hear
that it was not he who was responsible for the Armenian massacres,
but...I did not think any useful purpose could be served by our
meeting at that time." But the matter did not end there. Word of
Talat's letter found its way to Sir Basil Thomson, at Scotland Yard
(and the Directorate),[28] the man who had been coordinating all
wartime intelligence. Thomson decided there would be much to
gain by a meeting between Aubrey Herbert and Talat. Scotland
Yard and the Directorate had been keeping tabs on the former
Grand Vizier. Secret memos from October 1920 confirm that British intelligence knew where Talat was living, even if the Armenians didn't. They also knew that Talat had been very active,
meeting with his former government in Berlin and in Rome.

On February 18, 1921, Basil Thomson suggested that Herbert
meet with Talat in Germany. Though Soghomon Tehlirian could
not have known it on that freezing day when he doggedly chased
Dr. Shakir halfway across Berlin, Shakir's visit to the British
embassy marked the moment when communications between
Talat and the British resumed. This is why Talat had not lingered
in Rome. He was needed in Germany for the meeting with Herbert. It is also why he disappeared from sight a few days later.

Aubrey Herbert left Victoria Station in London on the afternoon of Friday, the twenty-fifth of February, 1921, took the ferry
from Dover to Calais, then boarded a train, arriving in Cologne
early the next morning. On the evening of the twenty-sixth, Herbert arrived in Hamm, a small town about four hours from Berlin,

which he describes as "a miserable industrial village, that seemed to be inhabited by potential suicides."[29] Herbert checked in at the hotel, and Talat joined him around nine p.m. They ordered dinner sent up to Talat's room in order to maintain secrecy. According to Herbert, Talat had grown thinner, his black hair streaked with gray. "His eyes were very bright, glittering while he talked like the eyes of a wild animal in the dusk." Herbert, evaluating Talat's overall dress, could see that he was "obviously poor." Finding Hamm shabby and lacking the proper facilities, Herbert suggested that the two men take a short train ride to Dusseldorf, where they could converse in more civilized surroundings. Over the two days they spent together, Talat explained his position as Herbert patiently listened.

Talat Pasha, perhaps believing that the British would welcome any scheme that caused distress for the Soviet Union, informed Herbert that he and Enver were planning to stir up Islamic revolution against the Russians in the Muslim Soviet republics. In describing the "six Red republics" (the Muslim states of the Communist Russian Federation), Talat observed, "They are red, but not deep red"—in other words, these former khanates were ready to break away from their Soviet masters if given the opportunity. Talat made threats (as quoted by Herbert): "Turkey is at war with England, and we are engaged in propaganda throughout the East, and inciting India, though not very effectually. Turkey is, in fact, pursuing a policy of enlisting as many people as she can against Great Britain and undertaking all possible reprisals open to her."

Talat made this menacing point only moments after claiming great affection for Britain, stating, "Before the war, I was anxious that England should be her [Turkey's] teacher."[30] In his next breath Talat explained how Turkey would fight Britain to the last man: "Our geography is a fortress to us, a very strong fortress. Our mountains are the strongest of our forces. You cannot pursue us into the mountains of Asia; and stretching back into Central Asia are six republics, composed of men of our blood, cousins, if not brothers, and united now by the bond of misfortune."

After hearing him out, Herbert assured Talat that he would

deliver the message to his superiors in England. Herbert also asked Talat a strangely prophetic question: "Aren't you afraid of assassination?" Talat answered that "he never thought of it. Why should anyone dislike him?" Herbert continues: "I said that Armenians might very well desire vengeance....He brushed this aside." This was not the first time Herbert had asked Talat about assassination. Years before, in Constantinople, he had queried him along the same lines. According to Herbert, Talat had then replied, "Life was so hard that, if one had to fear death also, the burden would be too heavy to bear."

Herbert returned to Scotland Yard, wrote out his report, and then met with Basil Thomson the next day. What happened next is unclear. Mim Kemal Oke (a prominent Turkish "denialist") claims:

> Talat Pasha also dared to make the threat that he was going to incite the Pan-Turanist and Pan-Islamist movements against England, unless she signed a peace treaty favorable for Turkey. This courageous action of Talat Pasha made the British very anxious. Their intelligence service established contact with its counterpart in the Soviet Union to evaluate the situation. Talat Pasha's plans made the Russian officials as anxious as the British. The two intelligence services collaborated and signed among them the death warrant of Talat Pasha. Information concerning his physical description and his whereabouts was forwarded to their men in Germany. However it was decided that Armenian revolutionaries carry out the verdict.

In other words, Oke claims that British intelligence was asking itself, "Why go through the trouble of killing Talat when the Armenians are ready to do the job?"[31]

An entry in Aubrey Herbert's journal is interesting:

> Friday March 4th, 1921. Reached London on Tuesday, wrote my report that night and Wednesday morning, sent it in yesterday. To-day, I went to see Sir Basil Thomson, to

tell him that I thought that he much better send it to Lord Curzon. It seemed to me much better to meet trouble half-way. Alan [sic] Leeper dined last night. I saw he knew something. He is a curious fellow, all light and no heat, all brain and no soul, and an Australian accent in his heart. Basil Thomson quite agreed with me. He also seemed to have given it away, pretty freely, on his own, but said that he had been going to write and ask me if he could not do what I suggested.[32]

There is definitive proof that assassination of Turkish leaders had been put on the table by the Brits as early as 1919. A cable dated August 12 of that year from the American ambassador to Great Britain, John W. Davis, to Secretary of State Robert Lansing reads in part: "I also met General Bridges who has just returned from scene of operations.... He also says that by his advice, British government has offered or will offer price of 35,000 sterling on the head of Enver Pasha who is now in Asia Minor leader of the Young Turks and growing pan Islamic movement. He, as well as Curzon, anticipates disorder following withdrawal of British troops. He remarked casually that 'The thing to do is for us to do the job and you to pay for it.' "[33]

Given Britain's obsessive anxiety about revolution among Muslims living in Arab territories as well as in Persia and India, Talat's threats, as reported by Herbert, were taken very seriously by Scotland Yard. What Talat didn't seem to understand was that although the British may have welcomed any plots against the Russians, Islamic revolution was their greatest fear. Britain had three prize possessions in that part of the world: the Arab mandates, with their rich oil reserves; the Suez Canal, the vital artery to India; and India itself. As each of these was either populated by millions of Muslims or surrounded by Muslim territories, they were especially vulnerable to Islamic revolt. In fact, with India, Egypt, and Mesopotamia under his command, King George V ruled over more Muslim subjects than any other monarch in the world. Should an Islamic revolution be sparked within the USSR, there was a great danger that such a movement could ignite rebellion in the British possessions as well. Pan-Turanism was an exciting idea for Turkish nationalists. It was a potential nightmare for the British.

What is known is that Herbert was debriefed by Basil Thomson upon his return to England (probably on the Monday, the twenty-eighth of February). Furthermore, British intelligence had pinpointed Talat's exact location two full months before Tehlirian arrived in Berlin. The address "4 Hardenbergstrasse" is mentioned explicitly in the briefs. Though there is little doubt that Tehlirian and his crew did track down Talat in Berlin, they could not absolutely confirm that "Ali Salih Bey" was in fact Talat Pasha. Caught up in Hamlet-like indecision, the conspirators sought some kind of concrete evidence that the man who lived at 4 Hardenbergstrasse was indeed the former leader of Turkey. Apparently they got the proof they needed.

A few days before the assassination, Tehlirian and his friends received a ciphered telegram from Geneva confirming that the man living at that address was their man. Was it possible that British intelligence tipped off the Tashnags? It would have been very easy for Scotland Yard to let the ARF leadership in Geneva know where Talat was living. Geneva could then contact Natali, and no connection could be traced back to the British.

Is it just a coincidence that Tehlirian moved to Hardenbergstrasse only a few days after Herbert met with Talat? What is also interesting is what Herbert does not say. Herbert obsessively kept a daily journal, but he writes nothing on the day Talat is killed. He claimed that he had food poisoning and could not write. The day after the assassination he states in an offhand manner, "This morning the papers told me of the murder of Talaat." This is an intriguing entry, given that Herbert had just spent two full days with the man only three weeks before his death. He had written a report on that meeting. He had discussed Talat with his superiors. But when Talat is murdered, he only learns about it in the *newspapers?* No one phoned him or sent a memo? He continues: "I am very sorry. I think that he was a great influence for peace." There is a strikeout and then: "He may or may not have been a criminal. I cannot tell, but he was a very unusual man, and had remarkable attraction."[34]

Until his death in 1923, Aubrey Herbert continued to receive very sensitive assignments. In 1922, weeks after the Smyrna debacle, he was asked to serve as liaison between Churchill and Mustapha Kemal. A. J. Sylvester, private secretary to the prime minister, advised Lloyd George in a memo on September 26, 1922: "Mr. Churchill thinks that the suggestion that Aubrey Herbert should go and see Kemal is very important. The difficulty in this respect is that Aubrey Herbert is almost blind, and from what I hear is practically out of the picture for this work."[35]

In Constantinople, the British ambassador begged Herbert to stay away from Kemal.[36] The British had promised the French that they would not deal with Kemal behind their back. In fact, the French were already secretly working with Kemal. Herbert never made it to Ankara and died a year later, eighteen months after the assassination of Talat. Perhaps he was not an out-and-out spy. But Herbert did serve as a model for the fictional character Sandy Arbuthnot in John Buchan's best-selling spy thriller *Greenmantle,* published in 1916. One character says of Arbuthnot: "I know the fellow—Harry used to bring him down to fish—tallish with a lean, high-boned face and a pair of brown eyes like a pretty girl's. I know his record too.... He rode through Yemen, which no white man ever did before. The Arabs let him pass, for they thought him stark mad and argued that the hand of Allah was heavy enough on him without their efforts. He's blood brother to every kind of Albanian bandit. Also he used to take a hand in Turkish politics, and got a huge reputation."[37]

It is not hard to see why British leaders would embrace the idea of working solely with Kemal. If Talat and Enver could be taken out of the picture (as they were), General Kemal would be the only man with whom Britain would have to negotiate. Though Talat was no longer in charge in Turkey, he had every intention of returning to power once the fighting had ceased in "the home-land." Talat believed that he was first in line to lead postwar Tur-key. From his vantage point, the energetic Mustapha Kemal was a general and no more than that. Talat could handle Enver Pasha, and he could handle Kemal. This put the two leaders on an inevi-table collision course—one that was obvious to any serious observer of postwar Turkey.

In early March 1921, Kemal had big plans for the future Turkish republic. The last thing he needed was for Talat to arrive on his door-step to claim leadership. (Decades after Talat's death, either Kemal or those interested in perpetuating the mythologies surrounding the Young Turk charter membership would maintain that there was a great friendship and respect between Talat and Kemal. There is no evidence of such a relationship.) To complicate matters, during exactly this same period, the British were securing their hold on Mesopotamia (Iraq), a vast region acquired during the war along with other Arab territories. Though British leaders, particu-larly Lord Curzon, would deny it at the time, it was well under-stood that valuable oil reserves lay under the Middle Eastern sands. Only one man had the armies and the strategic know-how to stand in the way of the British grand design for the Middle East. That man was General Mustapha Kemal.

Kemal had proven himself a resilient and able foe. It makes sense that the British would have wanted either to remove or to mollify this brilliant but problematic young general. Assisting the new Turkish leader with his domestic problems could smooth out any issues the British might have at the Arab-Turkish border (roughly where Mosul lies). Removing or undermining Talat and Enver would make Kemal happy. And the British wanted oil con-cessions. *Ergo, quid pro quo.*

Kemal was also extremely cautious. The Great Powers had become very sophisticated about stirring up trouble and deposing leaders who did not suit their needs. Kemal was well aware of the power wielded by the United States as it interfered in the Philip-pines and in Mexico, not to mention Britain's machinations in

Egypt, the Hijaz, and Mesopotamia. Once he had secured the borders of his state, the new leader of Turkey avoided confrontation with the West. Combining boldness with caution would be a trademark of Mustapha Kemal for his entire career. (Ataturk was so afraid of assassination that he stayed away from Constantinople/Istanbul for decades after his ascension to power in Turkey. His only real return to the imperial city came at the end of his life, when he was dying.)

The British understood Kemal. Kemal understood the British. Although there was probably never a direct line of communication between the two, it's interesting that Kemal did not launch guerrilla warfare against the British occupation of the Arab lands. Despite the deep antipathy the Arabs felt for the Turks, it remained an option. He carefully chose his battles, using the Chanak crisis as leverage at the bargaining table, while understanding that fighting for Mosul would put too much at risk. A brilliant pragmatist, Kemal Ataturk knew how far to push the British and when to give in.[38] A final tantalizing piece in this jigsaw puzzle is that the nation of Iraq was established by the British on March 16, 1921 — one day after Talat's assassination. And as we've seen, among Aubrey Herbert's best friends were Gertrude Bell, Mark Sykes, and T. E. Lawrence — all people who were deeply involved in British intervention in the Middle East.

The Armenian side of the assassination plot was complex as well. The ARF was an embattled nationalist organization, and though revenge was high on their priority list, survival of the nation was the primary concern of the Tashnag leadership in 1920–21. For this reason, cooler heads than Garo, Natali, and Tehlirian were firm with regard to establishing the target's identity while preserving absolute secrecy. It would be seen as a colossal blunder if the avenging assassins managed somehow to upset negotiations in Paris or in any way alienated the Allies and discouraged their assistance. For all these reasons, it is interesting that it was around this time that

Herbert met with Talat in Germany. Within days after that meeting, someone confirmed Talat's whereabouts to the Nemesis crew, sealing his fate. A few days later, Talat was dead.

According to the Tashnag narrative, in early March a coded letter arrived from Geneva reporting that "Talat had been seen in Geneva at the beginning of the month, in front of the British consulate."[39] The letter was postmarked ten days earlier. The timeline was shaky, but the Nemesis team decided it was still possible that Talat was the man living in Hardenbergstrasse and decided to move Tehlirian as close to his quarry as possible. This would facilitate surveillance with the least danger of discovery.

Within two hours of receiving the communiqué, Hazor had located a room across the street from 4 Hardenbergstrasse at number 37. (The numerical layout on older Berlin streets often runs in sequence up one side of the street and then down the other side.) The second-story window overlooked the street and had a clear view of the façade of number 4. The room would be vacated in three days. Tehlirian could move in on March 5.

The next day, Apelian, unaware of the imminent assassination, arrived from the consulate and delivered the bad news arriving from the Armenian-Turkish front: the tiny republic was about to be overrun. Despite Soviet occupation, the situation in the Caucasus was highly unstable. Tehlirian, too preoccupied with Talat to be upset by this news, informed Apelian that he would be moving soon. He asked his friend to explain to the landlady that his doctor insisted he find an apartment with electric lighting. The dim gaslight was affecting his nervous condition. Tehlirian begged Apelian to do his talking for him because his German was still so faulty. The following evening, while Apelian was out, Hazor came by and assisted Tehlirian in his move.

The landlady of the new apartment at 37 Hardenbergstrasse, Frau Dittman, was a young widow. Maintaining an immaculate and orderly household, she employed a female servant, and her residence was quiet and peaceful. Like most rented rooms of the period, Tehlirian's room was furnished with a dresser, a small desk and chair, an armchair, and a bed. The entrance from the street was through a gate, then through a courtyard to a door that led to a flight of stairs. The room itself was wide and airy, featuring a large window hung with drapes.

Alone in his room, Tehlirian was drawn to a gap in the curtains. He peered through. Below him lay the small avenue, bisected by a flower-embroidered median strip. The thoroughfare was dense with traffic that flowed between the important government buildings and institutions only a few blocks away. Students, office workers, and tradespeople formed a constant stream of humanity beneath the window. Many smoked or ate while walking. Across the way stood the residence of "Ali Salih Bey." Tehlirian's pulse quickened. A mere twenty-five meters separated him from the monster.

Tehlirian could not resist maintaining a constant vigil. The windows on the second floor remained lit for hours, but he could detect no movement within. In the middle of the night he woke up to find himself still seated at his post. The apartment across the way was now shrouded in darkness. Wearily, Tehlirian rose and finally made his way to bed. When daylight broke, he jumped out of bed and stationed himself again at the window. In case Frau Dittman should happen by, he opened a German lesson book on the desk before him.

The team was ready to act. Natali and Tehlirian took a long stroll together to review exactly how the killing was going to go down. Natali reiterated that after the assassination, Tehlirian must wait by the body and allow himself to be arrested. As they stood before Frau Dittman's house, the windows of 4 Hardenbergstrasse glowed with light. Hidden in shadow, Natali handed Tehlirian the Luger pistol, telling him, "It has been tried and is ready for the command of your index finger."[40]

The next morning, Frau Dittman's servant delivered tea, bread, and cheese. Tehlirian ignored the food as he focused on the building across the way with binoculars Natali had provided him. Like an eagle on a high perch, Tehlirian searched for any sign of his prey.

The clock had not struck nine when the front door of 4 Hardenberg-strasse opened and "Ali Salih Bey" jogged down the front steps, clutching a sheaf of papers. The heavyset man paused when he hit the sidewalk, glanced up and down the street, then turned left.

From his earlier reconnaissance, Tehlirian knew that this was not the usual pattern. Downing a glass of cognac, he grabbed his pistol and raced downstairs. As he took hold of the latch on the gate that led to the street, he found it was frozen. Tehlirian could not escape the courtyard. Running back into the house, he found the servant and dragged her into the courtyard, but as the minutes ticked by, the gate would not budge. By the time the latch was dismantled and Tehlirian lurched toward the Tiergarten, Talat was nowhere to be seen.

Tehlirian states in his memoirs, "Having lost my mind, I pulled at the door almost to the extent of destroying it—in vain."[41] He feared the worst—that Talat had been alerted to the plot and slipped through their fingers. In a funk, he headed for the stakeout outside Djemal Azmi's tobacco store. As he made his way there, he sensed a greater police presence on the street. Or was his mind playing tricks on him? Why had Talat broken with his usual schedule and left so early that morning? Had he been tipped off that he was being watched? The men outside the tobacco store reported no activity. Tehlirian returned home to find a locksmith repairing the street gate.

The following morning Tehlirian phoned Natali and in a shaky voice insisted on meeting with him. Natali rushed to Tehlirian's room, where the nervous young man described how the broken lock had prevented him from pursuing Talat and that he suspected Talat had left the city altogether. Natali assured his protégé that there was no reason to believe Talat was suspicious and that in fact it was better that things had gone as they did. Natali pointed out that Tehlirian had left piles of evidence around his room, evidence that would suggest the larger conspiracy. Better to clean things up, because once the deed was done, there would be no time to cover their tracks. Natali poured out a glass of cognac for Tehlirian and made a toast to "our sacred mission." When he left, he took with him the binoculars as well as a pile of letters and notebooks.

The following morning a bleary-eyed Tehlirian once again stationed himself at his desk, scrutinizing Talat's building through the narrow slit in the curtains. In the street beneath his window, all was normal as people dashed to their early-morning jobs. The servant arrived with Frau Dittman in tow. The landlady was freshly made up and spoke in a rapid chatter. Tehlirian felt panic. Had he been caught spying? He concentrated on her words. What was she saying? Something about the gate, the latch. Ah, she was apologizing for the broken latch! Frau Dittman pressed a new key into Tehlirian's hand. Relieved, he thanked her profusely. There was an uncomfortable silence and the young widow left, flustered. Tehlirian glanced around the room. It was bare; no evidence of his real occupation remained.

By noon, Talat had not yet reappeared. Number 4 Hardenbergstrasse seemed vacant. Had Talat ever returned at all? Another knock at the door. A messenger was delivering a note from his compatriots. A coded cipher received from Paris once again had confirmed that Talat was living at 4 Hardenbergstrasse under the name Ali Salih Bey. Tehlirian was feeling ill. All appearances indicated that the building across the street had been vacated. He had made a deal with Natali to call him every day. This would be the way he signaled his superior. On the day that he received no call, Natali would know that Tehlirian had gone into action, would know that it was time to abandon Berlin.

Another endless night followed the fruitless day. Across the way, behind the curtains, a lamp was switched on. Then off. Nothing more. The next day Tehlirian kept his vigil until eleven p.m. but saw no one. Now he was certain that Talat had escaped. Another night passed. Tehlirian became feverish. He was wracked with nightmares. He obsessed about the lock on the gate. Why had that happened? Was it fate? What did he think he was doing? Talat was gone, he had failed. Without Talat to focus on, the walls of his room closed in on him.

Thoughts of his mother haunted Tehlirian continuously. In his dreams they walked to church together, shared bread and honey. Tehlirian wrote, "She was like a blind woman, feeling my face, my body." In his dreams, the sun broke through the clouds and Tehlirian's mother ran from him. He would wake up in the morning to find his pillow wet with tears. "My nerves were wrecked." The constant vigilance and tension were taking their toll on a man who was not well to begin with. With each dawning day, he splashed cold water onto his face from the dresser washbasin, pulled on his clothes, and resumed his vigil at the window.

At one point during the days prior to the assassination, an automobile rolled up before 4 Hardenbergstrasse and the man the conspirators had named "dark face" emerged, accompanied by a beautiful woman. The two entered the building. There was no doubt in Tehlirian's mind that this woman was Talat's wife, Hayriye Talat Bafrali. This was evidence that Talat was still here. Two hours later, his body stooped with fatigue, Tehlirian allowed himself a phone call to the Tiergarten Hotel, where the others were staying. He was told that a ciphered letter had arrived by air mail from America. "The comrades confirmed that Talat lives in Berlin at Hardenberg 4 under the pseudonym Ali Salih Bey and asked that the Talat affair be ended through all possible measures. This telegram was the answer to our question sent in early February."[42] They understood this to mean that they were to bring the operation to a conclusion: kill Talat.

On the morning of March 14, the woman Tehlirian identified as Talat's wife emerged from the house and made her way up the street. He wrote in his autobiography thirty years later: "I knew from Istanbul that she had abilities and was involved in her husband's affairs.... It was said that she had a great influence on her husband." So he decided to abandon his observation post and follow her as she headed for the Tiergarten, where she made her way to a fountain. Tehlirian observed her from a distance. It was a surreal moment. Struck by her beauty, Tehlirian had to reconcile this with the fact that "with her knowledge and on the command of her husband, tens of thousands

Soghomon Tehlirian assassinated Talat Pasha in Berlin in March 1921 and was subsequently freed by the German court. *(Project SAVE Armenian Photograph Archives, Watertown, MA, archives@projectsave.org. Photograph by Arlington Studios. Courtesy of Helen Paragamian)*

Sultan Abdul Hamid II was the last sultan with any real power. He ruled for over thirty years, ever wary of assassination. He created the Hamidiye militias in the east and fostered a "culture of massacre" in the Armenian territories, leading to tens of thousands of deaths. Abdul Hamid was deposed by the Young Turks in 1909. *(Universal Images Group / SuperStock)*

William Gladstone served as British prime minister during the late nineteenth century. His views reflected the most virulent anti-Turkish sentiments. *(© Bettmann/Corbis)*

The fedayeen were paramilitary Armenian fighters who made it their "holy mission" to attack Turkish troops and Kurdish militias. General Adranik is seated in the center. *(CPA Media / Pictures From History)*

Kurdish Hamidiye were militias organized in the name of Sultan Abdul Hamid that were encouraged to commit massacres against the Armenian population in Eastern Asia Minor. *(CPA Media / Pictures From History)*

Armenian deportations southward to the Syrian desert were designed to be unsurvivable. Deportees were driven through harsh terrain while being systematically starved. Those who lagged behind were often killed on the spot. Armenians who endured to the end of the line found themselves condemned to a slow death by starvation or disease in concentration camps surrounded by desert. *(The Art Archive at Art Resource, NY)*

A gathering of the Committee of Union and Progress sometime in 1909. The three men seated in the center (Talat Pasha, Said Halim Pasha, and Djemal Pasha) were assassinated by Operation Nemesis agents. Behind them, center, is Enver Pasha, assassinated by Soviet troops. Also in attendance were former minister of finance Djavid Bey; Alusa Mussa Kiazim, former Sheik ul-Islam; Rifaat Bey, president of the Senate; and Halil Bey, foreign minister. The man standing on Enver's left has been identified as Mustapha Kemal. *(CPA Media / Pictures From History)*

Enver Pasha was an admirer of Prussian military culture. At the end of the war he escaped his conviction for war crimes by moving to Moscow. After attempting to foster Islamic revolution in Central Asia, he was hunted down and killed by Soviet troops. *(akg-images / Interfoto)*

General Otto Liman von Sanders was Germany's man in Turkey during World War I. He had little regard for the Ottoman military leadership and disagreed openly with Enver Pasha's tactics. Liman von Sanders would testify at Tehlirian's trial, denying German involvement in the destruction of the Armenians. *(© Hulton-Deutsch Collection / Corbis)*

Talat Pasha was interior minister of the Ottoman Empire during World War I. He was in effect the leader of the CUP and directly responsible for the Armenian Genocide. Talat was assassinated by Soghomon Tehlirian in Berlin in the spring of 1921. *(akg-images)*

Djemal Pasha was a key leader in the CUP government of World War I Ottoman Turkey. He commanded the military in Arab regions and governed the populations there. After the war he objected to his conviction by the war crimes tribunal held in Constantinople, claiming that he was a friend of the Armenians. He was assassinated outside secret Cheka headquarters in Tiflis, Georgia, by three Nemesis operatives on July 21, 1922. *(© Robert Hunt Library / Mary Evans)*

Along with Dr. Nazim, Dr. Behaeddin Shakir ran the "Special Organization" (Teshkilati Mahsusa), a secret paramilitary outfit that organized the lethal deportations. With the approval of Talat Pasha, Shakir's priority was a full eradication of the indigenous Armenians as part of a program of "Turkification." He was assassinated by Aram Yerganian on April 17, 1922. *(CPA Media / Pictures From History)*

Misak Torlakian was the Nemesis fedayee who assassinated Azerbaijani leader Khan Javanshir in Constantinople during the postwar occupation. Though he stood trial and was convicted, Torlakian was released because the court was convinced that he was mentally incapacitated at the time of the murder. Like Tehlirian and Shiragian, Torlakian would quietly spend his last years in the United States a free man. *(CPA Media / Pictures From History)*

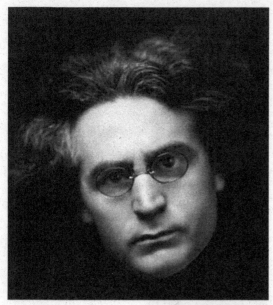

Shahan Natali (Hagop Der Hagopian) was a prolific author of short stories, plays, and poetry who ran the Operation Nemesis actions in Europe. Placing a pistol in Tehlirian's hand, Natali claimed to have said, "It has been tried and is ready for the command of your index finger." *(CPA Media / Pictures From History)*

Revolutionary Armen Garo (Karekin Pastermadjian) was the executive in charge of Operation Nemesis. Garo was a seasoned operative and statesman who participated in the Bank Ottoman attack, the Ottoman Parliament, and the first Armenian Republic. *(CPA Media / Pictures From History)*

While residing in the United States, Aaron Sachaklian oversaw strategy and kept the Nemesis books, managing cash flow for the organization. When the operation was disbanded, he hid letters and accounting and maintained silence on Operation Nemesis for the rest of his life. *(Marian Mesrobian MacCurdy / Transaction Publishers)*

Arshavir Shiragian was the most flamboyant of the Nemesis assassins, describing his exploits in his memoir, *The Legacy*. Shiragian gunned down Vahe Ihsan in Constantinople, Said Halim Pasha in Rome, and Djemal Azmi in Berlin. Though Shiragian wounded Dr. Behaeddin Shakir, Aram Yerganian is credited with that assassination. *(Sonia Shiragian / Hairenik Association)*

Johannes Lepsius was a German humanitarian who attempted to publicize atrocities committed against the Armenians in the Ottoman Empire. Testifying at Tehlirian's Berlin trial, Lepsius laid the blame for the Armenian deportations squarely on Talat's shoulders. *(CPA Media / Pictures From History)*

Krikoris Balakian was an Armenian archbishop arrested and deported in the roundup of key Armenians in late April 1915. Balakian managed to escape his caravan and Turkey. He was a star witness at Tehlirian's trial. *(CPA Media / Pictures From History)*

Calouste Gulbenkian was known as "Mr. Five Percent" because this was the commission he demanded for negotiating key oil concessions in the Middle East. Though Britain and other clients fought him in court, Gulbenkian eventually won his case, becoming one of the world's richest men. *(Photo 12 / Polaris)*

General Mustapha Kemal made his reputation as a bold commander in Gallipoli. At the end of World War I, as Young Turk leaders fled Turkey, Kemal successfully led what remained of the Ottoman army against Greek and Armenian forces, compelling Britain to sharply modify its postwar plans for the Ottoman Empire. Kemal would adopt the name Ataturk as founder of modern Turkey. *(The Art Archive at Art Resource, NY)*

Aubrey Herbert was a trusted British diplomat tasked with the most challenging assignments. Two weeks before Talat Pasha was assassinated, Scotland Yard
requested that Herbert interview the former Ottoman leader in Germany. Herbert was a close acquaintance of some of the most significant "Orientalists"
of the period, including T. E. Lawrence and Gertrude Bell. Though barely
mentioned in history books, Herbert was a key operator in Near East affairs.
(CPA Media / Pictures From History)

Hailed as a hero of the Armenian people, twenty-eight-year-old Soghomon Tehlirian, seen here with his young bride, Anahid, visited Paris in 1924, three years after he assassinated Talat Pasha. *(CPA Media / Pictures From History)*

In 1973, Gourgen Yanikian lured two Turkish diplomats to a hotel room in Santa Barbara, California, under the pretense of making a gift to the Republic of Turkey. Yanikian then murdered both men in a self-proclaimed act of revenge in the name of the Armenian Genocide. In a letter to the *Los Angeles Times* he urged Armenians to wage terror attacks against Turkey. *(Associated Press)*

The author's grandparents Megerdich and Lucy Jamgochian *(Eric Bogosian)*

Talat Pasha's dress shirt is on display at the Istanbul Military Museum (Askeri Muze) in the "Hall of Armenian Issue with Documents." A brass plaque explains: "Blood-stained shirt worn by Grand Vizier Talat Pasha when he was assassinated by an Armenian called Sogomon Tehlerian [*sic*] in Berlin on May [*sic*] 15th 1921." The display case is surrounded by photographic documentation of Armenian atrocities against Muslims. *(Eric Bogosian)*

Hrant Dink was an Armenian Turkish editor of the journal *Agos,* in which he argued for memorializing the Armenians who died during World War I. He was gunned down outside his Istanbul offices by a young man affiliated with Turkish extremists incensed by Dink's humanitarian views. At his funeral, thousands of people took to the streets of Istanbul with placards that said "We Are All Armenians" or "We Are All Hrant Dink." *(Associated Press)*

like her were condemned to die from starvation in the deserts and to wither away in Turkish harems."[43]

The following morning, as Tehlirian was finishing his tea, Talat stepped out onto his balcony across the way. "The monster" was still here. "Talat hung his head." Tehlirian mused, "Apparently life was not easy for him after the crime he committed in the desert."[44] The former minister slipped back into his suite. Since it was after ten in the morning, Tehlirian knew that Talat would soon exit the building and go for his stroll toward Uhlandstrasse. Sure enough, Talat, dressed nattily in a striped shirt, suit, and overcoat but no hat, appeared at the door of the building and descended to the street. Tehlirian found his pistol, checked it, thrust it in his pocket, and rushed down the stairwell. The landlady would later note that Tehlirian left the building around eleven a.m.

From across the boulevard, Tehlirian could see Talat was traveling along his usual southeasterly path. The moment of truth had arrived. Before pulling the trigger, it was crucial for Tehlirian to get a good look at Talat's face in order to make a positive identification. It was equally important not to alert his target in any way, to catch his quarry unawares so that he could not avoid the kill shot. Tehlirian had to hit his target square.

As the world speeded up, and with his pulse pounding in his temples, Tehlirian slipped along the opposite side of the street, duplicating Talat's path across the Hardenbergstrasse. The two men, each on his side of the street, progressed in this manner for almost three blocks. Tehlirian knew that Talat would cross the street at some point within the next hundred yards, probably after passing the imposing Berlin University of the Arts. Tehlirian was now fifty steps ahead of Talat. He jogged across the boulevard, then turned and began striding toward his victim. Swinging his cane as he walked, Talat displayed no sense of caution. Ten feet separated the men, now five, now they were almost upon each other. Their eyes met.

Moments later, Talat Pasha lay on the ground, dead.

CHAPTER SEVEN

The Trial

Glory to him who wielded the avenging thunderbolt! Soghomon Tehlirian exercised holy vengeance. He is the symbol of our Nemesis.

—Flyer circulated in the Armenian
American communities

Soghomon Tehlirian's June 1921 trial lasted only three days amidst a charged political environment. A young man had assassinated a world leader. Seven years earlier the Great War had been sparked when a twenty-year-old Serbian, Gavrilo Princip, assassinated Archduke Franz Ferdinand of Austria and his wife, Sophie, Duchess of Hohenberg, in late June 1914. Now, another young man in his twenties had killed another important political figure. This time the killer was from Armenia, which, like Serbia, had been a longtime territory of the Ottoman Empire. The powerless were killing the powerful and the world was transfixed.

The drama was riveting also because not just a young man but an entire nation was, by association, on trial. This trial was not only about Tehlirian and Talat but also about the Armenians and the Turks. And it was taking place in Berlin, of all places. The proceedings would shed light not only on Ottoman war crimes but on a particularly shameful aspect of the war that many Germans wanted to forget: the Reich's complicity in the destruction of the Ottoman Christians.

Many outside Germany believed that the Kaiser's military had aided and abetted the deportations and killings. At the very least, the German commanders had done nothing to stop the carnage. This was yet another item to add to Germany's unenviable résumé as a warmonger and aggressor state. The citizens of the Allied nations were almost unanimous in their belief that the "Huns" were inherently violent and brutal, and most non-Germans were certain that Germany should receive harsh punishment. Germany was responsible for millions of war dead; now, here was further proof of its barbarity, its alliance with Turkey. (In Leipzig, war crimes trials before the Reichsgericht, or Supreme Court, were taking place concurrently with Tehlirian's trial in Berlin.)

Germany's leaders could not afford to let the trial become an examination of their involvement with the murderous Ittihadists because at that very moment, terms that could dramatically affect the Fatherland were being negotiated at the Paris treaty conferences. Minimizing reparations was a top priority for German statesmen. Key to that effort was covering up Germany's role as accomplice. Since a trial was unavoidable, it was imperative to put full responsibility onto "the Turk" rather than "the Hun." This was not simply a matter of reputation; this was about the survival of the German nation. Germany could not move on until the treaties were signed. The trial must not be allowed to make matters worse.

As Tessa Hofmann explains in her 1989 essay "New Aspects of the Talat Pasha Court Case," the German government made an effort to steer the trial away from the political motivations for the assassinations while urging the prosecution to focus on the obvious guilt of the unstable young man who had pulled the trigger. Hofmann quotes the prosecutor in a communication to the

Prussian Ministry of Justice: "It is to be feared that the (coming) trial by jury of the Armenian, who assassinated the former Turkish grand vizier, Talat Pasha, on 15 March of this year, in Berlin, will escalate into a mammoth political case.... Perhaps the defense will even try to investigate the stance of the German government on the Armenian atrocities.... (As a result) of the (given) political reasons, the (Foreign Office) would greatly appreciate exclusion of the (public) in this matter."[1]

Any suggestions of wrongdoing on the part of the Germans had to be diluted. More than that, this trial must contribute to a new, more favorable public image for Germany. The prosecution needed to paint the Turks with the blackest brush possible. The Armenian defense team was well aware of this. In a secret memo to fellow Tashnags, Armen Garo announced with absolute certainty that Tehlirian would be acquitted, adding, "Our German friends are determined to make this trial a forum for our cause."[2]

The sensational killing had made headlines worldwide. A rootless immigrant had murdered a convicted war criminal. The assassin was a hardworking engineering student who suffered from chronic "epilepsy." It was even possible that the young man was mentally ill as a result of the fact that six years earlier he had witnessed the brutal executions of his entire family. The killer had few friends, no real plans, and apparently no means of employment. The murdered man had been one of the most powerful men in the world. The killer was an Armenian, the victim a Turk. The enmity between these two nationalities was legendary.

On the first day of his trial, this loner, this misfit, the man the *New York Times* described as an "undersized swarthily palefaced Armenian,"[3] exuded an aura of serenity and intelligence. Anyone could see that this was no crazed maniac. Neatly dressed in suit and tie, clean-shaven and poised, Tehlirian sat calmly at the defense table flanked by top-shelf lawyers and interpreters. The expensive defense team had been underwritten by a well-endowed fund covering all of the defendant's needs. Prominent members of the Armenian expat community, having no prior connection to the man, were eager to come to the aid of their new hero. This young student had avenged the brutal deaths of hundreds of thousands of his countrymen, and Armenians everywhere were rallying to his cause.

The trial took place in the high-ceilinged Victorian chamber of Berlin's Third District Court beneath a massive chandelier. Judge Erich Lehmberg, with his counselors Karl Locke and Ernest Bathe on his left, presided over a jury of twelve that included two landlords, a brick maker, a butcher, and a locksmith. District Attorney Gollnick; Tehlirian's three lawyers—Dr. Adolf von Gordon, privy legal counselor, Berlin; Dr. Johannes Werthauer, privy legal counselor, Berlin; and Dr. Kurt Niemeyer, privy legal counselor, professor of law, Cologne University—were arranged at tables below the judge, at floor level. Also present were the two interpreters for Tehlirian: Vahan Zakarian (his fellow conspirator Vaza) and Kevork Kaloustian. A gallery ran along the upper circumference of the chamber, and from there a dozen or so reporters tracked the proceedings. Only a handful of women were present.[4]

From the start, Tehlirian held the courtroom's full attention as the translator repeated his softly recounted story of the rape and murder of his sisters as well as the bloody killings of his brothers and mother. His interpreter translated into German and a court stenographer took notes. The young man's story was like an adventure novel. Left for dead, he had made an astonishing escape from the killing fields, managing to cross the wastelands of Kurdish territory and escape through the mountains. He was a thrilling example of the triumph of the spirit despite all odds. He was brave in so many ways, and now here he was, humbly standing trial, a man who had risen above the heaviest of burdens. Only the hardest heart could remain unmoved by a story so full of pathos.

The subtext was clear: Tehlirian had surmounted his victimhood. The skinny kid had mustered up amazing courage and confronted evil directly. He had survived the cruel deportation caravans and then outsmarted the Turkish security apparatus in Berlin. He had struck at the "head of the snake." His actions had been bold, fearless. In the world's eyes, Tehlirian was a David standing up to the powerful Turkish Goliath. To many he was more than sympathetic; he was heroic.

In contrast, it seemed that no one held any pity for the murdered man. First of all, Talat was a Turk, and every well-read person in the West was familiar with "the terrible Turk" and his perverse proclivities. Furthermore, he was an Ottoman leader, and everyone was familiar with what seemed to be an endless string of slaughters of the Armenians by Ottoman authorities. Since the nineteenth century, massacres of Christians had been making headlines in Europe and America almost weekly. Often, details of the atrocities were almost too horrible to recount. Church groups in the United States, Britain, and Germany had gathered and protested against the violence for decades. When Tehlirian detailed the specifics of his family's demise, his audience knew what he was going to say before he said it. All Tehlirian had to do was personalize it.

The judge, the jury, and the world also knew that about a year earlier, a postwar tribunal in Constantinople had convicted Talat of war crimes and sentenced him to death in absentia. But before the Great Powers had been able to find Talat and arrest him for "crimes against humanity," the former interior minister of the Ottoman Empire and his cronies had escaped from Constantinople in the dark of night on a German ship. The tribunal had proceeded without them and had delivered its verdict. Talat was a condemned man at the time of his assassination, and the court knew this.

Tehlirian's sickliness also made him sympathetic. The young man suffered from sudden fainting spells and nightmare-ridden insomnia. Several witnesses had seen him collapse in public. Doctors examining him concurred that these seizures, which arrived with no warning, were linked to the massacre of his family. His experience as a captive of the Turkish criminals was so severe that he had been psychologically damaged for the rest of his life. For the duration of the trial, the judge would treat Tehlirian with kid gloves, fearful of triggering an "epileptic fit."

Any one of those aspects of the case would have made it complex and difficult to judge. What capped the conundrum was the unimpeachable justification at the core of what appeared to be a premeditated murder. The man had seen his mother beheaded right before his eyes! For this reason the killing seemed to exist outside the bounds of established law, in another legal dimension altogether. And his mother had not been the only victim, nor only his immediate family, but an entire nation! The man had not simply pursued a personal vendetta; he had avenged the murder of his *people*.

As such an agent for retribution, Tehlirian represented not just himself but all of humanity. The crimes against the civilian Armenian population of Anatolia had been unprecedented in their scope and sadism. Never before in history had so many died in such a brief period of time. Indeed, there seemed to be no legal scale vast enough to measure what the Young Turks had done. Likewise, there was no legal precedent for Tehlirian's particular form of first-degree murder.

And since Talat had been the one who had given the orders for the destruction of the Armenians, since the lives of hundreds of thousands of people were on his head, wasn't Talat's life a small price to pay in exchange for the deaths of thousands upon thousands? The implications of the case before Judge Lehmberg strained the rule of law, went beyond strict legal concepts of guilt and innocence, generating moral, philosophical, even existential questions. Anyone could see that the man on trial had no guilty conscience. Tehlirian was so certain of his right to kill Talat that he could look the judge in the eye and confidently claim the moral high ground. As far as Tehlirian was concerned, he had no free will in the matter; he was compelled by his very soul to kill the man who had killed his family. Who could debate him?

For all these reasons, the trial favored Tehlirian. But there was one catch. If Tehlirian told the "whole truth and nothing but the truth," he didn't stand a chance. Premeditation might be overlooked, but acting as the spearhead of an international conspiracy to assassinate a world leader would send the young Armenian straight to the gallows. And even if Tehlirian was prepared to sacrifice himself on the altar of justice, it was nevertheless crucial that he lie. He had to provide cover for those who had financed and planned the killing—the operatives working in Boston, Syracuse, Paris, Berlin, Geneva, and Constantinople. He had to protect them so that they could plan and execute more reprisals.

One more factor, invisible to the court, loomed over the proceedings: the leaders of Operation Nemesis wanted to use this trial to reveal to the world what had happened to the Armenians in 1915 and 1916. This trial would be a means of laying bare the crimes committed by Talat and his Committee of Union and Progress. Tehlirian had been specifically instructed to linger by the body, to allow himself to be arrested so that he would be tried. In the tumult of the moment, he had panicked and run. But he had not run far. And now here he was, on trial, representing a nation's tragedy.

Tehlirian would be walking a tightrope as he balanced truth and fiction. He had to escape punishment while furthering the cause of the Armenian Revolutionary Federation. It was imperative that Operation Nemesis remain hidden from view. Even as Tehlirian was stepping into the defendant's box, his confederates in other major European cities were laying the groundwork for the next assassination, and the one after that.

To achieve this goal of obfuscation, a well-coached Tehlirian would offer mere fragments of "truth," snippets of narrative representing the alternative history he needed the court to accept. Because Tehlirian was presenting a version of events that had in fact never actually taken place, it was essential that the details dovetail and that no slipups be made. So he avoided specifics, never giving his interrogators an opportunity to uncover a flaw in his story.

For example, he had to explain his whereabouts between the time when he supposedly "escaped" the Turks (in 1915) and the date he arrived in Berlin (in December 1920). In an era before credit cards and automatic telephone logs, Tehlirian's defense attorneys knew that the Berlin prosecutors would never be able to track his travels in detail. When the prosecution did make an effort to question his movements, Tehlirian replied with a logic bordering on the absurd. When asked why, prior to arriving in Berlin, he had visited Geneva (where the ARF maintained its headquarters), Tehlirian, a country boy from Anatolia, answered that hadn't wanted to miss the opportunity to visit the Swiss city. Judge Lehmberg asked no follow-up questions. When queried about how he had passed his time in Berlin (since apparently he was neither a registered student nor employed), rather than explain that he spent all day stalking Turks, he gave vague answers about attending German language classes.

No one seemed to notice that this man who supposedly took German classes every day could hardly speak the language. At the same time, ironically, Tehlirian's mediocre language skills provided an additional layer of protection when he was testifying. He repeatedly misunderstood questions and requested they be asked again, buying time as he prepared an answer. This stratagem would prove especially invaluable whenever he was cornered in a fabrication. Caught in contradictory statements, he would stick to a hazy storyline, made even more vague by his awkward rhetoric. Often he refused to understand a question or avoided answering it at all. He was rarely challenged.

As the trial began in the early summer of 1921, Tehlirian held center stage in a state of super-consciousness while playing the part of a sweet and slightly incoherent man who had acted solely out of passion. He focused all of his attention on Judge Lehmberg, the most important individual in the room. Unlike trials in the United States, this trial would not be a contest between prosecution and defense. Instead, Lehmberg would lead a free-form investigation more like an inquest, asking questions as he saw fit. In Lehmberg, Tehlirian had an ally. The judge would repeatedly "lead" the defendant while brushing aside queries and objections made by the prosecution.

Judge Lehmberg opened the trial by establishing that Tehlirian was born on April 2, 1897, in the village of Pakarij (in his autobiography, he claims that he was born in 1896), moving to the larger town of Erzincan when he was a small boy. Tehlirian explained, through his interpreter, that the men in his family were coffee merchants, adding, as he mixed fact with fiction, that he had two brothers and three sisters. The judge asked, "Did all these brothers and sisters live in your parents' house until 1915?" To which Tehlirian replied, "They all lived there except one sister who was married." In fact, by 1915, not only was Tehlirian's father not living in Erzincan, but Tehlirian and his older brother were likewise long gone. Though he admitted that his brother Misak had been a soldier (ostensibly home on leave and "caught" by the Turks when the deportations began), Misak was in fact hundreds of miles away at the time, on the other side of the Russian front, fighting against the Turks. As was Tehlirian.

The prosecuting attorney repeatedly tried to get the judge to focus on the murder (and Tehlirian's part in it), but Lehmberg preferred to explore Tehlirian's story: "We wish to hear from the defendant in detail regarding what led to the massacres and what his family experienced."

According to the transcript of the trial, Tehlirian recounted a typical story of what we now call "ethnic cleansing":

After the war began in 1914 and Armenian soldiers were conscripted, in May 1915 came the news that the schools had to be shut and that the city's notables and teachers were going to be sent away to camps.... I was scared and didn't want to leave home. After these convoys were taken away, rumors started spreading that the people who'd been deported earlier had already been killed. And through a cable we learned that out of all the deported people from Erzincan, only one man was still alive: Martirossian.

In early June the order came that the people of Erzincan had to be ready to leave. We were also told that all our money and valuables could be handed over to the authorities for safekeeping. Three days later, early in the morning the residents were taken out of the city.... After the order came that the people had to leave the city, they were mustered and herded together outside. The line of people then moved forward in caravans and convoys.

The judge asked, "How many days did you march?" Tehlirian replied, "I do not know. After leaving the city, already on the first day my parents were killed."

Justice Lehmberg continued to lead the witness:

LEHMBERG: Who escorted the caravans?
TEHLIRIAN: Gendarmes, soldiers on horseback, and other soldiers.
LEHMBERG: A large number?
TEHLIRIAN: They came from both sides of the road.
LEHMBERG: They were also in front and behind?
TEHLIRIAN: They came from both sides.

Helpfully, the judge added, "To prevent someone getting away?" Tehlirian: "Definitely." Lehmberg then asked, "Now, how did your parents and your brothers and sisters die?"

TEHLIRIAN: When the column was some way from the city, we were ordered to stop. The gendarmes began to plunder and tried to get hold of the column's money and valuables.

When Lehmberg asked, "How did they justify this?" Tehlirian took advantage of the question to instruct the greater public who would be reading about the trial: "They didn't say. No one in the world can explain it. Things like that take place in Asia's interior." Lehmberg helped Tehlirian along: "So something like this takes place without people being able to understand the reasons?"

TEHLIRIAN: Yes. It happened.
LEHMBERG: With other nationalities as well?

Tehlirian promptly replied, "Only the Armenians were treated this way by the Turks." He continued, "During the plundering those of us in the column took rifle fire from up front. One of the gendarmes then dragged away my sister, and my mother cried out,

'Please, let me go blind!'—I can't remember that day any more. I don't want to keep on being reminded of that day. I'd rather die right now than continue describing that black day."

Tehlirian went silent.

Lehmberg, taking Tehlirian's distress at face value, was compassionate but firm: "I'm obliged to let you know that the court must lay the strongest importance on learning about these things from you, in particular as you are the only person who can say something about this deed. Perhaps you can pull yourself together and overcome your distress." Tehlirian's story drifted into a surreal concoction of place and time. "They took everyone away and beat me as well. Then I saw how my brother's skull was split apart with an ax."

LEHMBERG: Your sister was taken away? Did she return?

TEHLIRIAN: Yes, my sister was taken away and raped.

LEHMBERG: Did she return afterwards?

TEHLIRIAN: No.

LEHMBERG: Who split open your brother's skull with an ax?

TEHLIRIAN: When the soldiers and gendarmes began their massacre, ordinary people showed up too. That's when my youngest brother's skull was split open. My mother fell down.

LEHMBERG: Why did she fall?

TEHLIRIAN: I don't know why, if it was a bullet or something else that caused it.

LEHMBERG: Where was your father?

TEHLIRIAN: I didn't see my father; he was farther up ahead, where there was also fighting.

LEHMBERG: What did you do yourself?

TEHLIRIAN: I felt a blow to my head and fell down then. I don't know what happened afterwards.

Judge Lehmberg made no attempt to clarify in what order the rapes and bludgeonings occurred. Rather, he prodded Tehlirian to continue.

LEHMBERG: Did you remain lying in the spot where the massacre took place?

TEHLIRIAN: I don't know how long I lay there. Maybe two days. When I woke up I saw many corpses close by, because the entire caravan had been killed then. I saw very long piles of corpses. But I couldn't make out everything well since it was pretty dark. First, I didn't know where I was; then I saw the truth, that it was corpses.

LEHMBERG: Could you make out your parents, brothers, and sisters among the corpses?

TEHLIRIAN: I saw my mother's body lying on its face, and my brother's body lay on top of me. I couldn't make out anything else.... When I stood up I saw that my leg was wounded and that my arm was bleeding.

LEHMBERG: Was your head injured?

TEHLIRIAN: I was first hit on the head.

LEHMBERG: Do you know what kind of implement you were wounded with?

TEHLIRIAN: While the massacre was taking place I ducked my head down, so I couldn't know that. I only heard screaming.

LEHMBERG: You said the guards were gendarmes and soldiers on horseback. Then you said that ordinary people were also there. What do you mean by that?

TEHLIRIAN: The Turks living in Erzincan.

LEHMBERG: They were present and also participated in the massacre?

TEHLIRIAN: All I know is that when the gendarmes started to kill, those people were there.

LEHMBERG: And now after a day or two you regained consciousness and realized your brother's body was lying on top of you. But you didn't see your parents' bodies there as well?

TEHLIRIAN: I saw my oldest brother's body on top of me.

PROSECUTOR: I think it was the younger brother whose head
    had been split open with an ax.
LEHMBERG: Was it your younger brother's body?

Zakarian, the translator, clarified the point: "No, the oldest brother's."

LEHMBERG: But from behind you saw that your younger
    brother had been struck with the ax?
TEHLIRIAN: Yes.
LEHMBERG: Have you seen your parents since that day?
TEHLIRIAN: No.
LEHMBERG: And your brothers and sisters?
TEHLIRIAN: No, also not.
LEHMBERG: So they've vanished, disappeared?
TEHLIRIAN: Up to now I haven't found a trace of them.

It's hard to tell if Lehmberg was trying to trip up Tehlirian on his earlier testimony in which he says he saw his family murdered, indeed saw their corpses, or was simply trying to understand what he was saying. Clearly the testimony is inconsistent, and yet Judge Lehmberg (and the prosecuting attorney) gave Tehlirian a pass.

Tehlirian next recounted how he had eventually found his way back to his hometown of Erzincan (neglecting to mention that he did so as a volunteer soldier in the Russian army).

TEHLIRIAN: News came that Erzincan had been taken by the
    Russians—then I wanted to go back to look for my
    parents and relatives. I also knew very well there was still
    money at home and wanted to get it. . . .
       When I arrived I found all the doors shattered and part
    of the house was destroyed. And after I entered the house I
    collapsed. . . . After I came to, I went to two Armenian
    families who had converted to Islam; they were the only
    families in the entire city who had been saved . . . two

families and here and there individual people, altogether around twenty people, but only two families. . . . I found various utensils, everything else had been burnt and was gone. But there was still money there, buried in the ground. . . forty-eight hundred Turkish pounds.

LEHMBERG: You took that with you?

TEHLIRIAN: Indeed I did.

According to this version of the story, Tehlirian, after escaping Turkey, made it to Tiflis, Georgia, turned around, crossed the Caucasus once more, and returned to his home village in Turkey, covering a distance of five hundred miles, traversing a war zone twice. No one in the court questioned how he accomplished this. Whether Tehlirian actually retrieved hidden loot or not, this narrative would explain to the court how he'd gotten his hands on enough money to travel freely around Europe, find lodging in Berlin, and pay his expenses while apparently unemployed. The recovery of the 4,800 Turkish gold pieces (a small fortune) would have been more than enough to cover his traveling expenses for years.

By 1919, armistice had been declared and Constantinople, now under British control, was flooded with refugees. Tehlirian testified that he had traveled to the imperial capital because he wanted to place an advertisement in a newspaper in the hope of locating his lost relatives. He repeats this story in his autobiography. What he did not mention in court was that while he was in Constantinople, he assassinated the *muhtar* Megerdichian, establishing his credentials as a dependable "weapon" for the ARF.

Having delivered a disorderly and inexact account of his whereabouts prior to his sudden appearance in Berlin, Tehlirian was permitted to step down. At this point, Judge Lehmberg moved to take Tehlirian's plea. But before that could happen, there was one more attempt on the part of the defense team to shift blame onto the murder victim.

DEFENSE ATTORNEY VON GORDON: I would like to ask the
    accused if he had read in the papers that Talat Pasha had
    been sentenced to death by the military court in
    Constantinople on account of this atrocity.

TEHLIRIAN: I read it and was in Constantinople when Kemal
    [Kemal Bey, not to be confused with General Mustapha
    Kemal], one of the massacre's organizers, was hanged
    already. At the time the papers wrote that Talat and Enver
    Pasha had also been condemned to death.

The reporters in the courtroom took Tehlirian's testimony at face
value. Strangely, when the *New York Times* had first reported the
assassination over two months earlier, a greater conspiracy had
been hinted at: "The authorities are skeptical as to Tehlirian's boast
that his discovery of his victim's whereabouts and identity was
entirely his own work. They are inclined to the view [that] he is an
agent of the Armenian Revolutionary Committee and find support for this theory in the fact that his passport was issued in Paris
and has a Geneva visa." In a follow-up article, the *Times* reported
that "a check for 12,000 marks which Salomon [*sic*] Tehlirian the
assassin of Talat received two days before the crime was committed
leads the authorities to believe that this money was sent to him by
conspirators to enable him to fly after the deed."[5] The "newspaper
of record" mentioned a conspiracy and named as co-conspirator
the Tashnag (ARF) organization within *two days* of the killing.
Curiously, the *Times* never followed up on its own suspicions while
reporting at great length on the trial. And neither a conspiracy nor
the ARF was ever mentioned in court.

Judge Lehmberg preferred the uncomplicated narrative of atrocity and revenge to getting mired in the swampy complexities of
political terrain. The court refused to entertain the notion that
Tehlirian was anything more than what he said he was. That he
might be a pawn in a much larger game was also never hinted at.
The indictment was read by the court's clerk:

The alleged student of mechanical engineering Salomon [*sic*] Tehlirian, Charlottenburg, Hardenbergstrasse 37, c/o Dittman, since 16 March 1921 in pretrial custody, born 2 April 1897 in Pakarij, Turkey, Turkish citizen, Armenian Protestant, is accused of having intentionally killed the former Turkish Grand Vizier Talat Pasha on 15 March 1921 in Charlottenburg, and of having carried out the homicide with premeditation. Crime according to Article 211 of the Penal Code.

For reasons explained, custody is continued.

Berlin, 16 April 1921.

Regional Court III, Criminal Division 6.

The reading of the indictment triggered another visit to Tehlirian's version of reality.

LEHMBERG (to the interpreter): Please explain to the accused that the indictment accuses him of having killed Talat Pasha in a premeditated manner.

The defendant remained silent.

LEHMBERG: If you were to answer this accusation with yes or no, which answer would you give?

TEHLIRIAN: No.

LEHMBERG: On earlier occasions you indicated otherwise. You admitted having carried out the deed with premeditation.

TEHLIRIAN: When did I say that?

LEHMBERG: So today you prefer not having said that? Let's now go back to developments up to Paris. On various occasions, at various times, you admitted that you made the decision to carry out the deed, to murder Talat Pasha.

DEFENSE ATTORNEY VON GORDON: I request that the accused be asked why he considers himself not guilty.

Lehmberg directed the question to the defendant.

> TEHLIRIAN: I consider myself not guilty because my conscience
>   is clear.
> LEHMBERG: Why is your conscience clear?
> TEHLIRIAN: I have killed a man. But I wasn't a murderer.
> LEHMBERG: You say that you feel no remorse? Your conscience is
>   clear? You don't have any self-reproaches? But you certainly
>   have to ask yourself: Did you then intend to kill Talat Pasha?
> TEHLIRIAN: I do not understand this question. After all, I
>   killed him.
> LEHMBERG: Did you have a plan?
> TEHLIRIAN: I had no plan.
> LEHMBERG: When did the idea first occur to you?
> TEHLIRIAN: Around two weeks before the deed I felt lousy and
>   I again saw visions of the massacre. I saw my mother's
>   corpse. This body stood up and stepped over to me and
>   said, "You've seen that Talat is here and you're completely
>   disinterested? You're no longer my son."
> LEHMBERG (repeating those words to the jury): What did you
>   do now?
> TEHLIRIAN: I suddenly woke up and decided to kill the man.

Once again Lehmberg led the defendant.

> LEHMBERG: When you were in Paris and Geneva and when
>   you came to Berlin, had you not yet decided this?
> TEHLIRIAN: I'd made no decision.
> LEHMBERG: Did you even know that Talat Pasha was staying in
>   Berlin?
> TEHLIRIAN: No.

When the district attorney mused, "Just one thing seems odd
to me — that the accused man found an apartment in Hardenbergstrasse so quickly," the point was rapidly passed over and the line of

questioning dropped. Had this anomaly been given any attention by the police, they soon would have uncovered Tehlirian's associates.

Piece by piece, the facts at hand were either fitted into Tehlirian's version or discarded. When he was asked whether he had scars on his body, he replied, "Indeed I do!" implying that the scars were a result of his experience in the death caravan. But he had not received his wounds as a hostage; he had received them as a soldier. His fainting spells were attributed to the trauma of the deportation. He was not asked whether he had always suffered from these fits. No one questioned his version of how he came to have so much cash on him at the time of his arrest. No one questioned how a young man from the Anatolian countryside was able to travel around Europe with such easy familiarity. No one questioned how he spent his time in Berlin, hour after hour, day after day. Did he really study German all day, every day?

And where had the gun come from?

A gunsmith, "expert witness Barella," testified. "The pistol has an eight- to nine-millimeter-diameter barrel. It has been officially approved for use by the German army. It's a so-called 'self-loading weapon,' from which eight bullets can be fired. It is war surplus and carries the year nineteen fifteen from the Deutsche Waffen- und Munitionsfabrik. The ammunition is also war surplus." The pistol used was probably a Luger P-08. The 9mm Parabellum has more explosive kick than the normal 9mm because the automatic mechanism gives the bullet more of a surge. Also the bullet is larger than the normal 9mm. The Luger was a soldier's handgun.

LEHMBERG: Defendant, did you ever use the weapon earlier on?
TEHLIRIAN: No.

Tehlirian's first landlady stated that she never saw a pistol in Tehlirian's luggage. Testimony was provided that the pistol was in good condition if not new. So where did the Luger come from? Apparently there was no interest in providing an answer to this mystery either. Furthermore, Tehlirian, supposedly a student with no military background whatsoever, had killed a man with one shot. How had he been able to do that? No one bothered to ask.

In the most illogical reasoning of the trial, even when it was clear that Tehlirian had moved to a new apartment directly across the street from his victim only a few days before the killing, he insisted that there was no premeditation.

LEHMBERG: On the fifth of March you moved in at Frau Dittman's. For what reasons?

TEHLIRIAN: When my mother appeared before me, I made the decision to kill Talat. I changed apartments for this reason.

LEHMBERG: And, so to speak, prepared the deed?

TEHLIRIAN: After my mother ordered it, the next day I told myself I had to kill him.

LEHMBERG: And from that time on you tried to convert the thought into action?

TEHLIRIAN: After moving into the new apartment, to some extent I forgot what my mother told me.

LEHMBERG: Forgot?

TRANSLATOR ZAKARIAN: This can't be translated. We could say "dropped it," let the thought drop.

LEHMBERG: I think [you're saying] you'd just moved into the new apartment because your mother reproached you for being unconcerned.

TEHLIRIAN: I started to reflect. I told myself: How can you kill someone?

LEHMBERG: You asked yourself how you could be capable of killing Talat Pasha?

TEHLIRIAN: I told myself: I'm not capable of killing someone.

LEHMBERG: I don't really understand this. Earlier you answered that since that day you had decided to move to Hardenbergstrasse; so you must have known that Talat Pasha lived across from you.

TEHLIRIAN: Yes.

LEHMBERG: So you wanted to live near him?

TEHLIRIAN: When my mother said that to me.

LEHMBERG: Then you decided—and what was the decision?

TEHLIRIAN: That I want to kill him.

LEHMBERG: Now tell us: Is it correct that already beforehand you'd realized Talat Pasha was living in Berlin?

TEHLIRIAN: Yes, about five weeks earlier I saw him.

LEHMBERG: Where?

TEHLIRIAN: He was walking on the street with two other men from the direction of the zoo. I heard Turkish being spoken near me and one of the men being addressed as "pasha." I turned around and saw that this person was Talat Pasha. I walked behind them until I came to a cinema. Before the door of the cinema I saw that one of the other men was leaving. He kissed Talat's hand and addressed him as "pasha." The two other men entered a house.

LEHMBERG: At the time that you, so to speak, made this acquaintance, did the idea already occur to you to kill Talat?

TEHLIRIAN: The idea didn't occur to me. I only felt bad, and when I was walking into the cinema it seemed to me that all the pictures of the massacre were rising up before me, and I walked back out of the cinema and went home.

LEHMBERG: And that was, as you said today, four to five weeks before this move to Hardenbergstrasse?

TEHLIRIAN: Yes.

LEHMBERG: So it's not correct that you'd already learned earlier that Talat Pasha was staying in Berlin?

TEHLIRIAN: No.

Lehmberg addressed the court, clarifying, "I'm asking this because in earlier proceedings the defendant said at one point he came to Berlin because he wanted to study in Berlin and also had learned that Talat was staying in Berlin."

DEFENSE ATTORNEY VON GORDON: What's been said today roughly corresponds to the defendant's last previous statement that around two weeks before the deed the appearance of his mother's spirit sparked the decision to kill Talat Pasha. He thus also last indicated that he moved to Hardenbergstrasse for this reason.

TEHLIRIAN: Yes.

LEHMBERG: From that point onward, did you make it your business to observe and control Talat Pasha in his everyday life?

TEHLIRIAN: No, after moving into the new apartment I wanted to do my usual everyday work.

A smorgasbord of facts had been served up. The court was informed when Tehlirian first saw Talat, when he first decided to shoot Talat, and that he soon "forgot" about his decision. And yet he'd moved to an apartment directly across the street from Talat's residence. At this point von Gordon addressed the judge.

DEFENSE ATTORNEY VON GORDON: I didn't entirely understand a remark made a little while ago. Did I understand correctly that after finding the apartment in Hardenbergstrasse in order to be close to Talat, the defendant afterwards at times dropped the idea [of murdering Talat] because the thought occurred to him: You can't kill another person?! To put it briefly: Did this decision he made after the spirit's appearance stay firm, or did he sometimes drop it and then devote himself to his usual occupations, because he said to himself: You can't kill someone?

LEHMBERG: That's indeed what he said; he wavered in his decision.

TEHLIRIAN: I did waver. Whenever I felt sick, I wanted to honor my mother's command. But when I was well again, I said to myself: You can't really kill someone.

★   ★   ★

This "wavering," in combination with Tehlirian's proclivity for fainting, became the linchpin of the defense. This convoluted logic was argued back and forth to the very end of the trial. When did he decide to kill Talat? How confused was he when he experienced his fainting spells? The court, avoiding the problematic logic of Tehlirian's preparations to kill Talat, roamed to and fro while trying to gain some insight into the man himself. When directly asked why he had happened to move across the street from his victim, Tehlirian repeated an unsubstantiated medical reason, something having to do with the amount of light in his room. Again, he was never questioned directly about the clearly predatory nature of his actions.

The assassination was described, moment by moment. Tehlirian did not deny stalking Talat, passing him, shooting him in the back of the head, and throwing the pistol away. The court became entangled in trying to understand why Tehlirian had walked past Talat before shooting him. They found his actions confusing because they did not understand that they were dealing with a seasoned assassin. Seen from that perspective—that Tehlirian knew what he was doing—everything Tehlirian did made sense: He tracked his victim by walking in a parallel path on the other side of the boulevard. He then hurried forward, crossed the street, and walked past Talat, getting a good look at his face so he could be absolutely certain of his victim's identity. Immediately after passing his target, Tehlirian turned and shot Talat once in the base of his skull. He said so himself: "One shot." Intelligence agents the world over know that absolute reliability is obtained by severing the spinal cord in the cervical region. Tehlirian's efficiency was noted but disregarded.

Tehlirian was no amateur; his first priority was to complete his assignment. As he had explained to a police officer when he was first interrogated, shooting Talat from the front risked the possibility of Talat's making some sort of defensive maneuver. Shooting him from behind decreased the possibility that Talat might dodge or deflect the bullet. Tehlirian's job was to effect the man's death, not satisfy some personal emotional need. He was clear about this.

LEHMBERG: What sort of feeling did you have when Talat Pasha was dead? What did you think at that point?

TEHLIRIAN: Right afterwards, I don't know.

LEHMBERG: But sometime afterwards, what happened must have become clear to you?

TEHLIRIAN: After I was brought to the police station, I knew what had happened.

LEHMBERG: What did you think about the deed then?

TEHLIRIAN: I felt satisfaction in my heart.

LEHMBERG: And what about now?

TEHLIRIAN: Now as well, I'm satisfied with the deed.

LEHMBERG: Of course you know that under normal circumstances no one may take on the role of judge, even if many things have happened to him?

TEHLIRIAN: I don't know—my mother said I had to kill Talat Pasha because he was guilty of the massacre, and my soul was so transformed I didn't know I still was not allowed to kill.

LEHMBERG: But you certainly know that our laws forbid murder, forbid killing a human being.

TEHLIRIAN: I don't know the law.

LEHMBERG: Does the custom of blood vengeance exist among the Armenians?

TEHLIRIAN: No.

DEFENSE ATTORNEY NIEMEYER: You said something while the crowd was beating you and you were bleeding. Can you recall what you said at the time, a statement in your defense facing the crowd?

LEHMBERG: He has indicated that he did not run away, that he saw blood flowing, and that people stood around and some grabbed hold of him. (To Tehlirian) Now, do you know if one of the onlookers who'd come running confronted you, or if perhaps you spontaneously said something to one of those people in self-defense, because you'd been grabbed hold of and beaten?

TEHLIRIAN: I said I was a foreigner and the man I'd killed was also a foreigner: What did the Germans have to do with it?

LEHMBERG: You're supposed to have said you knew what you'd done. That it was no loss for Germany.

Tehlirian then repeated his previous words.

Character witnesses followed: the two landladies as well as Tehlirian's non-Tashnag friends, his tutor, and his doctor. Everyone described a melancholy, sweet man who would sit alone in his room, singing to himself in the dark, a traumatized refugee who refused to talk about what had happened during the war. The young student was clean and neat, even to the point of polishing his own shoes (usually the responsibility of the landlady)—a point both Tehlirian and Frau Dittman saw fit to mention. Dittman further testified that on the day before the murder, Tehlirian had been drinking cognac and crying.

His friend Levon Eftian summed it up: "He always looked sad."

When it was learned that Tehlirian had not mentioned sighting Talat in Berlin to any of his (non-Nemesis) Armenian cohorts, the prosecutor tried to force him to admit the logical contradiction.

LEHMBERG: Defendant, but you did run into Talat? After the encounter, why didn't you say anything about this important event to your countrymen?

TEHLIRIAN: I thought they'd make fun of me.

LEHMBERG: Why would they do that? If Talat was generally considered the main author? Witness [Christine] Terzibachian always wanted to talk about it. Why didn't you mention it?

TEHLIRIAN: I didn't speak about it.

LEHMBERG: Why did you keep it to yourself?

TEHLIRIAN: I didn't have any interest in speaking about it.

LEHMBERG: But we're interested in this.

TEHLIRIAN: If I had spoken about it, they would have asked many questions.

LEHMBERG: You didn't want your countrymen to become
   upset and assail you with curious questions?
TEHLIRIAN: I was in such a state that I didn't want this
   discussed.

One more thread was left dangling.

Next to testify was Geheimer Justizrat Schulze, a jurist as well
as an official, probably a reasonably high one, who had been present at Tehlirian's arrest.

SCHULZE: I still remember the defendant's statements rather
   precisely. He readily admitted having killed Talat
   intentionally and with premeditation. When asked for the
   reasons, he answered that Talat was the one responsible for
   having murdered his relatives, or some of his relatives, in
   Armenia. As a result he had decided to avenge his relatives
   and came here to Germany, to Berlin.
LEHMBERG: When did he make his decision?
SCHULZE: In his homeland. He bought a pistol. He tried to
   learn which apartment Talat was staying in, and after he
   succeeded, he rented a place across from him so that he
   could observe him furtively. He then did watch him
   furtively from his window, and, he indicated, when he saw
   Talat go out on the day in question, he took his revolver
   and followed him.
      He said that to make sure there was no mistake, he first
   walked past Talat, then turned around or walked back
   toward him, looked him more closely in the eye, then,
   when he was sure, shot him from behind in the head with
   the revolver. This is what he indicated.

The lawyers for the defense insisted that Schulze's testimony be
thrown out. They pointed out that Tehlirian had been running a
fever and his head was bandaged at the time of the questioning.

Clearly he had been incoherent when he was interrogated by the court officer. Lehmberg gently questioned Tehlirian.

LEHMBERG: Defendant, on the sixteenth of March you
   admitted that already at that time, in nineteen fifteen,
   when you had to flee from Erzincan, you decided to kill
   Talat.

TEHLIRIAN: I don't remember having said that.

LEHMBERG: So you didn't mean to state that a deed planned
   over a long period was involved here?

TEHLIRIAN: No, how could I have said that?

LEHMBERG: But you must have actually said that then. You
   were questioned by the interpreter, were you not?

TEHLIRIAN: It is *possible* that I stated something like that,
   because my head was still injured and bandaged.

The defense attorneys accused the original police station inter-preter of putting words in Tehlirian's mouth, charging that he was no friend of Tehlirian's. But apparently the opposite was true.

SCHULZE: The interpreter was very calm. But he had a pile of
   sweets for the prisoner—pastries, chocolate, and so
   forth—and asked him to help himself. I said, "What, you
   want to actually offer the murderer sweets?" Then he said,
   "What kind of murderer?! He's a great man we all
   admire!"

CHAPTER EIGHT

The Big Picture

THEY SIMPLY HAD TO LET HIM GO!
— *New York Times* headline

It was now time to tell the world about the destruction of the
Armenians living in the Ottoman Empire. A series of witnesses
was called to the stand to fill in the big picture. An Armenian
survivor, Christine Terzibashian, testified about her own, very real
ordeal. It would prove to be consistent with reports from missionaries and other observers.

> TERZIBASHIAN: When we had left the city and stood before the
> Erzurum fortress, the gendarmes came and searched for
> weapons. Knives, shields, and so on were taken away from
> us. From Erzurum we went to Bayburt. As we passed by
> this city we saw piles of corpses, and I had to step over
> corpses so my feet were stained with blood.
>
> LEHMBERG: Were the corpses from earlier groups that had
> come from Erzurum?

TERZIBASHIAN: No, these were from Bayburt. Then we arrived in Erzincan. We had been promised shelter, but we were not allowed to live there, and we were also not allowed to drink water. We even had to give up our oxen; these were driven into the mountains.

LEHMBERG: Now, what led up to the massacre in which your relatives perished?

TERZIBASHIAN: When we marched on, five hundred young people were selected from the groups. Including one of my brothers. But he managed to escape and join me. I dressed him as a girl so he could stay with me. The other young people were herded together.

LEHMBERG: What happened with those who had been selected?

TERZIBASHIAN: They were all tied together and thrown in the water.

LEHMBERG: How do you know this?

TERZIBASHIAN: I saw it with my own eyes.

LEHMBERG: That they were thrown in the river?

TERZIBASHIAN: Yes, they were thrown in the river, and the current was so strong that all those thrown in the water were carried away.

LEHMBERG: What happened with those remaining?

TERZIBASHIAN: We screamed and cried and did not know what to do. But we were not even allowed to cry but were driven forward by stabbing.

LEHMBERG: Who did that?

TERZIBASHIAN: Thirty soldiers, and a detachment of soldiers.

LEHMBERG: Were they beating you?

TERZIBASHIAN: Yes.

LEHMBERG: What happened next with your relatives?

TERZIBASHIAN: We arrived in Malatya with those we could carry on our backs. There we were taken to the mountain and the men were separated from the women. The women were now around ten meters away from the men and could see with their own eyes what happened to the men.

LEHMBERG: What happened with the men?

TERZIBASHIAN: They were murdered with axes and tossed from the land into the water.

LEHMBERG: Were the women and men really massacred in this way?

TERZIBASHIAN: Only the men were murdered in this way. When it was a little dark, the gendarmes came and sought out the most beautiful women and girls and took them for themselves as wives. A gendarme also came over to me and wanted to make me his wife. Those who did not wish to obey, who did not wish to give in, were pierced with bayonets and their legs torn apart. Even pregnant women had their ribs cut through and the children taken out and thrown away.

According to the transcript there was an "uproar in the courtroom" as Terzibashian raised her hand and said, "I swear to this." Lehmberg responded, "And is all of this really true: Is this not fantasy?" Her reply triggered another wave of commotion: "What I've told is still far less than the reality. It was much worse."

Terzibashian was followed by three "star witnesses": Dr. Johannes Lepsius, a revered humanitarian who had published books on the massacres of the 1890s; General Otto Limon von Sanders, the highest-ranking German military official in Turkey during the war;[1] and Krikoris Balakian, a refugee Armenian bishop who had traveled from Manchester, England, to testify. All three men had known Talat personally, and all three were comfortable in the spotlight.

Lepsius was the greatest Western expert on Armenian culture, history, and, specifically, the Hamidian massacres of twenty-five years earlier. In his reports, essays, and books, Lepsius had made every effort to call the world's attention to the plight of the Armenians in Asia Minor. Like England's William Gladstone, who had been prime minister in the 1880s, Lepsius believed that the Turkish government was a unique criminal enterprise that should be suppressed or removed altogether.

In the spring of 1915, when Lepsius learned what was happening to his Armenian friends in Anatolia, he did what he could to publicize the deportations. The German government quickly stepped in and warned the venerable scholar that as a German citizen, he was barred from disparaging the nation's wartime allies, the Ottoman Turks. For the duration of the conflict, Lepsius remained silent. Now the war was over, and the disgraced Kaiser's government was no longer in power. The Tehlirian trial gave Lepsius an opportunity finally to have his say.

For an Armenophile like Lepsius, making a clear case regarding the deportations and mass killings was not only about exposing what had happened. It was also an attempt to assist in establishing an independent Armenian nation. Yet even as he charged the Turks with destroying the Armenians, Lepsius whitewashed German complicity. In his testimony he was careful to edit himself and suggest by omission that Germany had had no control over the killings:

Approximately one million four hundred thousand Armenians were deported.

What did this deportation mean? In a decree signed by Talat, we find the statement, "The goal of the deportation is nothingness." In line with this order, it was seen to that from the entire population transported southwards from the eastern Anatolian provinces, only around ten percent arrived at the deportation's goal; the remaining ninety percent were murdered in transit or, to the extent that women and girls were not sold by the gendarmes and abducted by Turks and Kurds, killed by hunger and exhaustion. The Armenians were transported to the edge of the desert from western Anatolia, Cilicia, and northern Syria, so that gradually a substantial mass of human beings—in total several hundred thousand—were brought together in concentration camps; they were largely exterminated through systematic starvation and periodic massacres. Namely, as new trains filled up the concentration camps and there was no place left for the mass of people, they were brought to the desert in groups and slaughtered there. Turks have explained that the idea of the concentration camps came from the example of the English with the Boers in South Africa. What is officially declared is that the deportations involved preventive measures; but privately, authoritative persons have indicated with complete openness that the goal was to exterminate the Armenian people.

Lepsius scored points against British brutality as he described the Turkish use of deportations to destroy a population: "Until the present, the Armenians have only been a means to an end in the diplomatic game between England, Russia, and France. As the publication of the German documents will show, Germany has always taken a benevolent and understanding approach in the Armenian question since the Berlin Congress, and in response has been blackened by the entire world as that power behind which all wicked deeds of the sultan and the Turkish government stand."[2]

Lepsius went on to give a short history of Armenian-Turkish relations under the sultan, with specific reference to his fears about secession. (The empire had been losing territory continuously since the early nineteenth century.) Lepsius also talked about Great Power interference in the Ottoman Empire. He ended with the reforms that had been enacted just as World War I broke out:

Two European inspectors general were meant to be responsible for supervising the reforms. It never came to that. War broke out and both reformers were sent home. I was in Constantinople in 1913. During the negotiations, the Young Turks were extremely upset that the Great Powers were again concerned with the question of Armenian reform. And they were doubly embittered when the question was settled in a manner hoped for by the Armenians as a result of the agreement between Germany and Russia. At the time a statement came from the Young Turkish side: "If you Armenians don't keep your hands off the reforms, something will happen in comparison to which Abdul Hamid's massacres were child's play."

Next to take the stand was Lieutenant General Otto Liman von Sanders, who was such a renowned military leader that his very presence in the courtroom made the trial significant. He was also the direct link between Germany's war effort and the Ottoman command. In fact, he had been arrested by the British during the occupation. His first priority at the trial was to clear Germany's name. Two major indictments against the Germans stood. First of all, there were reports that German soldiers had participated in the rounding up and killing of Armenian civilians. Second, since the German government was well aware of the atrocities, and since it was the more powerful partner in the alliance with the Turks, by not stepping in and halting the killings, it was complicit. (In fact, Germany did intercede when doing so served its needs. The ongoing construction of the Berlin–Baghdad railway line underwritten by Deutsche Bank employed many Armenian railroad workers, who were protected.)

More sinister motives could be traced back to before the war, when German theorists considered Anatolia a vast unexploited territory waiting to be cleared of Armenians and other problematic indigenous peoples. With railroads and irrigation, Anatolia could become a fertile breadbasket for Germany. (As in the case of the United States and Africa, railroads were opening up substantial areas for settlement, agriculture, and mining. Indigenous peoples were seen as a problem to be solved.) These expansive theories were a favorite theme of the German philosopher Paul Rohrbach and related to notions made popular by General Friedrich von Bernhardi. Bernhardi had popularized the term *Lebensraum* in his 1911 book *Germany and the Next War,* in which he stated simply, "Without war, inferior or decaying races would easily choke the growth of healthy budding elements and a universal decadence would follow." "Lebensraum," "natural selection," "decaying races"—these were all ideas that German social philosophers subscribed to and would form the foundation of Adolf Hitler's thinking in the coming years.[3]

Liman von Sanders, like most Germans, especially those in the military, had little respect for the Turkish leadership or their armed forces.[4] Like most Europeans, he believed that the Turkish government was essentially corrupt. For Germany, Turkey was a resource to be exploited, inconveniently guarded by a wily old sultan and his retinue of crooked functionaries. It is true that the Kaiser had lavished praise on the Ottomans when visiting Constantinople fifteen years earlier. But for all his speeches about friendship between the countries and his love of Islam, the real relationship between Germany and Turkey was economic, and was secured by military men like Liman von Sanders. The Ottoman Empire was a client state of Germany and, as such, subordinate.

Now that the war had been lost, there was no longer any reason to pretend to admire the people of Turkey or its leaders. Never very happy with his relationship to the Turkish military, especially Enver Pasha, von Sanders was finally free to say what he thought. He took pains to shift any blame for massacres away from Germany and onto Turkey. He told the court:

> In my view, everything that took place in Armenia and that is summarized with the term "Armenian massacre" needs to be separated into two parts. The first part is in my opinion an order of the Young Turk government concerning the Armenian deportations. For this the Young Turk government can be held responsible, for this order *in itself, for the consequences only in part.* But the other part is comprised of the battles that took place in Armenia, because in the first place the Armenians defended themselves vigorously, didn't want to accede to the disarmament ordered by the Turkish government,[5] and because, second, as has been proven beyond any doubt, they partly came out on the side of the Russians against the Turks. This naturally led to battles and, as is commonplace, to mowing down the inferior side. I

believe these are matters that do need to be distinguished from each other. The government ordered the deportation, and indeed in response to both the highest military and civilian authorities, both of which considered the clearance of eastern Anatolia to be necessary on military grounds.

Liman von Sanders circumvented the unasked questions: Why didn't you stop the deportations when you understood that they were homicidal? In what way did German artillery abet the destruction of Armenian strongholds? And why was Talat, an exile convicted of war crimes, granted safe haven in Germany?

Liman von Sanders denied vehemently that any German soldiers had committed atrocities. He expanded on this theme:

> I would like to emphasize that the army leaders and commanding generals in the Caucasus were always Turks, because so much that is false and incorrect in this question [of guilt] has been asserted against the Germans. These army leaders and the civil authorities reported to Constantinople precisely what I have said previously, and the execution of the deportation order that was issued then fell into the worst conceivable hands!...Concerning ourselves, I can say — because as Herr Dr. Lepsius has been kind enough to point out, we have been subjected to boundless suspicion — that no German officer ever participated in a measure against the Armenians. To the contrary, we intervened when we could.

While Liman von Sanders defended Germany, he condemned Turkey. Of course, this is exactly what Tehlirian's defense attorneys wanted. The general's testimony established (1) that the government of Turkey had planned and executed the destruction of Armenian civilians, and (2) that there were dedicated death squads (the Special Organization) that had been directed by the Committee of Union and Progress (and Talat) to commit the most horrific atrocities.

Recently opened East German archives indicate, however, that

German officers actually were involved with the Turks, in a way that modern statecraft might describe as "counterinsurgency." The Germans assisted the Turkish army in destroying Armenian "strongholds" with Krupp heavy artillery. These operations focused on leveling Armenian neighborhoods and towns. The German leadership decided to ignore the deportations, despite their brutality. If the Turks wanted the Armenians out of the way, the Germans would not interfere.

Although Germany's leaders denied responsibility for assisting the Young Turks in their destruction of the Armenians, new evidence proves otherwise, and the parallels between the murder of one million Armenians and six million Jews thirty years later are numerous. Two ancient peoples, primarily identified by their religion, were methodically exterminated in what would be defined as "genocide." Though Raphael Lemkin was responding to the Jewish Holocaust when he coined the term in 1943, he specifically cited the destruction of the Armenians as a prime example. In fact, Lemkin had carefully followed Tehlirian's Berlin trial of 1921 and pondered the ethical dilemma created by Tehlirian's actions.[6]

There is no doubt that many Germans were familiar with what had occurred in Asia Minor. It is probable that hundreds of German soldiers who served in the Ottoman Empire during World War I went on to become Schutzstaffel or "SS" officers in Nazi Germany. In fact, Germany had set a precedent for deportation massacre earlier in the century in German South-West Africa (Namibia), where General Lothar von Trotha successfully pursued an eradication of the Herero by forcing the defenseless indigenous people into the desert, where they died. In addition, one of Hitler's closest friends, Max von Scheubner-Richter, had been a German officer in Turkey during World War I. He had also served as vice consul in Erzurum, placing him in the center of the action. Scheubner-Richter witnessed and later wrote about the attacks against the Armenians.[7] In fact, he was subpoenaed to appear at Tehlirian's trial but was not called to testify. If Hitler somehow missed the news of Tehlirian's trial in Berlin, certainly Scheubner-Richter, as a veteran who served in Ottoman territories, must have discussed the war with him. How close was Max von Scheubner-Richter to Adolf Hitler? Scheubner-Richter would be shot and killed, his arm linked through Hitler's, on the night of the 1923 Beer Hall Putsch.[8]

As National Socialism found its footing in Germany, the Committee of Union and Progress in Turkey, the Ittihad, stood as an example of what could and could not be accomplished within a modern "constitutional" government. An autocratic and clandestine political faction, the CUP had muscled its way into power. While stoking the furnaces of nationalism, this secretive cabal had arrested its detractors and murdered its foes. Having gained control of the government, these Young Turks liquidated a large and successful minority group and stole their assets. Adolph Hitler has been quoted as declaring, "Who remembers the Armenians?"[9] He was saying that there would be no significant reaction to an attack on Jewry in Europe because there had been no real punitive consequences following the destruction of the Armenians.

There are many parallels between the modus operandi of the Nazis and that of the Ittihad. First of all, though the CUP and the Nazis were supposedly political parties, both were born as underground organizations, and by the time they had consolidated their power, both "parties" were illegal by any definition of the term. The Nazis, like the Ittihadists, were nationalists who built their philosophy upon a foundation of myth and pseudoscience. Both were convinced that the minorities in their country were akin to an "infection" that was contaminating the body of the nation. The alleged "decadent" nature of the minority was contrasted with the purity and wholesomeness of the pureblooded majority.[10]

Both the Ittihad and the Nazis employed deception to eject victim populations easily from their villages and towns, telling them that they were being "moved." Once dislocated from the familiarity and safety of their home region, they became disoriented and more vulnerable to the killing machine. Both the Nazis and the Ittihad enslaved their minority victims. Both performed medical experiments on their victims.[11] And in both cases, it was religion that identified the target group. (In a sad irony, male circumcision was proof of faith. The majority Muslims on the one hand and the minority Jews on the other underwent ritual circumcision, unlike their neighbors, the Christian Armenians and Germans. So in Turkey, if you were circumcised, you might survive. In Germany, if you were circumcised, you were condemned.)

Despite the fact that both genocides were couched in theory, both the CUP and the Nazis used concrete and nontheoretical methods. Property belonging to the murdered minority populations was confiscated. It is well documented that the Nazi regime subsidized itself with money, art, and factories stolen from wealthy Jews. Likewise, the Ittihad stole land, businesses, and property from wealthy Armenians all over the empire.[12] According to Ittihad economic theory, these "Turkified" properties would provide the basis for a Turkish middle class, which in turn would lead the country to its destiny as a homogeneous Turkic nation.[13] The stolen wealth was also used to pay for the deportations and concentration camps themselves. When genocide is on the agenda, "leaders, planners, and killers need the sight of gold as well as the smell of ink."[14]

The Ittihad and the Nazis both took advantage of the latest technologies to intensify the killing. Mass media propaganda prepared the general population for the violence against the hapless civilians, convincing the average German or Turk that Jews or Armenians were wrongdoers if not actually evil. The telegraph sped up orders to the territories, increasing the element of surprise. (Talat had worked as a telegrapher before undertaking his political career. He had a personal telegraph installed in his home.[15]) In both the Ottoman Empire and the Third Reich, railroads (cattle cars specifically) were used to move large numbers of the condemned quickly and efficiently.

The Ittihad and the Nazis alike set out to "solve" a problem by exterminating a people who had lived peacefully within their borders for centuries. In both cases, it is possible that an original plan that called for ethnic evacuation (through deportation) devolved into mass murder. In both cases, "room" was being made for the majority populations. For example, Balkan refugees were settled in emptied Armenian villages; years later, Baltic Germans were moved to Poland to replace the Jews who had been forced from their homes.

It is not a coincidence that Heinrich Himmler, head of the Nazi SS and so directly in charge of the Holocaust, was made minister of the interior in 1943. Talat's official designation as a leader of the Ottoman Empire was also minister of the interior (until he took over the job of Grand Vizier in 1917). "Population control," as it was euphemistically called in both countries, was the responsibility of the Interior Ministry.

There were great differences, of course, between the two tragedies. Armenians were forced out of an ancestral homeland that existed within the borders of the Ottoman Empire, while the Nazi attempt at the total destruction of the Jews extended far beyond Germany's borders. Some Armenian political groups were seeking to establish an autonomous Armenian region, whereas it was beyond anyone's imagination that a Jewish state could rise within the borders of Germany. Still, the parallels stand. And the fact remains that methods for removing a population group were developed and refined by both the Ottomans and the Germans. Not only in its execution but in its theory and economics as well, the Armenian Genocide was instructive for prosecutors of the Jewish Holocaust.[16]

Expert testimony at Tehlirian's trial came from Armenians as well as Germans. The Reverend Krikoris Balakian was a worldly, educated Armenian cleric who had been living in Constantinople when he was arrested on the evening of April 24, 1915, along with hundreds of other members of the Armenian elite. Unlike the majority of his peers, Balakian survived.[17] And unlike Lepsius and Ambassador Henry Morgenthau, Balakian was an eyewitness to the atrocities, going so far as to interview Turkish soldiers during his own deportation. The soldiers freely described atrocities to Balakian because they didn't believe he would live to repeat what they had told him. Finally, Balakian knew Talat personally. For all of these reasons, he was an invaluable witness and was able to put the big picture together. Balakian described his time in a deportation caravan:

> Between Yozgat and Boghazlian alone, forty-three thousand Armenians were cut down, with children and women. We also were afraid we were going to be killed. Because although the official name was "deportation," what was really involved was a policy of organized extermination. But since we had money, together around fifteen thousand to sixteen thousand pounds in gold, we thought that in line with the general custom in the Orient of obtaining everything with "baksheesh," we could use it to save our lives. We hoped that with gold we could accomplish everything we could not accomplish otherwise. We were not mistaken. If I'm here alive today, it's because of baksheesh.
>
> When we came to Yozgat, which was the bloodiest place, we saw nearby, four hours away in a valley, a couple of hundred heads with long hair, which is to say heads of women and girls. A gendarmerie captain named Shukri was with us—he had led us. (We were around forty-eight men, and with us were perhaps sixteen gendarmes on horseback.) I asked the captain: I had heard that the Armenian *men* were being killed, *but not the women and girls*. Well, he answered, if we only kill men and not women and girls as well, then in fifty years there are again a few million Armenians. So we have to also kill women and children, so that there is no internal or external disorder forever.

Balakian, because of his status as a member of the elite, had greater freedom than most in the caravan and was allowed to have conversations with the soldiers guarding the deportees.

> The captain explained very simply, "We killed everyone, but not in the city." That was forbidden, because in eighteen ninety-five to ninety-six, Abdul Hamid had ordered

everyone in the city killed. The European nations learned about this, the entire civilized world, and did not want to allow this. So now no person was to remain, so that no one would appear as a witness in court.

"I can tell you about all of this because you're going into the desert and are going to die from hunger there and have no opportunity to bring this truth to light." He now gave us details. First of all, fourteen thousand men were taken out of the city of Yozgat and environs and killed in the valleys. The remaining families of those killed were told the men had arrived safely in Aleppo, they were doing well there, and they had asked the government to allow the families to join them. The government had allowed this, they were told, and also their taking all their movable property with them. The families would find apartments ready for them there. The families then packed everything up—their gold and silver items, their jewelry, carpets—they took all their movable property with them. The very same captain who dragged away the caravan told me about this. He himself, he explained, had had forty thousand Armenians killed between Yozgat and Boghazlian, as the gendarmerie commander. So the women now believed their husbands were living and they made preparations to join them. There were around eight hundred and forty wagons, including around three hundred and eighty ox carts, the rest being drawn by horses. Many women and children had to go on foot. A total of some sixty-four hundred women and children marched off to Aleppo.

I now asked the captain, "Why did you do this?" Then he said, "If we had killed the women and children in the cities, then we wouldn't have known where the valuables were being kept, whether they were buried in the ground or had been destroyed somewhere. For this reason we 'allowed' them to take all their jewelry with them. When we had moved forward another four hours," the captain continued his account, "we came to a valley which had three watermills. We had around twenty-five to thirty Turkish women with us." They now began to examine the clothing of the Armenian women and girls and take away their jewelry and gold things. Because there were so many women and girls, around sixty-four hundred, this examination took the Turkish women around four days.

When the examination was finished, the captain told the Armenian women a new order had come from the government, a "pardon": the women had permission to return to their homes.

Namely, on the way back, around an hour's distance, there was a great plain. The wagons and drivers had been sent back earlier. The women asked why. They were told that since the pardon had come allowing them to return, they of course no longer needed any wagons, since Yozgat was only four hours away.

(The captain himself told me this. He didn't speak like I am doing here, one thing after the other; rather, I always had to ask him in order to get an answer. My thought was that maybe I could use what I heard.)

Now, when the women tried to return to Yozgat on account of the "pardon," many gendarmes were sent into the provincial villages, and the peasants were invited to participate in a holy war. Around twelve or thirteen thousand peasants came with axes for chopping wood and other iron implements. They were allowed to kill everyone and take only the most beautiful girls.

Balakian specifically addressed Talat Pasha's guilt:

I am a member of the synod of the Armenian Patriarchate of Constantinople and for a long time have had many opportunities to become familiar with Turkish circumstances. I naturally also knew Talat personally. He had great influence.

He did everything in full awareness. When we wanted something from the Armenian Patriarchate, he would tell us, "You don't need to go first to the other ministers; just come straightaway to me. You don't need to put things in writing; you can explain everything to me personally and I'll take care of it!" He acted as if he had full responsibility and had no need to give anyone an accounting.

At another point in his testimony Balakian stated unequivocally about an incriminating telegram, "The telegram was signed 'Talat.' I saw it with my own eyes." At this point in the interrogation, other damning telegrams collected at the end of the war by Aram Andonian were introduced. A debate ensued as to whether the telegrams should be admitted as evidence. Defense attorney von Gordon made his case:

> But I must state what the wires contain. The wires are meant to demonstrate that Talat personally gave the order in these five wires to seize all Armenians, including Armenian children. Initially the order was given to keep alive only those children who were not in a position to remember what happened to their parents. Later, in March 1916, the order was narrowed, so that all those in orphanages were to be removed and exterminated because, after all, only elements damaging to Turkey would come from these children. The witness Andonian will be able to testify concerning the authenticity of these wires: he received these wires directly at the sub-directorate, which was made accessible to the Armenian delegation after occupation by the British. I personally consider it possible, even probable, and hope that the jury members believe the defendant in his insistence that he for his part was firmly and not without good reason convinced—not superficially but deep within his heart—that Talat was the author of these fearful

atrocities against the Armenians and is responsible for them.
I can waive presenting a motion to submit evidence only if
you become convinced of this.

The district attorney was tired of the lecturing on the part of
the defense. He addressed the judge:

I request that such a motion be denied. In a very extensive
manner, Your Honor has already allowed a discussion of
whether or not Talat is guilty of the Armenian atrocities.
But this question is entirely extraneous. For in my view
there can be no doubt that the defendant was of the opinion
that in Talat, the man bearing the guilt for these atrocities
stood before him. This fully explains his motive. I also
believe that clarifying the question of Talat's guilt is completely out of the question in this courtroom. For a historical judgment would have to be made, then, that requires
entirely different material from what is available here.

As the Tashnags had hoped, the trial of Tehlirian had become
the trial of Talat Pasha.

After the VIPs testified, five doctors and psychiatrists, including
those who had cared for Tehlirian before his arrest, took the stand.
They reported on his symptoms (fainting spells, nightmares) and
offered their theories. They attempted to define the term "epilepsy." Their testimony would determine from a medical perspective whether or not Tehlirian was in his right mind when he pulled
the trigger. According to a Dr. Stormer:

He was never seriously ill until nineteen fifteen, when he
was a witness to the massacre that has already been suffi-
ciently discussed today. In a deeply emotional way, he told
me that both his parents and all his brothers and sisters were

killed. Shuddering with terrible fear, he recalled the moment in which he saw the ax of a Turk descend on his brother's head and split it in two. He himself received injuries in the event, a head wound that is not serious but nevertheless is there, and injuries to his left arm and knee. The horrible impression of these murderous deeds, combined with the physical injuries and exertion, robbed him of consciousness. He was unconscious for three days and finally woke up covered with corpses and awakened by the intense corpse stench that has stamped him for all eternity and has gained a firm foothold in the organs of his soul. He says that whenever he reads of horrifying events, and above all when he recalls the massacre, the smell of the corpses repeatedly penetrates his olfactory organ—and in such a way that it is of decisive importance since he cannot get rid of it.

The doctors determined that Tehlirian's illness was not a figment of his imagination. The symptoms followed a pattern: subsequent to feeling weak and seconds before fainting, Tehlirian always smelled blood. There was no reason to doubt that he had had these experiences. People who had seen him fall into one of the seizures later reported that his whole body would tremble. He would then lose consciousness. Upon awakening, he would feel pain in his legs and arms. Exhausted, he would become very thirsty and eventually fall into a deep sleep. (Such symptoms could be typical of epilepsy.)

The doctors who had examined Tehlirian also found scars all over his body. He told them that the Turks had attacked him physically, and the wounds seemed to be definitive proof that he had in fact been attacked while a hostage in the caravan. The possibility that he might have received the wounds in another way—for instance, as a soldier in battle—was never brought up during the testimony.

Every single person in that courtroom knew that the war had brought with it horrors never before experienced. Over fifty percent of the soldiers serving in "the war to end all wars" were either killed or wounded. There had been World War I battlefields with casualties numbering in the hundreds of thousands. World War I veterans had been subject to types of warfare so terrible that these weapons would soon be outlawed. Poison gas alone left hundreds of thousands of men with severe facial scars, blindness, and respiratory problems that plagued them for the rest of their lives. Most had been exposed to the nonstop rattle of machine gun fire and bursting bombs, to grenade and mine shrapnel. Some had endured starvation or survived bouts of cholera or typhus. Young men returned home wrecked and stupefied from witnessing the massive carnage. A syndrome never before identified was added to the list of war injuries. It was called "shell shock."

By 1921, the science of the mind had captured the imagination of the medical world. This was the era of Freud. One year earlier, in February 1920, the Berlin Psychoanalytic Institute had been founded, and the idea that actions could be motivated by subconscious forces was gaining favor. Within this context, Tehlirian presented a fascinating case to the doctors tasked with examining him. Here was a man who had suffered trauma during a violent episode and apparently committed murder five years later as a result of that trauma. The vivid dreams in which his mother commanded him to kill added another layer of complexity for analysis. In addition, the five doctors who testified were taking the stand publicly; their reputations were at stake. For a few days, all eyes were on them, forcing them to defend their pet psychological theories. Each doctor felt obliged to weigh in with a lengthy and verbose analysis of the symptoms and what those symptoms might indicate.

The debate in the courtroom boiled down to determining exactly what level of "free will" Tehlirian possessed at the moment when he pulled the trigger and killed Talat. Was it possible that his epileptic fits could create a kind of insanity that would force him to do things against his will? Also, what about these "appearances" by his mother? Did he really believe she was actually standing there before him? When asked if he believed his mother was viscerally present, Tehlirian answered yes, adding another piece to the jigsaw puzzle of his mental illness. Doctors offered the theory of the "compulsive precept," defined as an overwhelming psychological compulsion that had grown out of the shock of the experience of seeing his family murdered (which in fact had never happened).

The consensus view was that Tehlirian had been traumatized by the experiences he claimed to have had in Anatolia. The verdict from a medical perspective was clear: the Turks had done terrible things to Tehlirian, he was psychologically damaged, and his condition had contributed to his murderous impulse. In sum, the doctors gave Tehlirian's defenders exactly what they were looking for.

In the end, the judge and jury being completely ignorant of Operation Nemesis, there was only one verdict they could hand down. In under two hours, the verdict was arrived at: "not guilty." At first Tehlirian didn't understand what was being said. He turned to Vaza, his co-conspirator and translator: "What does that mean?"

"It means you're free."

People in the courtroom applauded. Women rushed toward Tehlirian with bouquets of flowers. Zakarian moved Tehlirian out of the courtroom through the back and into a waiting car, requesting that no pictures be taken. He knew that from this day on, Tehlirian would be a target. No reason to give his hunters any more ammunition than they already had.[18]

In the words of a *New York Times* headline, "They Simply Had To Let Him Go." The opinion piece that followed was prescient: "The court before which the case was tried practically has given, not only to this young man, but to the many others like him and with like grievances, a license to kill at discretion any Turkish official whom they can find in Germany." The *Times* writer criticized the jury's decision, calling it "a queer view of moral rightness [that] opens the way to other assassinations less easily excusable than his or not excusable at all." Yet, the editorialist added, "what other verdict was possible?" The whole logic of the court was explained: "An acquittal on the ground of insanity, the usual device of jurors who do not want to punish a killing of which they approve, would have been more than ordinarily absurd in the case of a man as obviously sane as this Armenian is, and to have hanged him, or even to have sent him to prison, would have been intolerably to overlook his provocation." The commentator puts it in a nutshell: "The dilemma cannot be escaped—all assassins should be punished, this assassin should not be punished. And there you are! The solution lies further back and long ago, when German officers in Turkey permitted the massacres of Armenians, though they had the power to prevent them."[19]

The *Times* never returned to the theory, outlined only days after Tehlirian's arrest in March, that he might be a member of a revolutionary organization. There is no further mention of skepticism on the part of the authorities. The writer does not return to the loose threads the *Times* itself had tugged on earlier, such as Tehlirian's Paris passport and visa stamped in Geneva or the large amount of money he had in his possession.

If the authorities themselves had had any such suspicions, they were never raised in court. The ARF was not mentioned once during the proceedings. Tehlirian was never asked if he was a member of a revolutionary group or an assassination squad or even if he had received assistance from others. Vague references were made to the money that had been found on him after his arrest, his visit to Geneva, his knowledge of political events. Nothing more was ever asked of him in court.

Having been acquitted,[20] Tehlirian was set free in early June 1921. The Turkish expatriates living in Berlin were outraged. The Turkish nationalist newspaper *Yeni Gun* eulogized Talat: "Our great patriot has died for his country.... We salute his fresh tomb and bow low to kiss his eyes. Talat was a political giant. Talat was a genius. History will prove his immense stature and will make of him a martyr and an apostle.... Talat will remain the greatest man that Turkey has produced."[21] Talat's widow, Hayriye Talat Bafrali, requested an appeal but was refused. The acquittal stood.

In hindsight, given the new barbarity that would soon blanket Europe, defense attorney Adolf von Gordon's last words at the trial are ironic: "I should be far from passing a final judgment on Talat the man. What can be said objectively I said at the start. But I do wish to state one more thing: like many of his comrades, he certainly worked for the extermination of the Armenian people in order to create a purely pan-Turkish state; he certainly here used means that seem intolerable to us Europeans."

PART III

CHAPTER NINE

The Work Continues

Our organization had no extermination plan. It inflicted punishment on individuals who had been tried in absentia and found guilty of mass murder.

—Arshavir Shiragian

Within three years of its founding, the Nemesis conspiracy located and killed seven high-level Ittihadists and their confederates (Djemal Azmi, Said Halim Pasha, Khan Javanshir, Djemal Pasha, Khan Khoyski, Behaeddin Shakir, and Talat Pasha). At least ten armed assassins carried out the executions. (In addition to Tehlirian, the list includes Bedros Der Boghosian, Stepan Dzaghigian, Yervant Fundukian, Haroutiun Haroutiunian, Artashes Kevorkian, Misak Kirakosyan, Arshavir Shiragian, Misak Torlakian, and Aram Yerganian.) Another dozen lookouts, spies, and organizers assisted. In addition, diplomats and other behind-the-scenes personnel provided intelligence and funds. The Nemesis conspiracy operated in seven countries across three continents.

Tehlirian was deported to Turkey after his acquittal in order to prevent any "further investigations which otherwise would have been realized similar to those against Young Turk leaders in absentia." The twenty-five-year-old assassin was sent to Turkey via Serbia, where "Tehlirian could escape."[1] Jacques Derogy, who had access to secret ARF archives, reports that Tehlirian then traveled to Manchester, England, with Bishop Krikoris Balakian (one of the star witnesses at the trial), making it almost impossible for Turkish agents to find him. A few months later, Tehlirian crossed the Atlantic for a victory lap of Armenian communities in the United States. Everywhere he went, grateful Tashnags embraced him and kissed his hands. Small babies were placed in his arms, as if physical contact with this saint would bless their lives.[2]

Though Nemesis had more "work" to do in Europe, Armen Garo and Shahan Natali decided to retire their champion. The operation had succeeded beyond their wildest hopes. All over the world Tehlirian was now hailed as a sympathetic hero even by non-Armenians. To quote the *Philadelphia Inquirer*: "The verdict of the Berlin jury which acquitted the slayer of Talaat Pasha must be approved and even applauded as an act of substantial justice."[3] The Tashnag conspirators saw no reason to disturb that image. Preserving the myth of the lone gunman was also a pragmatic decision. The leadership couldn't risk Tehlirian's getting caught in another assassination attempt. Such an arrest would undermine his story and endanger other agents in the field. The effectiveness of Nemesis depended on the greater truth remaining hidden.

Within a year of his acquittal, Tehlirian returned to Serbia, where he married Anahid. In 1924 the young couple, accompanied by Anahid's sister Araxie, traveled to Paris for a vacation. Photos reveal a relaxed and happy man, apparently at peace with himself. Soghomon could finally rest. He had honored his family and killed "the monster." Despite the fact that Tehlirian had answered in the negative when Judge Lehmberg asked if he felt that he had participated in an act of revenge, he had found a kind of resolution, and he could now go on and live his life.

Tehlirian settled in Valjevo, Serbia, joining his father and uncles

in their wholesale coffee business. He changed his name to Soghomon Melikian and fathered two children with Anahid. Protected
by the Serbian Christian community, Tehlirian enrolled in the local
gun club, where he would occasionally take target practice with the
chief of police. Here his mild manner manifested itself. Though
Tehlirian was reputed to be a very good shot, he refused to join
hunting parties. He could not kill another living thing.

After World War II, Turkish agents continued their search for
Tehlirian in Marshal Tito's Yugoslavia, forcing him to emigrate to
Morocco with Anahid and his two sons, Shahen and Zaven. Perhaps
because of rising antipathy toward non-Muslims in Islamic countries
in the mid-fifties, the Tehlirians did not linger in Morocco. With a
final move to San Francisco in 1957, Tehlirian lived out the rest of
his days peacefully as "Saro Melikian," working for George Mardikian, the famous Armenian restaurateur who had "come over" in
1922. Mardikian was the nephew of an important Armenian revolutionary who had fought with Generals Antranig and Drastamat
Kanayan, better known as General Dro. Awarded the Medal of
Honor by President Harry Truman after World War II, George
Mardikian was happy to sponsor and protect "the Armenian eagle."

Despite Tehlirian's retirement, the "work" continued. Within
weeks of his acquittal, the Nemesis commandos resumed their
hunt and by late summer 1921 were in full pursuit of former Ittihad
leaders in Rome. Six or seven men, utilizing only a minimal but
sufficient support structure, hung out in coffee shops and tracked
the likes of Dr. Nazim and Enver Pasha, both of whom continued
to prove elusive. Shahan Natali crisscrossed Europe, as Aaron
Sachaklian in Syracuse, New York, continued to collect and disperse
funds, all the while maintaining the absolute secrecy that ensured
the survival of Nemesis.[4]

With the success of the Berlin operation, Tashnag leaders in
Boston and Constantinople lobbied their superiors to continue the
work of Nemesis on several fronts simultaneously. The Special Fund
had been fattened with contributions to Tehlirian's defense. These
donations included money from some of the most conservative

leaders in the Armenian diaspora, like Boghos Nubar, founder of the Armenian General Benevolent Union, a very non-Tashnag operation. Nubar was at the time living in Paris, where he and Avedis Aharonian jockeyed for participation at the peace conference. He also had known these CUP leaders personally, yet apparently had no reservations about sponsoring their demise.

As the defense funds were redirected, Armen Garo crowed, "Money is no problem." He instructed Sachaklian in Boston to continue to forward money directly to Natali in Paris, adding, "What is left over [from the defense of Tehlirian] will in fact be used to continue the work, but without the committee knowing."[5] The "committee" Garo was referring to was the "Body Responsible Abroad" or ABM (Ardasahmani Badaskhanadu Marmin), the Tashnag board that oversaw all of the ARF's affairs at the highest level. It was the final arbiter of the *Hadug Marmin,* or Special Corps, that is, the Nemesis operation.

The ABM suspected that Garo and Natali were acting independently of their oversight, so they clarified their instructions: "The money collected must be used for the purpose for which it was collected."[6] The ARF were demanding that any surplus funds be returned to the organization. Garo and Natali wanted to use this surplus to continue the pursuit of former Ittihadists.

The schism between Garo and Natali and the rest of the Tashnag leadership had deepened, and there was a clear disagreement as to how far this revenge conspiracy against the former CUP leadership should proceed. By the mid-1920s, the ABM felt that the primary mission had been accomplished and wanted Nemesis shut down.[7] (The ABM was even exploring an anti-Soviet pact with Turkey.)[8] Natali was livid. He believed that the "work" had only begun. But revenge was far from the minds of the Armenian leadership. While Nemesis was intent on assassinating Turkish leaders, the first Republic of Armenia was quickly becoming a historical footnote as the Soviets and Kemalist forces from Turkey surrounded and closed in on the tiny mountain nation.

Kemal had forced the British, in particular, to make a crucial decision: either give up on the Wilsonian notion of a partitioned postwar Turkey or commit to full-scale war with no end in sight. The seasoned general understood that the Allies had lost their taste for battle, while his men, though exhausted, would continue to fight for survival. There was no way of knowing what the consequences would be if a Wilsonian mandate or a Treaty of Sèvres could be effected. Kemal sensed that the British would jump at any excuse to abandon the front. On the other side of the border, Yerevan was teeming with starving, disease-ridden Armenian refugees and orphans. Thousands upon thousands were dying of hunger and typhus. It was in that context that Operation Nemesis continued its "work."

Khan Javanshir (Constantinople, July 18, 1921)

A few weeks after Tehlirian was acquitted, Misak Torlakian, assisted by Haroutiun Haroutiunian and Yervant Fundukian, gunned down Behbud Khan Javanshir outside the Pera Palace Hotel in Constantinople. Javanshir was the former Azerbaijani internal affairs minister in Baku. Because of the massive oil reserves there, Baku in Azerbaijan was a vital strategic city within the Russian Empire. Pan-Turanist Turks saw Azerbaijan as an extension of a potential Turkish empire, one that could extend eastward all the way to China. Javanshir was aligned with the Young Turks in this respect.

The Armenians of Baku had traditionally been the businessmen who traded in petroleum products. (Before oil was used for internal combustion engines, it was in demand for lamps and machine lubrication.) In this role they constituted a significant segment of the middle class and as such were the focus of Muslim resentment. The Soviets, to the degree that they had any ability to control the city, tried to suppress the constant Muslim-Armenian feuding, but in March of 1918, harsh fighting broke out. Atrocities were committed in Baku against the Muslim population.[9] Then in September 1918, as Enver Pasha's "Army of Islam" invaded the city, the local Azerbaijanis meted out payback to the Christian Armenians of Baku. Some ten to thirty thousand ethnic Armenians died in the violence. The Tashnags blamed Javanshir, who had been minister of internal affairs at the time, for the massacres. After the Soviets locked down Azerbaijan, Javanshir escaped Baku, moving to Constantinople, where he hoped to enjoy the protection of British occupation. The Tashnags knew he was residing in the Pera district of Constantinople and approved the hit.

Misak Torlakian was more experienced with firearms and combat than Tehlirian; in fact, he was given his first pistol when he was twelve years old. He had been a gunrunner for the Tashnags, a reconnaissance scout with the Russian army, and under General Dro had fought in the final battles to save Armenia. Like Tehlirian, he had returned to his home village to find it depopulated. Nearly everyone in his family had been murdered. The only survivor was a sister who had been taken by a Muslim as his wife. Like Tehlirian, Torlakian sought to avenge his family, and the Tashnags recruited him in Constantinople.

On July 18, 1921, Khan Javanshir was gunned down as he returned to his suite at the luxurious Pera Palace after seeing a show at the Petit Champ theater. Torlakian and his cohorts had spent hours lying in wait for Javanshir and his entourage in a nearby garden bistro, and when Javanshir appeared, Torlakian charged up to him and fired. Wounded, Javanshir grabbed Torlakian's wrist. The twenty-nine-year-old assassin fired two more rounds into his victim's chest. Javanshir fell to the ground with a groan. Chaos broke out on the crowded street, allowing Torlakian to slip away, but upon hearing the moans of the wounded Javanshir, he ran back and shot the Azerbaijani point-blank in the head.

French military police quickly arrived on the scene and arrested Torlakian. He was beaten into unconsciousness and awoke the next day locked in a cell, facing trial for murder in occupied Constantinople. Under instructions from his handlers, he commenced to feign the same symptoms of "epilepsy" that had worked so well for Tehlirian. He made sure that his fellow inmates saw him collapse and foam at the mouth. Like Tehlirian, he contrived a story about witnessing firsthand the slaughter of his family. (In his fictional narrative, Torlakian moved the location of his family's demise from Trebizond on the Black Sea to Baku, thus giving him a motivation to seek Javanshir's death.) In late August, only months after Tehlirian's acquittal, Torlakian was brought before a British tribunal arranged by the occupying government. His defense team exploited the intense British antipathy toward the Turkish.

This trial, like Tehlirian's in Berlin, was embraced by the Tashnags as a way to publicize Muslim atrocities, particularly the attacks on the Armenians of Baku. The Azerbaijanis, perhaps alert to what had transpired at the Berlin trial, summoned their own witnesses, who testified in court that the Armenians had committed atrocities against them first (in March of 1918) and that from their perspective the Armenians were exaggerating the Baku massacres of September 1918. The trial devolved into a he said/she said tug-of-war, with no clear resolution. Unlike the proceedings in Berlin, this trial operated under the auspices of an occupying military force, in a major Middle Eastern capital. Javanshir was unknown outside Turkey and Azerbaijan. No supporting testimony was provided by the likes of a Professor Lepsius or a General Liman von Sanders, and the international press showed little interest. Yet once again the focus of the trial was shifted from a political murder to a public forum on violence against Armenians.

As in the Tehlirian trial, a slew of doctors and fellow inmates testified to the accused's mental instability and fainting spells, and raised various theories as to whether such a person could act rationally and commit cold-blooded murder while under the influence of a psychological disease. Torlakian testified on his own behalf that in 1918, in Baku, when the massacres began, he had been confined to bed after having been shot on the street. He explained that while he lay in his room fading in and out of consciousness, Muslim paramilitaries had entered his apartment and murdered his entire family. When confronted with his own crime, he stated, "My conscience is completely at peace."[10]

In November 1921 the British tribunal found Torlakian guilty of murder but "unconscious and not responsible." He was released to the Armenian patriarch in Constantinople and a few days later boarded a steamer headed for Greece. The trial had barely touched on whether or not Torlakian had committed first-degree murder. In this way the Tashnags effectively made use of the defense strategy from Tehlirian's Berlin trial.[11]

Said Halim Pasha (Rome, December 5, 1921)

Nemesis struck again late that fall in Rome, a mere month after Torlakian's acquittal. Said Halim Pasha, the grandson of Egyptian leader Muhammad Ali and the acting Ottoman Grand Vizier throughout most of the war, was assassinated as he emerged from a horse-drawn coach only a few blocks from the Borghese Gardens. The killer was Arshavir Shiragian, only twenty-one years old, born and bred in Constantinople. Shiragian, like Tehlirian, was an experienced killer, having already carried out the Nemesis assassination of an Armenian collaborator named Vahe Ihsan (Yesayan), a man who had provided Turkish police with the names and locations of activists, and who, according to Shiragian, had a role in the April 24 arrests. In that killing, Shiragian had been assisted by Arshag Yezdanian, a veteran assassin who, on his own, had gunned down another "traitor," Hmayag Aramiantz.

Shiragian was the most dynamic of the Nemesis operatives. Barely a teenager when the war broke out, he was an active member of the underground resistance effort in Constantinople. Shiragian's boyishness was a useful cover as he moved weapons and fugitives from one clandestine location to the next in the wartime city. His family home was often used to hide young men from the relentless search for army recruits by the police. These young Armenian fugitives were the so-called "Army of the Attics."

In all the Armenian districts of Constantinople, the attics, the cellars, the spaces between outer and inner walls, the deep storage closets, and the indoor wells became hiding places; it was a kind of subterranean world, inhabited by thousands, into which the Turkish police, guided by damned Armenian traitors, would at times penetrate. Then the people in hiding—as well as the people who had offered them shelter—would be dragged off to jail, and there would be tortured and killed, or else they would be sent into the interior to become victims of the massacre that was in progress.[12]

During the war, many Armenians led desperate and frightened lives, and were careful to keep their heads down. But some Tashnags, like Shiragian, a born fighter who took delight in clashing with the police and their allies, relished the conflict. Where Tehlirian was sickly, Shiragian was robust. Where Tehlirian was hesitant, Shiragian was cocksure. Shiragian had no experience as a soldier, but he was a good shot and was comfortable around firearms. Also, he was well known to the Tashnag leadership. Years of experience outwitting the police while running weapons and fugitives had made him a wily asset in the Tashnag camp. When the possibility was discussed among Tashnag inner circles of an operation to assassinate former Ittihad leaders, Shiragian was one of the first to volunteer. The Tashnag bosses were reluctant to give such an important job to someone so young, but after several fruitless attempts on the life of Vahe Ihsan, Shiragian was given the order to stalk and kill the former policeman.

In his autobiography *The Legacy*, Shiragian describes shooting the informant Ihsan:

My second bullet got Ihsan in the arm. When he realized that he would not be able to use his gun, he started to run. I fired two more bullets after him as I chased him. There was quite a commotion in the street. Pedestrians were screaming and trying to take cover, and from nearby windows people were throwing things at me—flowerpots, shoes, anything. But no one dared to get in my way or grab me.

Ihsan fell; his head struck a stone. My third and fourth bullets had hit him, but he didn't seem human. He was still alive. He got to his knees and tried to stand. We were both being struck by the various objects which people were throwing at us from the shelter of their homes. Taking advantage of the confusion, Ihsan managed to get his revolver out of his pocket. He started to take aim. I jumped on him and fired my last two bullets into his head. Then I started to run away. But I couldn't leave. I had to turn back to make certain that he had stopped breathing. In my nervousness and because of my inexperience, I had done a sloppy job. His skull was shattered and his brains had splattered on the stones.[13]

Over the next few years, Shiragian would develop a more elegant killing technique.

Shiragian was later identified by Ihsan's bodyguard (who had run off when the shooting started), and a warrant was issued for the young man's arrest. Meanwhile, the "organization" gave him a new assignment: Find Enver Pasha and kill him. He was provided with a false alias and a "Nansen" passport (passports issued after World War I by the newly formed League of Nations, providing stateless refugees a means to travel). Strapping a Russian-made revolver to his leg, Shiragian was smuggled onto a Black Sea steamer heading for the Crimea, where the civil war between the Red and White Russian armies continued to rage. From there, he crossed into the newborn Republic of Armenia. From Armenia, he planned to sneak into Azerbaijan via Georgia, on the trail of Enver Pasha.

Though Enver Pasha, like Talat, had abandoned Turkey, once he eluded the British and French authorities, he formed the "Army of Islam" and entered Azerbaijan with his men. Enver was intent on uniting the pan-Turanistic and pan-Islamic forces in the region, after which he could take on the role of their leader within the new Soviet system. Or not. It would depend on which way the cookie crumbled. Once he had control of Azerbaijan, he could just as well form an alliance with the Turkish nationalists fighting in eastern

Turkey. Either way, his presence in the region was of great concern to both the Russians and the British.

Having arrived safely in Armenia, Shiragian was paired up with Aram Yerganian, a veteran Nemesis operative who had assassinated Fatali Khan Khoyski, another high-level Azerbaijani minister, in Tiflis, Georgia, earlier that year. With Armenian diplomatic passports in their pockets, Shiragian, twenty, and Yerganian, twenty-five, headed for Tiflis. Once in Georgia, they would exchange diamonds, gold, and cash for Azerbaijani rubles. They would assume Muslim aliases and present themselves as Turkish caviar merchants. They would then cross the border into Azerbaijan and travel on to Baku, where Enver had been sighted.

The two Tashnag would-be assassins of Enver Pasha arrived in Tiflis in November 1920. No sooner had they settled into their hotel room than police burst in and arrested them. In a matter of days, the two young men were swallowed up by the state apparatus of Georgia, at the time on unfriendly terms with Armenia. There was tension among the three "Transcaucasian" nations: Georgia, Armenia, and Azerbaijan. All three were struggling with their delicate geographical position as buffer zones between Turkey and Soviet Russia. Though they maintained relations with one another, each nation was fighting for its own survival as its agents moved from one territory to the next.

Once in prison, the young men lost contact with their confederates in the outside world. As far as their Armenian comrades back in Yerevan and Constantinople were concerned, the two were either dead or soon to be executed. Shiragian and Yerganian were brutally tortured and condemned to solitary confinement in a rat-infested dungeon. The night arrived when they were roused from bed and marched to the prison yard. It was time for their final disappearance. As they were being led to a crumbling wall where they would be lined up and shot, Shiragian grabbed hold of an old pump in the middle of the prison yard and began to scream, waking the entire inmate population. A riot ensued, and the clandestine execution was postponed. The incident was reported via the prison grapevine, and the news that the two men were still alive and in this prison made it back to their comrades in Armenia.

The Tashnag spy network contrived an elaborate escape plan. Upon learning that Shiragian and Yerganian would be moved from their prison to another, more formidable and probably fatal incarceration, they went into action. On the day of the transfer, as the prisoners left the building surrounded on all sides by soldiers, a humble fruit seller approached the entourage. Shiragian recognized the man as one of his fellow fedayeen. Weapons materialized, the Georgian soldiers were disarmed, and Shiragian and Yerganian were set free.

Unfortunately, by this time the political climate in Armenia had deteriorated for the Tashnags. The entire region was now under siege as fighting broke out all around Baku. Although Constantinople was still dangerous for Shiragian (since he was being sought for the murder of Ihsan), he and Yerganian had few options. So they returned to the imperial city and the de facto Tashnag headquarters, the editorial offices of the newspaper *Jagadamard*.

Pursuit of Enver was put on hold and a new target was assigned: Said Halim Pasha, the wartime Ottoman prime minister. Though Said Halim was one of the CUP leaders arrested by Britain after the war, he had been traded for British hostages held by the Kemalists and set free. Now he was residing in a well-appointed villa in Rome on a fashionable street not far from the Spanish Steps. Said Halim Pasha was, like the Armenian Boghos Nubar, a member of the old Ottoman elite. Both had roots in the Egyptian aristocracy established by Muhammad Ali, the man who had wrested Egypt from direct control of the sultan in the early 1800s. (Today Muhammad Ali is considered by many to be the "Father of Modern Egypt.") For this reason Said Halim was unlike the other Young Turks. He was not a military man, nor had he fought his way up the ranks. Neither a hotspur nor an ideologue, Said Halim actually had clashed openly with Enver and the "hawks" when Enver sought an alliance with Germany at the outset of the war in 1914.

Though he was a moderate by Ottoman standards, Said Halim had survived the revolution against the sultan in 1908 and was acting—some would say "figurehead"—Grand Vizier during the actions against the Armenian population. His signature had legitimized the deportation orders. When the Armenian patriarch Zaven appealed to Said Halim and begged him to spare his people, the Grand Vizier replied that reports of the arrests and deportations were greatly exaggerated. For this reason, the Tashnags considered him culpable and placed his name high on "the list."

In Rome, Said Halim presided over a group of exiled CUP leaders who awaited the inevitable victory of Mustapha Kemal and a triumphant return to Turkey. He led meetings of the Ittihad in exile and, unbeknownst to Nemesis, was about to sign off on a large loan with which to purchase arms for Kemal's rebels in Asia Minor. Secret British reports from the period are detailed:

> Enver had gone to Moscow and had obtained support for Mustapha Kemal in Armenia. Some two hundred thousand rifles and two and a half million pounds had been delivered and promises of more had been made. Enver's supporters had been given "carte blanche" to organize Moslems from Turkestan to Asia Minor to incite them to embarrass English everywhere in the East. He did not approve of the conditions which the Soviet Government was anxious to impose.... Reverting to the present situation Talaat said the treaty of Sevres was now driving the Turkish nationalists into the arms of the Bolshevists.[14]

In his introduction to *The Legacy,* Leon Surmelian writes: "It would be a mistake to consider these political assassinations by Arshavir [Shiragian] and his comrades—they were a handful of young men, six or seven altogether—merely acts of vengeance, though they were that too. Arshavir fought against the extension of Turkish power across the Caucasus and the Caspian to Central Asia and Afghanistan: the cherished dream of Pan-Turkism."[15]

Whether they supported a dream of an ethnically cleansed Anatolian homeland or that of a vast pan-Turkic empire, the

Muslims of postwar Turkey felt the powerful tug of nationalism. The Greek invasion of the Turkish coast (followed by Greek atrocities against Turkish citizens) hardened the solidarity of the Turks. The Greek invasion was a crime against *their* humanity, and every former leader would work to preserve what was left of the Ottoman Empire and hope to see a new Turkey rise from the ashes of the World War I debacle. Still, those residing outside Turkey, lacking the protection of a fully operational police and spy network, were vulnerable.

The CUP leadership may have presented a united face to the rest of the world—that of patriotic Turks committed to preserving the nation—but Enver, Talat, and Said Halim had disagreed strongly when it came to deciding how best to run the empire or any possible republic that might follow. Most Ittihadists were fervent nationalists, but not all of them were racists, especially when it came to Armenians. Some prominent Ittihadists were reluctant pragmatists when it came to violence, and most subscribed to some code of ethics. But others had committed war crimes with relish and were motivated by greed or an appetite for sadistic violence in their persecution of minorities. The men in the Central Committee of the CUP were for the most part from Balkan Ottoman territories. They were very familiar with the massacres of Muslims during the Balkan wars and had held little sympathy for the Armenians once the decision was made to wipe them out.

Memoirs indicate that high-ranking Young Turks in exile, like Bekir Sami Bey, Kemalist minister of foreign affairs, were aware of being hunted. On one or two occasions, in Berlin and in Rome, the quarry came face-to-face with their Armenian pursuers. The Ittihadists in exile knew that the Armenians were fluent in Turkish and could position themselves in public places like coffeehouses to overhear key discussions, so when possible they tried to meet in private. Dr. Nazim in particular was always on the alert, surveying his surroundings whenever he stepped outdoors, moving his place of residence often. (Nazim would be the one high-priority target who would elude Nemesis completely.) A review of memoirs by prominent Ittihadists living abroad at the time shows that their own spy networks were urging caution only a few months later, by the spring of 1922. "Just about everybody is changing their locations. Haci Adil Bey has left Munich, Nesimi and Halil Bey are about to leave soon, but not right away in these days. But a second assassination is to be expected after a period of calm. In here, I too survey everywhere at all the times."[16]

Shiragian's assassination of Said Halim was the most flamboyant of the Nemesis kills. After arriving in Rome, Shiragian befriended a young war widow named Maria, who invited him to live with her. While stringing Maria along, Shiragian located Said Halim's villa at 18 Via Bartolomeo Eustachio, only a short train ride from the city center. The former Grand Vizier had established for himself the life of an Italian gentleman with an entourage, having hired a full-time Italian chef, a Swiss woman as housekeeper, a bodyguard Tevfik Azmi, as well as "the Moor Bilal," a young man Halim had adopted in Turkey who was always at his side. Loitering in the neighborhood renowned as a lover's lane, Shiragian began to woo a young Greek girl who lived nearby, curbing any suspicions as to his perpetual presence in the neighborhood. He made himself familiar with Said Halim's habits and schedule, particularly when he was likely to leave or return to his villa.

Like Tehlirian, Shiragian was impatient to act. But unlike his fellow avenger, he was not going to wait forever for approval from higher-ups. Like Tehlirian, Shiragian was plagued by a fear of failure, but his solution was to move forward. (Perhaps because he had not been a soldier, he was not as obedient to the chain of command.) Fearing that Halim might suddenly decide to leave Rome, Shiragian made a decision to act. Unlike Tehlirian, who had spent the night before Talat's assassination alone in his room weeping as he sang sad songs, Shiragian went shopping. He bought eye-catching new clothes designed to create drama and distract observers from his personal features. He found a wide-brimmed black hat and a large black overcoat. Perhaps anticipating a possible inspection of his corpse by the police coroner, he made sure that everything he wore was brand-new, from his underwear outward.

The next morning Shiragian cleaned and checked his pistol, caught the train out to Said Halim's neighborhood, and posted himself outside the villa. Helena, his neighborhood girlfriend, happened by, and before Shiragian could avoid it, he found himself engaged in amorous conversation. Trying to keep his distance, he claimed that his father was arriving any minute and that he couldn't stop and talk to her. Helena was confused. Hadn't Shiragian told her that his father was dead? Also, why would he be meeting his father in this neighborhood? Hardly paying any attention to her, Shiragian kept a lookout for the approaching horse-drawn carriage.

According to his memoirs, having spied the carriage, Shiragian stepped away from Helena into the middle of the street and placed himself directly in its path. In one deft move, he raised his hand, forcing the horse to rear, then slipped around to the side, stepped up onto the running board, and, face-to-face with the startled former Grand Vizier, fired once. The bullet caught Said Halim square in the middle of his forehead, killing him instantly. Shiragian then turned his gun on the former Grand Vizier's bodyguard, Tevfik Azmi, and ordered him to throw his weapon out the window as the startled horse, with the carriage in tow (and Shiragian hanging on to its side), raced down the avenue. Shiragian, who was not only an able assassin but an effusive narrator, describes the moments after the assassination with the imagery of an action movie: "madly racing horses" and "the Pasha's head dangling out of the side of the carriage." He sees himself in the starring role: "The strong wind had caught my coat; it was flying straight out from my back and made me look like a huge, black bird."[17]

Contemporary newspaper accounts of the murder are not so colorful, describing a more perfunctory killing, with Shiragian stepping up to Said Halim as he paid his driver and shooting him in the head. However he accomplished his task, Shiragian did kill

Said Halim with one shot before he ran. The coachman managed to give chase in his carriage, but traffic got in his way and Shiragian made a clean escape. Though Shiragian does not mention an accomplice on the day, eyewitnesses stated that when he lost his coat and hat, another man quickly picked the items up and ran off in another direction. Fortunately for Shiragian, "the Moor Bilal" rushed out of the house just a few moments too late, telling a reporter for *Il Messaggero,* "If I had reached him, I would have devoured him."[18]

In his memoir Shiragian muses:

> Many persons, informed of the details of my work and behavior, have asked why I did not kill Azmi or others. I thought the answer obvious: Azmi had no responsibility for the planning or the execution of the massacres of the Armenian people. He had fought as a colonel during the Gallipoli campaign, and as a reward for his bravery he had been promoted and afterwards made secretary and bodyguard to Said Halim. Our organization had not embarked on a program of mass extermination-genocide. We were meting out punishment to persons who had been tried in absentia and who had been found guilty of mass murder. There were Armenian traitors high on this list as well.[19]

Shiragian found his way out of the neighborhood and back to Maria's place in the city. It was clear to him upon his girlfriend's arrival home that she had seen the banner headlines in the afternoon newspapers and had deduced that her lover was the assassin. She dropped hints about a "murderous Pasha" being assassinated, then teased the young killer about what "bad boys" can and can't do. Then she suggested the two retire to her villa in the country for a couple of days to "rest," an offer Shiragian couldn't refuse.[20] Despite a massive manhunt for the assassin in the black hat, he was never apprehended.

Behaeddin Shakir and Djemal Azmi
(Berlin, April 17, 1922)

Though he was eager to return to Baku to continue his pursuit of Enver, Arshavir Shiragian was handed a different assignment: he and five others would head for Berlin to "finish the job" that Tehlirian had begun: eliminating the other members of Talat Pasha's council in exile. Shahan Natali would accompany Shiragian and bring along his trusted cohort Aram Yerganian (with whom Shiragian had shared the Georgian dungeon).[21]

The Nemesis team resumed their reconnaissance in Berlin. Again Hrach "Hrap" Papazian posed as Mehmed Ali, Turkish playboy. Along for the ride was Seto Jelalian and Arshag Yezdanian (Yezid Arshag). Seto, who had been the Yerevan police chief during the short-lived republic, would be a problem due to his unreliable reports. For every Shiragian or Tehlirian there was an operative like Seto, who reminded Shiragian of the nameless agent "M" (possibly Grigor Merjanov) in Rome. Arrogant and preoccupied, "M" felt that the younger men should shoulder most of the burden of stalking the targets. Shiragian complains in his memoir of "M" coming up short time and time again.

Yezid Arshag had problems, too, with anger management. When he drank, his temper would flare up, potentially bringing unwanted attention to the plotters. After the assassination of Talat, the game had become much more dangerous in Berlin, and the tiniest slip-up could be fatal. Police all over Europe were on the lookout for suspicious activity associated with Turks, having concluded that the killings of Talat and Said Halim Pasha were not isolated incidents but the work of an organized conspiracy. Yezid Arshag was sent home.

To get closer to the targets, Hrap Papazian befriended Djemal Azmi's son Kemal, as well as Talat's widow. This job was particularly difficult because as "Mehmed Ali," Papazian was expected to share stories from the old country. The attacks on the Armenians were a favorite subject. At one dinner, Papazian was forced to listen to Azmi's boast that when he was governor of Trebizond, "the fishes ate well that year," referencing the mass drownings of Armenians in the Black Sea.

Arshavir Shiragian, always eager to court danger, was residing with the family of a local German policeman known to him as "Herr Sack." Shiragian had convinced Sack that he was the son of a rich Romanian Armenian oil baron, and in that way gained the policeman's trust. Shiragian even befriended the family's German shepherd, Robert, volunteering to take the dog out for his daily walk. This familiarity with Sack would prove handy when Shiragian needed to register as a foreign visitor to the city. It was exactly this sort of registration that could expose Shiragian for what he was, a secret agent. Sack, believing that he was doing nothing more than a harmless favor, pushed the paperwork through, never suspecting that his young tenant was a seasoned killer.

It was on a pleasant April night that the team, led by Shiragian, prepared its attack. Shiragian and Yerganian shared a meal in a restaurant, morbidly joking that it might be their "last supper." Knowing that Shakir and his entourage usually went for a walk after dinner, the two men hung around the crowded avenue. About ten p.m. they caught sight of Djemal Azmi and Dr. Shakir strolling with their usual entourage amidst the crowd streaming from the local cinemas. This group, led by Dr. Rusuhi Bey, was followed by Azmi's wife, daughter, mother, and eldest son's fiancée, in turn followed by Azmi and Shakir, who strolled arm in arm. Bringing up the rear was Talat's widow, Hayriye Talat Bafrali, who accompanied Shakir's wife. A blond man, probably a hired German bodyguard, followed at a discreet distance.

Suspecting that Rusuhi Bey was armed, and wary of the blond German, the assassins kept their distance, hidden in the shadows of an elm. The entourage wended its way along Uhlandstrasse, not far from the Kurfürstendamm. People streamed from every direction, smoking, chatting. Shiragian notes that the great silent film *Dr. Mabuse the Gambler* was playing at one of the film houses. The small knot of Turks seemed relaxed, at ease in the crowd. Yerganian nervously whispered to Shiragian that they should call it off, that the presence of the two armed men and the large crowds would make the hit impossible.

Shiragian simply made the sign of the cross over his chest and, ignoring Yerganian's pleas, replied that Yerganian could join him or not but he was going in for the kill, the only option being to attack the group from behind. Drawing his weapon, Shiragian stepped out into the street. Yerganian followed. Shiragian nodded and they ran full tilt toward the Turkish entourage. Talat's widow, seeing Shiragian's pistol, screamed and tried to grab him. He shoved her to one side, thrust his arm forward, and shot Azmi below his left eye. Azmi fell dead.

Shiragian then turned to Shakir, who in terror simply cried, "Ah, ah, ah." Shiragian replied, "Yes, 'ah'!" He fired, wounding Shakir. Yerganian shouldered past Shiragian, fired his Mauser, and delivered the coup de grâce. "Shakir fell across the body of his comrade murderer; their corpses formed a hideous cross," Shiragian writes in his memoir. Dr. Rusuhi fainted. Shiragian does not say what happened to the blond German.

Shiragian and Yerganian ran. The crowd chased after them, shouting, "Catch them! Stop them!" Recollecting the moment, Shiragian says he was amused by his partner's anger. "Like many other comrades, he had never worked in a European city before....Here in Europe, these strange Germans were actually trying to catch us. 'What do these people want?' Aram shouted angrily. 'What are they saying?'"

Shiragian couldn't resist circling back to the scene of the crime. There he found the women crouched over the lifeless bodies of Azmi and Shakir. He continues: "Nor did I feel sorry for their women, who were sobbing and hysterical, bending over their corpses. Had these women shed one tear for all the Armenian children, women and men who had been murdered by their husbands and sons?" Understanding that the police were establishing a cordon around the area, Shiragian struck up a conversation with a German family standing in the midst of the onlookers. As the family moved on, Shiragian exchanged a few words with one of the little girls, took her by the arm, and together they slipped through the police cordon.

Djemal Pasha (Tiflis, Georgia, July 21, 1922)

The last high-level official remaining on the Nemesis list was Djemal Pasha, who, along with Talat and Enver, had been one of the
"ruling triumvirate" of the Young Turk Ottoman Empire. Djemal
had been in charge of the navy, as well as commander of the Fourth
Ottoman Army in the Arab lands south of Anatolia. As such, he had
overseen the forced *surgun* (population relocation) of Armenians
into Syria. Djemal was a member of the Central Committee and
was intimately involved in the decision-making process of the Ittihad. Nonetheless, in 1922, when he published his account of his
wartime activities in a book, *Memories of a Turkish Statesman,*[22] Djemal argued that, rather than being a driving force behind the deportations, he was dedicated to protecting and saving Armenians.[23]

The story was far more complex. In December of 1915, with
the empire fully embroiled in the First World War, an attempt at a
secret truce was brokered by a Tashnag, Dr. Hagop Zavrian
(Zavriev). This truce, which could have ended the war on the
southern (Ottoman) flank, was founded on a plan whereby Djemal
would stage a coup against his cohorts, particularly Enver and
Talat. In exchange for a massive bribe and the guarantee that he
would be granted reign over a new state composed of "an independent Asiatic Turkey consisting of Syria, Mesopotamia, a Christian
Armenia, Cilicia and Kurdistan as autonomous provinces," Djemal
would sue for peace and end the slaughter of the Armenians.
Wealthy Armenians outside of Turkey stood ready to provide the
cash for the bribe. Russia, Britain, and France agonized over the
proposal for months. Finally, "in their [the Allies'] passion for
booty," the proposal was abandoned, since it deprived them of
the opportunity to take over those territories themselves. Djemal
Pasha would later point to this unconsummated deal as evidence of
"protecting" Armenians. In the end, however, he supported the
government effort to eradicate the Christian population in Turkey,
or at least move it out of Asia Minor.[24] If Djemal convinced anyone

of his paternal attitude toward the deportees, Tashnag ears were deaf to his pleas. His name remained on "the list."

When the Regional Central Committee of the Tashnag Party operating in Georgia learned that Djemal was en route to Moscow via Tiflis, it assigned Stepan Dzaghigian to find and kill the former leader. Dzaghigian was a veteran who had successfully carried out executions against "war criminals." Upon his arrival in Tiflis, Dzaghigian met with the agents who had been tracking Djemal, and they informed him that Djemal always traveled with two bodyguards.

Dzaghigian was backed up by his nephew Artashes Kevorkian, and by Bedros Der Boghosian. When Djemal went for his daily stroll at four p.m. on July 21, 1922, the killers moved in, surrounding the former leader and his two bodyguards as they passed the secret Soviet Cheka headquarters. Djemal Pasha and his young bodyguards died in a fusillade of bullets. Two hundred Tashnags in Tiflis, Dzaghigian among them, were rounded up by Soviet Georgian Chekists. Though General Dro, an Armenian fighter with influence in Soviet circles, interceded on behalf of those arrested, Dzaghigian was thrown into prison. There were rumors that, while in prison, Dzaghigian created an underground organization to aid Armenian prisoners in the Soviet Union. "Provisions and clothing were sent as far as Siberia."[25] But that's about the last we know of him. In time, Dzaghigian was exiled to the gulag. There is no record of his death.

Enver Pasha (Cegen, Tajikistan, August 4, 1922)

Enver Pasha and Dr. Nazim were, of course, high on "the list." Operation Nemesis tracked both men but did not succeed in assassinating them. Since they were targets, and because they died violent deaths, they must be mentioned here.

Enver Pasha had developed a tenuous relationship with the Soviet authorities while living in Moscow (where he befriended and was interviewed by the journalist Louise Bryant, consort of John Reed). Enver had at first entangled himself in Soviet politics at the 1920 Congress held in Baku. But as he attempted to insinuate himself into Moscow's good graces, he found himself cut off from the center of power in Turkey. Mustapha Kemal viewed Enver as a real threat to his authority. They were rivals in the military hierarchy, and on March 12, 1921, only days before Talat's assassination, the Turkish Grand National Assembly issued a decree "to the effect that Enver and Halil Pasha were prohibited from returning to Anatolia," as this would be "detrimental" to the workings of Kemal's new government.[26] Louise Bryant also reports that Enver seemingly had little affection for his fellow CUP leader Talat. In March, upon receiving word that Talat had been gunned down in Berlin, "he read the message with no show of emotion," Bryant observed, "commenting only that, 'His time had come!' "[27]

Understanding that he had to consolidate his power using means outside the control of Kemal, Enver traveled to Bukhara in Central Asia as a representative of the Soviet authorities. Ostensibly he was there to help suppress Islamic uprisings against the local Bolsheviks. Once he was in Tajikistan, however, on the pretext of going hunting, Enver slipped away from his Russian escorts and joined up with the local Basmachi rebels, Central Asian and Turkic Muslims who were rising up against Bolshevik rule. He assembled a new "Islamic Army," comprised of Basmachi fighters who accepted him as leader because of his credentials. In these ancient Muslim khanates, it was meaningful to the faithful that Enver was the son-in-law of a previous caliph, Sultan Abdul Hamid.

The Russians had had enough of a man they considered a dangerous loose cannon and began operations to eliminate Enver. At the same time, his Basmachi followers began to melt away. In early August 1922, a young Armenian Chekist named Georges Agabekov (Nerses Ovsepyan) led an attack team into the heart of the daunting Central Asian desert.[28] Agabekov tracked Enver to his lair and then alerted Red cavalry stationed nearby, who surrounded and ambushed his group. The story that an Armenian, Hagop Melkumov (Melkonian), actually fired the rifle that killed Enver is apocryphal.[29] Other versions claim that Enver was so mutilated by machine gun fire that it took two days to identify his body definitively. In 1996 Enver's body was exhumed from its grave in Ab-i-Derya and returned to Istanbul. Today his memorial gravesite stands a few yards from Talat's on Eternal Liberty Hill in Sisli, testimony to the restored reputations of both leaders among the Turkish public.[30]

Dr. Nazim

Dr. Nazim Bey Selanikli (b. 1870) was a founding member of the Central Committee of the CUP and a key leader of the Special Organization. He was also instrumental in covering the CUP's tracks before the leadership fled Constantinople, destroying incriminating files taken from their headquarters. Lacking the missing documents, the Turkish trials held in Constantinople were hobbled and incomplete. The missing documents on the inner workings of the CUP have left a gaping hole in the history of the organization ever since.

Nazim managed to elude the Nemesis killers, but in the 1920s Mustapha Kemal, as the supreme leader of the young Republic of Turkey, took steps to stamp out any potential opposition to his power as he tightened his grip on his nation. In 1926, in the wake of an apparent and probably fabricated attempt on Kemal's life, important former CUP members were rounded up. After a dramatic and well-publicized tribunal, Dr. Nazim was implicated in the conspiracy to assassinate Kemal. The man who had been so successful in evading the Armenian hunters was found guilty of treason and hanged by the Turkish government itself.[31] Mehmed Djavid Bey, another original Young Turk Central Committee member, was also implicated in the assassination attempt and hanged. With the executions of Nazim and Djavid Bey and a dozen others, Mustapha Kemal secured his hold on power. And another two names were scratched off the Nemesis list.

CHAPTER TEN

Aftermath and Ataturk

The memoirs of Soghomon Tehlirian are not the true and full story of the death of Talat. The time has not yet come to give the public the true history of the assassination. That will be the work of the next generation.

—V. Navasartian,
Executive Bureau of the Tashnag Party

On September 9, 1922, General Mustapha Kemal triumphantly entered the city of Smyrna, where the rout of the Greek army had come to its terrible conclusion. The vibrant Greek and Armenian neighborhoods of the multicultural metropolis had been reduced to piles of rubble and blackened timbers. Thousands of Christian civilians had been massacred or consumed by the conflagration. Naval officers on board British ships at anchor in Smyrna's magnificent harbor calmly observed the carnage through binoculars as hordes of terrified Christians crowded the quay, jumping into the water to escape the fires raging behind them. Most drowned. The guns of the warships stood silent as sailors onboard snapped pictures of the great city dying.

Kemal's Turkish republican army had successfully pushed the Greeks, the Armenians, the French, and the Italians out of Asia Minor. In the end, the Allies did nothing to intervene. A decision had been made: Europe would no longer directly interfere in Turkey. In the United States, Congress drifted toward isolationism. In the Caucasus, border fighting between the Russians and the Turks came to a standstill as the Soviets turned their attention on their immediate neighbors. New alliances were being struck: Italy would sell arms to Kemal's nationalists; the Soviets would lend Kemal gold with which to buy those arms. Britain would find ways to reach out to the Kemalists as it prepared for the pumping of mineral wealth out from under the sands of Mesopotamia and Arabia.

General Mustapha Kemal had become a national hero in Turkey. He and his generals had succeeded in preventing Britain, France, and their allies from parceling out and consuming their *vatan* (homeland). The 1920 Treaty of Sèvres (which had conceded territory to the Armenians and distributed the rest of Anatolia to the Greeks and Kurds) was scrapped. From his position of strength, Kemal negotiated new terms. The Lausanne Treaty signed in Paris in 1923 would establish the new Republic of Turkey. As part of this treaty, a massive and harsh population exchange of Christian (Greek) Turks for Muslims living in Greece was sanctioned and put into motion, further "purifying" the Turkish homeland.

Despite its success, the Nemesis operation was problematic for the ARF by 1922. Sooner or later the plot would be discovered, putting Armenia at a further disadvantage.[1] There had been emotional satisfaction in revenge, but the assassinations did not feed or clothe or heal the thousands of refugees stranded in the highlands of the Armenian Republic. Pursuit of an ongoing program of institutionalized assassination had no further upside, especially now that Kemal had begun to strengthen Turkey's connections with the West. The ARF leadership ordered Garo and Natali to mothball Operation Nemesis.

No longer the firebrand he had been decades earlier, and crushed by the devastation of the Armenian population, Garo did not fight the order to stand down. Shahan Natali, enraged by the decision, accused the ARF leadership of placating the Turks in the hope of furthering relationships between Armenia and Turkey. Like many Armenians, he felt that any future dealings with Turkey were unthinkable. Natali's objections fell on deaf ears. The operation was shut down with the simple explanation that it was too expensive.

The international Armenian community welcomed the news of the assassinations. War criminals who had escaped Turkey had finally been punished. More than that, the killings had shown the world that Armenians were not "sheep," that they could fight back. For those who had lost family and friends during the genocide, taking an eye for an eye could give little comfort, but it did provide some sense of justice. Barely fifty, the passionate but weary Garo died in 1923. Natali returned to the United States and would depart the ARF altogether by 1929. Soghomon Tehlirian moved to Serbia, Arshavir Shiragian to the United States. Misak Torlakian would end up joining General Dro's forces fighting the Soviets during World War II. Aaron Sachaklian, the finance and logistics manager, sealed his ARF records in Syracuse and never spoke of the operation again, not even letting his own family know what he had been part of. Hagop Zorian (Hazor) would end up in Soviet Armenia, where he would be purged by Stalin and die in exile in 1942. Aram Yerganian would move to Argentina, where he died of tuberculosis in 1934.

Those privy to the British side of these events had also made their exit by the early 1920s. A year after Aubrey Herbert's aborted trip to meet with Kemal in 1922, in an attempt to alleviate his blindness, Herbert had a number of teeth pulled (the operation had been suggested as a cure) and subsequently died of blood poisoning at the age of forty-three. Basil Thomson, the man who had sent Herbert to meet with Talat, was accused in 1921 of wasteful spending in the Directorate. When he refused to agree to the Special Branch coming under the control of another department, he was "in his own words, 'kicked out by the P.M.' " When he was arrested while soliciting a prostitute in Hyde Park in 1925, Thomson's allies claimed that he'd been "framed."[2]

The Protestant charitable organization Near East Relief raised $100 million in aid for orphans and displaced Armenians and other Christian refugees (mostly in Syria). But with the almost complete eradication of the Christians in Turkey, the missionary establishment, like the Tashnags, had to redefine its mandate. With almost no Armenians, Greeks, or Syriac Christians to attend to, attention had to be turned elsewhere. (A prominent Tashnag, Hovannes Katchznouni, first prime minister of the Armenian Republic, published a manifesto in 1923 titled *The Armenian Revolutionary Federation [Dashnagtzoutiun] Has Nothing to Do Anymore!*) As the U.S. mandate was debated in Congress, American Protestant missions modified and softened their support for the Armenian cause. In the end, the missions were forced to step lightly around the new Kemalist government. The missionary organizations owned a great deal of property in Turkey. They didn't want it taken from them.[3]

Eleven days before Talat was killed, Warren G. Harding was sworn in as the twenty-ninth president of the United States. Harding's landslide victory ushered in a deeply corrupt administration as well as a radically different approach to foreign policy. During his campaign, the handsome Republican nominee had promised a "return to normalcy," casting aside the progressive style of previous administrations, particularly that of the ailing incumbent, Democrat Woodrow Wilson. Harding specifically rejected the concept of a League of Nations. During Harding's brief tenure (he died in 1923, before he could complete his term of office), he would set an agenda in American domestic and foreign policy that endures to this day. Harding's cronies and the likes of the Dulles brothers would make the needs of big business the first priorities of foreign policy. Big oil became priority number one.

By the end of World War I, all the major powers understood that the acquisition of petroleum resources was essential to preservation of the status quo. Lacking a secure source of oil, armies, navies, and air forces could not move. Without oil, commerce could not function. The tremendous reserves of the Near East, what we now call the Middle East, had to be secured for the West. When the World War I armistice was declared, British forces in Mesopotamia did not lay down their arms but illegally advanced northward, taking possession of the region surrounding Mosul, fairly sure that major oil reserves lay there. As treaties were hammered out, the British claimed all the Arab lands as part of their "mandate," despite vigorous protestations from the Turkish government (not to mention the Arabs). Maps were marked off with red lines, and the territories were opened up for exploration and extraction of the "liquid gold."

Harding's cronies' appropriation of the massive Teapot Dome oil rights and other domestic sites would trigger a major scandal in Washington. But this didn't reduce what would eventually become an insatiable appetite for the world's oil reserves. Allen Dulles would move to Paris to assist in the peace talks; there he would develop a close relationship with the British high commissioner of Turkey, Admiral Mark Bristol, and retired admiral William Colby Chester. All of these men were committed to creating strong economic ties with the new Republic of Turkey, seeing Kemal's new nation as key to providing a base of operations in the Middle East.

The new men in power in Washington were savvy enough to allow bygones to be bygones as far as the crimes committed by the CUP during the war were concerned. Colby Chester's characterization of the Armenian deportations was breathtaking in its deliberate ignorance: "There are no prejudices against Christians in Turkey, let alone killings of Christians. Massacres of the past were enormously exaggerated by prejudiced writers and speakers." Referring to the deportations that killed hundreds of thousands of people, Chester made the case that the Turkish government had done the Armenians a favor by deporting them to the desert: "Those [Armenians] from the mountains were taken into Mesopotamia, where the climate is as benign as in Florida and California, whither New York millionaires journey every year for health and recreation. All this was done at great expense of money and effort."[4]

★   ★   ★

Americans' attitude toward intervention in Turkey would be influenced by propaganda and lobbying. Two films, *Auction of Souls* and the aborted *Forty Days of Musa Dagh,* illustrate the changing dynamic between Americans and Turkey.

Auction of Souls, or *Ravished Armenia* (1919), was based on the story of one young Armenian woman who had been captured by Muslims during the genocide. After the war, Aurora Mardiganian was "saved" through a program that existed between the end of World War I and the founding of Ataturk's republic in 1923. During this time, missionaries were able to operate relatively freely in Anatolia, gathering up orphans or, in the case of abducted Armenian women, buying their freedom. The missions would literally purchase the young women outright from their captors. The price was one gold piece for each "soul."

Sixteen-year-old Aurora was the most famous of all the liberated girls. She escaped capture, made it to Erzurum (around the same time Tehlirian was passing through), then on to Tiflis and finally Saint Petersburg. She immigrated to Oslo, where missionaries assisted her and then sent her to New York City.

In New York, Mardiganian was in the charge of Nora Wahn, publicity secretary of the American Committee for Armenian and Syrian Relief (or "Near East Relief," renamed the Near East Foundation in 1930).[5] Because of public interest in what had happened to the Armenians during the Great War, Mardiganian was interviewed by the *New York Sun* and the *New York Tribune,* whereupon she came to the attention of a screenwriter named Harvey Gates, who had her tell him the story of her trials. Gates and his wife, who would become Mardiganian's legal guardians, arranged for the publication of her story in the United States and Britain. This narrative, *Ravished Armenia,*[6] became a best-seller. The book was then sold to Hollywood. Renamed *Auction of Souls,* the silent black-and-white film, directed by Oscar Apfel, was released in 1919. Much of the film stock has been lost, but portions have survived and are available on the Internet.

Aurora was cast to play herself in the film version of her memoir, an unpleasant assignment for the traumatized young woman. On her first day on the set on a Santa Monica beach, she had an emotional meltdown when she suddenly found herself surrounded by a hundred extras dressed as Turkish military. Believing she was back in Turkey, she thought her nightmare was beginning all over again. She had only the vaguest idea what a movie was.

According to Anthony Slide, a film scholar who exhaustively researched the creation of the film and interviewed Mardiganian in 1988, the producers worked Aurora relentlessly, paying her only fifteen dollars a week. On one occasion she broke an ankle while shooting a scene. After it was bandaged, she was forced to continue filming. Upon completion of the film, which featured scenes of "ravishment" and massacre, the producers distributed it as a high-minded examination of the Armenian massacres. At the time, the American public was happy to embrace anti-Turk and pro-Armenian propaganda. The producers set up black-tie fund-raisers all around the country, using this sensational film as a centerpiece.

Aurora Mardiganian was compelled to make a personal appearance at each of these events, heightening the excitement. Although the film was racy, critics approached it as an earnest, socially conscious work and wrote approving notices. Aurora Mardiganian found a certain level of stardom; however, the pressure of the public appearances finally grew too much for her, and she ran away. Seven Aurora Mardiganian look-alikes were hired to make appearances along with showings of the film.

Ravished Armenia was released before Turkish denialists were conscious of the value of film as propaganda, but as Hollywood grew in its power to inform, and as the Turkish government began to focus on its Armenian public relations problem, the next major film slated for production would be stopped altogether. One of the most popular best-sellers of the early twentieth century was Franz Werfel's novel The Forty Days of Musa Dagh, a fictional retelling of the story of an embattled Armenian village that fought off the Turkish military. It is based on the true story of a village near the Mediterranean coast whose residents resisted deportation and were eventually rescued by the French navy.

In 1933 *The Forty Days of Musa Dagh* was a huge critical and commercial success worldwide. In 1934, as the American edition was about to reach the bookstores, Louis B. Mayer snapped up the rights for a film adaptation by Metro-Goldwyn-Mayer. David O. Selznick, sensing that the material might be of concern to the Turks, came up with the idea that the film could avoid tarring all Turks with the same brush by featuring one particularly evil antagonist. (This was a departure from the tone of the book.) As a courtesy, through an intermediary, Selznick contacted the Turkish ambassador and informed him that a production of the adaptation was imminent.

The wheels of production began to turn, and Irving Thalberg assigned Carey Wilson to write the *Musa Dagh* screenplay, with William Wellman as director (later Rouben Mamoulian would be enlisted to direct) and William Powell in the lead. Before the first book was sold in the United States, the Turkish ambassador, Mehmet Munir Ertegun Bey, was in contact with Wallace Murphy, chief of Near Eastern affairs at the State Department, expressing his concern. Murphy in turn got in touch with Will Hays, head of the powerful Motion Picture Producers and Distributors of America (MPPDA) in Washington, also known as the "Hays Office," which acted as the official censor for the industry. Hays didn't see why Turkey would have a problem with the script and gave it his OK.

Turkish government officials let it be known, however, that they wished production to cease. When this did not happen, objections became threats. Through intermediaries, the Turkish government made it clear that the film would be banned in Turkey and that "the Turkish authorities were prepared to expend every effort all over the world to prohibit the picture."[7] Turkish professionals and businessmen weighed in and warned the studio that in their opinion, release of this film would only exacerbate tensions in

Turkey. At one point an MGM executive actually met with the Turkish ambassador. In addition, MGM's man in Turkey advised his bosses that the studio's business interests in Turkey would suffer. Even the tiny Armenian community in Istanbul was pressured. Turkish Armenians contacted MGM to ask that the film be shelved.

MGM would not relent. The story became front-page news in Turkey and even "threatened Franco-Turkish relations via Muslims in North Africa." Eventually, Secretary of State Cordell Hull was drawn into the fray. He contacted Will Hays and asked him to "dispose of the issue." Though MGM had a lot of money invested in the picture, in the end the Hays Office (utilizing its power via the Production Code of 1930) supported the Turkish government and refused to give approval for production to commence. MGM-Loew's executive William A. Orr "personally informed the Turkish embassy of his complete support for the Turkish position. He agreed that filming the novel would be harmful whatever the modifications. Preferably, it would be better for all parties to drop the scheme altogether." *The Forty Days of Musa Dagh* would not be produced by a major Hollywood studio. Ambassador Munir Bey saw the victory as confirmation that the story told in the novel was fiction and he said as much. A version of the novel was finally produced in 1982, though it fell short of the major studio production that had been envisioned. The precedent had been set: with enough pressure, Turkish authorities could affect how their nation was represented in other countries, including the United States.[8]

—ɯ—

Behind each decision made in and around the region, the United States and its allies had always had oil in mind. Long before the onset of World War I, Winston Churchill, then serving as First Lord of the Admiralty, knew that for his navy to remain powerful, it must have a plentiful supply of oil. Millions of barrels of petroleum were needed to float a navy that had as its centerpiece the "super-dreadnought" battleship, the cutting-edge naval weapon of its time. These massive ships could not run on coal.[9] Churchill's observation still stands: "Mastery itself was the prize of the venture."[10] International oil cartels had been formed to distribute the oil and share the wealth. The Americans and the French, who were the only other loud voices here, were party to these cartels, so they did not interfere with British acquisition of the Arab lands.

Great Britain relied on its vast navy to control the ports of its empire and to make war on its enemies.By October 1911, Great Britain had 189 seagoing vessels requiring fuel oil. Britain needed 200,000 tons of petroleum per annum, but had no fully secure source for this natural mineral resource. Neither did Germany. Baku in Azerbaijan had very large proven reserves, but it lay within the Russian sphere of influence. As the years ticked by and oil exploration became more sophisticated, the need to exploit the massive petroleum reserves lying under Turkish, Arab, and Persian deserts became irresistible.

This thirst for oil compelled a deeper involvement in the Ottoman Empire. Complex negotiations over oil rights took place almost nonstop in the decade preceding World War I. "The advantages conferred by liquid fuel were inestimable," said Churchill. "Fortune brought us a prize from fairyland beyond our wildest dreams."[11] British, American, French, and German leaders and businessmen felt that they had the rights to the mineral resources in the former Ottoman Empire because they had "discovered" the oil in the first place. It seemed obvious to the Europeans that the people who had settled amidst the sand and rocks lying on top of these vast reserves were irresponsible and backward and had no idea how to exploit what they had. England, France, and Germany had the muscle to take what they needed. But then there was the matter of legality. If oil was going to be extracted from foreign territories, it was essential that this be done in a way that would be legally binding. Forever.

Turkey's leaders were aware of the value of this underground treasure, but they did not have the technology or the engineers to exploit it. It made better sense to license the lands to the highest bidder. But holding a straightforward auction was no simple matter. First of all, in the years leading up to World War I, the Ottoman government was in flux. The sultan, still wielding power until 1909, had a personal fortune, the Liste Civile, which included all the oil rights of Arabia. (The Liste Civile or Privy Treasury was traditionally administered by an Armenian. Under Abdul Hamid II, the minister of the Liste Civile was Hagop Kazazian Pasha.) Second, negotiations in the Middle East were always complicated and multilayered, especially when one was dealing with a bureaucracy as labyrinthine as that of the Ottoman Empire. Bribes and backroom negotiations were de rigueur. A middleman was needed.

Enter Calouste Sarkis Gulbenkian, a Turkish-born Armenian engineer educated in London, who was a seasoned trader in kerosene and machine lubricant. The sultan had consulted with Gulbenkian regarding the untold wealth lying under his empire's deserts and chose him as the man who would act as the go-between for financial interests in London and Constantinople. All Gulbenkian asked in return for his agency was five percent of the proceeds. At the time, this didn't seem like an outlandish request. The respective boards of directors of corporations representing English, French, and American interests agreed to this arrangement.[12]

As these contracts became more and more valuable, and as the world realized the enormous extent of the Middle Eastern oil reserves (to this day, the oil in the Middle East represents about fifty percent of all known world reserves), Gulbenkian's partners moved to renegotiate their arrangement with him. Their reasoning was simple: five percent of the value of the oil gushing from the sands would amount to billions of dollars and the net percentage going to Gulbenkian was too much money for one man. Gulbenkian refused to trim his percentage. So the national oil cartels, with the backing of their governments, declared Gulbenkian's contracts null and void and walked away from their deal with him. Gulbenkian went to court. Afraid of losing their legal grip on the concessions, the parties entered protracted negotiations with Gulbenkian and eventually reached an agreement.

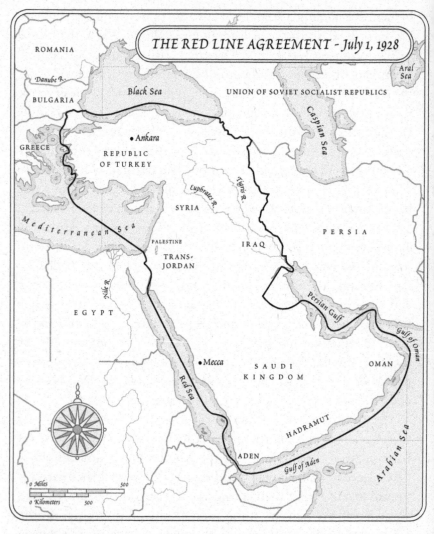

The Red Line Agreement bound its partners to a "self-denial clause" or non-compete agreement in which the major powers would share the petroleum resources of the Middle East. Calouste Gulbenkian claimed to have drawn the original red-line map.

In 1928 these contracts, in the form of the infamous "red line agreement" which Gulbenkian would later claim to have authored, created a zone in the Middle East in which the consortium could operate without interference. For decades no one but the partners (the national cartels) could extract oil from the region circumscribed by the red line. This region included all of Iraq, Syria, Turkey, Saudi Arabia, and the Emirates. The British already had Persia (Iran) and Kuwait in their pocket.

The agreement was finalized just as the massive "Baba Gurgur" strike near Kirkuk in northern Iraq began to flow. The field had been known since ancient times for its eternal (natural gas) fires, but now it would become a key source of petroleum for the modern world. The Kirkuk fields would produce hundreds of millions of tons of oil, one of the many massive strikes that would follow in the years to come. By the time of his death in 1955, Gulbenkian's fortune was estimated at between $280 million and $840 million, making him one of the richest men in the world. It's interesting to note that the man who originally helped Gulbenkian make contacts with the Turkish elite was Nubar Pasha, Boghos Nubar's father. Gulbenkian called Nubar Pasha "Uncle," which says a lot about the networks that existed between the wealthiest Armenians and the highest-level Ottomans.[13] The man who brokered Middle Eastern oil and the man best known as the epitome of dignified Armenian diplomacy were, for lack of a better term, cousins.[14]

It has often been argued that Armenia was "sold out" for oil. The loudest voice here belonged to Vahan Cardashian, who made it his personal crusade to let the world know how Standard Oil and the Harding administration had colluded to abandon the Armenian cause in their drive to acquire a foothold in the Middle East. And as it became more and more clear that Turkey was digging in its heels and would fight to keep its last territories (namely, eastern Asia Minor, what many Armenians call "western Armenia"), all parties understood implicitly that what was important was *Iraq*. To sum up, by 1923, the Armenians didn't have anything that the West desired, but the Republic of Turkey did.

Iraq, particularly northern Iraq, home to hundreds of thousands of Kurds, was wild country. It was land that over the centuries had been ruled by Ottomans, Arabs, Mongols, and Persians.

What made it so very valuable now was oil. Not that the British would ever admit that fact. Speaking in 1922, the British foreign secretary, Lord Curzon, couldn't have made it more clear that Britain's seizure of Mesopotamia/Iraq was not about oil: "I do not know how much oil there may be in the neighborhood of Mosul or whether it can be worked at a profit, or whether it may turn out after all to have been a fraud."[15] It is doubtful that Curzon was unaware of the value of northern Iraq.

Perhaps no direct connection can be made between the loss of the "Armenian mandate," or the genocide itself, and the world's appetite for oil and other mineral rights. But once the war was over, once the territories of the former Ottoman Empire were divvied up to everyone's satisfaction, any lingering outrage and the impetus on the part of the West to defend and fight for Armenian rights simply evaporated. Now that the exploitation of Turkey was a fait accompli and access to oil (guaranteed by international agreements) enriched all the parties involved, the tragedy of the Christians in the Ottoman Empire became a footnote of history, one that many would work hard to erase altogether.

—◊◊◊—

Governments were moving on, but the abandonment of the Armenians was felt far beyond the borders of Turkey. Only a few years after the war, Armenians and other "ethnics" from southern Europe found that the welcome mat so invitingly laid before America's front door at the end of the nineteenth century had been suddenly whisked away. When there had been a crying need for factory workers, thousands upon thousands of immigrants were allowed to flow into the United States. Hundreds of thousands of "Mediterranean types" (Italians, Greeks, Armenians, Jews) had settled in the United States between the late 1800s and the end of World War I. Who were these people? Were they trustworthy? Or were they a corrupting influence? After the war, Americans began to lose their fondness for these swarthy immigrants who fried their food in olive oil and seasoned it with garlic.

The newcomers were "dirty." They often had darker skin than most Americans of northern European descent, many of whom wrongly suspected that these "unclean" immigrants were the ones responsible for the devastating "Spanish flu" that killed tens of millions of people after the war. Perhaps worst of all, these immigrants were stealing scarce jobs away from "real" Americans struggling in the postwar recession. In the South, the Ku Klux Klan expanded its war on minorities to include persecution of the new arrivals. Though the Klan originated as a hate group focused on black Americans, it vigorously attacked Italians, Jews, and Catholics in the 1920s.

In response to a demand for action, Congress enacted immigration quotas, with some officials citing the pseudoscience of eugenics, which had risen in popularity in America, and which would eventually flourish in Nazi Germany. During the 1920s, impoverished Americans were sterilized so they could not transmit their defective genes to future generations.[16]

Were Armenians "white"? As absurd as this question sounds, it was widely discussed in the early twentieth century. Since Armenians came from lands east of the Bosphorus (the cartographical dividing line between Europe and Asia), they could have been considered "Asians." But after World War I, the United States began to close off immigration from Asia, as a strict quota was set with the aim of limiting the flow of Chinese entering the country; so establishing the racial differentiation of Armenians from other Asians would help preserve their right to immigrate. Thus the story of how Armenian "whiteness" entered the annals of American jurisprudence in 1924 in a federal court in Seattle, in the case of *United States v. Cartozian*.

Tatos O. Cartozian had to defend his right to American citizenship in court to prevent his deportation, even though an earlier ruling in 1909 *(In re Halladjian)* had already found that "scientific evidence" proved that Armenians were white. Nevertheless, attorney John S. Coke argued, "It is the contention of the government that it makes no difference whether a man is a Caucasian or not or what the racial and language history of his people may be if the man on the street does not recognize him as white."[17] In other words, Armenians are not white because they don't look white. The court supported the earlier ruling. The deciding factor seemed to be that Armenians practiced a "Western" religion, Christianity, and thus they were white. In this way, Christian identity came to help define race.[18]

In Turkey, identity was also on Mustapha Kemal's mind. In 1927 Kemal gave a speech that, with intermissions, took three days to deliver. This speech, presented at a political party convention, is so famous in Turkey that it is simply called "Nutuk" (The Speech). In this marathon exposition of his ideas, Kemal defined his nation and outlined his plans. He systematically ironed out any problematic historical wrinkles by expunging or avoiding facts like the CUP's destruction of the Armenians or the existence of a Kurdish people in the east.[19] He also took all the credit for establishing the new republic, giving none to his peers and comrades. Taking on the role of the great paternal leader, Kemal explained to the Turkish people where they had come from and where he saw them going. He outlined a blueprint for the future of the nation.

The speech was delivered in the midst of the cultural revolution Kemal had initiated after establishing the new Republic of Turkey in 1923. Once the Lausanne Treaty was signed, Turkey was recognized by the major powers and international relationships were normalized, Kemal began his program of modernization. He abolished the six-hundred-year-old sultanate and, not long after that, the caliphate itself, a major symbol of Islam for millions. Kemal enacted suffrage for women, modernized the alphabet, and imposed European-style clothing for all Turkish citizens (replacing the fez with the hat). He negotiated and validated the borders of the new nation, borders that have endured up to this day. He initiated the rewriting of the official history of the country, placing the

Turks squarely in the center of world civilizations. In 1935 Kemal ordered the people of Turkey to adopt first and last names. He himself took the name Ataturk, or "Father of the Turks."

The charismatic Kemal Ataturk never missed an opportunity to share his ideas with his nation and the world, becoming one of the most quoted men in history. He sought to instill in his countrymen a sense of national identity, repeatedly reminding them that they were "Turks," a term that before this time was mainly used by Ottomans to refer to country bumpkins. He explained to his audience that they were an illustrious people who had established one of the greatest empires in the history of the world. They were conquerors, *ghazi*. (Kemal himself was hailed as "Ghazi" early in his career. The word means "holy warrior.") They were a people, a nation, a powerful force of history. They were more than just Muslims. They were the inheritors of a great legacy: Ottoman-Turkish culture, strength, and enterprise. To maintain their vitality, it was imperative that they remain pure and proud.

In the early years of the republic, for the sake of international public relations, Turkey officially expressed sympathy for the lost Christian populations. Legislation was passed that seemed to welcome any surviving Armenians back to their homes, and at least on paper, Christians and Jews were to be treated like any other citizens in Turkey. But this was a very cold and toxic embrace. The Turkish government was no longer engaged in an organized system of deportation, but with Kemal's endorsement, the ethnic cleansing of Anatolia would continue. Even after the tragedy of World War I, there would be no equality for non-Turks in Turkey. Armenians, Greeks, and Muslim Kurds would be treated as second-class citizens and continue to suffer. Laws regarding language, inheritance, religious expression, and education put continual negative pressure on minority groups.[20] Unequal taxation, organized race riots, and persistent genocidal policies (particularly against the Kurds) would make life very difficult if not impossible for non-Turks in Turkey, whether they be Christian or Muslim.

Unlike Enver, Kemal showed no enthusiasm for an imagined

Turkic empire stretching across Eurasia. But he was a skillful pragmatist and understood how important nationalism was to his revolution. In the new Kemalist republic, all Muslims were welcome as
long as they called themselves Turks, and many communities of
Muslims—Circassians, Tartars, Allevi, Chechens, Laz, even
Arabs—were allowed to officially claim Turkic "roots" in Anatolia whether they had them or not.

Kurds made up as much as twenty percent of the total population in the new republic at the time of its formation. (Today, Kurds
form the vast majority in the southeast regions of Turkey.) Kurds
are Muslim but not Turkic, and so presented a conundrum for the
Kemalists. The solution was that Kurds would no longer officially
be considered a separate people. In Ataturk's republic, Kurds were
simply Turks who had lost their way; they were "mountain Turks."
On the ground, Kurds had a choice: be assimilated or be eradicated. Like the Armenians before them, Kurds were discouraged
from speaking their own language. After World War I, their settlements would be attacked repeatedly and viciously.

Greeks who lived in western Anatolia (most of whom were
Turkish-speaking) continued to present an entirely different quan-
dary for the nationalists. Although the 1922 debacle in Smyrna had
erased a major Christian population center and terrorized those
who had managed to survive, there were still hundreds of thousands of Greek Christians living in Turkey. As part of the Lausanne
Treaty, a massive population swap was negotiated. For outsiders
watching from Europe, such a swap seemed logical. The plan was
simple: all the "Greeks" in Turkey would "return" to Greece and
all the "Turks" in Greece "return" to Turkey. Sadly, these "Greeks"
and "Turks" were defined by religion only. Often the Muslim
"Turks" in Greece did not speak Turkish and the Christian "Greeks"
in Turkey did not speak Greek. As a result, the deportees faced discrimination when they were "returned" and eventually, like the
Kurds in the east, were forced to live as less than full citizens.

The few Armenians who had survived the debacle and who

tried to return only found more hardship, sometimes death. Even Armenians who had converted to Islam continued to suffer discrimination. As a final blow, the Armenians as a people were excised from the official history of Turkey in what Donald Bloxham has called "a systemic, state-sponsored rewriting of Armenian and Turkish history."[21]

Kemal's revision of the historical narrative was formalized in 1932 at a Turkish Historical Congress in Ankara. From this convention was born a three-year project resulting in a spurious "Outline of Turkish History." The "thesis" on which it was based was complete fantasy, proclaiming that Turkey was the "original" civilization giving birth to all other civilizations, including Greek, Egyptian, and Roman. This "history" was backed up with a pseudoscientific language analysis called "the Sun Language theory" (*gunes-dil teorisi*), which claimed that all world languages had evolved from a Turkic root language. With their radical distortion of the truth, these theories never gained much traction, and were mostly abandoned after Kemal's death.[22]

Vestiges of these theories nevertheless persist in contemporary Turkish culture. A tourist visiting the Archeological History Museum of Anatolia, a major attraction adjacent to Topkapi Palace in Istanbul, receives an in-depth survey of the history of the land now called Turkey (more or less Asia Minor) spanning thousands of years. Bizarrely, the Armenians, who were settled in the region for two thousand years before the Seljuk Turks arrived, are not mentioned once. This museum is only one of more than fifty such museums that exist all over the Republic of Turkey,[23] contributing, along with schools and publishing houses, to the education and mind-set of all Turkish students. These institutions teach Turkish citizens the "truth" about their country's history with displays of artifacts and charts and maps. Because of this concerted effort to misinform, most citizens of Turkey have only the vaguest idea of who the Armenians were and what happened to them.[24]

Not far from Taksim Square, where in the summer of 2013

protests against the Erdogan administration were met with police violence, stands the immense Istanbul Military Museum, "dedicated to one thousand years of Turkish military history." Along a dark corridor deep within the building is a large room labeled simply "Hall of the Armenian Issue with Documents" (Belgelerle Ermenia Sorunu Salonu). This compact exhibition features along its walls dozens of photographs of atrocities purportedly committed by Armenian "gangs." Many are dated in the summer of 1915, the very period when the worst acts of violence were taking place against the Armenian population living in eastern Asia Minor. In the center of the room is a large glass case. In the case is a striped dress shirt, still stained with patches of blood. This is the shirt Talat was wearing when he was shot. A plaque outlines Talat's biography. There is no mention of his conviction for war crimes by the Ottoman courts in 1919. The final sentences simply say: "He was killed in Berlin by an Armenian called Sogomon Tehlerian [*sic*] in 1921. His remains were taken to Istanbul in 1943 and reburied in the cemetery at Hurriyet-I Ebediye Hill [Monument of Liberty Hill]." The message of the hall is clear: Armenians constituted a real danger to Turkey during World War I, culminating in the murder of a Turkish patriot. (Enver's remains are also interred on Liberty Hill.)

If you fly Turkish Airlines from one area of Turkey to another, the in-flight magazine will feature a map of the region. Although all adjacent countries are labeled on the map, only an empty unlabeled outline of the modern country of Armenia can be found. On another flight within the country of Turkey, I watched an in-flight video about the city of Van, the fortress city once a bastion for Armenians which at the beginning of the genocide was attacked and overwhelmed by the Turkish military. This city is today a tourist destination, featuring lovely medieval Armenian Christian architecture. Though Van was once a thriving center for Turkish Armenians, there are no Armenians living there today. The promotional video, like so much of the media that make up our modern history, makes no mention of Armenians whatsoever.

*   *   *

The cult of Kemal grew alongside the concept of "Turkishness."[25] Even when visiting Turkey today, it is impossible to venture very far without seeing Ataturk's ruggedly handsome face gazing down upon you. His portrait hangs behind the counter in nearly every shop, on the wall of every office. His image is printed on all currency. He is omnipresent. In this secular state, Ataturk has replaced God as the ultimate authority. It is true that Islam discourages naturalistic representation in religious art and architecture, and for that reason Ataturk's image stands out even more. But in some respects Ataturk transcends even Islam, because he symbolizes Turkey itself.

The pervasive nature of Kemal Ataturk in Turkey is the product of his own self-promotion. Like other world leaders of his period, he harnessed the power of the mass media to win over a public vulnerable to the influence of film and radio. For example, in interviews and speeches, he redefined his role as an effective and able general at Gallipoli to "the man who saved Constantinople." This legend would only grow, and by the end of his life, Ataturk was known to his countrymen as "the man who saved Turkey" and "the father of the country." For the rest of Ataturk's life, every speech and interview he gave would erode the reputations of his contemporaries while elevating his own stature. Schoolchildren would begin each day pledging, "O Ataturk the great! I swear that I will enduringly walk through the path you opened and to the target you showed. May my personal being be sacrificed to the being of the Turkish nation. How happy is the one who says: 'I am a Turk.'"[26] To this day, Law 5816 makes disparaging Ataturk a criminal act. This law has been used against journalists.[27]

To be the father of a people, there has to be "a people." This is an essential element of nationalism. "A people" can be defined culturally, linguistically, religiously. But there is usually an underlying notion of "pure blood." The entire ideology of the Young Turks was built on this racist notion of pure-bloodedness. Perhaps people with "pure blood" do exist in the most northern reaches above the Arctic Circle or on some isolated Pacific island. But the last place on earth where genetic "purity" could ever exist would be in the territories of the former Ottoman Empire. Not only was this region an enormous melting pot, but also the very nature of Turkish society and its institutions guaranteed that non-Turkic "blood" would be continuously intermixed with the genetic repository of the original invaders from the Far East. Ataturk himself, with his blue eyes and light skin, appears to have been descended from Slavic Europeans, not Turkic invaders.

Not only would Turkish history be rewritten by Ataturk, not only would the Turkish government take the position that no coordinated extermination of the Armenians had ever taken place, but also any previous written history became essentially unavailable because it was literally unreadable. Until 1929, Turkish was written in an Arabic script; after 1929, a twenty-nine-character Western alphabet would be employed. (Ironically, this new alphabet was created by an Armenian, Hagop Martayan Dilicar, a favorite of Ataturk's.) Words themselves were altered to make them more "Turkish." Vocabulary was deleted, new words added.

Place-names all over the country were Turkified (for example, "Smyrna" became "Izmir"), which only added confusion and another obfuscating layer to the buildup of historical sediment. In fact, the Turkish language has changed so radically since the time of Kemal's "Nutuk" that a Turk living today would not be able to understand his actual words. The speech literally has to be *translated* for contemporary Turkish speakers. Most important, any record, history, or document created prior to 1929 is totally unreadable by all Turks and even most scholars. The impact of this makeover has been to significantly impede historical research, and it is one of Ataturk's most devastating accomplishments.

In 1938 Kemal Ataturk's lifestyle, fueled by little sleep, high-octane raki, chain-smoking, and endless cups of black coffee brought his intense life to an end. He was fifty-seven when he died of cirrhosis of the liver. By this time his godlike status in Turkey was unassailable. Like Stalin and Mao, he had held his country in thrall for decades, and when he died, new personalities and institutions would try unsuccessfully to fill the void he left behind. The struggle within Turkey that continues to this day is the legacy of Kemal Ataturk's radical reformation, made possible by his tremendous vitality and charisma and his commitment to the goals of the Ittihad. That vision, of the Ittihadists and, by extension, Kemal Ataturk, did not include the non-Muslim population of what was once the Ottoman Empire.

CHAPTER ELEVEN

Post-Ataturk

What matters in life is not what happens to you but what you remember and how you remember it.
— Gabriel García Márquez

In the decades following World War I, the Republic of Armenia became fully integrated into the Soviet Union. At the same time, the newborn Republic of Turkey reinforced its alliance with the United States. Christians in Turkey continued to be persecuted, while the Turkish government actively refused to acknowledge the organized destruction of the Ottoman Empire Armenians during the war. The prospect of violence constantly loomed. In 1933, an Armenian archbishop in New York City was murdered by members of the ARF for his pro-Soviet posture. In the 1940s and 1950s, organized harassment and killing of Armenians and Greeks in Turkey led to further "purification" of the population. Military coups unseated at least three Turkish governments. In the 1970s and 1980s, radical Armenian terror cells calling themselves the Armenian Secret Army for the Liberation of Armenia and the

Justice Commandos murdered dozens of Turkish diplomats and their associates. In 1991, in the midst of a war with neighboring Azerbaijan, the Republic of Armenia broke free from the defunct Soviet Union. When the outspoken Armenian humanist Hrant Dink, editor of the Turkish periodical *Agos,* was assassinated in broad daylight outside his offices in Istanbul in 2007, some saw the killing as a long-delayed reprisal for the murder of Talat.

As the decades have passed, Kemal's former opponents in the CUP, all dead by 1930, were resuscitated as heroes in the Turkish national consciousness. As a first step, on March 31, 1923, Turkey declared a general amnesty for all those accused of planning the massacres.[1] Families of the victims of the "Armenian hit men" were bequeathed pensions and property, very often property that had belonged to wealthy Armenians killed during the genocide. In the 1940s, during the Nazi period in Germany, as his body was ceremoniously returned to Istanbul, Talat was hailed as a hero of the republic and a monumental gravesite was commissioned. Schools continued to teach an alternative history in which no crimes were ever committed against Armenians in Turkey. Turkish historians with few or no scholarly credentials wrote long tracts "proving" that there was no such thing as an Armenian people, let alone a genocide against them (just as it would also become government policy to say that the Kurds were in fact "mountain Turks"). Turkey claimed that Armenians had never existed, while the official Turkish history of World War I reported that Armenians had committed massacres against the Turks.

After Ataturk's death, the Kemalist bias against Christian minorities continued. In 1942, a special "wealth tax," the *Varlik Vergisi,* was enacted by Ataturk's successor, Ismet Inonu. It was "a form of state racketeering that found a particularly easy target in the vulnerable religious minorities."[2] The tax, never enforced against Muslims, was ruinous for any Christian or Jew who had somehow managed to hang on to property or a business in Turkey. Those who would not or could not pay the tax were literally packed off in chains to concentration camps in the mountains. There they spent their days breaking rocks. Even the historian Bernard Lewis, who has taken a stand against using the term "genocide" when describing the events of 1915 and 1916,[3] has stated, "It soon became apparent that the really important data determining a taxpayer's assessment were his religion and nationality."[4]

The Turkish public accepted this brutal treatment of minorities because anti-Semitism and anger over war profiteering were trumpeted nonstop in the Turkish press. From an opinion piece:

> If you don't believe it, stop by a bazaar, a covered market. [A consignment of] wool arrived. You would order a sweater for your daughter but the shop owner tells you "All out!" Our Jewish compatriot has purchased it. Some printed linen has arrived. You would like to have a bathrobe made for your daughter-in-law, but the shop owner tells you "All out!" Our Jewish compatriot has purchased it. Rouge has arrived. There's none left. Our Jewish compatriot has purchased it. Some powder has arrived. There's none left. Our Jewish compatriot has purchased it. Socks have arrived. They're all gone. Our Jewish compatriot has purchased them.[5]

Newspapers ran political cartoons featuring scowling hook-nosed Jews and Armenians licking their chops over obscene profits extracted from poor Muslims. Later, when middle-aged businessmen were sent to the labor camps, they were depicted in cartoons boasting of their skill at stacking rocks because they were so good at stacking gold.

Over a thousand men were arrested and sent to hard labor. Many died. At its peak in 1943, the program attracted the attention of foreign diplomats and press. According to a British embassy report: "Thirty-two wealthy Istanbul non-Moslems were deported to East Anatolia January 27 for hard outdoor labor as punishment for non-payment of individual assessments of the recent Turkish capital levy.... These 32 average over fifty-five years of age, although the legal age limit for deportees is fifty-five. They include 15 Jews, 8 Armenians, 9 Greeks and no Turks. The deportation was marked by the maximum psychological torture."[6] Scrutiny by the United States and Great Britain embarrassed Turkey into rescinding the law in late 1943. Turkish officials later denied that it had ever existed in the first place, painting a new layer of secrecy over the old.

When World War II ended, Soviet Armenians lobbied Moscow to reconsider its abrogation of pro-Armenia treaties with Turkey. (During World War I, Russia had occupied eastern Anatolia, land that the Armenians considered rightfully theirs. After World War I, the USSR relinquished this territory to Turkey.) Victorious against the Nazis, Armenians saw no reason why Soviet Armenia should not now reclaim these eastern Turkish territories. As Russia massed its troops along the Turkish-Armenian SSR border, preparing to reoccupy the "Armenian homelands" of Turkey, President Harry S. Truman interceded in a way that would fundamentally alter the world's political landscape. Fearing that a Russian invasion of Turkey would destabilize the Middle East (read: threaten the oil supply) while furthering the spread of communism, Truman announced that any attack on Turkey would be seen as an attack on the United States and would receive the appropriate response. Russia backed down.

The era of the "Truman Doctrine" had begun. It bound Turkey and the United States into a strategic partnership. Though this bond has been strained at times, it has served the United States well and provided Turkey with a vast source of arms and funding. Not long after the doctrine was initiated, the United States began to pump money into the Republic of Turkey, with totals eventually rising to hundreds of millions of dollars annually. (Combined economic and military aid to Turkey since the inception of the Truman Doctrine has reached almost $30 billion.) This money not only assisted Turkey economically but also announced to the world that Turkey was now a member of the postwar "family of nations" headed by the United States. In addition to direct aid, Turkey received millions more as a participant in the postwar Marshall

Plan to rebuild Europe—this despite the fact that Turkey sat out most of the war and no Turkish troops ever faced combat in World War II. As a member of NATO, Turkey maintains the organization's largest standing army outside the United States.

After the war, as relations with the United States grew warmer, the harassment and destruction of non-Muslim communities continued. On the night of September 6–7, 1955, state-organized riots against Greek homes and businesses in Istanbul (triggered by an alleged terrorist bombing of Ataturk's ancestral home in Salonika) brought a total end to the Greek presence in Turkey. "In relatively few hours, forty-five Greek communities in the greater Istanbul area had been savagely attacked by extensive arson and vandalism, and the larger Greek community lay ruined in its homes, shops and businesses, churches, cemeteries, medical clinics, schools and newspapers."[7] Following the attacks, many Greeks remaining in Turkey departed. The few Armenians living in Istanbul were also viciously attacked during these riots. The eradication of a Christian business presence in Turkey was complete.[8]

Though the actions of Nemesis committed during the 1920s had been far from legal, the ARF found ways to advertise its clandestine activities. Tehlirian's autobiography, written in Armenian with Vahan Minakhorian (a Tashnag minister of education who had been among those chased out of Soviet Armenia in the 1920s) was published in Cairo in 1953. Soon other memoirs and interviews would follow. These remained part of underground lore but could not compensate for the fact that there had yet to be any real recognition of the genocide in any official capacity. Armenians everywhere feared that the memory of this colossal tragedy might be buried altogether by the Turkish government's concerted disinformation effort.

—◊—

In 1951 a massive statue of Stalin was erected in Yerevan, the capital city of Armenia. It was so huge that Vasily Grossman would write: "This monument towers over Yerevan and the whole of Armenia. It towers over Russia, over the Ukraine, over the Black and Caspian seas, over the Arctic Ocean, over the forest of eastern Siberia, over the sands of Kazakhstan. Stalin and the state are one and the same."[9] This statue symbolized the iron grip that the Soviets had on the Armenians. From its inception, this grip had led to bloody confrontations, the most dramatic being the murder of an Armenian archbishop in New York City in 1933, which in turn created a schism in the diaspora that would endure for decades.

The genesis of this schism lay in the nature of Armenia's "salvation" by the Soviets. For the Armenian diaspora, the new Armenian Soviet Socialist Republic was a glass half-full. Here was a "soviet republic" made up almost entirely of Armenians, many of whom had been either refugees from Anatolian Turkey or children of those refugees. Though the fighting and killing had finally ended, Armenia was a landlocked state with almost no resources other than its weary populace. Yerevan could trace its history back over two thousand years. Within its boundaries stood Etchmiadzin, the fifteen-hundred-year-old holy city founded by Gregory the Illuminator. Etchmiadzin was the home to the Catholicos of all Armenian Apostolic Christians, making the city and the tiny SSR a kind of mecca for Armenians scattered across the world. Yet for many Armenians living in the West, the Republic of Armenia was on the wrong side of what would soon be labeled the "iron curtain."

The Armenian revolutionaries who had led the republic during its short life at the end of World War I had been ousted when the Armenian SSR was founded. Most had sought safety in Iran or the new French and British protectorates in the Levant. To further complicate the matter, while securing the new SSR, Stalin broke off Armenian territories and "gave" them to Azerbaijan (also an SSR). This move would preserve a violent enmity between the nations which endures to this day. Those Tashnags remaining in Armenia were disposed of by Lenin's security forces, the Cheka.

An equal number of Armenians lived in the United States, France, Lebanon, Syria, Greece, Serbia, and Bulgaria (former possessions of the Ottoman Empire) as lived in Armenia proper. Within each community were thousands of survivors who had mixed feelings about Tashnags. Some sided with the ARF, believing that in the years leading up to and including World War I, the only appropriate Armenian response to Turkish violence was strong revolutionary, often violent action. Others (and among these I would include my own grandparents) felt that the politically activist Armenians were troublemakers who willingly courted violence. These "moderate" Armenians wanted to put the past behind them and live peaceably in their adopted country, whether it be the United States, the Soviet Union, or Lebanon.

As Turkey "emerged" as a state, Armenia had to contend with its own complex kaleidoscope of truth. Stalin's hold on Armenia was absolute. Appealing to the nationalistic feelings of many diasporans, Stalin had invited the scattered Armenians to return to the homeland, and many had accepted the invitation. Unfortunately, this invitation was as much a trap as an opportunity. As he would do so often, Stalin gathered up his imagined enemies so he could more easily dispose of them. The secret police worked relentlessly to root out anyone with even the slightest inclination toward independent thought or self-determination, and thousands of these Armenian returnees were exiled to Siberia. It is estimated that ten thousand Armenians died or were sent to Siberia in the first two decades of the Armenian SSR. Life in urban Armenia, as in all of Stalinist Russia, became paranoid and insecure.[10]

In the period between the wars, the Armenian communities in the United States centered on the church. Virtually every Armenian attended church, through which most social events were organized. Around the world, the hierarchy of the church was complex, with patriarchs residing in Etchmiadzin (near Yerevan), Jerusalem, and Istanbul, and Catholicoi in Sis (then in Antelias, Lebanon) and Etchmiadzin. (Confusingly, the "Catholicos of All Armenians" in Etchmiadzin also has the title of patriarch.) Since the Holy See of Etchmiadzin was located within the Armenian SSR, the Catholicos embraced the Soviet system for the sake of harmony with the mother country. This position was unacceptable to the Tashnags, who held fast to their dream of a totally independent Armenia. The Tashnags honored an alternative Catholicos living outside the Soviet Union.

In the United States, Tashnags and moderate Armenians fought openly. In New England, the Tashnags badgered Archbishop Ghevont Tourian, the church's representative in the eastern United States. Arriving at church-sponsored events, nationalists would unfurl the flag of the short-lived first Armenian Republic. Fights would break out. Archbishop Tourian held to the position that since Etchmiadzin was the Armenian holy city, and since it existed within the USSR, it was essential to maintain peaceful relations with Moscow. The Tashnags were adamant, insisting that "a free, independent, and united Armenia has been, and continues to be, the goal of Tashnag and Armenian national aspirations."[11]

On Christmas Eve 1933, Archbishop Tourian performed mass at the Holy Cross Armenian Apostolic Church in Upper Manhattan. As he made his way down the center aisle, blessing the congregation as part of the Badarak, the holy liturgy of the Armenian Apostolic Church, a parishioner in an overcoat stood up from his pew and stepped toward the cleric. This man in the overcoat was followed by another and then another. The men shouldered their way past the acolytes on either side of Tourian and surrounded him. Blocking the view of the congregation, Tourian was stabbed repeatedly with a long butcher knife. As the holy father collapsed onto the Oriental carpeting, the men made for the exits. Tourian would soon bleed to death as the terrorized churchgoers fled onto 187th Street.

Several men were arrested, convicted of first-degree murder, and sent to prison. Two received death sentences, later commuted to life imprisonment by the governor of New York State. But the damage had been done. From this point on, the diaspora in the United States would be split into clearly defined Tashnag and non-Tashnag camps. New churches were built for the Tashnag congregations. As a youngster I remember passing the Watertown Tashnag church, Saint Stephen's, and asking my father why there were two Armenian churches only a few blocks apart. I'm not sure he knew himself.

The ARF was now isolated, yet it continued to see itself as the champion of Armenian destiny. Armenian nationalism became the religion of the Tashnag organization, with the Soviet state replacing the Ottoman Empire as enemy. Then, in the late 1930s, the very same church fathers living in Soviet Armenia who had tried to make peace with Moscow were rounded up by the GPU, heirs to the Cheka security forces and forerunners of the KGB. "Catholicos Khoren [I Muradbekyan] did not survive the Great Purges of 1936 to 1938. . . . [H]is death, on April 6, 1938, is believed to have been ordered by the secret police."[12] A new sense of desperation set in.

In time, Tashnag and non-Tashnag Armenians would see that some kind of uneasy unity was inevitable, especially since a new consciousness was rising within Soviet Armenia itself. In the spring of 1962, the massive statue of Stalin described by Grossman was replaced by an equally impressive statue of "Mother Armenia." On April 24, 1965, Armenians in Yerevan memorialized the fiftieth anniversary of the genocide with a massive demonstration. Uncharacteristically, the local apparatchiks refrained from cracking down on the demonstrators. Political awareness and activism in Armenia grew.

In the late 1980s, a series of major events ushered in a new era for Armenia. A massive earthquake hit the country, leaving at least thirty thousand people dead; war broke out with Azerbaijan over the disputed territories; and Gorbachev's policies of glasnost and perestroika stimulated the birth of freedom movements all over the Soviet sphere, especially in Armenia. Seemingly overnight, the Soviet Union came to an end in 1991, as it broke up into its constituent pieces. The Republic of Armenia was reborn.

As the Nemesis killings receded deeper into the past, the conspirators began to publicly discuss those events more brazenly. Aram Yerganian's memoir, *We Killed This Way,* had been posthumously published in Armenian by Shahan Natali in 1949. Tehlirian's memoir was published in 1953. Misak Torlakian's *The Course of My Life* was published in Beirut in 1963. In 1964 Natali published an extended article explaining in impossibly lyrical language how Operation Nemesis assassinated Talat. In 1965 Arshavir Shiragian, by this time a successful American businessman (reputed to have made millions selling parachute silk to the U.S. government during World War II), appeared on American Armenian television and, speaking in Armenian, described his involvement. Also around this time, Lindy V. Avakian, the son of a close friend of Tehlirian's, published *The Cross and the Crescent,* a loose account of the conspiracy, much of it written in the first person, in Tehlirian's voice. This was followed by the publication of *The First Genocide of the 20th Century* by James Nazer in 1968, a disturbing collection of photographs and articles exposing the crimes against the Armenians. The book concludes with portraits of Shiragian, Misak Torlakian, Yerganian, and Tehlirian, labeling each an "Armenian National Hero." In 1976, a few years after his death, Arshavir Shiragian's *The Legacy* was published in Armenian, French, and English by the Tashnag organization. It describes in detail how Shiragian's assassinations were committed. Other memoirs would follow, mostly published in Armenian, some translated. In 1986 the eminent French journalist Jacques Derogy researched Nemesis thoroughly, augmenting Tehlirian's account in his Armenian autobiography with details gleaned from the secret ARF archives in Watertown, Massachusetts, to which he had gained access through the archivist Gerard Libaridian. In 1991 Edward Alexander, a former U.S. diplomat, would publish *A Crime of Vengeance,* making Tehlirian's story accessible to the English-speaking American public. Not all the details in these memoirs jibed, but the cat was out of the bag. Armenians had confessed to a campaign of assassination against Turkish leaders in the 1920s.

Although Tehlirian had kept a relatively low profile in the years after he moved to the United States, he continued to consort with fellow Nemesis commandos. According to Vartkes Yeghiayan, who has published a translation of the Tehlirian trial transcript, *The Case of Soghomon Tehlirian,* "the three of them [Tehlirian, Tor-lakian, and Shiragian] always sat together at the functions [at the Armenian Center in San Francisco's Haight-Ashbury district], and without exception always occupied the last row of seats at the very back of the hall....[T]hey were very unassuming, inconspicuous and modest to the point of timidity, and acted as if they were unac-customed to socializing."[13]

Nemesis had been disbanded and its agents were either aged or dead, but its spirit continued to inspire new avengers. The per-sistent Turkish denial of the genocide became intolerable for cer-tain survivors and their descendants. Some Armenians decided to go beyond the annual protests held around the world each year on April 24 and organized new violence. Young men in southern Cal-ifornia and Lebanon, furious that the tragedy of their murdered grandparents had been forgotten, found one another as their col-lective anger compressed into a powder keg of pent-up fury. All that was missing was the spark.

That spark was provided in 1973 by a seventy-seven-year-old Californian, a survivor of the genocide named Gourgen Yanikian. In many ways, Yanikian's story was similar to Tehlirian's. He was from the same region of Asia Minor and, like Tehlirian, was born during the waning decades of the Ottoman Empire. He had lost many members of his family during the genocide. After the war, he settled in Iran. On moving to the United States, Yanikian found that life did not get any easier. In January 1973, sickly and out of funds, Yanikian made the decision to avenge the Armenian Geno-cide on his own.

On January 27, 1973, Gourgen Yanikian contacted the Turkish consulate in Los Angeles and, impersonating an Iranian expat, claimed to have in his possession a painting that had been stolen from the sultan's palace more than a century earlier. Yanikian offered to make a gift of the painting (and other items) to the Republic of Turkey, but insisted that the consul general, forty-seven-year-old Mehmet Baydar, meet him in person to accept the items. Baydar and his thirty-year-old vice consul, Bahadir Demir, agreed to the rendezvous with Yanikian.

Once Yanikian was alone with the two diplomats in his room at the Santa Barbara Biltmore Hotel, he confessed that he was originally from Turkey and that he was an Armenian. He argued with the men, produced a Luger pistol, and shot them both several times. As the two diplomats lay wounded on the floor of his hotel room, Yanikian calmly opened a dresser drawer, removed a Browning pistol, and fired two more shots into each man's head.

As reprehensible as his actions were, Yanikian's arrest and trial became a cause célèbre for many Armenians, serving as a focus for the frustration that had built up over decades of nonrecognition of a major crime against humanity. (This bitterness had only been compounded by the sorrowful recognition accorded to the Jewish Holocaust after World War II.) Many Armenians found a certain satisfaction in the fact that because of Yanikian, people were finally talking about the genocide. The killings were appalling, but to many Armenians they seemed not that different from the endless horror stories all had heard from their grandparents. Few could condone Yanikian's actions, but weren't these violent deaths just one more consequence of the genocide?

During his trial, echoing the attitude of his hero Soghomon Tehlirian,[14] Yanikian admitted to killing the men but said he did not feel that he was guilty of any crime. Claiming that his actions were designed to bring attention to the genocide, he noted that other victimized peoples had had "their Nuremberg" but the Armenians had not. He was indifferent to the fact that his victims were too young to have had anything to do with the deportations. Yanikian had come "to view the men not as human beings, but as symbols of decades of injustice."[15] Before killing the diplomats, he posted a letter to an Armenian-language paper urging Armenians to wage war on Turkish diplomats.[16]

Yanikian was found guilty on two counts of first-degree murder and received a life sentence. While he was incarcerated, his cause was adopted by a new wave of terrorists. Originally calling themselves the Prisoner Gourgen Yanikian Group, ASALA (the Armenian Secret Army for the Liberation of Armenia) consisted primarily of Lebanese-born Armenians dedicated to terror bombings and the assassination of Turkish diplomats and politicians. Their first victim was Danis Tunaligil in Vienna on October 22, 1975. By the mid-1970s, ASALA had launched a worldwide wave of terror bombings and shootings. Before long it was competing with other Armenian terrorist groups, particularly the Armenian Revolutionary Army, or Justice Commandos, a group believed to have been created by the ARF in response to ASALA.

By the time the killing ended in the 1990s, thirty-six Turkish diplomats and those close to them (including wives, children, bodyguards, and drivers) had been murdered. Dozens of others were injured. Four killings took place in the United States, while other attacks occurred in Paris, Belgrade, Ottawa, Tehran, and Sydney. One of the best-known incidents took place at the Turkish Airlines check-in desk at Orly Airport in 1983, where a half kilo of Semtex plastic explosive attached to bottles of gas packed into a suitcase exploded prematurely, killing eight and injuring fifty-five others. Most of the victims had no relationship to Turkey or Armenia. The Orly bombing created a schism within the ASALA organization as disagreements broke out over objectives and the underlying rationale for extremely violent acts.

ASALA members had received training and inspiration from the Palestine Liberation Organization (PLO) in Beirut. In the PLO, ASALA saw a model for terrorism as a political tool: a disenfranchised people who had no political muscle would make their case through violence. Neither ASALA nor the Justice Commandos ever hid the fact that Operation Nemesis was an important model for their groups.[17] Yanikian had set things in motion. In two decades, ASALA, the Justice Commandos, and other groups committed literally hundreds of "actions."

In time, ASALA's best-known leader, Hagop Hagopian (probably an alias), would break from the PLO. Hagopian then allied himself with the notorious Abu Nidal, founder of Fatah, and

ASALA would become even more ruthless and sinister. (Nidal's trade-mark was random killing.) Alienated members finally assassinated Hagopian in April 1988, whereupon ASALA disintegrated. By this time the vast majority of Armenians were disgusted by the killings of innocent people, and many spoke out clearly against the actions of ASALA and other terrorist groups. The violence had made the world more aware of the genocide, but murdering those who had had no direct hand in the tragedy was sickening.

Bombings and killings within Turkey strained Turkish-American relations, too. Turkey felt that the Western governments were not making a genuine effort to apprehend the culprits. A U.S.-Turkish Committee on Armenian Terrorism was formed in 1982 with an eye toward legislation to curtail the operations.[18] But ASALA and the Justice Commandos had fallen into disarray on their own, and by the early 1990s, they were no longer active. Nonetheless, many members of the Turkish diplomatic corps had become hardened by the killing of their colleagues. Most people in Turkey had forgotten the crimes of their elders, but a new generation of Turkish officials would never forget the Armenian terror actions of the 1970s and 1980s. An indifference toward Armenians turned into a deep animosity, stiffening a resolve never to admit to the "so-called genocide."

—ᴍ—

In the early hours of November 3, 1996, on a dark and desolate stretch of the Istanbul-Izmir highway near Susurluk, a speeding Mercedes rammed into a gasoline tanker truck and exploded into a ball of fire. Three bodies were pulled from the scorched wreck: a former deputy head of the Istanbul Police Department; a fugitive hit man and heroin trafficker; and his "beauty queen" lover. The sole survivor was Sedat Bucak, a member of the Turkish parliament and a Kurdish tribal landlord who had formed his own militia to fight Kurdish rebels.

False passports, pistols equipped with silencers, and machine guns were found in the trunk of the wreck. The hit man, Abdullah

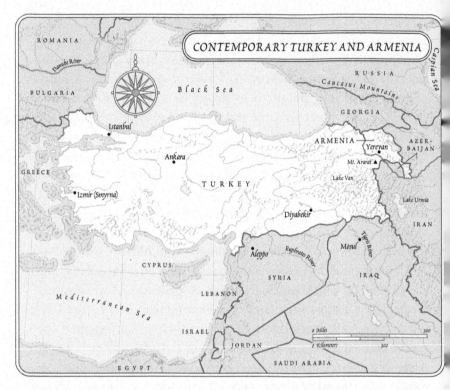

In size, contemporary Turkey and Armenia are fractions of their former realms, the Ottoman Empire and the Kingdom of Armenia. Today, the two republics share a closed border.

Catli, was not only a drug runner but also a former leader of the ultranationalist "Grey Wolves." ("Grey Wolf" is a term of affection synonymous with Kemal Ataturk.) For years he had been wanted by the authorities for his involvement in the 1978 murder of seven leftist university students. On Catli's body was found a false diplomatic passport as well as a gun license signed by the Turkish interior minister, Mehmet Agar.

After it was learned that Agar had met with the group just prior to the accident, he was forced to resign. The "Susurluk Incident" ignited an uproar in Turkey because it definitively revealed for the first time links between the government, terrorist organizations, and drug traffickers. It exposed a long-suspected underlying "Deep State" *(Gizli Devlet)* that secretly ran Turkey behind an appealing façade of official democracy. It seemed that an invisible network made up of politicians, military officers, and intelligence operatives was collaborating with criminal organizations to form the true leadership of the world's "only Islamic democracy." After Susurluk, the center of power shifted in Turkey, and in subsequent elections an Islamic-oriented government took over.

That was twenty years ago, and the political landscape of Turkey remains in flux. As governmental factions struggle with one another, it is very clear that Turkey is not a democracy in the sense that the West understands the term. Censorship and cronyism, torture and corruption are the rule, not the exception.[19] "Islamist" leaders have not yet given way to "jihadist" leaders in Istanbul, because to embrace religious groups too closely would be the wrong move in "secular" Turkey. The veneration of Ataturk remains supreme, while Kemalism as a political philosophy is seen to be in decline under the current leadership.

Perhaps the "Deep State" is losing its grip as well. The trial beginning in 2008 involving the so-called Ergenekon conspiracy (a supposed secularist clandestine group accused of plotting against the Turkish government) may or may not be directed at a genuine organization. Many believe that the Ergenekon arrests, in which hundreds, including journalists, military officers, and opposition lawmakers, have been taken into custody and charged with crimes against the state, are targeting a paper tiger for the purposes of undermining enemies of the current regime.[20]

In January 2007, Hrant Dink, the Armenian Turkish editor of *Agos,* an Armenian journal published in Istanbul, was gunned down as he stepped outside his office. His killer was Ogun Samast, a seventeen-year-old Turk with links to the nationalist, pro-Turanist organizations Great Union Party and the Grey Wolves. Dink was a man of tremendous integrity who risked his life by writing editorial appeals for reconciliation between Armenians and Turks. His reasonableness and courage became an irritant to radical elements in Turkey. His murder came after a year of death threats. After Samast's arrest, photographs of the killer were posted online. In one photo he is flanked by genial Turkish policemen posing before a Turkish flag.

The Turkish public responded to Dink's killing with a massive protest. At Dink's funeral, two hundred thousand mourners crowded the streets of Istanbul carrying signs stating simply "We Are All Hrant Dink" and "We Are All Armenians." In September 2010, the European Court of Human Rights concluded that the Turkish government had violated Dink's right to life by not trying to prevent his murder and, in addition, taking no concrete action to punish the police for their inaction. Despite parliamentary, judicial, and civil efforts to further expose this apparent action by the "Deep State" network, there have been no significant consequences as a result of these investigations.

—❧—

As I write these last words of this book, I realize that in the end it is impossible to communicate the immensity of the crime I've come to know through my research. Though this effort is a tapestry of history and politics, of leaders and soldiers and assassins, the core of what this book is really about is almost unfathomable. As I checked my last edits of the manuscript and rechecked some of my source materials, particularly Raymond Kévorkian's massive work on the genocide, Wolfgang Gust's collection of memoirs, and Verjiné Svazlian's collection of eyewitness testimony, I was overwhelmed by the vastness and sheer brutality of the crime.

Genocide is a word. Like the words "love" or "God," it seems to be comprehensible. But in fact it cannot be grasped, it cannot be taken in. It is the unspeakable made verbal. Yet it is very much a part of our lives. Every week we read in the newspaper about violence in the form of massacres and terror attacks. And for this reason, we think we understand the meaning of the word when we hear of genocide. But war or environmental calamity has the quality of circumstances out of control. Genocide is different. What happened to the Armenian population in Turkey during World War I was intentional. Men made decisions, men made plans, and those men executed those plans.

The immensity of the Armenian Genocide is beyond conception. How can human beings commit such atrocities? The crime defies an answer. What we do know is that such a crime against humanity must be reacted to and that it must be memorialized. Thus Operation Nemesis. Though the men and women of Operation Nemesis broke the laws of man, they did so to bring some portion of sanity to an insane world. The unthinkable actually cannot be answered, but in the case of Armen Garo, Shahan Natali, Soghomon Tehlirian, and others, to act was the only way to continue living. Otherwise they too would have been consumed by the insanity.

The Nemesis fedayeen did not see themselves as terrorists. From their point of view, their actions were driven by motives that far surpassed simple retribution or revenge. As holy warriors, they believed their domain to be spiritual, not political. Their job was to exact some fraction of justice. In other words, killing Talat Pasha, Djemal Pasha, Behaeddin Shakir, and Said Halim Pasha was an attempt to bring some kind of balance to the universe. The CUP leadership, in the eyes of Garo and Natali, had evaded just punishment for mass murder. Though the perpetrators were convicted by a court of law in Constantinople, those convictions were later thrown out by the new Ankara government. A new Turkish regime was taking shape, and it was clear that the men who had organized and carried out the genocide would participate in it. To let these men walk free would be wrong in the deepest sense.

That does not make what Operation Nemesis did legal. One question that surrounds these assassinations is this: If you desire a world where justice prevails, then you must rely on laws. If you rely on laws, they must be universal. Laws cannot be superseded simply because some feel that they are wrong or because a person "knows" he has the right to break them. We live in a world where we attempt to achieve consistency in rule of law. The concept of "law" demands it. Yet the men and women of Operation Nemesis did what governments could not. They were appealing to a higher, final justice. One that exists somewhere between heaven and earth.

—ᴍ—

My grandfather told me stories from his life. It was his gift to me. Memory lies at the center of the Nemesis story. It is the engine of an intense bloodlust. We remember, but we remember differently. Our respective narratives lead to different actions. Thus the conundrum of history. Were you there? Did you actually see it? Who told you about it? How can you be sure?

Operation Nemesis is only one link in a historical chain that began long before its actors were born and that continues to this day. The Hamidian massacres of the late nineteenth century gave birth to Armenian revolutionary groups that fought the Ottoman government in eastern Anatolia. The Ottoman government under the Young Turks, shrouded by the fog of war, used this activity as a justification for liquidating an entire indigenous population. And though tribunals were held after the war, little was done in the end to bring the perpetrators to justice. Operation Nemesis was born and carried out its mandate. And then, a half century after the genocide, as the Turkish government persisted in its refusal to acknowledge one of the greatest mass murders in history, a new generation rose up and initiated an anarchic string of assassinations. In 2007 one more link in the chain was forged with the tragic assassination of the Armenian Turkish editor Hrant Dink.

And so memory and retribution are linked. But why? Why is it so important to remember what happened? All people who live will die someday, and in a few generations most of us will be forgotten altogether, so why does it make any difference whether the details of our particular deaths are remembered, violent or not?

Perhaps the answer lies in the very fact that we *do* all die, that no one cheats death. We come into this world with nothing and we leave with nothing. We all know, either implicitly or explicitly, that all we really have is our place in the memories of others. We exist to the degree that we know and remember one another. Even the most isolated among us. We share a collective understanding that we are all part of a greater whole. Perhaps we will not be remembered as individuals, but we, the living, move through life surrounded by what the dead have left for us. The dead live on in the pages of thousands of books, in the bricks of countless buildings, in the flickering shadows of old movies, in virtually everything we see and touch, including our own children.

For this reason, we must respect the dead. It is this contract of respect we have with those who have gone before us that demands we acknowledge how they died and, if they died violently, to seek redress. The question that is almost impossible to answer is what should we do if those who committed the original crime go unpunished? What if those who follow in the footsteps of those who committed the original crime insist on hiding the truth? What then? In the end, is there such a thing as justice?

This book is an attempt to meditate on an answer, not only by providing the facts as best we know them, but also by research and authorship, and through your willingness to read what I have to offer. In that way we honor those hundreds of thousands who were condemned to anonymous death and burial, whose memory lasts only as long as our memories do.

POSTSCRIPT

The year 2015 marks one hundred years since Talat Pasha and the CUP ruled over the last days of the Ottoman Empire. One hundred years ago, millions of Armenians lived in Asia Minor. Today, fewer than ninety thousand people living in Turkey call themselves Armenian. In many ways, the destruction of the Christians in the Ottoman Empire began a trend. Throughout the Middle East, fewer and fewer Christians make their home where Islam is the majority religion. Year by year, Turkey plays a greater role as a major representative of the United States in the Middle East. Turkey is now considered to be an irreplaceable component of American foreign policy. The Turkish government has more than enough incentive to remain silent about the genocide of one hundred years ago.

Whether Turkey wants to be part of the European Union or not, it binds itself ever more tightly to the West with each passing year. What began as a military relationship has become a deeply economic one, and that in turn has affected civic life in Turkey. The institutions of the republic, particularly its university system and judiciary, as well as its social life, can no longer exist in concert with manufactured history. The truth is easily accessible, and Turkish scholars and writers, young people using social media, anyone watching television, must in time be exposed to it, despite the law forbidding discussion of the genocide. Some brave souls are writing about it and investigating it. The tide of truth is rising.

A rising tide floats all boats. And that includes the full history of the Armenians who lived within and outside the Ottoman Empire. The Armenian Genocide is a part of that history, but so is the story of the Armenian revolutionary groups and their actions. And so are the contributions Armenians made for centuries to Ottoman civilization. And so is Operation Nemesis. We can only hope that serious scholars will someday be allowed to enter the shuttered archives, Turkish and Armenian, to uncover the memories we're losing, the history we've lost, including the full and complete story of this brave group of men possessed of remarkable will and courage.

ACKNOWLEDGMENTS

First and foremost, I must thank Aram Arkun for his dedication and invaluable guidance during this long journey. Aram provided the translations of Armenian and Turkish which were essential to a full investigation of the story. He was there with an answer to my every question on Armenian and Turkish history and politics. He vetted the manuscript several times. He was there from start to finish. Thank you, Aram.

Thanks to Ted Bogosian and Marc Mamigonian, who made themselves available from the very first with desperately needed informational and emotional support. Thanks to Leslie Peirce for invaluable expertise.

Thanks to those people who shared with me their personal knowledge of Operation Nemesis and Armenian revolutionary activity: Viken Hovsepian, Gerard Libaridian, Marian Mesrobian MacCurdy, Sylva Natali Manoogian, and Melineh Verma.

Thanks to my history-writing coach and buddy Sarah Vowell, who was also ready with strategy and a backslap when the going got rough. Thanks to my old friend Joel Golb, who provided the rock-solid German translation of the Berlin trial and hosted my visit to Berlin. Thanks to Eddy Vicken Noukoujikian for a warm introduction to Armenian Paris. And to all the folks at NAASR.

Special thanks to my agent Simon Green, who was always

there for me when I was ready to give up. And thanks to George Lane and Ronald Taft, my longtime associates, who once again provided their invaluable guidance.

Thanks to Geoffrey Shandler, who invited me into the Little, Brown fold and encouraged a more ambitious book. Thank you to Reagan Arthur for believing in this book, to John Parsley for his calm, steadfast presence, and very, very importantly David Sobel, who diligently solved the unsolvable and did not despair when faced with hundreds of pages of disorganized manuscript.

Special thanks to those who provided research and editorial assistance: Annette Vowinckel (Berlin), Dana Vowinckel, Maria Alegre, Ewan Roxbourgh, Liz Seramur at Wyss Photo, Melissa Levine at the University of Michigan, and at Little, Brown, Allie Sommer, Malin von Euler-Hogan, Amanda Heller, Ruth Cross, and Betsy Uhrig. Thanks to the promotion team, Catherine Cullen and Meghan Deans. Thank you to Jeffrey Ward for his impeccable cartography.

Special thanks to the Manoogian Simone Foundation and the Alex and Marie Manoogian Foundation, for granting me an Armenian Studies Program Fellowship at the University of Michigan. The time I spent there exploring the broader themes with experts in the field was an invaluable aid. Very special thanks to Kathryn Babayan and Ronald Grigor Suny for inviting me. Thanks to Kevork Bardakjian, Melanie Tanielian, and Tamar Boyadjian as well as the postdoctoral fellows who provided much-needed interrogations: Ruken Sengul, Michael Pifer, and Hayarpi Papikyan. Thanks to Zana Kweiser and Michelle Andonian for enlarging my visit to Ann Arbor and Detroit. Finally, special thanks to Fatma Muge Gocek for the long discussions and support.

A number of experts in the fields of Ottoman and Armenian history donated their precious time to answer my questions and engage in naked discussions of the topic. Thank you to Taner Akcam, Anny Bakalian (Middle East and Middle Eastern American Center, CUNY), Peter Balakian, Michael Bobelian, Lerna Ekmekcioglu, Ayda Erbal, Basak Ertur, Ara Ghazarians (Armenian

Cultural Foundation), Vartan Gregorian, Christopher Gunn, Rolf Hosfeld (Lepsius Institute, Berlin), Jean Claude Kebabjian (Center for Armenian Diaspora Studies, Paris), Raymond Kévorkian (AGBU Nubarian Library, Paris), Stephen Kinzer, Vartan Matiossian, Khatchig Mouradian (Hairenik), Nora Nercessian, Gregory P. Nowell, Donald Quataert, Verjiné Svazlian, Alina and Zareh Tcheknavorian, and Ruth Thomasian (Project SAVE).

During my visits to Istanbul, special thanks to Arzu Turkomen (Bogazici University), Agah Okay Alkan, and Robert Koptas (*Agos*) for extending the most generous hospitality and opening doors for me that would have otherwise remained closed.

Thanks to Rolf Hosfeld and his staff at Lepsiushaus for their generous contributions of time and material.

Thanks to the New York Public Library and Kay Westcott and Jill Clements at the Watertown Public Library.

I must thank Mark Stahlman, Grayson Fertig, and Radenko Miskovic, who kept me in fighting shape and heard every word of this book before it was written.

Finally, there is a mixture of friendship and concrete help that's impossible to quantify. Thanks to Philip Rinaldi, Vahak Janbazian, Sarah Leah Whitson, Karren Karagulian, Debbie Ohanian, Lily Gulian-Bogosian, Michael Morris, Jesse Drucker, Onick Papazian, Atom Egoyan, Arsinee Khanjian, Kimberly Ryan, and Fred Zollo.

Thanks to Warren Leight. He knows I couldn't have afforded to write this book without his inspired sense of casting.

Thanks to my amazing sons, Harry and Travis Bogosian, who supported the production of this book with encouragement and concrete assistance.

Finally, thank you Jo, my love, who is always there for me.

A SHORT GLOSSARY OF
NAMES AND TERMS

Armenia—A homeland to the Christian Armenians straddling the borders of
  Turkey, Iran, and Russia. Two thousand years ago, Armenia was a
  kingdom and a power to be reckoned with. After World War I, the
  landlocked Republic of Armenia, comprising a fraction of its original
  territory, was founded in the Caucasus. This republic was annexed to the
  Soviet Union in 1922, and since 1991 it has existed as an independent
  nation.

The Ottoman Empire—The Islamic empire established by the Turkish
  Osmanli dynasty. It endured for over six centuries. At its peak, the
  empire stretched from the Balkans to Persia, as well as Egypt and North
  Africa. The Ottoman Empire formally ceased to exist at the end of
  World War I.

The Republic of Turkey—The Turkish nation established by Kemal
  Ataturk and other Young Turks after the demise of the Ottoman Empire.
  It is roughly congruent to the region called Asia Minor, which stretches
  from the Mediterranean to the Caucasus and northern Iran and is
  bordered on the north by the Black Sea.

  Many names have changed over the centuries. The most significant is
  that Constantinople officially became Istanbul in the 1920s. Smyrna
  became Izmir, Salonika became Thessalonika, and so on. Sometimes the
  new name sounds nothing like the old: today's Elazig was Kharpert. In
  this book I use the names that were prevalent in the respective periods.

The Hai Heghapokhakan Tashnagtsutiun refers to the Armenian
  Revolutionary Federation, or ARF, founded in 1890. Members of this
  organization are referred to as Tashnags.

The Osmanli Ittihad ve Terakki Cemiyeti refers to the Ottoman Committee of Union and Progress (CUP). Members are often known as Ittihadists, Unionists, and sometimes Young Turks. The term "Young Turks" originally referred to a variety of Turkish political activists, not only the CUP.

Central Committee — The ruling junta of the CUP from 1908 to 1918. Talat Pasha, Enver Pasha, and Djemal Pasha were members of the Central Committee.

Hnchags — Members of a socialist Armenian revolutionary group (the Social Democrat Hunchakian Party, or SDHP), founded in the late nineteenth century, a few years before the ARF.

Hamidiye — Kurdish paramilitary fighters responsible for massacres of Armenians in rural eastern Anatolia, particularly in the 1890s. These units were named in honor of Sultan Abdul Hamid.

Sultan Abdul Hamid II (Abdulhamid; Abd al-Hamid) was the last sultan with any real power. He presided over the Ottoman Empire for the thirty years prior to World War I.

Talat Pasha (Mehmet Talat) was interior minister of the Ottoman Empire during the CUP years, including World War I. By the end of the war he had assumed the position of Grand Vizier (1917–18). He fled Constantinople at the end of the war and was subsequently convicted in absentia of war crimes.

General Mustafa Kemal/Ataturk — The key Ottoman military leader during World War I. Later he would command the nationalist insurgency that fought the Greeks and the Armenians. He would found the Turkish Republic in 1923. As Ataturk, Kemal led his nation until his death in 1938. Depending on the period, I use the name he was known by during that time.

Anatolia (Asia Minor) — A general term used in this book for loosely describing the peninsula of land that roughly corresponds to today's Turkey. Also known as Asia Minor. "Anatolia" is a political term used by the Turkish government to describe all of its lands. Originally, Anatolia's eastern border was the Euphrates, and the farthest eastern reaches of what is now called Anatolia were originally known as the Armenian plateau.

Smyrna/Izmir — Major city along the Turkish Aegean coast, destroyed by Kemalist troops as they entered the city in September 1922.

The Special Organization (Teshkilati Mahsusa) — A secret paramilitary organization formed by the Committee of Union and Progress to perform extralegal operations, particularly conducting guerrilla warfare and overseeing the Armenian Genocide.

Mahomet, Mehmet, Mohammed, Muhammad are equivalent names in Turkish and Arabic.

Patriarch refers to a leader of a Christian church. The Catholicos is the supreme head of the Armenian Apostolic Church.

The Franks are the French and are equivalent in the Ottoman mind to the Catholic Crusaders who arrived in the Middle East from Europe in the late Middle Ages.

Softas — Muslim students.

Caliph — Leader of the Islamic world.

Imam — In Islam, religious leader, specifically prayer leader.

Vilayet — Province.

Vali — Governor of a vilayet.

Sultan — Padishah. Supreme leader of the Ottoman Empire.

Pasha, Bey — Terms of respect equivalent to "Mr." or "sir." Pasha denotes a member of the highest level of an elite.

Sublime Porte — A term referring to the Ottoman government, especially the offices of the Grand Vizier.

Grand Vizier — The most powerful leader in the Ottoman Empire after the sultan, equivalent to a prime minister.

Kurds — Muslim tribal people of eastern Turkey, northern Persia, and Iraq, sometimes led by warlords and chieftains, who harassed Christian Armenians as well as fought Turkish troops.

Chete — A member of a guerrilla band. During World War I the term refers to the paramilitaries who were particularly violent members of the Special Organization, often convicts released specifically to employ terrorism against local populations.

Apostolic or Gregorian Church — The original Armenian Christian Church. "Monophysite" refers to a doctrinal distinction that separated the Armenian Church from some other early churches, particularly the Byzantine Church and what would later become the Roman Catholic Church.

Sharia — Islamic law. The Ottoman Empire was governed by Sharia in combination with sultanic law.

Zapiteh, **gendarmes** — Police.

Muhacir — Muslim refugees who emigrated into Turkey just prior to and during World War I, primarily from the Balkans.

Millet — Community defined by its religious affiliation.

Raya — Flock, common folk subject to poll tax. Also derogatory, meaning "sheep," when referring to Armenians.

A NOTE ON LANGUAGE

Almost every town and vilayet referred to here is known by at least three names: its old Ottoman name, its Armenian name, and its current Turkish name. When possible I have tried to use the Ottoman name, since most of this story takes place during the era of the Ottoman Empire. To further complicate things, spellings are phonetic versions derived from either old Ottoman script or Armenian. These phonetic spellings vary from source to source. I've tried to be consistent: I use "Kharpert" for "Harpoot" and so on. In addition, today's Turkish employs a different alphabet that is similar but not equivalent to the alphabet we use in English. I've dropped the Turkish special characters and used the accepted Western spelling, so, for example, "Talat," which would normally need a diacritical mark over the second "a," is spelled here as "Talat" rather than "Talaat" (or with the mark). Finally, Western Armenian and Eastern Armenian are different versions of the same root language. Western Armenian refers to the language of the Ottoman (Turkish) Armenians. I have opted for Western Armenian when possible here.

NOTES

PROLOGUE

1. Aubrey Herbert, *Ben Kendim: A Record of Eastern Travel,* ed. Desmond MacCarthy (London: Hutchinson & Co., 1924), p. 318.
2. This account is drawn from Soghomon Tehlirian, *Verhisumner Hoosaber* [Memoirs], ed. Vahan Minakhorian, tr. Aram Arkun (Cairo, 1953), pp. 307–8; hereafter cited as Tehlirian memoir.
3. Ibid. p. 310.
4. Ibid.
5. Greeks, Syriacs, and other Christian people living in the Ottoman Empire were persecuted under the Ittihad regime.

CHAPTER 1: THE RISE OF EMPIRE

1. The term "Asia Minor/Anatolia" has historically meant the territory up to the Euphrates River—meaning everything *but* the Armenian plateau; the Republic of Turkey favors the term to describe its entire territory in Asia, thus eliminating mention of Armenia. This usage has altered the generally accepted understanding of the term, and for the sake of simplicity in this volume I will use the terms interchangeably to describe the entire peninsula extending from the Caucasus to the Mediterranean Sea.
2. See Hovann H. Simonian, ed., *The Hemshin: History, Society, and Identity in the Highlands of Northeast Turkey* (New York: Routledge, 2007).
3. Noel Malcolm, *Kosovo: A Short History* (New York: New York University Press, 1998), p. 95.
4. The head of the Armenian faith carries the title "Catholicos of All Armenians." It is not clear when this term was first used. The first Christian churches were headed by bishops. See Malachia Ormanian, *The*

Church of Armenia (London: A. R. Mowbray & Co., revised ed., 1955), pp. 8–13.

5. Fred C. Conybeare, "The Survival of Animal Sacrifices inside the Christian Church," *American Journal of Theology* 7 (1910): 63.

6. Sean McMeekin, *The Berlin-Baghdad Express: The Ottoman Empire and Germany's Bid for World Power* (Cambridge: Belknap Press of Harvard University Press, 2010), p. 28.

7. Daniel Goffman, *The Ottoman Empire and Early Modern Europe* (Cambridge: Cambridge University Press, 2002), p. 13.

8. The summary of Armenian history given here is a simplification of a complex era in which the Romans/Byzantines vied for control of the region with the Persians. For a complete history, see Richard G. Hovanissian, *The Armenian People from Ancient to Modern Times: The Dynastic Periods; From Antiquity to the Fourteenth Century,* 2nd ed., vol. 1, and *The Armenian People from Ancient to Modern Times: Foreign Dominion to Statehood; The Fifteenth Century to the Twentieth Century,* 2nd ed., vol. 2 (New York: St. Martin's Press, 2004).

9. For a complete explication of the term "monophysite," see *The New Catholic Encyclopedia,* 2nd ed., vol. 9 (Washington, DC: Thomson Gale in association with the Catholic University of America, 2001), s.v. "monophysitism." Also Malachia Ormanian, *The Church of Armenia* (London: A. R. Mowbray & Co., 1955), pp. 96, 97.

10. There have been successive caliphates, Islamic governments headed by the caliph, going back to the time of Mohammed. These would include the Rashidun Caliphate, the Umayad Caliphate, and the Abbasid Caliphate. All were considered *dar al-Islam.* These preceded the Ottoman Caliphate, of which the sultan was head. The history of Islamic dynasties is complex. For a complete history of Islam, see Karen Armstrong, *Islam: A Short History* (New York: Modern Library, 2000).

11. The Mongols flourished during the thirteenth and fourteenth centuries. At its height, the Mongol Empire was the largest in contiguous landmass the world has seen. Though feared and destructive during their invasions, the Mongols were an important civilization as well. See David Morgan, *The Mongols* (London: Wiley, 2007).

12. "Pilgrims came from different clutures and spoke different languages— German, Flemish, Norman, French, Provencal, and Italian—but their shared experiences instilled in them a common identity: Now all were Franks." Jay Rubenstein, *Armies of Heaven: The First Crusade and the Quest for Apocalypse* (New York: Basic Books, 2011), p. xii.

13. Speros Vryonis Jr., *Byzantium and Europe* (London: Thames & Hudson, 1967), p. 152.

14. Serbs, Bulgars, and Bosnians were the people of the Balkans. Many other groups populated the Ottoman Empire. See chapter 1, p. 19.

15. Goffman, *The Ottoman Empire and Early Modern Europe*, p. 68.

16. Lord Patrick Douglas Balfour, Baron Kinross, *The Ottoman Centuries: The Rise and Fall of the Turkish Empire* (New York: Harper Perennial, 2002), p. 329.

17. Carter Vaughn Findley, *The Turks in World History* (New York: Oxford University Press, 2005), p. 115.

18. Quoted in Noel Barber, *The Sultans* (New York: Simon & Schuster, 1973), p. 46.

19. See Leslie P. Peirce, *The Imperial Harem: Women and Sovereignty in the Ottoman Empire* (New York: Oxford University Press, 1993), for a complete examination of the imperial harem; quotation p. 76.

20. *The Oxford Encyclopedia of the Modern Islamic World,* ed. John L. Esposito, 4 vols. (New York: Oxford University Press, 1995), s.v. "harem."

21. Philip Mansel, *Constantinople: City of the World's Desire, 1453–1924* (London: John Murray Publishers, 1995), p. 96.

22. Halil Inalcik, *The Ottoman Empire: The Classical Age, 1300–1600* (London: Phoenix, 2000), p. 85.

23. Alber Hourani, *A History of the Arab Peoples* (Cambridge: Belknap Press of Harvard University Press, 1991), p. 47.

24. Mansel, *Constantinople,* p. 21.

25. The history of nineteenth-century Ottoman politics as they relate to the Armenians is a complex and demanding topic, far beyond what I can get into here. For a clear overview, see Aram Arkun, "Into the Modern Age, 1800–1913," chapter 4 of *The Armenians: Past and Present in the Making of National Identity,* ed. Edmund Herzig and Marina Kurkchiyan (London: RoutledgeCurzon, 2005), pp. 65–88.

Chapter 2: Rushing Headlong into the Modern Era, 1800–1914

1. See *Washington Times,* July 28 and August 17, 1914.

2. Ian Kershaw, *Hitler: A Biography* (New York: W. W. Norton & Co., 2008), p. 106.

3. Daily life would for the most part appear unchanged. But larger systemic changes in economics and the distribution of manufactured goods would alter the relationship between the Christians and Muslims of the Ottoman Empire, exacerbating friction between communities. See Donald

Quataert, *The Ottoman Empire, 1700–1922* (New York: Cambridge University Press, 2005), chap. 7 for an introduction to the topic.

4. Compare Hamidye raiders to the "official" Janjaweed paramilitary in the Darfur region of Sudan today. For descriptions of Janjaweed raids, see Dave Eggers, *What Is the What* (New York: Vintage, 2007) pp. 85–95.

5. Vahakn N. Dadrian, *The History of the Armenian Genocide: Ethnic Conflict from the Balkans to Anatolia to the Caucasus* (New York: Berghahn Books, 1995), p. 121.

6. Though the terms "terror" and "terrorist" can be found throughout ARF literature from its earliest days, the leaders of the Tashnags and their fedayeen were absolutely against attacks on innocent civilians, and so the modern use of the term "terror" is *not* congruent with the ARF use of the word. Assassinations of officials and "traitors" were the mainstay, though there could be exceptions, as seen in the paragraphs that follow.

7. Mikayel Varandian, *Murad of Sepastia,* trans. Ara Ghazarians (Arlington, MA: Armenian Cultural Foundation, 2006), p. 30fn.

8. Gerard J. Libaridian, *Modern Armenia: People, Nation, State* (New Brunswick, NJ: Transaction Publishers, 2007), p. 7.

9. "Kurdish Fiendish Cruelty," *New York Times,* March 19, 1895, reprinted in Richard Diran Kloian, *The Armenian Genocide: News Accounts from the American Press: 1915–1922,* 4th ed. (Richmond, CA: Heritage Publishing, 2007), pp. 1–30.

10. W. E. Gladstone, MP, *Bulgarian Horrors and the Question of the East* (London: John Murray, 1876), p. 9.

11. Von Trotha quoted in Clive Ponting, *Progress and Barbarism: The World in the Twentieth Century* (London: Chatto and Windus, 1998), p. 43. In 1904, the German army under von Trotha forced the Herrero people, including women and children, into the desert to die.

12. Al. Carthill, *The Lost Dominion* (London: Blackwood, 1924), p. 94. "Al. Carthill" was the pen name of Bennet Christian Huntingdon Calcraft-Kennedy, a mid-level administrator who had been stationed in India.

13. Piers Brendon, *Decline and Fall of the British Empire* (New York: Vintage, 2010), p. 12.

14. "Mr. Herbert Morrison Replies to Critics of Empire," *Manchester Guardian,* January 11, 1943.

15. Caglar Keyder, *State and Class in Turkey: A Study in Capitalist Development* (London: Verso, 1987), p. 64.

16. Yves Troshine, "A Bystander's Notes of a Massacre," *Scribner's Magazine,* January 21, 1897, 48–69.

17. Armen Garo, *Bank Ottoman* (Detroit: Topouzian, 1990; originally published Boston: Hairenik Press, 1948), p. 155.

18. Louise Nalbandian, *The Armenian Revolutionary Movement: The Development of Armenian Political Parties through the Nineteenth Century* (Berkeley: University of California Press, 1963), pp. 110, 168. Nalbandian's history of the genesis of the Armenian political parties of the nineteenth century is the most complete reference to date.

19. Libaridian, *Modern Armenia*, p. 83.

20. Edward Joris's mystery-laden participation in the assassination attempt has been for the most part ignored by English-speaking historians. Most references can be found in Belgian or Dutch publications. See Mete Ozturk, "Edward Joris: De Belgische anarchist achter de verijdelde Yildiz-aanslag," *Zaman Vandaag* (Rotterdam), July 19, 2013.

21. Though the sultan was the leader of an Islamic empire, his role as caliph was a political rather than a religious one. There is very little evidence of sultans ever being particularly religious. In fact, not one sultan in the history of the Ottoman Empire ever went on the hajj, the pilgrimage to Mecca.

22. Quoted in Shirley W. Smith, *James Burrill Angell: An American Influence* (Ann Arbor: University of Michigan Press, 1954), p. 265.

23. M. Şükrü Hanioglu, *Preparation for a Revolution: The Young Turks, 1902–1908* (Oxford: Oxford University Press, 2001), p. 312.

24. Keyder, *State and Class in Turkey*, p. 59.

25. Hanioglu, *Preparation for a Revolution*, p. 313.

26. Erik J. Zürcher, *The Young Turk Legacy and Nation Building: From the Ottoman Empire to Atatürk's Turkey* (London: I. B. Tauris, 2010), p. 103.

27. Rolf Hosfeld, "The Armenian Massacre and Its Avengers," *IP Journal* (Transatlantic Edition), Fall 2005 (original German edition, June 2005), http://www.armenews.com/IMG/original_TIP_3-05_Hosfeld_1_.pdf.

28. Hanioglu, *Preparation for Revolution*, p. 283.

29. Henry Morgenthau, *Secrets of the Bosphorus* (London: Hutchinson & Co., 1918), p. 13.

30. Vahakn N. Dadrian, *German Responsibility in the Armenian Genocide: A Review of the Historical Evidence of German Complicity* (Watertown, MA: Blue Crane Books, 1996), p. 217.

31. In 2010, *Chienne d'Histoire*, a short animation based on the eradication of the dogs of Constantinople, won a Palme d'Or at the Cannes Film Festival. https://www.youtube.com/watch?v=YMzp8v1AvzU.

Chapter 3: Blood Flows

1. For a complete recounting of the start of World War I with emphasis on Ottoman Empire participation, see David Fromkin, *A Peace to End All*

Peace: The Fall of the Ottoman Empire and the Creation of the Modern Middle East (New York: Henry Holt and Co., 2001).

2. Grigoris Balakian, *Armenian Golgotha: A Memoir of the Armenian Genocide, 1915–1918,* trans. Peter Balakian (New York: Alfred A. Knopf, 2009), p. 42.

3. The story of Major Hovannes Karnik Papazian, an Armenian artillery officer stationed in Gallipoli, is worth noting. Throughout the war, Armenians who were seen as irreplaceable were not deported; instead they were retained to perform essential services. Though he was Armenian, Papazian had risen up through the ranks during the short period after the reinstatement of the constitution when Armenians were allowed to serve. In fact, he had gone to military academy at the same time as Mustapha Kemal Ataturk. Papazian's efforts on the battlements were significant enough to earn him a medal for valor, the Harp Medalyasi. By 1915, realizing that his life was in danger, Papazian escaped to Aleppo and in time settled in the United States. Author's interview with Papazian's grandson Onick Papazian. See also http://www .tanerakcam.com/debates/sarkis-torossian-debate for information on another Armenian Ottoman officer, Sarkis Torossian.

4. For a more complete investigation of property seizure, see Ugur Umit Ungor and Mehmet Polatel, *Confiscation and Destruction: The Young Turk Seizure of Armenian Property* (London: Continuum International Publishing Group, 2011).

5. Mae M. Derdarian, *Vergeen: A Survivor of the Armenian Genocide; Based on a Memoir by Virginia Meghrouni* (Los Angeles: ATMUS Press Publications, 1996), p. 38.

6. "Frequently, heaps of used Armenian clothing and sometimes children's shoes were auctioned. Auctions were conducted by town criers who received half of a 5 percent tax on auctioned goods (the other 2½ percent was transferred to the government). Christian Gerlach, *Extremely Violent Societies: Mass Violence in the Twentieth-Century World* (Cambridge, UK: Cambridge University Press, 2010), pp. 97, 98.

7. To give an air of legitimacy to the massacres and theft of Armenian property, two laws were enacted by the Ittihad government. The Temporary Law of Deportation and the Temporary Law of Confiscation and Appropriation were announced in the early summer months as villages were emptied and property collected. The first law did not specify that the Armenians in particular were to be moved, but it laid the foundation for the later argument that the Armenians were being moved because of the ongoing war activity in their provinces. The second "law" was for the purposes of providing an alibi. Denialists of the genocide note

that laws concerning "abandoned property" included clauses providing for the "safekeeping" of deportees' possessions as well as procedures for the eventual return of goods and land. These laws were only window dressing only. First of all, the property was not "abandoned." Second, even if people managed to survive, nothing was returned to them. For additional information, see Peter Balakian, *The Burning Tigris: The Armenian Genocide and America's Response* (New York: HarperCollins, 2003).

8. See Raffi Khatchadourian, "A Century of Silence," *The New Yorker* (January 5, 2015), pp. 32–53.

9. Giacomo Gorrini, *Il Messaggero* (Rome), August 1915, quoted in James Bryce and Arnold Toynbee, *The Treatment of Armenians in the Ottoman Empire, 1915–16: Documents Presented to Viscount Grey of Fallodon by Viscount Bryce*, ed. Ara Sarafian (Reading, UK: Taderon Press, 2000), pp. 317, 318; hereafter cited as Viscount Bryce, "Blue Book."

10. The United States did not enter the war until April 1917 and at that time made a declaration of war only against Germany. The United States was never at war with the Ottoman Empire (Turkey), and so its representatives retained a certain freedom of movement within the empire.

11. Morgenthau, *Secrets of the Bosphorus* (London: Hutchinson & Co., 1918), pp. 215, 216 .

12. See Sarah Vowell, *Unfamiliar Fishes* (New York: Riverhead, 2011).

13. See Joseph L. Grabill, *Protestant Diplomacy and the Near East: Missionary Influence on American Policy, 1810–1927* (Minneapolis: University of Minnesota Press, 1971), p. 19.

14. Ibid., p. 7.

15. Ibid., pp. 11, 12.

16. H. G. O. Dwight, *Christianity in Turkey: A Narrative of the Protestant Reformation in the Armenian Church* (London: James Nisbet and Co., 1854), pp. 8, 10.

17. Elie Kedourie, *The Chatham House Version and Other Middle-Eastern Studies* (1970; reprint, Hanover, NH: University Press of New England, 1984), pp. 287–88.

18. James L., Barton, comp., *Turkish Atrocities: Statements of American Missionaries on the Destruction of Christian Communities in Ottoman Turkey, 1915–1917* (Ann Arbor: Gomidas Institute, 1998), pp. 12, 15.

19. From Maria Jacobsen, *Diaries of a Danish Missionary: Harpoot, 1907–1919*, ed. Ara Sarafian, trans. Kristen Vind (Princeton: Gomidas Institute Books, 2001), p. 65 (May 30), p. 83 (July 29), p. 86 (August 7), pp. 86, 87 (August 14), p. 93 (October 2).

20. The quotations that follow are from Leslie A. Davis, *The Slaughterhouse Province: An American Diplomat's Report on the Armenian Genocide,*

1915–1917, ed. Susan K. Blair (New Rochelle, NY: Aristide D. Caratzas, 1989), pp. 8, 81.

21. *United States Official Records on the Armenian Genocide,* comp. Ara Sarafian (Princeton: Gomidas Institute, 2004).

22. Military Mission B, no. 1950 Secret, Constantinople, November 17, 1916, in *The Armenian Genocide: Evidence from the German Foreign Office Archives, 1915–1916,* ed. Wolfgang Gust (New York: Berghahn Books, 2014), p. 686.

23. Heinrich Vierbücher, *Armenia 1915: What the German Imperial Government Concealed from Its Subjects; The Slaughter of a Civilized People at the Hands of the Turks,* ed. Ara Ghazarians (Arlington, MA: Armenian Cultural Foundation, 2006), p. 52.

24. Gust, *The Armenian Genocide,* p. 329.

25. From the Gust Guide (document 1915-07-21-DE-012), an extract from his publication on the Armenian Genocide. See http://www.sci.am /downloads/musgen/WolfgangGust.pdf, p. 59.

26. Gust, *The Armenian Genocide,* document 1916-02-09-DE-001, pp. 542–55.

27. Khatchig Mouradian, "The Ottoman Archives Are Open…Almost: An Interview with Hilmar Kaiser," *Aztag Daily* (Lebanon), September 22, 2005.

28. Vahakn Dadrian, *The History of the Armenian Genocide: Ethnic Conflict from the Balkans to Anatolia to the Caucasus* (New York: Berghahn Books, 2008), p. 205.

29. Ibid., including p. 209, n. 8.

30. These accounts are all from Verjiné Svazlyan, *The Armenian Genocide: Testimonies of the Eyewitness Survivors,* trans. Tigran Tsulikian and Anahit Poghikian-Darbinian (Yerevan: "Gitoutoyun" Publishing House of NAS RA, 2011), pp. 384, 443, 270–71, 289.

31. The Kurds have officially recognized the Armenian Genocide as well as their part in it. They have issued numerous apologies. See en.wikipedia .org/wiki/Kurdish_recognition_of_the_Armenian_genocide for a complete listing with quotes.

32. Balakian, *The Burning Tigris,* p. 169.

33. Morgenthau, *Secrets of the Bosphorus,* p. 108.

34. The perpetrators understood at the time that the war would end someday and that this mass killing would be viewed as a "crime against humanity." On May 24, 1915, the Triple Entente nations had warned the Ottoman Empire that "in view of these new crimes of Turkey against humanity and civilization, the Allied Governments announce publicly to the Sublime Porte that they will hold personally responsible for these crimes all

members of the Ottoman Government, as well as their agents who are implicated in such massacres." See Ulrich Trumpener, *Germany and the Ottoman Empire, 1914–1918* (1968; repr., Delmar, NY: Caravan Books, 1989), p. 210. A full English translation of the original text can be found in U.S. Department of State, *Foreign Relations of the United States, 1915,* supplement, p. 981.

35. Taner Akcam, *The Young Turks' Crime against Humanity: The Armenian Genocide and Ethnic Cleansing in the Ottoman Empire* (Princeton: Princeton University Press, 2013).

CHAPTER 4: TEHLIRIAN GOES TO WAR

1. Mikayel Varandian, *Murad of Sepastia,* trans. Ara Ghazarians (Arlington, MA: Armenian Cultural Foundation, 2006), p. 5. The full quote reads, "Since Murad had not received any education, he was almost illiterate, like Antranig and many others of our fighters."

2. Tehlirian memoir, p. 50.

3. See Yervant Odian, *Accursed Years: My Exile and Return from Der Zor, 1914–1919,* trans. Ara Stepan Melkonian (London: Gomidas Institute, 2009); also Raymond Kévorkian, *The Armenian Genocide: A Complete History* (London: I. B. Tauris, 2011), pp. 251–53.

4. In addition to Gomidas, almost an entire generation of Armenian writers were rounded up and killed. Significant authors on this list include Yervand Srmakeshkhanlian, Artashes Harutiunian, Ruben Zardarian, Tigran Chrakian, Gegham Barseghian, Daniel Varuzhan, Tigran Cheokiurian, Ruben Sevak, and Atom Yarchanian (Siamanto). See Agop J. Hacikyan, coordinating ed., *The Heritage of Armenian Literature,* vol. 3 (Detroit: Wayne State University Press, 2005), pp. 658–853.

5. *Der Prozess Talaat Pascha: Stenographischer Prozessbericht* [The Talat Pasha Trial], foreword by Armin Wegner (Berlin: Deutsche Verlagsgesellschaft für Politik, 1921), p. 60. This is the original courtroom transcript, supplied to me by Rolf Hosfeld of Lepsiushaus, Berlin, and translated by Joel Golb.

6. Ibid., p. 60.

7. Michael Bobelian, *Children of Armenia: A Forgotten Genocide and the Century-Long Struggle for Justice* (New York: Simon & Schuster, 2009), pp. 13–15.

8. Tehlirian memoir, p. 67.

9. Rafael de Nogales, *Four Years beneath the Crescent,* trans. Muna Lee (London: Sterndale Classics, 2003), chap. 7, "The Siege of Van," pp. 69–87.

10. Tehlirian memoir, pp. 75, 80.

11. Ibid., p. 90.

12. Jacques Semelin, Claire Andrieu, and Sarah Gensburger, eds., *Resisting Genocide: The Multiple Forms of Rescue,* trans. Emma Bentley and Cynthia Schoch (New York: Oxford University Press, 2013), p. 205.

13. Omer Bartov and Phyllis Mack, eds., *In God's Name: Genocide and Religion in the Twentieth Century* (New York: Berghahn Books, 2001), p. 8.

14. The account that follows is drawn from Fethiye Cetin, *My Grandmother: A Memoir,* trans. Maureen Freely (London: Verso, 2008), pp. 61–80, 86–88.

15. Ibid., p. ix.

16. Jacobsen, *Diaries of a Danish Missionary,* pp. 78, 102, 201.

17. The account that follows is from Kévorkian, *The Armenian Genocide,* pp. 309–10.

18. Tehlirian memoir, p. 95.

19. Ibid.

20. Ibid., p. 103.

21. Ibid., p. 115.

22. Ibid., p. 116.

23. James B. Gidney, *A Mandate for Armenia* (Kent, OH: Kent State University Press, 1967), pp. 64, 65.

24. This was the original name of the communist state that followed the Bolshevik Revolution. In 1922 a larger entity was born: the Union of Soviet Socialist Republics.

25. Richard Hovanissian, ed., *The Republic of Armenia,* 4 vols. (Berkeley: University of California Press, 1996), 1:21.

26. Tehlirian memoir, pp. 111–12.

27. Ibid., p. 157.

Chapter 5: The Debt

1. Trumpener, *Germany and the Ottoman Empire,* p. 359.

2. Margaret MacMillan, *Paris 1919: Six Months That Changed the World* (New York: Random House, 2002), p. 372.

3. The former version of this newspaper, *Azadamard* (*Struggle for Freedom*), was shuttered on April 24, 1915. Its editor, Kegham Parseghian, was arrested on that date and subsequently murdered.

4. Tehlirian memoir, p. 190.

5. Quoted in Joan George, *Merchants in Exile: The Armenians in Manchester, England, 1835–1935* (London: Gomidas Institute, 2002), pp. 184–85.

6. The British were reluctant to bang the drum too loudly regarding "crimes against humanity" now that the war was over. They did not want to call attention to their own record in the colonies.

7. Vahakn N. Dadrian and Taner Akcam, *Judgment at Istanbul: The Armenian Genocide Trials* (New York: Berghahn Books, 2011), p. 196.

8. Tehlirian memoir, p. 206.

9. Sylvia Kedourie, ed., *Seventy-Five Years of the Turkish Republic* (London: Frank Cass Publishers, 2000), p. 48.

10. Andrew Mango, *Ataturk: The Biography of the Founder of Modern Turkey* (Woodstock, NY: Overlook Press, 1999), p. 196.

11. Marian MacCurdy credits Manoog Harpartsoumian, an attorney who was active in ARF conferences, with compiling the "list." Marian Mesrobian MacCurdy, *Sacred Justice: The Voices and Legacy of the Armenian Operation Nemesis* (New Brunswick, NJ: Transaction Publishers, 2015), p. 100.

12. Nemesis is the ancient Greek goddess often described as the distributor of retribution for evil deeds, thus creating justice or balance in the world.

13. Jacques Derogy, *Resistance and Revenge: The Armenian Assassination of the Turkish Leaders Responsible for the 1915 Massacres and Deportations*, trans. A. M. Berrett (New Brunswick, NJ: Transaction Publishers, 1990), p. 71.

14. Shahan Natali, "On the Trail of the Great Criminal [Medz vojrakordin hedk`erov]," trans. Aram Arkun, *Nayiri* (Beirut) 12, no. 1 (May 24, 1964), pt. 1, pp. 4–5.

15. Tehlirian memoir, p. 232.

16. The account that follows is drawn from Tehlirian memoir, pp. 236–39.

17. Sarkis Atamian, "A Portrait of Immortality," pt. 1, "Soghomon Tehlirian," *Armenian Review* 13, no. 3 (Autumn 1960): 50.

18. Tehlirian memoir, p. 248.

19. See Andon Kosh in *Badmakrut'iwn Hay H'eghap'okhagan Tashnagts'ut'ean*, vol. 2, p. 110.

20. Author interview with Marian MacCurdy April 15, 2013; see also MacCurdy and Libaridian, *Sacred Justice*.

CHAPTER 6: THE HUNT

1. Christopher J. Walker, *Armenia: The Survival of a Nation*, 2nd ed. (New York: St. Martin's Press, 1990).

2. Derogy, *Resistance and Revenge*, p. 74.

3. Kershaw, *Hitler*, p. 96.

4. Ibid.

5. George Grosz, *An Autobiography* (Berkeley: University of California Press, 1998), p. 119.

6. Aaron Sachaklian (1879–1964) was an immigrant to the United States who had established his credentials as a CPA at a large insurance firm in

Syracuse at the time of the conspiracy. His full story is told in Marian Mesrobian MacCurdy's book *Sacred Justice: The Voices and Legacy of the Armenian Operation Nemesis.*

7. Hrach Papazian (1892–1960) would serve in the Syrian parliament in 1932 and 1943 and was a member of the ARF Bureau from 1947 to 1959.

8. Vahan Zakarian (1883–1980). In Germany he was one of the founders of the German-Armenian Society, presided over by Johannes Lepsius. He was counselor of economic affairs at the Republic of Armenia mission in Berlin. He would also serve as Tehlirian's interpreter at the subsequent Berlin trial.

9. Hagop Zorian (1894–1942) was a history student at the University of Berlin. In later life he would become one of the leading economic historians of Soviet Armenia from 1925 until 1937, when he was arrested during the Stalinist purges. He was tried in 1939 and sentenced on the charge of having collaborated in Talat Pasha's assassination. He died in exile.

10. Haig Ter-Ohanian (1883–?) was an active ARF member and author.

11. I am indebted to Vartan Matiossian for allowing me to read his unpublished lecture on Haigo, presented at the National Association for Armenian Studies and Research in Belmont, Massachusetts, on June 5, 2014, from which the biographical information on these figures was drawn. In this lecture he reveals for the first time the previously unknown true identity of agent Haigo. Matiossian identifies one of the collaborating resident artists in Berlin as the renowned poet Avetik Isahakian (1875–1957).

12. From a letter from Natali to Sachaklian, dated September 30, 1920. Marian Mesrobian MacCurdy, *Sacred Justice: The Voices and Legacy of the Armenian Operation Nemesis* (New Brunswick, NJ: Transaction Publishers, 2015), p.166.

13. Interview with the author at the Nubarian Library, Paris, September 8, 2011.

14. Herbert, *Ben Kendim,* p. 321.

15. Tadeusz Swietochowski, *Russian Azerbaijan, 1905–1920: The Shaping of National Identity in a Muslim Community* (Cambridge: Cambridge University Press, 2004), p. 160.

16. Lawrence James, *The Golden Warrior: The Life and Legend of Lawrence of Arabia* (London: Paragon House, 1993), p. 373.

17. Sir Andrew Ryan would also serve as chief dragoman, or high-level translator, during the peace talks in Lausanne in 1921.

18. British National Archives, From Directorate of Intelligence, marked "SECRET," C.P. 2192/A Monthly Review of Revolutionary Movements

in British Dominions Overseas and Foreign Countries [no. 24, October 1920], 2, Whitehall Gardens, S.W., 30 November 1920: "Talaat Pasha, who lives at Hardenbergerstrasse [*sic*] 5 or 6 Berlin, is said recently to have been very active. He presides over the Turkish Egyptian organization, which has 10 prominent members, one of them a cousin of Enver Pasha. The German Foreign office is indirectly subsidising Egyptian students in Berlin. The money passes through the hands of a certain Herr von Kardoff and Sheikh Shawish, and is finally distributed by Talaat in order that the Egyptians and everyone else may believe that the money comes from Pan-Islamic sources. The students in this way are induced to carry out Pan-Islamic propaganda."

19. Derogy, *Resistance and Revenge,* p. 77.
20. Tehlirian memoir, p. 290.
21. Ibid.
22. For quotations in this passage, see ibid., pp. 267–68.
23. Ibid., p. 272.
24. The quotations that follow are from Tehlirian memoir, pp. 274–76.
25. Many of the buildings on Hardenbergstrasse were destroyed during World War II. Number 4 Hardenbergstrasse is listed as *"durch Sprengwirkung zerstörte,"* or destroyed by bombing.
26. Priya Satia, *Spies in Arabia: The Great War and the Cultural Foundations of Britain's Covert Empire in the Middle East* (Oxford: Oxford University Press, 2008), pp. 33, 34.
27. Unless otherwise noted, all quotations in this portion of the chapter are from Herbert, *Ben Kendim,* pp. 307–28.
28. Sir Basil Thomson was for a time both an assistant commissioner at Scotland Yard and director of intelligence at the Home Office.
29. Aubrey Herbert, *Ben Kendim: A Record of Eastern Travel* (London: Hutchinson & Co., 1924), p. 308.
30. Herbert, *Ben Kendim,* p. 318.
31. Mim Kemal Oke, *The Armenian Question, 1914–1923* (Nicosia: K. Rustem & Brother, 1988), p. 269. Oke provides no citation for what he reports as "fact": that the intelligence service made contact with the Soviets.
32. Aubrey Herbert papers, British National Archives, London. Sir Reginald Wildig Allen Leeper, born in Sydney, Australia, would eventually become head of Britain's Political Intelligence Department. During World War I he was an intelligence officer. He was also a member of the Lausanne delegation.
33. U.S. Department of State, Papers Relating to Foreign Relations, 1919, vol. 2, p. 830, University of Wisconsin Digital Collection. General Bridges was Sir George Tom Molesworth Bridges, who had extensive experience in the Greek and Turkish campaigns. Curzon was Lord

Curzon, who was foreign secretary at the time. Special thanks to Nora Nercessian for her assistance in this research.

34. Aubrey Herbert papers, British National Archives, London.

35. Parliamentary archives, British National Archives, London, LG/F/93/4/11. Churchill was at the time secretary of state for the colonies.

36. Margaret Fitzherbert, *The Man Who Was Greenmantle: A Biography of Aubrey Herbert* (London: J. Murray, 1983).

37. John Buchan, *Greenmantle* (New York: George H. Doran Company, 1916), p. 23.

38. Kemalist Turkey did eventually share in the Mosul oil wealth via its shares in the Turkish Petroleum Company, which would be renamed the Iraq Petroleum Company.

39. Derogy, *Resistance and Revenge,* p. 82.

40. Shahan Natali, "On the Trail of the Great Criminal," *Nayiri* 12, no. 4, June 14, 1964, pt. 4, p. 4.

41. The account that follows is drawn from Tehlirian memoir, p. 298.

42. Tehlirian memoir, p. 304.

43. Ibid.

44. Ibid., p. 306.

Chapter 7: The Trial

1. Tessa Hofmann, "New Aspects of the Talat Pasha Court Case," *Armenian Review* 4, no. 168 (1989): 41–53.

2. Derogy, *Resistance and Revenge,* p. 111.

3. *New York Times,* June 3, 1921, "Says Mother's Ghost Ordered Him to Kill," reprinted in Kloian, *The Armenian Genocide,* p. 344.

4. All quotes from the trial are from *Der Prozess Talaat Pascha.* Also see Christoph Dinkel, "German Officers and the Armenian Genocide," *Armenian Review* 44, no. 1/173 (Spring 1991): 91.

5. "Assassin Boasts of Talaat's Death," *New York Times,* March 17, 1921; "Talaat Is Mourned as Germany's Friend," *New York Times,* March 18, 1921. Both articles appear in Kloian, *The Armenian Genocide,* p. 343.

Chapter 8: The Big Picture

1. General Liman von Sanders was arrested in February 1919 by the British occupying force. He was held for a brief time to stand trial himself for war crimes but was released before any trial could take place. Dinkel, "German Officers and the Armenian Genocide," p. 78.

2. I did not have access to the "German documents" Lepsius refers to here. The debate on the exact nature of Germany's cooperation is ongoing. See

Vahakn Dadrian, *German Responsibility in the Armenian Genocide: A Review of the Historical Evidence of German Complicity* (Watertown, MA: Blue Crane Books, 1996); and the sources cited by Hilmar Kaiser and Donald Bloxham for the two sides of the issue.

3. Dadrian, *History of the Armenian Genocide,* p. 254; see also Friedrich von Bernhardi, *Germany and the Next War,* trans. Allen H. Powles (New York: Longmans, Green and Co., 1914), p. 19.

4. "As for the Turks, the German military personnel had so much mastery over them that no Turk, irrespective of rank, position or class, dared to challenge them. Let one example suffice: When the Turkish major in charge of the Mamure station dared to show reluctance to put a whole [train] car at the disposal of forty German soldiers, an ordinary German soldier killed him with a shot of his pistol. The matter—a German soldier having killed the Turkish station commander—was not even brought before a court-martial." Balakian, *Armenian Golgotha,* p. 312.

5. Liman von Sanders is referring here to embattled areas where the Armenians dared to resist pressure from Ottoman troops. German artillery was decisive in the destruction of these holdouts. See Raphael de Nogales, *Four Years beneath the Crescent,* translated by Muna Lee (London: Sterndale Classics, 2003); Paul Leverkuehn, *A German Officer during the Armenian Genocide: A Biography of Max von Scheubner-Richter,* translated by Alasdair Lean (London: Taderon Press for the Gomidas Institute, 2008); Vahakn N. Dadrian, *German Responsibility in the Armenian Genocide: A Review of the Historical Evidence of German Complicity* (Watertown, MA: Blue Crane Books, 1996).

6. The exact definition of the term "genocide" is still being debated. The following from Wikipedia: "Genocide is the systematic destruction of all or a significant part of a racial, ethnic, religious or national group" via "(a) Killing members of the group; (b) Causing serious bodily or mental harm to members of the group; (c) Deliberately inflicting on the group conditions of life calculated to bring about its physical destruction in whole or in part; (d) Imposing measures intended to prevent births within the group; (e) Forcibly transferring children of the group to another group." Genocide also entails conspiracy to commit genocide; direct and public incitement to commit genocide; attempt to commit genocide; and complicity in genocide. It is important to note that the term "genocide" is not rooted in "genetics." Also, "genocide" is a legal term. Once it has been established that genocide has occurred, legal attempts at reparations are possible. Actions do not have to be one hundred percent effective to be a genocide. Denial has been called the last stage of genocide.

7. Paul Leverkuehn, *A German Officer during the Armenian Genocide: A Biography of Max von Scheubner-Richter* (London: Gomidas Institute, 2009).

8. Dinkel, "German Officers and the Armenian Genocide," p. 94; Kershaw, *Hitler,* p. 131.

9. For a thorough investigation into this attribution, see Kevork B. Bardakjian, *Hitler and the Armenian Genocide* (Cambridge, MA: Zoryan Institute, 1985). The entire book deals with the veracity and implications of the quote. On p. 1 (and in the footnote, p. 37) Bardakjian cites the source of the quote as *Documents on British Foreign Policy, 1919–1939,* ed. E. L. Woodward and Rohan Butler, 3rd ser., vol. 7 (1939; London, 1954), p. 257.

10. See Vahakn N. Dadrian, "The Armenian Genocide: An Interpretation" in Jay Winter, ed., *America and the Armenian Genocide of 1915* (Cambridge, UK: Cambridge University Press, 2003), p. 70.

11. Vahakn Dadrian, *The Role of Turkish Physicians in the World War One Genocide of Ottoman Armenians* (New York: Pergamon Press, 1986), 169–92.

12. See both Ugur Umit Ungor and Mehmet Polatel, *Confiscation and Destruction: The Young Turk Seizure of Armenian Property* (London: Continuum International Publishing Group, 2011); and Ungor, *The Making of Modern Turkey: Nation and State in Eastern Anatolia* (Oxford: Oxford University Press, 2012).

13. See Ugur Umit Ungor and Mehmet Polatel, *Confiscation and Destruction: The Young Turk Seizure of Armenian Property* (London: Continuum International Publishing Group, 2011), pp. 31–32.

14. Timothy Snyder, *Bloodlands: Europe between Hitler and Stalin* (New York: Basic Books, 2010), p. 117.

15. See Akcam, *The Young Turks' Crime against Humanity,* p. 383.

16. Israel does not officially recognize the Armenian genocide. Many Jews see Hitler's destruction of European Jewry as a unique historical event, and any comparison to other genocides is viewed as degrading to the memory of the Holocaust. The resistance to recognition is also grounded in geopolitics. Israel is an on again, off again ally of Turkey, and both nations are major allies of the United States. See Yair Auron, *The Banality of Denial: Israel and the Armenian Genocide* (New Brunswick, NJ: Transaction Publishers, 2003), p. 127.

17. For Balakian's full story see his *Armenian Golgotha,* translated by his grand-nephew Peter Balakian.

18. From a letter to Shahan Natali from Zakarian, dated June 11, 1921, in MacCurdy, *Sacred Justice,* pp. 195–196.

19. "They Simply Had to Let Him Go," *New York Times,* June 5, 1921.
20. The specific law that allowed Tehlirian's acquittal can be found in paragraph 51 of the German Penal Code. For a full examination of the legal aspects of the trial, see the unpublished thesis by Osik Moses, "The Assassination of Talaat Pascha in 1921 in Berlin: A Case Study of Judicial Practices in the Weimar Republic" (submitted to California State University, Northridge, May 2012), p. 1. It is available for viewing on the Internet at https://www.yumpu.com/en/document/view/2103368 /california-state-university-northridge.
21. From Levon Marashlian, "Finishing the Genocide," in *Remembrance and Denial: The Case of the Armenian Genocide,* ed. Richard Hovannisian (Detroit: Wayne State University Press, 1999), p. 127.

CHAPTER 9: THE WORK CONTINUES

1. Hofmann, "New Aspects of the Talat Pasha Court Case," pp. 47, 52 n. 25.
2. See Edward Alexander's postscript to *A Crime of Vengeance: An Armenian Struggle for Justice* (Lincoln, NE: IUniverse.com, 2000), p. 206: "But father, why were those women kissing his hand?...Because with that hand he avenged our people. Never forget him!"
3. "The Slayer of Talaat Pasha Acquitted," *Philadelphia Inquirer,* June 6, 1921.
4. See MacCurdy, *Sacred Justice.* Marion Mesrobian MacCurdy is the granddaughter of Sachaklian.
5. Derogy, *Resistance and Revenge,* p. 111.
6. Ibid.
7. Author interview with Gerard Libaridian, former ARF archivist, April 17, 2013.
8. The plan of the "Prometheus Pact" was "to use Kemalist Turkey as the agent for overthrowing the Bolsheviks in the Caucasus. It was established in Tabriz in mid-July 1921." Walker, *Armenia,* p. 353.
9. Ronald G. Suny, *The Baku Commune, 1917–1918: Class and Nationality in the Russian Revolution* (Princeton: Princeton University Press, 1972), pp. 336–37.
10. See Vartkes Yeghiayan and Ara Arabyan, *The Case of Misak Torlakian* (Glendale, CA: Center for Armenian Remembrance, 2006), p. 180.
11. Ibid., p. 273.
12. See Arshavir Shiragian, *The Legacy: Memoirs of an Armenian Patriot,* trans. Sonia Shiragian (Boston: Hairenik Press, 1976), p. 13.
13. Ibid., p. 47.
14. Political and Secret Department Records (IOR/L/PS/11/170–IOR/L/ PS/11/309), India Office Records, Asia, Pacific and Africa Collections,

British Library, London, vol. 192, p. 225/1921, Turkey: Views of Talaat
Pasha, Communication, 5 December 1920, D'Abernon to FCO (Lord
Curzon). Also see references to transfer of funds by Enver and Talat from
German banks to Swiss banks in memo marked "Very Secret," dated June
3, 1920 (1885 HA/615), and other activity in concert with Kemal and the
Bolshevik movement in "Mesopotamia Causes of Unrest Report No. II"
by Major N. N. E. Bray, special intelligence officer attached to Political
Department, India Office, dated October 18, 1920, in British National
Archives, London.

15. Shiragian, *The Legacy,* p. x.
16. See article published online at AVIM website by Professor Hikmet
    Ozdemir titled "Revanchism as Blind Faith and the Dashnak-Asala
    Assassinations" (http://www.avim.org.tr/yorumnotlarduyurular/en
    /REVANCHISM-AS-BLIND-FAITH-AND-THE-DASHNAK
    -ASALA-ASSASSINATIONS-/3216), posted March 18, 2014, which
    goes into detail on CUP fears, and the citation from that report: Huseyin
    Cahit Yalcin, *Ittihatci Liderlerin Gizli Mektuplari,* p. 456.
17. Shiragian, *The Legacy,* p. 132.
18. "Un ex gran visir assassinato a Roma: Si tratta di un delitto politico?" ["A
    Former Grand Vizier Assassinated in Rome: Was It a Political Crime?"],
    Il Messaggero, December 8, 1921.
19. Shiragian, *The Legacy,* p. 136. Though the word "genocide" appears in
    this quote published in 1976, at the time of Said Halim's assassination the
    term had not yet been coined by Raphael Lemkin.
20. Ibid., pp. 114, 115.
21. For the account in this section of the chapter, see ibid., pp. 145–80.
22. Djemal Pasha, *Memories of a Turkish Statesman, 1913–1919* (London:
    Hutchinson & Co., 1922), pp. 277–79.
23. Deportations moved through areas Djemal Pasha oversaw, in what we
    now call Syria. However, he was not in charge of the concentration
    camps.
24. Fromkin, *A Peace to End All Peace,* p. 214; also Peter Hopkirk, *Like Hidden
    Fire: The Plot to Bring Down the British Empire* (New York: Kodansha
    International, 1994), pp. 129, 130.
25. Hrach Dasnabedian, *History of the Armenian Revolutionary Federation,
    Dashnaktsutiun, 1890–1924* (Milan: Oemme Edizioni, 1989), p. 191.
26. Suhnaz Yilmaz, "An Ottoman Warrior Abroad: Enver Pasha as an
    Expatriate," in Kedourie, *Seventy-Five Years of the Turkish Republic,* p. 53,
    and n. 75, citing Turkish Republican Archives, Decree of the Parliament
    concerning Enver and Halil Pasha, 3 December 1921, no. 731/385.

27. Louise Bryant, *Mirrors of Moscow* (New York: Thomas Seltzer, 1923), pp. 158–59.
28. See chap. 6 of Georges Agabekov's memoirs, *Tche Kah za Rabatoi* [The Cheka at Work] (Berlin: Strela, 1930).
29. Fromkin, *The Peace to End All Peace,* p. 487.
30. The man who tracked down Enver Pasha, Georges Agabekov, is historically notable because he was the first high-level Soviet intelligence agent to defect to the West. He was himself hunted by the NKVD and killed in March 1938. See Boris Volodarsky, "Unknown Agabekov," Intelligence and National Security, June 28, 2013, 890–909, DOI: 10.1080/02684527.2012.701440. http://www.lse.ac.uk/european Institute/research/canadaBlanch/PDF/Press%202013/6Nov13INS.pdf.
31. Andrew Mango, *Ataturk: The Biography of the Founder of Modern Turkey* (Woodstock, NY: Overlook Press, 1999), p. 451.

CHAPTER 10: AFTERMATH AND ATATURK

1. Also see chapter 9, p. 240, n. 8 re: the Prometheus Pact.
2. Christopher Andrew, *Defend the Realm: The Authorized History of MI5* (New York: Alfred A. Knopf, 2009), pp. 119–20.
3. See Grabill, *Protestant Diplomacy,* pp. 274, 275; also John A. DeNovo, *American Interests and Policies in the Middle East: 1900–1939* (Minneapolis: University of Minnesota Press, 1963), pp. 160, 161.
4. Colby Chester, "Turkey Reinterpreted," *Current History* 16 (April– September 1922): 344.
5. The following narrative is from Anthony Slide's introduction to his book *Ravished Armenia and the Story of Aurora Mardiganian* (Lanham, MD: Scarecrow Press, 1997), pp. 1–18.
6. Aurora Mardiganian, *Ravished Armenia: The Story of Aurora Mardiganian, the Christian Girl Who Lived Through the Great Massacres* (New York: Kingfield Press, 1919).
7. See Edward Minasian, "The Forty Years of *Musa Dagh*: The Film That Was Denied," *Journal of Armenian Studies* 3, nos. 1–2 (1986–87): 63–73.
8. Pressure on media companies and the United States government continues to this day. In 1988, three weeks before Ted Bogosian's documentary *An Armenian Journey* was to be broadcast on PBS stations across the United States, Turkey began a concerted campaign to block the broadcast by lobbying the State Department and pressuring local PBS stations. As a result, some stations did not air the program. Some of the few that did received death and bomb threats (for example, WGBH in Boston and KCET in Los Angeles).

9. By 1910, the most significant armaments were the "fast battleship" and the "super-dreadnought." "Super-dreadnought" battleships, weighing over twenty thousand tons, were the atomic bomb of their day, the ultimate weapon. Each ship was very expensive to produce but seemed worth the expenditure because a super-dreadnought anchored in the harbor of any major city would ensure control of that city. Super-dreadnoughts, as opposed to conventional coal-fueled battleships, could not run without oil. Even for conventional warships, oil packed more energy per ton. Thus an oil-burning ship had a "40 per cent larger radius of action." Oil-fueled ships also had greater speed. Oil was much more easily moved and stored than coal and, even more important, was more easily injected into the engines. Half as many human stokers were necessary for smooth operation. The ship could be refueled "with the greatest of ease" at sea. Finally, oil didn't smoke like coal when it burned, maintaining invisibility of the ship on the horizon. See Anton Mohr, *The Oil War* (New York: Harcourt, Brace and Company, 1926), p. 114.

10. Winston Churchill, *The World Crisis, 1911–1918* (New York: Free Press, 2005), pp. 74–76.

11. Churchill quoted in Stephen Kinzer, *Reset: Iran, Turkey, and America's Future* (New York: Times Books, 2010), p. 26.

12. See "Memoirs of Calouste Sarkis Gulbenkian with Particular Relation to the Origins and Foundation of the Iraq Petroleum Company Limited," testimony before the U.S. Congress, 1945, National Archives, Washington, DC. Also see Edwin Black, *British Petroleum and the Redline Agreement: The West's Secret Pact to Get Mideast Oil* (Washington, DC: Dialog Press, 2011).

13. The Turkish Petroleum Company, which would later morph into the Iraq Petroleum Company, was substantially owned by the National Bank of Turkey. The National Bank of Turkey featured a board of directors in 1908 composed of both high-ranking CUP members and Armenians. This board would include the Armenian Egyptian Nubar Pasha and a "Mr. Essyan" as well as Said Halim and Djemal Pasha. See Marian Kent, *Moguls and Mandarins: Oil, Imperialism and the Middle East in British Foreign Policy, 1900–1940* (1993; New York: Routledge, 2011), p. 90 n. 8.

14. See Ralph Hewins, *Mr. Five Per Cent: The Story of Calouste Gulbenkian* (New York: Rinehart & Company, 1958), appendix, p. 259. Gulbenkian's wife, Nvart, was related to Nubar.

15. Edwin Black, *British Petroleum and the Red Line Agreement: The West's Secret Pact to Get Mideast Oil* (Oshkosh, WI: Dialog, 2011), p. 153. See also my discussion in chapter 6 implicating Curzon in a contract on Enver Pasha's life.

16. See Edwin Black, *War against the Weak: Eugenics and America's Campaign to Create a Master Race* (New York: Four Walls Eight Windows, 2003).

17. As quoted in an essay by Joshua Binus on the Oregon Historical Society website: http://www.ohs.org/education/oregonhistory/historical_records/dspDocument.cfm?doc_ID=c5f74925-d75d-54f1-e441ea279f7a9402.

18. Matthew Frye Jacobson, *Whiteness of a Different Color: European Immigrants and the Alchemy of Race* (Cambridge: Harvard University Press, 1998), p. 240.

19. Early in his career as leader of the new Republic of Turkey, Kemal did publicly denounce the genocide, calling it a "scandal" and a "lowly act." See Vahakn N. Dadrian and Taner Akcam, *Judgment at Istanbul: The Armenian Genocide Trials* (New York: Berghahn Books, 2011).

20. The Foundations Law of 1935 and other laws pertaining to taxes, ownership of property, and inheritance are complex and barely investigated aspects of the Ottoman/Turkish institutional structure. "Foundations" were a significant part of that structure. The idea was that certain facets of social life, such as bathhouses, charitable institutions, soup kitchens, and the like, as well as religious buildings, should not belong to anyone in particular. They belonged to God. And so these and other material manifestations of charitable endeavors, from parks and public fountains to mosques, were established by foundations. Royalty would finance foundations to build and preserve the buildings and other elements. Foundations could include contributions from earned income (for instance, a bazaar), which could be used to perpetuate the foundation. The foundations were created under the auspices of the sultan in his role as caliph. They were created at his pleasure. Since millets also had churches and other charitable elements, millets also needed foundations.

    When the republic was created by Kemal Ataturk, the issue of foundations had to be addressed for at least two reasons. First of all, Ataturk's was a secular state, and so the state controlled religious activity. Thus the state had to control the foundations that held the religious equities. In this way, the power of Islam could be checked. Second, minority religions could be suppressed by laws that addressed the foundations. Also, some foundations were barely solvent, so other foundations traditionally could be created to aid them. But the Foundations Law of 1935 forbade one foundation from aiding another. See "2012 Declaration: The Seized Properties of Armenian Foundations in Istanbul," published by the Hrant Dink Foundation, Istanbul, for a more complete look at the subject.

21. Donald Bloxham, *The Great Game of Genocide: Imperialism, Nationalism, and the Destruction of the Ottoman Armenians* (Oxford: Oxford University Press, 2005), p. 209.

22. M. Sukru Hanioglu, *Ataturk: An Intellectual Biography* (Princeton: Princeton University Press, 2011), p. 164.

23. Esra Ozyurek, ed., *The Politics of Public Memory in Turkey* (Syracuse: Syracuse University Press, 2007), p. 42.

24. Visiting a pottery shop while touring in Turkey, I mentioned to the gracious owner that my family originally came from Turkey and that they were Armenian. He nodded and said with a smile, "Many Armenians lived here once. They all went away."

25. "Insulting Turkishness" (Article 301 of the Turkish Penal Code) became a punishable crime in Turkey in 2006. Authors Orhan Pamuk and Elif Safak have faced prison time for their mention of the Armenian genocide in their writing.

26. Ahmet T. Kuru and Alfred Stepan, eds., *Democracy, Islam, and Secularism in Turkey* (New York: Columbia University Press, 2012), p. 166.

27. The actual wording of the law is as follows:

> Article 1. To anyone offending or insulting Ataturk's memory, a sentence from one year to three years of prison should be applied.
>
> To anyone breaking, destroying, or soiling statues, busts, and monuments representing Ataturk or Ataturk's grave, a sentence from one year to five years in prison should be applied.
>
> To anyone encouraging others to perform the above-mentioned crimes, the sentence will be the same as for the actual crime.
>
> Article 2. For the crimes listed in Article 1: if the crimes are performed by two or more people in a collective fashion, or in public or in places open to the public or through the press, the sentence to be applied is augmented by half.

See Human Rights Watch website: http://www.hrw.org/reports /1999/turkey/turkey993-09.htm.

Chapter 11: Post–Ataturk

1. Vahakn N. Dadrian and Taner Akcam, *Judgment at Istanbul: The Armenian Genocide Trials* (New York: Berghahn Books, 2001), p. 265.

2. Nicole Pope and Hugh Pope, *Turkey Unveiled: A History of Modern Turkey* (Woodstock, NY: Overlook Press, 1997), p. 76.

3. In April 1985 Lewis was one of sixty-nine scholars who co-signed a petition requesting Congress not to support a resolution condemning the Armenian Genocide. The petition was published in two-page ads in the *New York Times* and the *Washington Post*. In 1993 he made statements in

France that resulted in a civil proceeding against him. See Yair Auron, *The Banality of Denial: Israel and the Armenian Genocide* (New Brunswick, NJ: Transaction Publishers, 2003), pp. 227, 228.

4. Bernard Lewis, *The Emergence of Modern Turkey,* 3rd ed. (New York: Oxford University Press, 2002), p. 298.

5. Rifat N. Bali, *The "Varlik Vergisi" Affair: A Study on Its Legacy with Selected Documents* (Piscataway, NJ: Gorgias Press, 2011), p. 47.

6. Ibid., p. 93.

7. Speros Vryonis Jr., *The Mechanism of Catastrophe: The Turkish Pogrom of September 6–7, 1955, and the Destruction of the Greek Community of Istanbul* (New York: Greekworks.com, 2005), p. xxvi.

8. For a more complex take on how the city changed, see Orhan Pamuk, *Istanbul: Memories and the City,* trans. Maureen Freely (New York: Vintage International, 2004).

9. Vasily Grossman, *An Armenian Sketchbook,* trans. Robert Chandler and Elizabeth Chandler (New York: New York Review of Books, 2013), p. 5.

10. See the 1990 documentary film by Zareh Tjeknavorian, *Enemy of the People,* https://www.youtube.com/watch?v=EV3H4YxdSfs&list= UU8mkGExJ3OEWkbaJ_dxr5OQ.

11. This motto of the Tashnag organization has been quoted many times. I'm quoting here from Levon Thomassian, *Summer of '42: A Study of German-Armenian Relations during the Second World War* (Atglen, PA: Schiffer Publishing, 2012), p. 36.

12. Simon Payaslian, *The History of Armenia* (New York: Palgrave Macmillan, 2007), p. 179.

13. Yeghiayan and Arabyan, *The Case of Misak Torlakian,* p. x.

14. Author Lindy Avakian sent an inscribed copy of *The Cross and the Crescent* to Yanikian. Internal FBI report dated February 24, 1973; courtesy Christopher Gunn, who has obtained FBI and CIA reports on ASALA and other Armenian terrorist groups with a FOIA query.

15. Michael Bobelian, *Children of Armenia: A Forgotten Genocide and the Century-Long Struggle for Justice* (New York: Simon & Schuster, 2009).

16. *Los Angeles Times,* January 30, 1973.

17. One cell called itself the Shahan Natali Guerrilla Group (ASALA publication of interviews, 1982, courtesy Christopher Gunn). See also Markar Melkonian and Seta Melkonian, *My Brother's Road: An American's Fateful Journey to Armenia* (London: I. B. Tauris, 2007). Markar was the sibling of one of the more remarkable members of ASALA, Monte Melkonian, a young Armenian American from southern California who had embraced Armenian nationalism and moved to Lebanon to join the

radical groups operating there. Monte Melkonian would commit violent acts and go to prison in France as a member of ASALA. As Monte's brother Markar explained in the 2008 biography/memoir of his brother, Monte chastised himself after killing a young Turkish woman but continued to believe in the "cause." In time he would break away from ASALA altogether and form a splinter group, the ASALA Revolutionary Movement. During the Armenian war with Azerbaijan in the 1990s, Monte Melkonian volunteered to fight, becoming an important military leader. In a battle that is still shrouded in controversy, he was gunned down in an ambush and died in Karabagh in 1993 at the age of thirty-five. He is revered as a national hero in Armenia.

18. See the CIA reports "Global Terrorism: The Justice Commandos of the Armenian Genocide," September 1984 (GI 84-10148); and "The Armenian Secret Army for the Liberation of Armenia: A Continuing International Threat," January 1984 (GI 84-10008 and EUR 84-10004).

19. For a description of torture practices in modern Turkey, see Mehdi Zana, *Prison No 5: Eleven Years in Turkish Jails* (Watertown, MA: Blue Crane Books, 1997).

20. For the most complete discussion of Ergenekon, see Gareth H. Jenkins, "Between Fact and Fantasy: Turkey's Ergenekon Investigation," Silk Road Paper, Central Asia–Caucasus Institute Silk Road Studies Program, August 2009.

BIBLIOGRAPHY

BOOKS AND ARTICLES

Abulafia, David. *The Great Sea: A Human History of the Mediterranean*. New York: Oxford University Press, 2011.

Agabekov, George. *Tche Kah za Rabatoi*. Berlin: Strela, 1931.

Ahmad, Feroz. *The Making of Modern Turkey*. London: Routledge, 1993.

———. *The Young Turks: The Committee of Union and Progress in Turkish Politics, 1908–1914*. New York: Columbia University Press, 2010.

Akcam, Taner. *Armenien und Der Völkermord: Die Istanbuler Prozesse und die Türkische Nationalbewegung*. Hamburg: Hamburger Edition, 1996.

———. "Deportation and Massacres in the Cipher Telegrams of the Interior Ministry in the Prime Ministerial Archive (Basbakanlik Arsivi)." *Genocide Studies and Prevention: An International Journal* 1, no. 3 (December 2006): 305–25.

———. *Dialogue across an International Divide: Essays towards a Turkish-Armenian Dialogue*. Cambridge, MA: Zoryan Institute, 2001.

———. *From Empire to Republic: Turkish Nationalism and the Armenian Genocide*. London: Zed Books, 2004.

———. "The Ottoman Documents and the Genocidal Policies of the Committee of Union and Progress (Ittihat ve Terakki) toward the Armenians in 1915." *Genocide Studies and Prevention: An International Journal* 1, no. 2 (September 2006): 127–48.

———. *A Shameful Act: The Armenian Genocide and the Question of Turkish Responsibility*. Translated by Paul Bessemer. New York: Metropolitan Books, 2006.

———. *The Young Turks' Crime against Humanity: The Armenian Genocide and Ethnic Cleansing in the Ottoman Empire.* Princeton: Princeton University Press, 2012.

Aksakal, Mustafa. *The Ottoman Road to War in 1914: The Ottoman Empire and the First World War.* Cambridge: Cambridge University Press, 2008.

Alexander, Edward. *A Crime of Vengeance: An Armenian Struggle for Justice.* Lincoln, NE: iUniverse.com, 2000.

Allen, William Edward David, and Paul Muratov. *Caucasian Battlefields: A History of the Wars on the Turco-Caucasian Border, 1828–1921.* Cambridge: Cambridge University Press, 2010.

Altinay, Ayse Guul. *The Myth of the Military Nation: Militarism, Gender, and Education in Turkey.* New York: Palgrave Macmillan, 2004.

Anderson, Scott. *Lawrence in Arabia: War, Deceit, Imperial Folly, and the Making of the Modern Middle East.* New York: Doubleday, 2013.

Anush, Armen. *Passage Through Hell: A Memoir.* Studio City, CA: H. and K. Manjikian Publications, 2005.

Apkarian, Sooren. *My Armenian Heritage.* Eastbourne, Sussex, UK: Gardners Books, 2007.

Apramian, Jack. *The Georgetown Boys.* Toronto: Zoyran Institute, 2009.

Arendt, Hannah. *Eichmann in Jerusalem: A Report on the Banality of Evil.* New York: Penguin Books, 2006.

Arkun, Aram. "Into the Modern Age, 1800–1913," in *The Armenians: Past and Present in the Making of National Identity.* Edited by Edmund Herzig and Marina Kurkchiyan. London: RoutledgeCurzon, 2005.

Arlen, Michael J. *Passage to Ararat.* New York: Farrar, Straus & Giroux, 1975.

Armenian Review 44, no. 1/173 (Spring 1991).

Armstrong, Karen. *Holy War: The Crusades and Their Impact on Today's World.* New York: Anchor Books, 2001.

———. *Islam: A Short History.* New York: Modern Library, 2000.

Arnaiz-Villena, Ara, et al. "HLA Alleles and Haplotypes in the Turkish Population: Relatedness to Kurds, Armenians, and Other Mediterraneans." *Tissue Antigens* 57 (2001): 308–17.

Atamian, Sarkis. *The Armenian Community: The Historical Development of a Social and Ideological Conflict.* New York: Philosophical Library, 1955.

———. "Soghomon Tehlirian: A Portrait of Immortality—Part I." *Armenian Review* 13, no. 3 (Autumn 1960): 40–51.

———. "Soghomon Tehlirian: A Portrait of Immortality—Part II." *Armenian Review* 13, no. 4 (1961): 10–21.

———. "Soghomon Tehlirian: A Portrait of Immortality—Part III." *Armenian Review* 14, no. 1 (1961): 16–36.

————. "Soghomon Tehlirian: A Portrait of Immortality—Part IV." *Armenian Review* 14, no. 1 (1961): 44–49.

Atkinson, Tacy. *The German, the Turk, and the Devil Made a Triple Alliance: Harpoot Diaries, 1908–1917.* Princeton: Gomidas Institute, 2000.

Auron, Yair. *The Banality of Denial: Israel and the Armenian Genocide.* New Brunswick, NJ: Transaction Publishers, 2003.

Avakian, Lindy V. *The Cross and the Crescent.* Los Angeles: DeVorss & Co. Publishers, 1965.

Baghdjian, Kevork K. *The Confiscation of Armenian Properties by the Turkish Government Said to Be Abandoned.* Edited by A. B. Gureghian. Beirut: Antelias, 2010.

Bakalian, Anny. *Armenian-Americans: From Being to Feeling Armenian.* New Brunswick, NJ: Transaction Publishers, 1993.

Balakian, Grigoris. *Armenian Golgotha.* Translated by Peter Balakian. New York: Alfred A. Knopf, 2009.

Balakian, Peter. *Black Dog of Fate: A Memoir.* New York: Basic Books, 2009.

————. *The Burning Tigris: The Armenian Genocide and America's Response.* New York: HarperCollins, 2003.

Balakian, Peter, et al. "Turkey: Writers, Politics and Free Speech: In Memoriam, Hrant Dink (1954–2007)." Edited by David Hayes. *OpenDemocracy Quarterly,* 1st ser., 2 (April 2007).

Balancar, Ferda, ed. *The Sounds of Silence: Turkey's Armenians Speak.* Istanbul: Uluslararasi Hrant Dink Vakfi Yayinlari, 2012.

Bali, Rifat N. *The "Varlik Vergisi" Affair: A Study on Its Legacy with Selected Documents.* Piscataway, NJ: Gorgias Press, 2011.

Barber, Noel. *The Sultans.* New York: Simon & Schuster, 1973.

Bardakjian, Kevork B. *Hitler and the Armenian Genocide.* Cambridge, MA: Zoryan Institute, 1985.

Barkey, Karen. *Empire of Difference: The Ottomans in Comparative Perspective.* New York: Cambridge University Press, 2008.

Barootian, Haroutiun. *Reminiscences from Tomarza's Past.* London: Taderon, 2006.

Barton, James L. *Story of Near East Relief (1915–1930): An Interpretation.* New York: Macmillan, 1930.

————, comp. *Turkish Atrocities: Statements of American Missionaries on the Destruction of Christian Communities in Ottoman Turkey, 1915–1917.* Ann Arbor: Gomidas Institute, 1998.

Bartov, Omer, and Phyllis Mack, eds. *In God's Name: Genocide and Religion in the Twentieth Century.* New York: Berghahn Books, 2001.

Bauman, Zygmunt. *Modernity and the Holocaust.* Ithaca: Cornell University Press, 2000.

Bay, Austin. *Ataturk: Lessons in Leadership from the Greatest General of the Ottoman Empire.* New York: Palgrave Macmillan, 2011.

Bellow, Saul. *To Jerusalem and Back: A Personal Account.* New York: Viking, 1976.

Bernhardi, Friedrich von. *Germany and the Next War.* Translated by Allen H. Powles. New York: Longmans, Green and Co., 1914.

Bierstadt, Edward Hale. *The Great Betrayal: A Survey of the Near East Problem.* Edited by Helen Davidson Creighton. Bloomingdale, IL: Pontian Greek Society of Chicago, 2008.

Black, Edwin. *Banking on Baghdad: Inside Iraq's 7,000-Year History of War, Profit, and Conflict.* Hoboken: John Wiley & Sons, 2004.

———. *British Petroleum and the Redline Agreement: The West's Secret Pact to Get Mideast Oil.* Washington, DC: Dialog Press, 2011.

———, *War against the Weak: Eugenics and America's Campaign to Create a Master Race.* New York: Four Walls Eight Windows, 2003.

Blaichman, Frank. *Rather Die Fighting: A Memoir of World War II.* New York: Arcade Publishing, 2009.

Bloxham, Donald. *The Final Solution: A Genocide.* Oxford: Oxford University Press, 2009.

———. *The Great Game of Genocide: Imperialism, Nationalism, and the Destruction of the Ottoman Armenians.* Oxford: Oxford University Press, 2005.

Bobelian, Michael. *Children of Armenia: A Forgotten Genocide and the Century-Long Struggle for Justice.* New York: Simon & Schuster, 2009.

Boyar, Ebru, and Kate Fleet. *A Social History of Ottoman Istanbul.* Cambridge: Cambridge University Press, 2010.

Braude, Benjamin, and Bernard Lewis. *Christians and Jews in the Ottoman Empire: The Functioning of a Plural Society.* Vol. 1. New York: Holmes & Meier Publishers, 1982.

Brendon, Piers. *The Decline and Fall of the British Empire.* New York: Vintage, 2010.

Brown, L. Carl, ed. *Imperial Legacy: The Ottoman Imprint on the Balkans and the Middle East.* New York: Columbia University Press, 1996.

Bryant, Louise. *Mirrors of Moscow.* New York: Thomas Seltzer, 1923.

Bryce, James, and Arnold Toynbee. *The Treatment of Armenians in the Ottoman Empire, 1915–16: Documents Presented to Viscount Grey of Fallodon by Viscount Bryce.* Edited by Ara Sarafian. Reading, UK: Taderon Press, 2000.

Buchan, John. *Greenmantle.* London: Hodder & Stoughton, 1916.

Bullough, Oliver. *Let Our Fame Be Great: Journeys among the Defiant People of the Caucasus.* New York: Basic Books, 2010.

Burbank, Jane, and Frederick Cooper. *Empires in World History: Power and the Politics of Difference.* Princeton: Princeton University Press, 2010.

Campos, Michelle U. *Ottoman Brothers: Muslims, Christians, and Jews in Early Twentieth-Century Palestine.* Stanford: Stanford University Press, 2011.

Caprielian, Ara. "The Armenian Revolutionary Federation and Soviet Armenia." *Armenian Review* 28, no. 3 (Autumn 1975): 283–311.

Cardashian, Vahan. *The Ottoman Empire of the Twentieth Century.* Albany: J. B. Lyon Company, 1908.

Carthill, Al. [Bennet Christian Huntingdon Calcraft-Kennedy]. *The Lost Dominion.* London: Blackwood, 1924.

Catherwood, Christopher. *Churchill's Folly: How Winston Churchill Created Modern Iraq.* New York: Carroll & Graf Publishers, 2004.

Cetin, Fethiye. *My Grandmother: A Memoir.* Translated by Maureen Freely. London: Verso, 2008.

Chalabian, Antranig. *Dro (Drastamat Kanayan): Armenia's First Defense Minister of the Modern Era.* Translated by Jack Chelebian. Los Angeles: Indo-European Publishing, 2009.

———. "General Andranik and the Armenian Revolutionary Movement." Privately published, 1988.

Chalk, Frank, and Kurt Jonassohn. *The History and Sociology of Genocide: Analyses and Case Studies.* New Haven: Yale University Press, 1990.

Chester, Colby. "Turkey Reinterpreted." *Current History* 16 (April–September 1922): 936–47.

Chorbajian, Levon, Patrick Donabedian, and Claude Mutafian. *The Caucasian Knot: The History and Geo-politics of Nagorno-Karabagh.* Atlantic Highlands, NJ: Zed Books, 1994.

Churchill, Ward. *A Little Matter of Genocide: Holocaust and Denial in the Americas, 1492 to the Present.* San Francisco: City Lights Books, 1997.

Churchill, Winston. *The World Crisis, 1911–1918.* New York: Free Press, 2005.

Clark, Christopher. *The Sleepwalkers: How Europe Went to War in 1914.* New York: HarperCollins, 2013.

Conybeare, Fred C. "The Survival of Animal Sacrifices inside the Christian Church." *American Journal of Theology* Vol. 7, No. 1 (Jan. 1903), pp. 62–90.

Courtois, Sébastien de. *The Forgotten Genocide: Eastern Christians, the Last Arameans.* Translated by Vincent Aurora. Piscataway, NJ: Gorgias Press, 2004.

Croutier, Alev Lytle. *Harem: The World behind the Veil.* New York: Abbeville Press, 1989.

Dadrian, Vahakn. "The Armenian Genocide in Official Turkish Records." *Journal of Political and Military Sociology* 22, no. 1 (Spring 1995): 1–210.

———. *German Responsibility in the Armenian Genocide: A Review of the Historical Evidence of German Complicity.* Watertown, MA: Blue Crane Books, 1996.

———. *The History of the Armenian Genocide: Ethnic Conflict from the Balkans to Anatolia to the Caucasus.* New York: Berghahn Books, 2008.

———. *The Role of Turkish Physicians in the World War One Genocide of Ottoman Armenians.* New York: Pergamon Press, 1986.

Dadrian, Vahakn N., and Taner Akcam. *Judgment at Istanbul: The Armenian Genocide Trials.* New York: Berghahn Books, 2011.

Daniel, Robert L. *American Philanthropy in the Near East, 1820–1960.* Athens: Ohio University Press, 1970.

Dasnabedian, Hrach. *History of the Armenian Revolutionary Federation, Dashnaktsutiun, 1890–1924.* Milan: Oemme Edizioni, 1989.

———. "The Hunchakian Party." *Armenian Review* 41, no. 4 (Winter 1988): 17–39.

Davenport, E. H., and Sidney Russell Cooke. *The Oil Trusts and Anglo-American Relations.* London: Macmillan, 1923.

Davidson, Khoren K. *Odyssey of an Armenian of Zeitoun.* New York: Vantage Press, 1985.

Davis, Leslie A. *The Slaughterhouse Province: An American Diplomat's Report on the Armenian Genocide, 1915–1917.* Edited by Susan K. Blair. New Rochelle, NY: Aristide D. Caratzas, 1989.

Davison, Roderic H. *Essays in Ottoman and Turkish History, 1774–1923: The Impact of the West.* Austin: University of Texas Press, 2011.

Davison, Roderic H., and C. H. Dodd. *Turkey: A Short History.* 3rd ed. Huntingdon, UK: Eothen Press, 1998.

De Amicis, Edmondo. *Constantinople.* Translated by Stephen Parkin. London: Alma Classics, 2013.

De Bellaigue, Christopher. *Patriot of Persia: Muhammad Mossadegh and a Tragic Anglo-American Coup.* New York: Harper, 2012.

———. *Rebel Land: Unraveling the Riddle of History in a Turkish Town.* New York: Penguin Press, 2010.

De Las Casas, Bartolomé. *An Account, Much Abbreviated, of the Destruction of the Indies, with Related Texts.* Edited by Franklin W. Knight. Translated by Andrew Hurley. Indianapolis: Hackett Publishing Company, 2003.

de Nogales, Rafael. *Four Years beneath the Crescent.* Translated by Muna Lee. London: Sterndale Classics, 2003.

DeNovo, John A. *American Interests and Policies in the Middle East: 1900–1939.* Minneapolis: University of Minnesota Press, 1963.

Derdarian, Mae M. *Vergeen: A Survivor of the Armenian Genocide; Based on a Memoir by Virginia Meghrouni.* Los Angeles: ATMUS Press Publications, 1996.

Derderian, Shahen. *Death March: An Armenian Survivor's Memoir of the Genocide of 1915.* Translated by Ishkhan Jinbashian. Studio City, CA: H. and K. Manjikian Publications, 2008.

Der Minasian, Rouben. *Armenian Freedom Fighters: The Memoirs of Rouben Der Minasian.* Translated by James G. Mandalian. Boston: Hairenik Associates, 1963.

Derogy, Jacques. *Resistance and Revenge: The Armenian Assassination of the Turkish Leaders Responsible for the 1915 Massacres and Deportations.* Translated by A. M. Berrett. New Brunswick, NJ: Transaction Publishers, 1990.

Dinkel, Christoph, "German Officers and the Armenian Genocide." *Armenian Review* 44, no. 1/173 (Spring 1991): 77–133.

Djemal Pasha. *Memories of a Turkish Statesman, 1913–1919.* London: Hutchinson & Company, 1922.

Dobkin, Marjorie Housepian. *Smyrna 1922: The Destruction of a City.* Reprint. Kent, OH: Kent State University Press, 1988.

Dunn, Robert. *World Alive.* New York: Crown, 1956.

Dündar, Fuat. *Crime of Numbers: The Role of Statistics in the Armenian Question (1878–1918).* New Brunswick, NJ: Transaction Publishers, 2010.

Durak, Attila. *Ebru: Reflections of Cultural Diversity in Turkey.* Edited by Ayse Guul Altinay. Istanbul: Metis Publishing, 2007.

Dwight, H. G. O. *Christianity in Turkey: A Narrative of the Protestant Reformation in the Armenian Church.* London: James Nisbet and Co., 1854.

Edib, Halide. *Conflict of East and West in Turkey.* Delhi: Jamia Press, 1935.

———. *House with Wisteria: Memoirs of Turkey Old and New.* New Brunswick, NJ: Transaction Publishers, 2009.

———. *Turkey Faces West: A Turkish View of Recent Changes and their Origin.* New Haven: Yale University Press, 1930.

Eggers, Dave. *What Is the What.* New York: Vintage, 2007.

Einstein, Lewis. *A Diplomat Looks Back.* New Haven: Yale University Press, 1968.

Elbrecht, Anne Elizabeth. *Telling the Story: The Armenian Genocide in the New York Times and Missionary Herald, 1914-1918.* London: Gomidas Institute, 2012.

Elkins, Caroline. *Imperial Reckoning: The Untold Story of Britain's Gulag in Kenya.* New York: Henry Holt and Company, 2005.

Engdahl, William. *A Century of War: Anglo-American Oil Politics and the New World Order.* London: Pluto Press, 2004.

Erickson, Edward J. *Ordered to Die: A History of the Ottoman Army in the First World War.* Westport, CT: Greenwood Press, 2001.

Esfandiari, Haleh, and A. L. Udovitch, eds. *The Economic Dimensions of Middle Eastern History: Essays in Honor of Charles Issawi*. Princeton, NJ: Darwin Press, 1990.

Euben, Roxanne L., and Muhammad Qasim Zaman, eds. *Princeton Readings in Islamist Thought: Texts and Contexts from Al-Banna to Bin Laden*. Princeton: Princeton University Press, 2009.

Faroqhi, Suraiya. *Subjects of the Sultan: Culture and Daily Life in the Ottoman Empire*. London: I. B. Tauris, 2005.

Ferrier, R. W. *The History of the British Petroleum Company*. Cambridge: Cambridge University Press, 1982.

Field, James A., Jr. *America and the Mediterranean World, 1776–1882*. Princeton: Princeton University Press, 1969.

Figes, Orlando. *The Crimean War: A History*. New York: Metropolitan Books, 2010.

Findley, Carter Vaughn. *Turkey, Islam, Nationalism, and Modernity: A History, 1789–2007*. New Haven: Yale University Press, 2010.

———. *The Turks in World History*. New York: Oxford University Press, 2005.

Finkel, Caroline. *Osman's Dream: The Story of the Ottoman Empire, 1300–1923*. New York: Basic Books, 2005.

Fisk, Robert. *The Great War for Civilisation: The Conquest of the Middle East*. New York: Vintage Books, 2005.

Fitzherbert, Margaret. *The Man Who Was Greenmantle: A Biography of Aubrey Herbert*. London: J. Murray, 1983.

Fletcher, Richard. *The Cross and the Crescent: The Dramatic Story of the Earliest Encounters Between Christians and Muslims*. New York: Penguin, 2003.

Freely, John. *Inside the Seraglio: Private Lives of the Sultans in Istanbul*. London: Penguin Books, 2000.

Fromkin, David. *A Peace to End All Peace: The Fall of the Ottoman Empire and the Creation of the Modern Middle East*. New York: Henry Holt and Company, 2001.

Fuller, Graham E. *The New Turkish Republic: Turkey as a Pivotal State in the Muslim World*. Washington, DC: United States Institute of Peace Press, 2008.

Gaunt, David. *Massacres, Resistance, Protectors: Muslim-Christian Relations in Eastern Anatolia during World War I*. Piscataway, NJ: Gorgias Press, 2006.

George, Joan. *Merchants in Exile: The Armenians in Manchester, England, 1835–1935*. London: Gomidas Institute, 2002.

Gerlach, Christian. *Extremely Violent Societies: Mass Violence in the Twentieth-Century World*. Cambridge: Cambridge University Press, 2010.

Germany, Turkey and Armenia: A Selection of Documentary Evidence Relating to the Armenian Atrocities from German and Other Sources. London: J. J. Keliher, 1917.

Gerretson, F. C. *History of the Royal Dutch*. 4 vols. Leiden: E. J. Brill, 1957.

Gibb, George Sweet, and Evelyn H. Knowlton. *The Resurgent Years, 1911–1927*. New York: Harper & Brothers, 1956.

Gidney, James B. *A Mandate for Armenia*. Kent, OH: Kent State University Press, 1967.

Gladstone, W. E., MP. *Bulgarian Horrors and the Question of the East*. London, 1876.

Glassé, Cyril. *The Concise Encyclopedia of Islam*. San Francisco: HarperSan Francisco, 1991.

Göçek, Fatma Müge. *Denial of Violence: Ottoman Past, Turkish Present, and Collective Violence against the Armenians, 1789–2009*. Oxford: Oxford University Press, 2015.

———. *The Transformation of Turkey: Redefining State and Society from the Ottoman Empire to the Modern Era*. London: I. B. Tauris, 2011.

Goffman, Daniel. *The Ottoman Empire and Early Modern Europe*. Cambridge: Cambridge University Press, 2002.

Goldberg, Ellis Jay, ed. *The Social History of Labor in the Middle East*. Boulder, CO: Westview Press, 1996.

Gopoian, Khazaros. *The Diary of Khazaros Gopoian*. Translated by Stephan Gopoian. Teaneck, NJ, 2002.

Gordon, Mel. *Voluptuous Panic: The Erotic World of Weimar Berlin*. Port Townsend, WA: Feral House, 2006.

Grabill, Joseph L. *Protestant Diplomacy and the Near East: Missionary Influence on American Policy, 1810–1927*. Minneapolis: University of Minnesota Press, 1971.

Gravett, Christopher. *Medieval Siege Warfare*. London: Osprey Publishing, 1990.

Gregorian, Vartan. *Islam: A Mosaic, Not a Monolith*. Washington, DC: Brookings Institution Press, 2003.

Gross, Jan T. *Neighbors: The Destruction of the Jewish Community in Jedwabne, Poland*. New York: Penguin Books, 2002.

Gross, Jan Tomasz, and Irena Grudzińska-Gross. *Golden Harvest: Events at the Periphery of the Holocaust*. New York: Oxford University Press, 2012.

Grossman, Vasily. *An Armenian Sketchbook*. Translated by Robert Chandler and Elizabeth Chandler. New York: New York Review of Books, 2013.

Grosz, George. *An Autobiography*. Berkeley: University of California Press, 1998.

Gulbenkian, Nubar. *Portrait in Oil: The Autobiography of Nubar Gulbenkian*. New York: Simon and Schuster, 1965.

Gulesserian, Papken. *The Armenian Church*. Translated by Terenig Vartabed Poladian. New York: Gotchaag Press, 1939.

Gunter, Michael M. *Armenian History and the Question of Genocide.* New York: Palgrave Macmillan, 2011.

———. *The Kurds and the Future of Turkey.* New York: St. Martin's Press, 1997.

Gurbilek, Nurdan. *The New Cultural Climate in Turkey: Living in a Shop Window.* London: Zed Books, 2011.

Gurdjieff, George Ivanovitch. *Meetings with Remarkable Men.* New York: Penguin Compass, 2002.

Gurun, Kamuran. *The Armenian File: The Myth of Innocence Exposed.* Istanbul: Turkiye Is Bankasi Kultur Yayinlari, 2007.

Gust, Wolfgang, ed. *The Armenian Genocide: Evidence from the German Foreign Office Archives, 1915–1916.* New York: Berghahn Books, 2014.

Hacikyan, Agop J., coordinating ed. *The Heritage of Armenian Literature.* Vol. 3. Detroit: Wayne State University Press, 2005.

Hanioglu, M. Sukru. *Ataturk: An Intellectual Biography.* Princeton: Princeton University Press, 2011.

———. *A Brief History of the Late Ottoman Empire.* Princeton: Princeton University Press, 2008.

———. *Preparation for a Revolution: The Young Turks, 1902–1908.* Oxford: Oxford University Press, 2001.

Hartunian, Abraham H. *Neither to Laugh nor to Weep: An Odyssey of Faith; A Memoir of the Armenian Genocide.* Translated by Vartan Hartunian. 3rd ed. Belmont, MA: Armenian Heritage Press, 1999.

Headrick, Daniel R. *The Tools of Empire: Technology and European Imperialism in the Nineteenth Century.* Oxford: Oxford University Press, 1981.

Heath, Ian. *Byzantine Armies, AD 1118–1461.* Oxford: Osprey Publishing, 1995.

Herbert, Aubrey. *Ben Kendim: A Record of Eastern Travel.* Edited by Desmond MacCarthy. London: Hutchinson & Co., 1924.

———. *Mons, Anzac and Kut.* Edited by Edward Melotte. South Yorkshire, UK: Pen & Sword Books, 2009.

Herzog, Dagmar, ed. *Brutality and Desire: War and Sexuality in Europe's Twentieth Century.* Basingstoke, UK: Palgrave Macmillan, 2011.

Heussler, Robert. *Yesterday's Rulers: The Making of the British Colonial Service.* Syracuse: Syracuse University Press, 1963.

Hewins, Ralph. *Mr. Five Per Cent: The Story of Calouste Gulbenkian.* New York: Rinehart & Company, 1958.

Hewsen, Robert H., and Christopher C. Salvatico. *Armenia: A Historical Atlas.* Chicago: University of Chicago Press, 2001.

Hikmet, Nazim. *Poems of Nazim Hikmet.* Translated by Randy Blasing and Mutlu Konuk. New York: Persea Books, 2002.

Hodgson, Marshall G. S. *The Secret Order of Assassins: The Struggle of the Early Nizârî Ismâ'îlîs against the Islamic World*. Philadelphia: University of Pennsylvania Press, 2005.

Hofmann, Tessa. *Der Völkermord an den Armeniern vor Gericht: Der Prozess Talaat Pascha*. Göttingen: Gesellschaft für bedrohte Völker, 1985.

———. "New Aspects of the Talat Pasha Court Case." *Armenian Review* 4, no. 168 (1989).

Hopkirk, Peter. *The Great Game: The Struggle for Empire in Central Asia*. New York: Kodansha International, 1990.

———. *Like Hidden Fire: The Plot to Bring Down the British Empire*. New York: Kodansha International, 1994.

———. *Setting the East Ablaze: Lenin's Dream of an Empire in Asia*. London: John Murray Publishers, 2006.

Horton, George. *The Blight of Asia: An Account of the Systematic Extermination of Christian Populations by the Mohammedans and of the Culpability of Certain Great Powers; with the True Story of the Burning of Smyrna*. 2nd ed. London: Sterndale Classics, 2008.

Hosfeld, Rolf. *Operation Nemesis: Die Türkei, Deutschland und der Völkermord an den Armeniern*. Köln: Kiepenheuer & Witsch, 2005.

Hourani, Albert. *A History of the Arab Peoples*. Cambridge: Belknap Press of Harvard University Press, 1991.

Hovannisian, Garin K. *Family of Shadows: A Century of Murder, Memory, and the Armenian American Dream*. New York: HarperCollins, 2010.

Hovannisian, Richard, ed. *The Armenian Genocide: Cultural and Ethical Legacies*. New Brunswick, NJ: Transaction Publishers, 2007.

———, ed. *The Armenian Genocide in Perspective*. New Brunswick, NJ: Transaction Books, 1986.

———. *The Armenian Holocaust: A Bibliography Relating to the Deportations, Massacres, and Dispersion of the Armenian People, 1915–1923*. Cambridge, MA: Armenian Heritage Press, 1980.

———. *The Armenian People from Ancient to Modern Times: The Dynastic Periods; From Antiquity to the Fourteenth Century*. 2nd ed. Vol. 1. New York: St. Martin's Press, 2004.

———, ed. *The Armenian People from Ancient to Modern Times: Foreign Dominion to Statehood; The Fifteenth Century to the Twentieth Century*. 2nd ed. Vol. 2. New York: St. Martin's Press, 2004.

———, ed. *Looking Backward, Moving Forward: Confronting the Armenian Genocide*. New Brunswick, NJ: Transaction Publishers, 2003.

———, ed. *Remembrance and Denial: The Case of the Armenian Genocide*. Detroit: Wayne State University Press, 1999.

————. *The Republic of Armenia.* 4 vols. Berkeley: University of California Press, 1996.

Hovannisian, Richard G., and Simon Payaslian, eds. *Armenian Constantinople.* Costa Mesa, CA: Mazda Publishers, 2010.

Hull, Isabel V. *Absolute Destruction: Military Culture and the Practices of War in Imperial Germany.* Ithaca: Cornell University Press, 2005.

Imber, Colin. *The Ottoman Empire, 1300–1650: The Structure of Power,* 2nd ed. New York: Palgrave Macmillian, 2009.

Inalcik, Halil. *The Ottoman Empire: The Classical Age, 1300–1600.* London: Phoenix, 2000.

Jacobsen, Maria. *Diaries of a Danish Missionary: Harpoot, 1907–1919.* Edited by Ara Sarafian. Translated by Kristen Vind. Princeton: Gomidas Institute Books, 2001.

Jacobson, Matthew Frye. *Whiteness of a Different Color: European Immigrants and the Alchemy of Race.* Cambridge: Harvard University Press, 1998.

Jahoda, Gloria. *The Trail of Tears: The Story of the American Indian Removals, 1813–1855.* 1975. New York: Wing Books, 1995.

James, Lawrence. *The Golden Warrior: The Life and Legend of Lawrence of Arabia.* London: Paragon House, 1993.

Jenkins, Gareth H. "Between Fact and Fantasy: Turkey's Ergenekon Investigation." Silk Road Paper, Central Asia–Caucasus Institute Silk Road Studies Program, August 2009.

Jerjian, George. *The Truth Will Set Us Free: Armenians and Turks Reconciled.* London: GJ Communications, 2003.

Jernazian, Ephraim K. *Judgment unto Truth: Witnessing the Armenian Genocide.* Translated by Alice Haig. New Brunswick, NJ: Transaction Publishers, 1990.

Johnson, Ian. *A Mosque in Munich: Nazis, the CIA, and the Muslim Brotherhood in the West.* Boston: Houghton Mifflin Harcourt, 2010.

Jung, Dietrich, and Wolfango Piccoli. *Turkey at the Crossroads: Ottoman Legacies and a Greater Middle East.* London: Zed Books, 2001.

Kaiser, Hilmar. *At the Crossroads of Der Zor: Death, Survival, and Humanitarian Resistance in Aleppo, 1915–1917.* Reading, UK: Taderon Press, 2002.

Kaiser, Hilmar, ed. *Eberhard Count Wolffskeel von Reichenberg, Zeitoun, Mousa Dagh, Ourfa: Letters on the American Genocide.* 2nd ed. Princeton, NJ: Gomidas Institute, 2004.

————. *Imperialism, Racism, and Development Theories: The Construction of a Dominant Paradigm on Ottoman Armenians.* Ann Arbor: Gomidas Institute, 1997.

Kaligian, Dikran Mesrob. *Armenian Organization and Ideology under Ottoman Rule: 1908–1914.* New Brunswick, NJ: Transaction Publishers, 2009.

Kaminsky, Alexander H., as told to Michael Stern. "The Murder of the Archbishop." *Master Detective* 12 (July 1935): 6–12, 65–70.

Karagueuzian, Hrayr S., and Yair Auron. *A Perfect Injustice: Genocide and Theft of Armenian Wealth.* New Brunswick, NJ: Transaction Publishers, 2009.

Karpat, Kemal H. *The Ottoman State and Its Place in World History.* Leiden: E. J. Brill, 1974.

———. *The Politicization of Islam: Reconstructing Identity, State, Faith, and Community in the Late Ottoman State.* New York: Oxford University Press, 2001.

Karsh, Efraim, and Inari Karsh. *Empires of the Sand: The Struggle for Mastery in the Middle East, 1789–1923.* Cambridge: Harvard University Press, 1999.

Kasaba, Resat. *The Ottoman Empire and the World Economy: The Nineteenth Century.* Albany: State University of New York Press, 1988.

Kayali, Hasan. *Arabs and Young Turks: Ottomanism, Arabism, and Islamism in the Ottoman Empire, 1908–1918.* Berkeley: University of California Press, 1997.

Kazancigil, Ali, and Ergun Ozbudun, eds. *Ataturk, Founder of a Modern State.* Hamden, CT: Archon Books, 1981.

Kedourie, Elie. *The Chatham House Version and Other Middle-Eastern Studies.* 1970. Reprint. Hanover, NH: University Press of New England, 1984.

———. *England and the Middle East: The Destruction of the Ottoman Empire, 1914–1921.* 2nd ed. Brighton, UK: Harvester Press, 1978.

———. *Nationalism.* 4th ed. Oxford: Blackwell, 1993.

———. *Politics in the Middle East.* Oxford: Oxford University Press, 1992.

Kedourie, Sylvia, ed. *Seventy-Five Years of the Turkish Republic.* London: Frank Cass Publishers, 2000.

Kent, Marian, ed. *The Great Powers and the End of the Ottoman Empire.* London: George Allen & Unwin, 1984.

———. *Moguls and Mandarins: Oil, Imperialism and the Middle East in British Foreign Policy, 1900–1940.* 1993. New York: Routledge 2011.

Kerr, Stanley E. *The Lions of Marash: Personal Experiences with American Near East Relief, 1919–1922.* Albany: State University of New York Press, 1973.

Kershaw, Ian. *Hitler: A Biography.* New York: W. W. Norton & Co., 2008.

Kévorkian, Raymond. *The Armenian Genocide: A Complete History.* London: I. B. Tauris, 2011.

Kévorkian, Raymond H., and Vahé Tachjian, eds. *The Armenian General Benevolent Union: One Hundred Years of History.* Vol. 1. *1906–1940.* Translated by G. M. Goshgarian. Cairo: AGBU Central Board, 2006.

Keyder, Caglar. *State and Class in Turkey: A Study in Capitalist Development.* London: Verso, 1987.

Kinross, Lord Patrick Douglas Balfour, Baron. *Atatürk: The Rebirth of a Nation.* London: Weidenfeld and Nicolson, 1964.

———. *The Ottoman Centuries: The Rise and Fall of the Turkish Empire.* New York: Harper Perennial, 2002.

———. *Within the Taurus: A Journey in Asiatic Turkey.* New York: William Morrow and Company, 1955.

Kinzer, Stephen. *The Brothers: John Foster Dulles, Allen Dulles, and Their Secret World War.* New York: Times Books, 2013.

———. *Crescent and Star: Turkey between Two Worlds.* New York: Farrar, Straus and Giroux, 2008.

———. *Reset: Iran, Turkey, and America's Future.* New York: Times Books, 2010.

Kirakossian, Arman J., ed. *The Armenian Massacres, 1894–1896: British Media Testimony.* Dearborn: Armenian Research Center, University of Michigan, 2008.

———, ed. *The Armenian Massacres, 1894–1896: U.S. Media Testimony.* Detroit: Wayne State University Press, 2004.

———. *British Diplomacy and the Armenian Question: From the 1830s to 1914.* Princeton: Gomidas Institute Books, 2003.

Kloian, Richard Diran. *The Armenian Genocide: News Accounts from the American Press: 1915–1922.* 4th ed. Richmond, CA: Heritage Publishing, 2007.

Knapp, Grace H., Grisell M. McLaren, and Myrtle O. Shane. *The Tragedy of Bitlis: Being Mainly the Narratives of Grisell M. McLaren and Myrtle O. Shane.* London: Sterndale Classics, 2002.

Künzler, Jakob. *In the Land of Blood and Tears: Experiences in Mesopotamia during the World War (1914–1918).* Edited by Ara Ghazarians. Arlington, MA: Armenian Cultural Foundation, 2007.

Kurban, Dilek, and Kezban Hatemi. *The Story of an Alien(ation): Real Estate Ownership Problems of Non-Muslim Foundations and Communities in Turkey.* Istanbul: TESEV Publications, 2009.

Kuru, Ahmet T. *Secularism and State Policies toward Religion: The United States, France, and Turkey.* New York: Cambridge University Press, 2009.

Kuru, Ahmet T., and Alfred Stepan, eds. *Democracy, Islam, and Secularism in Turkey.* New York: Columbia University Press, 2012.

Kuyumjian, Rita Soulahian. *The Survivor: Biography of Aram Andonian.* London: Gomidas Institute, 2010.

Landau, Jacob M. *Pan-Turkism: From Irredentism to Cooperation.* Bloomington: Indiana University Press, 1995.

Lang, David Marshall. *Armenia: Cradle of Civilization.* 3rd ed. London: George Allen & Unwin, 1980.

Laqueur, Walter. *Terrorism.* Boston: Little, Brown, 1977.

Lemkin, Raphael. *Axis Rule in Occupied Europe: Laws of Occupation, Analysis of Government, Proposals for Redress.* 2nd ed. Clark, NJ: Lawbook Exchange, 2008.

————. *Raphael Lemkin's Dossier on the Armenian Genocide: Turkish Massacres of Armenians.* Glendale, CA: Center for Armenian Remembrance, 2008.

————. *Totally Unofficial: The Autobiography of Raphael Lemkin.* Edited by Donna-Lee Frieze. New Haven: Yale University Press, 2013.

Levene, Mark. *Genocide in the Age of the Nation State: The Rise of the West and the Coming of Genocide.* Vol. 2. London: I. B. Tauris, 2005.

Leverkuehn, Paul. *A German Officer during the Armenian Genocide: A Biography of Max von Scheubner-Richter.* Translated by Alasdair Lean. London: Taderon Press for the Gomidas Institute, 2008.

Lewis, Bernard. *The Assassins: A Radical Sect in Islam.* New York: Basic Books, 2003.

————. *The Emergence of Modern Turkey.* 3rd ed. New York: Oxford University Press, 2002.

————. *The Middle East: A Brief History of the Last 2,000 Years.* New York: Scribner, 1995.

————. *The Multiple Identities of the Middle East.* London: Phoenix, 1999.

Lewy, Guenter. *The Armenian Massacres in Ottoman Turkey: A Disputed Genocide.* Salt Lake City: University of Utah Press, 2005.

Libaridian, Gerard J. *The Challenge of Statehood: Armenian Political Thinking since Independence.* Cambridge, MA: Blue Crane Books, 1999.

————. *Modern Armenia: People, Nation, State.* New Brunswick, NJ: Transaction Publishers, 2007.

Longrigg, Stephen Hemsley. *Oil in the Middle East.* 3rd ed. London: Oxford University Press, 1968.

MacCurdy, Marian Mesrobian. *Sacred Justice: The Voices and Legacy of the Armenian Operation Nemesis.* New Brunswick, NJ: Transaction Publishers, 2015.

MacMillan, Margaret. *Paris 1919: Six Months That Changed the World.* New York: Random House, 2002.

————. *Peacemakers: The Paris Conference of 1919 and Its Attempt to End War.* London: John Murray, 2001.

Malcolm, Noel. *Kosovo: A Short History.* New York: New York University Press, 1998.

Mamdani, Mahmood. *Good Muslim, Bad Muslim: America, the Cold War, and the Roots of Terror.* New York: Three Leaves Press, 2004.

Mandelstam, Osip. *Journey to Armenia and Conversation about Dante.* Translated by Sidney Monas, Clarence Brown, and Robert Hughes. London: Notting Hill Editions, 2011.

Mango, Andrew. *Ataturk: The Biography of the Founder of Modern Turkey.* Woodstock, NY: Overlook Press, 1999.

———. *From the Sultan to Ataturk: Turkey*. London: Haus Publishing, 2009.

———. *The Turks Today*. Woodstock, NY: Overlook Press, 2004.

Mann, Charles C. "The Birth of Religion." *National Geographic*, June 2011, 34–59.

Mann, Michael. *The Dark Side of Democracy: Explaining Ethnic Cleansing*. New York: Cambridge University Press, 2005.

Mansel, Philip. *Constantinople: City of the World's Desire, 1453–1924*. London: John Murray Publishers, 1995.

———. *Sultans in Splendour: Monarchs of the Middle East, 1869–1945*. London: Parkway Publishing, 1988.

Mardiganian, Aurora. *Ravished Armenia: The Story of Aurora Mardiganian, the Christian Girl Who Lived through the Great Massacres*. Translated by H. L. Gates. New York: Kingfield Press, 1918.

Mardin, Serif. *The Genesis of Young Ottoman Thought: A Study in the Modernization of Turkish Political Ideas*. Syracuse: Syracuse University Press, 2000.

Mazower, Mark. *Salonica, City of Ghosts: Christians, Muslims, and Jews, 1430–1950*. New York: Alfred A. Knopf, 2005.

McCarthy, Justin. *The Armenian Rebellion at Van*. Glen Canyon: University of Utah Press, 2006.

———. *Death and Exile: The Ethnic Cleansing of Ottoman Muslims, 1821–1922*. Princeton: Darwin, 2008.

———. *The Turk in America: Creation of an Enduring Prejudice*. Salt Lake City: University of Utah Press, 2010.

McCartney, Laton. *The Teapot Dome Scandal: How Big Oil Bought the Harding White House and Tried to Steal the Country*. New York: Random House, 2008.

McDowall, David. *A Modern History of the Kurds*. 3rd ed. London: I. B. Tauris, 2004.

McMeekin, Sean. *The Berlin-Baghdad Express: The Ottoman Empire and Germany's Bid for World Power*. Cambridge: Belknap Press of Harvard University Press, 2010.

———. *The Russian Origins of the First World War*. Cambridge: Belknap Press of Harvard University Press, 2011.

Mejcher, Helmut. *The Struggle for a New Middle East in the 20th Century: Studies in Imperial Design and National Politics*. Edited by Camilla Dawletschin-Linder and Marianne Schmidt-Dumont. Berlin: Lit Verlag, 2007.

Melkonian, Markar, and Seta Melkonian. *My Brother's Road: An American's Fateful Journey to Armenia*. London: I. B. Tauris, 2007.

Melkonian, Monte. *The Right to Struggle: Selected Writings by Monte Melkonian on the Armenian National Question*. San Francisco: Sardarabad Collective, 1993.

Mendelson, Robert. *Revolution and Genocide: The Origins of the Armenian Genocide and the Holocaust.* Chicago: University of Chicago Press, 1992.

Meyer, Karl E., and Shareen Blair Brysac. *Kingmakers: The Invention of the Modern Middle East.* New York: W. W. Norton & Co., 2008.

Miller, Donald E., and Lorna Touryan Miller. *Survivors: An Oral History of the Armenian Genocide.* Berkeley: University of California Press, 1999.

Milton, Giles. *Paradise Lost: Smyrna, 1922; The Destruction of a Christian City in the Islamic World.* New York: Basic Books, 2008.

Minasian, Edward. "The Forty Years of *Musa Dagh:* The Film That Was Denied." *Journal of Armenian Studies* 3, nos. 1–2 (1986–87).

Mishra, Pankaj. *From the Ruins of Empire.* New York: Farrar, Straus and Giroux, 2012.

Mohr, Anton. *The Oil War.* New York: Harcourt, Brace and Company, 1926.

Monroe, Elizabeth. *Britain's Moment in the Middle East, 1914–1956.* London: University Paperbacks, 1965.

Montefiore, Simon Sebag. *Young Stalin.* New York: Vintage, 2008.

Morgenthau, Henry. *Ambassador Morgenthau's Story.* New York: Doubleday, Page & Co., 1919.

———. *Secrets of the Bosphorus.* London: Hutchinson & Co., 1918.

Morley, Bertha B. Marsovan. *1915: The Diaries of Bertha B. Morley.* Edited by Hilmar Kaiser. 2nd ed. Ann Arbor: Gomidas Institute, 2000.

Mugerditchian, Esther. *From Turkish Toils: The Narrative of an Armenian Family's Escape.* London: George H. Doran Company, 1918.

Nalbandian, Louise. *The Armenian Revolutionary Movement: The Development of Armenian Political Parties through the Nineteenth Century.* Berkeley: University of California Press, 1963.

Nash, Gerald D. *United States Oil Policy, 1890–1964: Business and Government in Twentieth Century America.* Pittsburgh: University of Pittsburgh Press, 1968.

Nassibian, Akaby. *Britain and the Armenian Question, 1915–1923.* New York: St. Martin's Press, 1984.

Natali, Shahan. "On the Trail of the Great Criminal." Part I. Translated by Aram Arkun. *Nayiri* 12, no. 1 (May 24, 1964): 4–5.

———. "On the Trail of the Great Criminal." Part II. Translated by Aram Arkun. *Nayiri* 12, no. 2 (May 31, 1964): 4.

———. "On the Trail of the Great Criminal." Part III. Translated by Aram Arkun. *Nayiri* 12, no. 3 (June 7, 1964): 4–5.

———. "On the Trail of the Great Criminal." Part IV. Translated by Aram Arkun. *Nayiri* 12, no. 4 (June 14, 1964): 4.

———. "On the Trail of the Great Criminal." Part V. Translated by Aram Arkun. *Nayiri* 12, no. 5 (June 21, 1964): 4.

———. "On the Trail of the Great Criminal." Part VI. Translated by Aram Arkun. *Nayiri* 12, no. 6 (June 28, 1964): 4–5.

Natalie, Shahan. *The Turks and Us.* Nagorno-Karabakh: Punik Publishing, 2002.

Nazer, James, comp. *The First Genocide of the 20th Century: The Story of the Armenian Massacres in Text and Pictures.* New York: T & T Publishing, 1968.

Nercessian, Baruir. *I Walked through the Valley of Death.* New York, 2003.

The New Catholic Encyclopedia. 2nd ed. Vol. 9. Washington, DC: Thomson Gale in association with The Catholic University of America, 2001.

Nicolle, David. *Armies of the Ottoman Turks, 1300–1774.* Oxford: Osprey Publishing, 1983.

———. *The Fourth Crusade, 1202–04: The Betrayal of Byzantium.* Oxford: Osprey Publishing, 2011.

———. *The Janissaries.* London: Osprey Publishing, 1995.

Nicolson, Harold. *Curzon: The Last Phase, 1919–1925; A Study in Post-war Diplomacy.* London: Constable, 1934.

Niepage, Martin. *The Horrors of Aleppo: Seen by a German Eyewitness; A Word to Germany's Accredited Representatives.* London: T. Fisher Unwin, 1917.

Novello, Adriano Alpago. *The Armenians.* New York: Rizzoli, 1986.

Nowell, Gregory Patrick. *Mercantile States and the World Oil Cartel: 1900–1939.* Ithaca: Cornell University Press, 1994.

Odian, Yervant. *Accursed Years: My Exile and Return from Der Zor, 1914–1919.* Translated by Ara Stepan Melkonian. London: Gomidas Institute, 2009.

Oke, Mim Kemal. *The Armenian Question, 1914–1923.* Nicosia, Cyprus: K. Rustem & Brother, 1988.

Okte, Faik. *The Tragedy of the Turkish Capital Tax.* Translated by Geoffrey Cox. London: Croom Helm, 1987.

Oktem, Kerem. *Turkey since 1989: Angry Nation.* Blackpoint, Nova Scotia: Fernwood Publishing, 2011.

Oren, Michael B. *Power, Faith, and Fantasy: America in the Middle East, 1776 to the Present.* New York: W. W. Norton & Co., 2007.

Orga, Irfan. *Portrait of a Turkish Family.* London: Eland, 2006.

Ormanian, Malachia. *The Church of Armenia: Her History, Doctrine . . . and Existing Condition.* Edited by Terenig Poladian. Translated by G. Marcar Gregory. 2nd ed. London: A. R. Mowbray & Co., 1955.

The Oxford Encyclopedia of the Modern Islamic World. Edited by John L. Esposito. 4 vols. New York: Oxford University Press, 1995.

Ozanian, Andranig. *The Battle of Holy Apostles' Monastery.* Translated by Ara Stepan Melkonian. London: Taderon Press, 2008.

Ozdemir, Hikmet. "Revanchism as Blind Faith and the Dashnak-Asala Assassinations." *Center for Eurasian Studies Report* 6 (March 2014): 5–14. http://www.avim.org.tr/uploads/raporlar/RAPOR-6.pdf.

Ozkan, Behlul. *From the Abode of Islam to the Turkish Vatan: The Making of a National Homeland in Turkey.* New Haven: Yale University Press, 2012.

Ozyurek, Esra, ed. *The Politics of Public Memory in Turkey.* Syracuse: Syracuse University Press, 2007.

Pamuk, Orhan. *Istanbul: Memories and the City.* Translated by Maureen Freely. New York: Vintage International, 2004.

———. *Snow.* Translated by Maureen Freely. New York: Vintage International, 2004.

Pamuk, Sevket. *The Ottoman Empire and European Capitalism, 1820–1913: Trade, Investment and Production.* Cambridge: Cambridge University Press, 1987.

Panossian, Razmik. *The Armenians: From Kings and Priests to Merchants and Commissars.* New York: Columbia University Press, 2006.

Papazian, K. S. *Patriotism Perverted: A Discussion of the Deeds and the Misdeeds of the Armenian Revolutionary Federation, the So-Called Dashnagtzoutune.* Boston: Baikar Press, 1934.

Papers Relating to the Foreign Relations of the United States. The Lansing Papers 1914–1920, Volume I. Washington: United States Government Printing Office, 1939.

Parla, Taha. *The Social and Political Thought of Ziya Gökalp, 1876–1924.* Leiden: E. J. Brill, 1985.

Pastermadjian, Karekin [Armen Garo]. *Armenia a Leading Factor in the Winning of the War.* New York: Armenian Committee for the Independence of Armenia, 1919.

———. *Bank Ottoman: Memoirs of Armen Garo, the Armenian Ambassador to America from the Independent Republic of Armenia.* Translated by Haig T. Partizian. Edited by Simon Vratzian. Detroit: Armen Topouzian, 1990.

Payaslian, Simon. *The History of Armenia: From the Origins to the Present.* New York: Palgrave Macmillan, 2007.

———. *United States Policy toward the Armenian Question and the Armenian Genocide.* New York: Palgrave Macmillan, 2005.

Peirce, Leslie P. *The Imperial Harem: Women and Sovereignty in the Ottoman Empire.* New York: Oxford University Press, 1993.

Penzer, N. M. *The Harem: An Account of the Institution as It Existed in the Palace of the Turkish Sultans, with a History of the Grand Seraglio from Its Foundation to Modern Times.* London: Spring Books, 1965.

Phillips, David L. *Unsilencing the Past: Track Two Diplomacy and Turkish-Armenian Reconciliation.* New York: Berghahn Books, 2005.

Phillips, Terry. *Murder at the Altar: A Historical Novel.* Bakersfield, CA: Hye Books, 2008.

Pipes, Richard. *A Concise History of the Russian Revolution.* New York: Alfred A. Knopf, 1995.

Ponting, Clive. *Progress and Barbarism: The World in the Twentieth Century.* London: Chatto and Windus, 1998.

Pope, Hugh. *Sons of the Conquerors: The Rise of the Turkic World.* New York: Overlook Duckworth, 2006.

Pope, Nicole, and Hugh Pope. *Turkey Unveiled: A History of Modern Turkey.* Woodstock, NY: Overlook Press, 1997.

Power, Samantha. *A Problem from Hell: America and the Age of Genocide.* New York: Basic Books, 2002.

Poynter, Mary Augusta. *When Turkey Was Turkey: In and Around Constantinople.* London: George Routledge and Sons, 1921.

Der Prozess Talaat Pascha: Stenographischer Prozessbericht. Preface by Armin Wegner. Berlin: Deutsche Verlagsgesellschaft für Politik, 1921. [Translated for the author by Joel Golb.]

Quataert, Donald, ed. *Consumption Studies and the History of the Ottoman Empire, 1550–1922: An Introduction.* Albany: State University of New York Press, 2000.

———. *The Ottoman Empire, 1700–1922.* New York: Cambridge University Press, 2005.

Radzinsky, Edvard. *Stalin.* Translated by H. T. Willets. New York: Doubleday, 1996.

Raffi. *The Golden Rooster.* Translated by Donald Abcarian. London: Taderon Press, 2008.

Ramsaur, Ernest Edmondson Jr. *The Young Turks: Prelude to the Revolution of 1908.* Princeton: Princeton University Press, 1965.

Redgate, A. E. *The Armenians.* Oxford: Blackwell Publishers, 2000.

Reed, John. *The War in Eastern Europe.* New York: Charles Scribner's Sons, 1916.

Reid, Donald Malcolm. *Cairo University and the Making of Modern Egypt.* Cambridge: Cambridge University Press, 1990.

———. "Political Assassination in Egypt, 1910–1954." *International Journal of African Historical Studies* 15, no. 4 (1982): 625–51. http://www.jstor.org/stable/10.2307/217848?ref=no-x-route:339e3747894331784d293b5033e9fdbb.

Reisman, Arnold. *Confronting the Armenian Conundrum.* By the author, 2010.

Reiss, Tom. *The Orientalist.* New York: Random House, 2006.

Reynolds, Michael A. *Shattering Empires: The Clash and Collapse of the Ottoman and Russian Empires, 1908–1918.* Cambridge: Cambridge University Press, 2011.

Riggs, Alice Shepard. *Shepard of Aintab.* Princeton: Gomidas Institute, 2001.

Riggs, Henry H. *Days of Tragedy in Armenia: Personal Experiences in Harpoot, 1915–1917.* Ann Arbor: Gomidas Institute, 1997.

Rosenberg, Emily S., ed. *A World Connecting, 1870–1945.* Cambridge: Belknap Press of Harvard University Press, 2012.

Rubenstein, Jay. *Armies of Heaven: The First Crusade and the Quest for Apocalypse.* New York: Basic Books, 2011.

Rustow, Dankwart A., ed. *Philosophers and Kings: Studies in Leadership.* New York: George Braziller, 1970.

Safrastian, Arshak. *Kurds and Kurdistan.* London: Harvill Press, 1948.

Said, Edward W. *Orientalism.* New York: Vintage Books, 1978.

Sakayan, Dora. *An Armenian Doctor in Turkey: Garabed Hatcherian; My Smyrna Ordeal of 1922.* Montreal: Arod Books, 1997.

Sampson, Anthony. *The Seven Sisters: The Great Oil Companies and the World They Made.* London: Coronet, 1976.

Sanders, Liman von. *Five Years in Turkey.* Translated by Carl Reichmann. East Sussex: Naval & Military Press, 2012.

Sarafian, Ara. *Talaat Pasha's Report on the Armenian Genocide, 1917.* London: Gomidas Institute, 2011.

———. *United States Official Records on the Armenian Genocide, 1915–1917.* Princeton: Gomidas Institute, 2004.

Sarafian, Nigoghos. *The Bois de Vincennes.* Translated by Christopher Atamian. Detroit: Wayne State University Press, 2011.

Satia, Priya. *Spies in Arabia: The Great War and the Cultural Foundations of Britain's Covert Empire in the Middle East.* Oxford: Oxford University Press, 2008.

Semelin, Jacques, Claire Andrieu, and Sarah Gensburger, eds. *Resisting Genocide: The Multiple Forms of Rescue.* Translated by Emma Bentley and Cynthia Schoch. New York: Oxford University Press, 2013.

Shamtanchian, Mikayel. *The Fatal Night: An Eyewitness Account of the Extermination of Armenian Intellectuals in 1915.* Translated by Ishkhan Jinbashian. Studio City, CA: H. and K. Majikian Publications, 2007.

Shaw, Stanford J., and Ezel Kural Shaw. *History of the Ottoman Empire and Modern Turkey.* Vol. 1. *Empire of the Gazis: The Rise and Decline of the Ottoman Empire, 1280–1808.* Cambridge: Cambridge University Press, 1976.

———. *History of the Ottoman Empire and Modern Turkey.* Vol. 2. *Reform, Revolution and Republic: The Rise of Modern Turkey, 1808–1975.* Cambridge: Cambridge University Press, 1977.

Shipley, Alice Muggerditchian. *We Walked, Then Ran*. Phoenix: By the author, 1983.

Shiragian, Arshavir. *The Legacy: Memoirs of an Armenian Patriot*. Translated by Sonia Shiragian. Boston: Hairenik Press, 1976.

Shirinian, George N., ed. *The Asia Minor Catastrophe and the Ottoman Greek Genocide: Essays on Asia Minor, Pontos, and Eastern Thrace, 1912–1923*. Bloomingdale, IL: Asia Minor and Pontos Hellenic Research Center, 2012.

Simonian, Hovann H., ed. *The Hemshin: History, Society, and Identity in the Highlands of Northeast Turkey*. New York: Routledge, 2007.

Simpson, Christopher. *The Splendid Blond Beast: Money, Law, and Genocide in the Twentieth Century*. New York: Grove Press, 1993.

Slide, Anthony. Introduction to *Ravished Armenia and the Story of Aurora Mardiganian*, ed. Anthony Slide. Lanham, MD: Scarecrow Press, 1997.

Smith, Albert. *A Month at Constantinople*. London: David Bogue, 1850.

Smith, Shirley W. *James Burrill Angell: An American Influence*. Ann Arbor: University of Michigan Press 1954.

Snyder, Timothy. *Bloodlands: Europe between Hitler and Stalin*. New York: Basic Books, 2010.

Sonyel, Salahi R. *Atatürk: The Founder of Modern Turkey*. Ankara: Turkish Historical Society Printing House, 1989.

———. *Turkish Diplomacy, 1918–1923: Mustafa Kemal and the Turkish National Movement*. London: Sage Publications, 1975.

Srodes, James. *Allen Dulles: Master of Spies*. Washington, DC: Regnery Publishing, 1999.

Stone, Dan, ed. *The Historiography of Genocide*. Basingstoke, UK: Palgrave Macmillan, 2010.

Stoneman, Richard. *A Traveller's History of Turkey*. 5th ed. Northampton, MA: Interlink Books, 2009.

Sumner-Boyd, Hilary, and John Freely. *Strolling through Istanbul: The Classic Guide to the City*. London: Tauris Parke Paperbacks, 2012.

Suny, Ronald Grigor. *The Baku Commune, 1917–1918: Class and Nationality in the Russian Revolution*. Princeton: Princeton University Press, 1972.

———. *Looking toward Ararat: Armenia in Modern History*. Bloomington: Indiana University Press, 1993.

Suny, Ronald Grigor, Fatma Muge Gocek, and Norman M. Naimark, eds. *A Question of Genocide: Armenians and Turks at the End of the Ottoman Empire*. Oxford: Oxford University Press, 2011.

Surmelian, Leon Z. *I Ask You, Ladies and Gentlemen*. New York: E. P. Dutton & Co., 1945.

Sykes, Mark. *Through Five Turkish Provinces.* London: Bickers and Son, 1900.

Svazlian, Verjiné. *The Armenian Genocide: Testimonies of the Eyewitness Survivors.* Translated by Tigran Tsulikian and Anahit Poghikian-Darbinian. Yerevan: "Gitoutoyun" Publishing House of NAS RA, 2011.

Swietochowski, Tadeusz. *Russian Azerbaijan, 1905–1920: The Shaping of National Identity in a Muslim Community.* Cambridge: Cambridge University Press, 2004.

Tehlirian, Soghomon. *Verhishumner (T'aleati ahapegume)* [Memoirs (The assassination of Talat)]. Edited by Vahan Minakhorian, translated by Aram Arkun. Cairo: Housaper, 1953.

Temelkuran, Ece. *Deep Mountain: Across the Turkish-Armenian Divide.* London: Verso, 2010.

Ternon, Yves. *The Armenian Cause.* Delmar, NY: Caravan Books, 1985.

———. *Armenians: History of a Genocide.* Translated by Rouben C. Cholakian. 2nd ed. Ann Arbor: Caravan Books, 1990.

Thomassian, Levon. *Summer of '42: A Study of German-Armenian Relations during the Second World War.* Atglen, PA: Schiffer Publishing, 2012.

Toledano, Ehud R. *Slavery and Abolition in the Ottoman Middle East.* Seattle: University of Washington Press, 1998.

Toner, Jerry. *Homer's Turk: How Classics Shaped Ideas of the East.* Cambridge: Harvard University Press, 2013.

Totten, Samuel, William S. Parsons, and Israel W. Charny, eds. *Century of Genocide: Eyewitness Accounts and Critical Views.* New York: Garland Publishing, 1997.

Toumani, Meline. *There Was and There Was Not: A Journey through Hate and Possibility in Turkey, Armenia, and Beyond.* New York: Metropolitan Books, 2014.

Toynbee, Arnold J. "The Ottoman Empire's Place in World History." In *The Ottoman State and Its Place in World History,* ed. Kemal H. Karpat. Leiden: E. J. Brill, 1974.

Toynbee, Arnold Joseph, and James Bryce, Viscount. *Armenian Atrocities: The Murder of a Nation.* London: Hodder & Stoughton, 1915.

Trask, Roger R. *The United States Response to Turkish Nationalism and Reform, 1914–1939.* Minneapolis: University of Minnesota Press, 1971.

Troshine, Yves. "A Bystander's Notes of a Massacre." *Scribner's Magazine,* January 21, 1897, 48–69.

Trumpener, Ulrich. *Germany and the Ottoman Empire, 1914–1918.* Princeton: Princeton University Press, 1968.

Turnbull, Stephen. *The Walls of Constantinople, AD 324–1453.* Oxford: Osprey Publishing, 2004.

Ungor, Ugur Umit. *The Making of Modern Turkey: Nation and State in Eastern Anatolia, 1913–1950.* Oxford: Oxford University Press, 2012.

Ungor, Ugur Umit, and Mehmet Polatel. *Confiscation and Destruction: The Young Turk Seizure of Armenian Property.* London: Continuum International Publishing Group, 2011.

Urquhart, David. *Turkey and Its Resources: Its Municipal Organization and Free Trade; the State and Prospects of English Commerce in the East; the New Administration of Greece, Its Revenue and National Possessions.* London: Saunders and Otley, 1833.

Ussher, Clarence D., and Grace H. Knapp. *An American Physician in Turkey: A Narrative of Adventures in Peace and in War.* Boston: Houghton Mifflin, 1917.

Uyar, Mesut, and Edward J. Erickson. *A Military History of the Ottomans: From Osman to Ataturk.* Santa Barbara, CA: Praeger Security International, 2009.

Varandian, Mikayel. *Murad of Sepastia.* Translated by Ara Ghazarians. Arlington, MA: Armenian Cultural Foundation, 2006.

Vidal-Naquet, Pierre. *A Crime of Silence: The Armenian Genocide; The Permanent Peoples' Tribunal.* Cambridge, MA: Zoryan Institute, 1985.

Videlier, Philippe. *Nuit Turque.* Paris: Gallimard, 2005.

Vierbücher, Heinrich. *Armenia 1915: What the German Imperial Government Concealed from Its Subjects; The Slaughter of a Civilized People at the Hands of the Turks.* Edited by Ara Ghazarians. Arlington, MA: Armenian Cultural Foundation, 2006.

Volodarsky, Boris. "Unknown Agabekov." Intelligence and National Security. Published online June 28, 2013, 890–909. DOI: 10.1080/02684527.2012.701440.

Voss, Huberta von, ed. *Portraits of Hope: Armenians in the Contemporary World.* Translated by Alasdair Lean. New York: Berghahn Books, 2007.

Vowell, Sarah. *Unfamiliar Fishes.* New York: Riverhead, 2011.

Vryonis, Speros, Jr. *Byzantium and Europe.* London: Thames & Hudson, 1967.

———. *The Mechanism of Catastrophe: The Turkish Pogrom of September 6–7, 1955, and the Destruction of the Greek Community of Istanbul.* New York: Greekworks.com, 2005.

———. *The Turkish State and History: Clio Meets the Grey Wolf.* 2nd ed. Thessaloniki: Institute for Balkan Studies, 1993.

Walker, Christopher J. *Armenia: The Survival of a Nation.* Rev. 2nd ed. New York: St. Martin's Press, 1990.

———. *Visions of Ararat: Writings on Armenia.* London: I. B. Tauris, 2005.

Washburn, George. *Fifty Years in Constantinople and Recollections of Robert College*. Boston: Houghton Mifflin, 1909.

Weiner, Tim. *Enemies: A History of the FBI*. New York: Random House, 2013.

Weitz, Eric D. *A Century of Genocide: Utopias of Race and Nation*. Princeton: Princeton University Press, 2003.

Werfel, Franz. *The Forty Days of* Musa Dagh. Translated by Geoffrey Dunlop. Edited by James Reidel. Boston: David R. Godine, 2012.

Wheatcroft, Andrew. *The Ottomans*. London: Viking, 1993.

———. *The Ottomans: Dissolving Images*. London: Penguin, 1993.

Willey, Peter. *The Castles of the Assassins*. Fresno, CA: Linden Publishing, 2001.

Winter, Jay, ed. *America and the Armenian Genocide of 1915*. Cambridge: Cambridge University Press, 2003.

Yalcin, Kemal. *You Rejoice My Heart*. Translated by Paul Bessemer. London: Tekeyan Cultural Association, 2007.

Yavuz, M. Hakan. *Islamic Political Identity in Turkey*. New York: Oxford University Press, 2003.

Yeghiayan, Vartkes. *The Armenian Genocide and the Trials of the Young Turks*. La Verne, CA: American Armenian International College Press, 1990.

———, comp. *British Reports on Ethnic Cleansing in Anatolia, 1919–1922: The Armenian-Greek Section*. Glendale, CA: Center for Armenian Remembrance, 2007.

———. *The Case of Soghomon Tehlirian*. 2nd ed. Glendale, CA: Center for Armenian Remembrance, 2006.

———, comp. *Vahan Cardashian: Advocate Extraordinaire for the Armenian Cause*. Glendale, CA: Center for Armenian Remembrance, 2008.

Yeghiayan, Vartkes, and Ara Arabyan. *The Case of Misak Torlakian*. Glendale, CA: Center for Armenian Remembrance, 2006.

Yeghiayan, Zaven Der. *My Patriarchal Memoirs: Zaven Der Yeghiayan, the Armenian Patriarch of Constantinople, 1913–1922*. Translated by Ared Misirliyan. Edited by Vatche Ghazarian. Barrington, RI: Mayreni Publishing, 2002.

Yergin, Daniel. *The Prize: The Epic Quest for Oil, Money, and Power*. New York: Free Press, 1992.

Yilmaz, Hakan, ed. *Placing Turkey on the Map of Europe*. Istanbul: Bogazici University Press, 2005.

Yilmaz, Suhnaz. "An Ottoman Warrior Abroad: Enver Pasha as an Expatriate." In *Seventy-Five Years of the Turkish Republic,* ed. Sylvia Kedourie. London: Frank Cass Publishers, 2000.

Young, George. *Constantinople*. New York: Barnes & Noble Books, 1992.

Zana, Mehdi. *Prison No. 5: Eleven Years in Turkish Jails.* Cambridge, MA: Blue Crane Books, 1997.

Zarinebaf, Fariba. *Crime and Punishment in Istanbul, 1700–1800.* Berkeley: University of California Press, 2010.

Zürcher, Erik J. *The Young Turk Legacy and Nation Building: From the Ottoman Empire to Atatürk's Turkey.* London: I. B. Tauris, 2010.

———. *Turkey: A Modern History.* London: I. B. Tauris, 2007.

PAMPHLETS

American Friends Service Committee. *Speak Truth to Power: A Quaker Search for an Alternative to Violence: A Study of International Conflict.* American Friends Service Committee, 1955.

Four Seasons Hotel Istanbul. *A History of the Sultanahmet Prison.* Istanbul.

Katchznouni, Hovannes. *The Armenian Revolutionary Federation [Dashnagtzoutiun] Has Nothing to Do Anymore: The Manifesto of Hovhannes Katchaznouni, First Prime Minister of the Independent Armenian Republic.* Translated by Matthew A. Callender. Edited by John Roy Carlson [Arthur A. Derounian]. New York: Armenian Information Service, 1923.

Les Musée des Civilisations Anatoliennes. Ankara: Dönmez, 1987.

OTHER SOURCES

2012 Declaration. "The Seized Properties of Armenian Foundations in Istanbul." Hrant Dink Foundation, Istanbul, November 2012. ISBN978-605-86570-0-7.

"Memoirs of Calouste Sarkis Gulbenkian with Particular Relation to the Origins and Foundation of the Iraq Petroleum Company Limited." Testimony before the U.S. Congress, 1945. National Archives, Washington, DC.

Privately published collection of ASALA interviews (1982), provided by Christopher Gunn.

CIA reports: "Global Terrorism: The Justice Commandos of the Armenian Genocide," September 1984 (GI 84-10148); and "The Armenian Secret Army for the Liberation of Armenia: A Continuing International Threat," January 1984 (GI 84-10008 & EUR 84-10004).

FBI report: YENIKIAN report, 1973.

The Gust Guide (document 1915-07-21-DE-012). http://www.sci.am/downloads/musgen/WolfgangGust.pdf, p. 59.

INDEX

Shane, Myrtle O., 80
Sharia-based law. *See* Islam
Shiragian, Arshavir, 12, 156, 237, 244–49, 251–56, 263, 293–94
Siberia, Armenian prisoners in, 12, 258, 290
slavery/serfdom, 36, 47; colonial subjugation, 52–53; conscription as, 71; Janissaries as slave soldiers, 34–35; minorities in, 221, (Armenians) 20, 76
Smyrna, 29, 44, 46, 125, 130; fire destroys, 131, 177, (Christians slaughtered) 261–62, 278; renamed Izmir, 282
Soviet Union (USSR): annexes Armenia, 13, 151, 180, 240, 284, 289–91, 327n8, (treatment of population) 118; Armenian prisoners in, 258; Britain and, 173, 175, 287; communist regime, 72, 116, 173, (Western fears of) 287; defection to West, 333n29; founded, 118, (ends, Armenia breaks from) 285, 292; and Islam, 173, 176, (Muslim-Armenian feuds) 157, 241–42; secret police (Cheka) of, 12, 258, 259, 289, (followed by GPU and KGB) 292; as threat, 120, (anti-Soviet pact considered) 240; Turkey and, (buffer zone) 247, (and Kemal) 262, (nationalist Turks, Enver and Talat Pasha) 143, 157–58, 160, 174, 246–47, 249, 258–59, (pro-Armenian treaties) 287; in World War II, 263. *See also* Russia; Stalin, Joseph
"Special Corps" *(Hadug Marmin),* "Special Fund" *(Hadug Kumar),* "Special Mission" *(Hadug Kordz),* 136–37, 139, 239–40
"Special Organization" *(Teshkilati Mahsusa). See* CUP (Committee of Union and Progress)
Stalin, Joseph, 50–51, 158, 263, 283, 290, 327n8; statue erected, 288–89, (replaced) 292. *See also* Soviet Union
Standard Oil company, 273
"Storm, The" (kidnapping operation), 50
Sublime Porte. *See* Ottoman Empire
Suez Canal, 68, 175
Suleiman "the Magnificent" (sultan), 29–30, 31, 36, 38

sultans, sultanate. *See* Ottoman Empire
Suni, Babken (Bedros Parian), 56
"Susurluk Incident," 297–99
Svazlian, Verjiné, 87
Sykes, Mark, 171, 179
Sykes-Picot accord (1916), 126, 130, 171
Syria, 126, 130, 257, 264, 273, 289; deportations to and from, 65, 135, 214, 257

Talat Bafrali, Hayriye, 184, 233, 255–56
Talat Pasha, Mehmet, 222; and Armenian extermination, 65–66, 69, 76–77, 106, 260, (disavows responsibility) 171–72, (guilt of) 191, 219, 226–28, 233, ("population control") 223, 257, (Turkification) 73, 118; as CUP leader, 61, 63–64, 144–45; death sentence, 10, 132, 158, 174, 190, 200; in exile, 9, 125, 127, 131, 147, 154, 171, (as "Ali Salih Bey") 10, 168–69, 176, 181–84, (Armenian fears of losing) 160, (British eye on) *see* Britain, (defense of) 164, (German funding of) 151, 161, 219, 332n14, (and Kemal) 178, (and USSR) 158, 174, 249; on Nemesis list, 136–38, 143, 162, 180, (photos of) 145–46, 169–70, (and public trial) 139, 166, 190, 192; as posthumous national hero, 232–33, 260, 280, (reprisal for murder of) 285; Tehlirian assassinates, 5–8, 10–13, 185, 237, 251, 254, 259, 301, 327n8, (full story untold) 261, (plot) 137–48, 150–57, 161–70, 176–77, 179–84, (published accounts of) 293, (Tehlirian quoted on) 17; trial, 5–7, 84, 113, 139–40, 186–211, 212–20, 223–30, 243–44, 326n7, (acquittal) 5, 12, 231–33, 237, 241
Tamurlane (or Timur), 29, 31
Tashnags. *See* ARF (Armenian Revolutionary Federation)
Tatigian, Anahid, 101–2, 119, 121–22, 138, 147, 238–39
Teapot Dome scandal (U.S.), 265
Tehlirian, Khatchadur, 98–99
Tehlirian, Misak, 110, 112, 115, 194

Also by Eric Bogosian

NOVELS
Mall

Wasted Beauty

Perforated Heart

SOLOS
Men Inside

funHouse

Drinking in America

Sex, Drugs, Rock & Roll

Pounding Nails in the Floor with My Forehead

Wake Up and Smell the Coffee

100 (monologues)

PLAYS
Talk Radio

subUrbia

Red Angel

1+1

NOVELLA
Notes from Underground